Aesthetic Experience and Literary Hermeneutics

Theory and History of Literature

Edited by Wlad Godzich and Jochen Schulte-Sasse

WITHDRAWI

Aesthetic Experience

and

Literary

Hermeneutics

Hans Robert Jauss

Translation from the German by Michael Shaw

Introduction by Wlad Godzich

Theory and History of Literature, Volume 3

University of Minnesota Press, Minneapolis

Publication of this book was assisted by a grant from the
publications program of the National Endowment for the
Humanities, an independent federal agency.

Copyright © 1982 by the University of Minnesota
All rights reserved.
Published by the University of Minnesota Press,
2037 University Avenue Southeast, Minneapolis MN 55414
Printed in the United States of America
This book was originally published as *Äesthetische Erfahrung
und literarische Hermeneutik I* (Munich: Wilhelm Fink Verlag, 1977).
"The Swan" is reprinted from *Charles Baudeliare, The Flowers of Evil*,
a selection edited by Marthiel and Jackson Mathews, copyright © 1955 by
New Directions, with the permission of the translator, Anthony Hecht.

Library of Congress Cataloging in Publication Data

Jauss, Hans Robert.
    Aesthetic experience and literary hermeneutics.
    (Theory and history of literature ; v. 3)
    Translation of: Ästhetische Erfahrung und
literarische Hermeneutik, Bd. 1: Versuche im Feld der
ästhetischen Erfahrung.
    Bibliography: p. 343.
    Includes index.
    Contents: Sketch of a theory and history of aesthetic
experience — Interaction patterns of identification
with the hero — On why the comic hero amuses — [etc.]
    1. Literature — Aesthetics. I. Title. II. Series.
PN45.J313   801'.93   82-4786
ISBN 0-8166-1003-7   AACR2
ISBN 0-8166-1006-1 (pbk.)

The University of Minnesota
is an equal-opportunity
educator and employer.

Contents

Introduction
Wlad Godzich

"Literature, its history and its study, have, in recent times, fallen into greater and greater discredit," wrote Hans Robert Jauss some eleven years ago in the preface to the book in which he set forth his program for the revival of literary studies.[1] It should be noted at the outset that, between literature and its study, Jauss inserts history, a point made not only syntactically but with considerable theoretical vigor and erudition in the key chapter of the book, the justly famous "Literary History as a Challenge to Literary Theory," originally delivered as the inaugural lecture of his seminar at the University of Constance in 1967.[2] Yet, during the ten years that elapsed between that day and the original publication of *Ästhetische Erfahrung. Literatur und Hermeneutik I.*, whose translation follows these introductory remarks, history did not stand still but rather, as it is wont to do, problematized even further its relationship to literature and its study. Some may have felt discomfited by such a development, but not Jauss who had just argued for a dynamic view of history which would govern the reception of texts. From the perspective of his own theory, he found himself in the highly enviable position of studying the reception of his own pronouncements and of responding to that reception, thereby giving concrete evidence, in his own procedures and writings, of the very processes that he had theoretically elaborated and then described in the works of others. Although too modest, and too mindful of scholarly decorum, to admit it, Jauss must have reflected upon this dialectic more than once in the writing of *Aesthetic Experience and Literary Hermeneutics*. Since the English-language reader may not be familiar with this history, I shall sketch it out briefly and then speculate on what Jauss's reception is likely to be among us. I shall conclude with some comments on the central claims of this book.

I

It is not easy to characterize Jauss's place on the German critical scene for, in many ways, it is eccentric to the dominant centers of his day. Although he has worked, for the past fifteen years, within the framework of a group of scholars united by similar methodological concerns, his original thinking developed almost idiosyncratically and did not follow any previously traced paths until it burst upon the national scene with his appointment to the new interdisciplinary university at Constance, whereupon it contributed to a major transformation of the German critical landscape.

Literary criticism in Germany, in the immediate post-World War II period, was dominated by approaches derived from American New Criticism. There was ample justification for the adoption of techniques of close reading against the prevailing tradition of positivism which treated texts as either biographical or historical documents or as the sum total of the influences that had determined them. But there was also the advantage to the *Werk-immanente* approach that it permitted the bracketing of all historical questions and thus obviated the need to address painful questions of recent political allegiance. This became the dominant methodological practice among students of German literature, but Jauss remained largely unaffected by it since he is a scholar of Romance literatures, and, in this discipline, the situation was different. As Harald Weinrich, himself a Romanist of note as well as an early theoretician of reader's response, recently noted in a personal memoir, many young Germans were struck by the publication of Ernst Robert Curtius's *European Literature and the Latin Middle Ages* in 1948 for it provided them with "the unsuspected chance to be all at once reintegrated, together with [their] nation, into the good old family of civilized and cultivated mankind."[3] Although descriptions of Curtius as a Cold War humanist, and of his version of humanism as "a strategic ideology with the aim of covering the restoration of capitalism in the Western world"[4] may strike the English reader as farfetched and extreme, it is nevertheless true that Curtius's influence upon the Germany of Adenauer—of whose brain-trust he was a member—coincided with the avoidance of any sociological reflection and the construct of history as handed down tradition. But again Jauss was eccentric to the movement. Having studied under Hans-Georg Gadamer, who was then reexamining the structure and function of hermeneutics, he saw the inescapability of a problematic relationship between the past and the present, and therefore the necessity of confronting the question of history; further, he understood that confrontation as taking place within a framework of communication, and therefore requiring consideration of both the individual and social dimensions of that encounter. He began to address the first, the historical, in his writings on medieval French literature and in a brilliant book with, so far, a very restricted readership, on the relationship of time and remembrance to the structure of the novel in Proust's *A la Recherche du Temps perdu*.[5] The occasion for the second, the examination of the psychosocial dimensions of communication, was provided by the rapid transformation of German society in the early sixties, and especially the rise of mass media and the ensuing crisis of education. Since this is a hotly debated topic in Germany upon which agreement is not likely to be reached in the near future, no more than a brief sketch of Jauss's stand on this matter can be offered here.

The traditional methods and aims of humanistic education, whether drawn along the lines of Curtius's ideal of Romania or the stylistic formalism of the *Werk-immanente* approach, proved vulnerable and incapable of resistance to the new media. Conceived for the leisurely and considered study and transmission of masterpieces, they offered no guidance for dealing with the sophisticated, and frequently aesthetically subtle, messages of the media, which, by their sheer mass and accelerated reception-time, overwhelmed high literature. Jauss took this as a sign of the failure of literary education to perform a "critical social function." It should be the function, he argued, of a literary education to endow the individual with sufficient discrimination and moral power of judgment to protect himself/herself against the influence of the "hidden persuaders." It is clear that Jauss conceived of the development of such a critical social function within the framework of existing society. He was, and continues to be, prepared to argue that literature, especially past literature, has a formative social function. Politically, his attitude could be characterized as liberal-reformist.

What such a project required was the reformulation of the way in which we conceive of our relationship to literature, past and present. Curtius's model, already disqualified by its failure to resist the trivialization of culture, is far too reverential and makes no provision for us except as celebrants of a richness past. The formalism of close reading is found wanting on two scores: (1) it aims at an ascesis of the reader who must, in her or his encounter with the text, bracket all personal interests and predilections so that the text may deploy its intentional structure unhindered; (2) by stressing the autonomy of each text, this methodological approach is incapable of reintegrating the text into a history. At this juncture, Jauss did something quite bold for a West German student of literature of his day: he decided to look at the model of history provided by Marxism. While he rejected it because of its dependence upon economic determinism, he opened up a debate among literary scholars on the value of the Marxist view of history, taking at times what were seen as highly ambiguous positions, such as his claim that Marxist literary critics had not replaced the Romantic model of literary history with a conceptualization adequate to Marx's view of history. Similarly, he noted that Lukács's focus on the way in which literature reflects reality (but is not a constituent factor in the shaping of reality) resulted in studies of literary creation but not in any awareness of the effect of literature upon the reader. Jauss then turned to the newly translated work of the Russian Formalists, and especially the notion of literary evolution advanced by Jakobson and Tynjanov.[6] Although he approved of their description, derived from phenomenology but couched in a more linguistic terminology, of the processes whereby individual works set themselves off from their predecessors, absorbed and automatized some of their features, or sought to react against them by the conscious alteration of some devices, he rejected their overall view for it claimed that works of literature evolve in their own autonomous series without reference to extraliterary history.

Coming back to his point of departure, Jauss reexamined the specific communicational situation that we call reading. If the reader is considered a part of the reading operation, the function of a reading cannot be the establishment of some objective, forever valid, meaning of the text. Rather, any conception of reading must start with the recognition that the reader is already fully awash in the tradition that has given rise to the object of his/her reading, and, indeed, that the text is itself an articulation in its mode of reception. No reader of Keats, e.g., approaches a poem of his without some sense of what it is to read a high Romantic poem. But once we begin to think in this manner, a whole host of questions descends upon us: What happens when we read? Do we bring ourselves to the work or do we get something from it? What sort of prejudgments do we bring to our readings?

Do we expect, e.g., certain things in certain genres? Are we intimidated by certain works, certain authors, certain reputations? What is the nature of such intimidations? What is the image of the author that we bring to a reading? Do we, as the reading audience, exercise some influence upon the author as s/he writes for us? Do we have immediate access to literature or not, and if not what mediations can we repertory? To what extent can we be manipulated so that we respond in an expected manner? How can it be determined that we will respond aesthetically to something that may not have been intended that way? All these questions, and more, especially those having to do with value, emerge in the forefront of attention as soon as a reader- or a recipient-centered approach to literature is attempted.

Jauss drew upon the teachings of Gadamer in order to establish the foundational categories of his *Rezeptionsästhetik*.[7] Gadamer is concerned with the nature of understanding, ostensibly philosophical, although he begins by conflating the distinction between philosophical and everyday understanding. For him, understanding is an event in which we are implicated but which we do not dominate; it is something that happens to us. We never come to cognitive situations empty but carry with us a whole world of familiar beliefs and expectations. The hermeneutic phenomenon encompasses both the alien world we suddenly encounter and the familiar one we carry. Whereas most philosophical conceptions of the hermeneutic phenomenon require that we overcome our own boundedness (historical, psychological, social, etc.), Gadamer argues that this is impossible and that what matters is to use the hermeneutic phenomenon to recognize what we brought into it, so that we gain knowledge of ourselves by discovering our own unsuspected preformed judgments (*Vorverständnis*), as well as gain knowledge of the alien by extending our horizons until they meet with its own so that a fusion of horizons takes place.

Gadamer's best known model for this encounter is that of question and answer. The relationship of interpreter to text must be conceived as a dialogue in which both participate on an equal footing. Such a dialogue presupposes that its participants share a common concern and are not merely intent upon each other. As a result, the interpreter must not concentrate on the text but rather must adopt an orientation toward the problem that concerns the text, and address the problem along *with* the text. In this way, the interpreter does not identify with the author—a delusion in any case—but explores the text's concern and finds himself/herself interrogated further in the direction that the text's initial question traces. A horizon of interrogation emerges but not in the guise of a new objectivity; rather it is a way of rendering the text actual to me existentially for I am now concerned with its questions and have brought my concerns to bear upon it.

Jauss takes over the notion of horizon which he names "horizon of expectation" and means by it the sum total of reactions, prejudgments, verbal and other behavior that greet a work upon its appearance. A work may fulfill such a horizon by confirming the expectations vested in it or it may disappoint the expectations by creating a distance between itself and them. This Jauss labels "aesthetic distance." Aesthetic distance becomes an important factor in the constitution of literary history for it may result in one of two major processes: either the public alters its horizon so that the work is now accepted—and a stage in the aesthetics of reception is set—or it rejects a work which may then lie dormant until it is accepted, i.e., until a horizon for it is forged (such was the case of medieval literature which had to await Romanticism to find a horizon in which it could be received again). In some instances, particularly in Modernism, the public splits into groups of willing recipients and adamant refuseniks. From the perspective of a social critical function for literature, Jauss sees in this ability of literary texts to alter horizons of expectation a stong liberating force which works both upon the recipient for it frees him/ her of the views s/he held without necessarily being aware of them, and upon literature, and especially classical literature, for it permits us to recover its initial impact which had been eroded by centuries of veneration and monumentalization.

Such a conception of the interaction of reader and text restores the historical dimension, claims Jauss, for the public of recipients, past and present, is fully involved as the mediator of the texts. The pitfall that the Russian Formalists could not avoid, namely the separation of literature and life, is thus overcome, for it is in their daily lives that readers build up their horizons of expectations and it is in the same lives that any work-induced changes will have to take place. The public also serves as the mediator between an older work and a more recent one, and thus provides the basis for understanding the formation of the literary sequences which historiography will record. A history of literature undertaken according to these principles would appear to be eminently empirical and value-free, for it would not obey some foreordained logic but merely record what it notes without succumbing to the totalizing views of positivism because it need recognize its own historical inscription. So that, for all practical purposes, each generation of readers must rewrite history. This is not a defect of the theory but its most liberating feature, for it ensures that no fixed view ever prevails and that each generation must read the texts anew and interrogate them from its own perspective and find itself concerned, in its own fashion, by the work's questions.

Because they stress the need to overcome the excessive mediatization of cultural life, it is ironic that Jauss's pronouncements should have emerged against a horizon that ensured their misinterpretation. The very misgivings that had led Jauss to formulate a research program for the renewal of the pedagogy of literary studies had by then become a major and social political force in the unrest of German universities and indeed the society at large. This is a history that remains to be written and its complexities are certainly beyond the scope of a sketch such as this one, but, for our purposes, it suffices to note that, with its emphasis upon a reauthentification of the experience of reception in literature; the legitimation of an active role for the reader, hitherto conceived of as passive recipient; the critique of the media; the call for the reorganization of humanistic studies; and the advocacy of a social-critical role for literary education; Jauss's ideas presented superficial analogies with the calls for educational and social transformation emanating from far more radical quarters. Or rather, Jauss was perceived by conservatives within the university and without, as not only legitimizing the oppositional forces of the S.D.S. and the A.P.O. (Ausserparlamentarische Opposition: extraparliamentary opposition), but as serving as their Trojan horse, for, unlike, the famous Frankfurt Institute for Social Research whose critique of the existing order was well known, Jauss appeared to be in the mold of the traditional German scholar. For the Right, then, this senior professor (an *ordinarius*, a member of the ultimate hierarchy in the German university system) was a traitor in its midst. But the excoriation from the Right differed in no manner of degree from the denunciations of the Left, which recognized readily that Jauss's project was reformist and not revolutionary in orientation and which tended to see in his enterprise an attempt at co-optation by the dominant group. How virulent these passions can become was shown when students occupied Adorno's seminar in Frankfurt and eventually had to be removed by the police.[8] Jauss's position thus became quite difficult. The Right, as is its wont, used its power against him, or more precisely against his junior associates so that on several occasions he had to threaten resignation — a threat made the more credible by his acceptance of visiting professorships in the United States. The attacks from the Left he dealt with in his own writings so that, rather paradoxically and misleadingly, Jauss's publications after 1970 give the impression of one intent upon combating the Left only, and therefore of an ally of the Right, whereas Jauss's response was more nuanced and addressed criticism from both sides with the weapons each would recognize: ideas against the Left; such power as he had against the Right.

Aesthetic Experience and Literary Hermeneutics is therefore a polemical work, an aspect which is at times quite apparent, at others less so. It polemicizes most of all against what Jauss perceives as the dominant left view of art: Adorno's aesthetics of negativity and the *Ideologiekritik* movement which accompanied it. Adorno is explicitly mentioned in the text a number of times and a full-fledged critique of his views is presented, but even when there is no direct reference to him, he is very much present. For example, Jauss reserves some of his severest criticism of contemporary writers for Samuel Beckett, who happens to be the author to whom Adorno intended to dedicate his *Ästhetische Theorie* had he been able to complete it prior to his death. Similarly, one may well wonder at Jauss's selection of the theme *Douceur du foyer* for his discussion of the lyric in the mid-nineteenth century, for the strongly affirmative value he places on this theme is in direct contradiction to Adorno's construct of the role played by a variant of the same theme, namely that of *intérieur* (also expressed in French) in the writings of S. Kierkegaard.[9] Were the purpose of these remarks not introductory but investigatory, it would be tempting to substitute for their *rezeptionsästhetische* orientation one drawn from Harold Bloom's agonistics of influence.

The difference between Jauss's views and Adorno's is substantial, even though both share a concern for the current state of culture. Adorno's thinking, always dialectical in the extreme, is equally concerned with the manipulation of art, but it immediately extends into a critique of the ideological means that are invoked to justify that manipulation. For him, aesthetic theory, as indeed any philosophical activity, must be not only theoretical but critical, for only a critical theory can have an impact in the social sphere. With respect to art, the task—but we shall see that it is a utopian one—is to restore its rightful existence, which can happen, if at all, in a liberated society. Since Adorno did not address the question of the concrete means of such a liberation, all that is left is the critical moment, which of necessity is impregnated with the pessimism caused by the present.

Art then, for Adorno, is, at the inscription of social conflicts, unfree and subject to ideological control, so that, for all practical purposes, art takes on the aspect of an element of the superstructure. On the basis of his previous studies of advanced capitalism, Adorno wants to bring out how, in its very form, art is compelled to embody social conflicts. A denunciation of the present treatment of art must therefore be formulated from a perspective which does not exist, which, as utopian thought, would lay the ground for a conception of art in a world in which conflicts would be sublated. But the situation of art today is, in Adorno's own term, "aporetic." For if, in the past, art had been in the service of rituals or other religious beliefs and practices, its achievement of autonomy in the age of the Enlightenment was but the prelude to a new enslavement. Our society, which Adorno sees ruled by instrumental reason, whose insitutional hallmark is the bureaucracy, is totally, and structurally, unwilling to let art have its autonomy, or, more precisely, it uses its autonomy to give it the motility of a commodity, which becomes subject to the operations of a market, and thus functions as the vehicle of dominant ideology. The market itself is the object of controls, among which is the scholarly study of art which serves to establish hierarchies of (marketable) values and thus provides the ground for market strategies.

Turning art into a commodity leads to a valorization of concepts that insists on its form as closed, on its aspect as finished or polished product. Such closure is achievable, under present socioeconomic circumstances, only by doing violence to the form of the art object which otherwise necessarily reproduces the conflicts and contradictions of the society. True art resists commodification by refusing this closure. It insists on its unfinished character, and on its overall uselessness, its incapacity to serve any end, for, in the radical affirmation of its uselessness, it calls into question the claims to harmonious totalization that our society advances ideologically. In practice, this signifies that the study of art, and *a fortiori* of literature, should not take the form of a traditional aesthetics but rather that of an analytics which, in the immediate study of individual art objects, would elicit the mode of their apprehension of history, i.e., the way in which they reproduce the social agonistics of their moment. This requires a strong denunciation of all approaches to art that wish to reestablish an ideal and separate position for it. What matters most, in Adorno's view, is that each individual analysis bring out the fundamentally critical moment in the artefact, whereby it stands in opposition to, and negates, the order and ideology of its society. For only in this manner can we recover the truth of art, which is that art is the inscription of history and therefore contains the promise of a future liberation.

What is at play in Adorno's aesthetic theory or indeed in his thought at large is negativity, a concept which he endowed with special richness, first in the formulation of the cognitive principle of nonidentity which then served as the basis of his philosophy of "negative dialectics" against which Jauss's entire critique is directed. In Hegelian dialectics, negativity is the movement of the concept toward its 'other', and a necessary stage in the passage to *Aufhebung*, the overcoming or sublation of the initial concept. But for Adorno, the Hegelian synthesis was, in its ideality, impossible. Reason is incapable of capturing reality, not so much because of its own finitude but because reality, always social in nature, is, in its very objective conditions, far too contradictory to be encompassed by reason without imparting contradictions to it. Thus, for Adorno, a concept and reality exist differentially with respect to each other. Rather than having the concept mirror the reality, as is the case in all idealistic epistemologies, Adorno has the concept refer to the reality by virtue of its nonidentity to it; the process may be envisaged, with the same results, with reality as the starting point. The cognitive force of art is, then, but an instantiation of the operation of a general principle of nonidentity, that is, negativity.

Jauss's critique of Adorno's views is cogently and forcefully expressed in section A2 of the book, and it needs no anticipatory summation here. Yet it appeals to a notion, which is then elevated to a major analytic concept in the study, whose logical emergence in this context may not be apparent to an English-language reader, namely *identification*. It happens that German disposes of two words to designate what we refer to by the simple term 'experience', and it becomes possible to signal an important conceptual difference by preferring one term over the other. In the context of aesthetics, and specifically within the framework of *Lebensphilosophie*, the term *Erlebnis* has been preferred. Generally translated as 'lived experience', it postulates the primacy of experience over reflection, and figures prominently in existentialism in the foundational axiom of the precedence of existence over essence. Earlier, in Dilthey's hermeneutics, *Erlebnis* was the object of the subject's quest for understanding. Adorno, by contrast, has recourse to the word *Erfahrung* by which he means to signal that reflection itself is lived experience and that it concerns the entire individual, not merely his/her capacity as knowing subject. The distinction here could be most easily apprehended through a reference to Kant. Adorno's rejection of the *Aufhebung* of Hegelian dialectics rested to a great extent on his extreme valorization of the individual whose singularity he wished to protect against Hegel's conflation in the collective subjectivity that is Absolute Spirit. To do this, he returned to Kant's phenomenology and its notion of autonomous subject. But Adorno critiqued Kant's conception of the relation of subject to object, for it seemed to him to lead to the kind of postulate of identity that his own principle of non-identity was meant to displace. In effect, he argued, Kant's notion of the individual was too formal and abstract, and therefore easily subsumable in reified thought, which is apparent in the master category of the transcendental subject, from the perspective of which every individual subject is, like a commodity, exchangeable for another, and thus not an individual, in the sense of specific, at all. If reflection is conceived of as *Erfahrung*, it will not stand in an abstract relation to lived experience and not become the locus of reification. At the same time, this implies that cognition is not merely an intellectual matter but one that involves the entire person, including the body. So that, in conclusion, it is the whole human person, as an empirically existing individual, that is engaged in *Erfahrung*, whereas *Erlebnis* is but the fodder of reflection. Jauss retains the term *Erfahrung* to designate aesthetic experience and thus gains for his discussion the reference to the somatic aspects of *aesthesis*, which permits the masterful discussion of pleasure. But, against Adorno, Jauss returns to another aspect of Kant's conception of the individual and his/her cognitive powers. For Kant, the fact that the individual could not experience the object as it was in itself required the postulation of another dimension among individuals: intersubjectivity. This was retained by both Hegel and Marx in their respective concepts of the master-slave dialectic and the class struggle. But Adorno's insistence on the radical and never subsumable individuality of each subject prevented any solution to what appears to be a monadic existence for the individual. Against this notion, Jauss restores the intersubjective dimension of Kant's concept of the subject and grounds it in a communicational framework within which it becomes possible for individuals to share experience. The effect is that of recapturing the hermeneutic dimension of Dilthey's *Erlebnis* without surrendering, at least ostensibly, the coprimacy of reflection implied by *Erfahrung*. The intersubjective dimension of *Erlebnis* is to be found in mechanisms of *identification* which thus come to replace Dilthey's *Einfühlung*, or empathy. In sum, Jauss replaces the Negation/Affirmation polarity of Adorno by stressing that the negativity of the work of art is mediated by identification, which thus emerges as the key counterconcept of the aesthetics of reception.

II

Some of the controversies that I have attempted to summarize here by somewhat forcedly, yet nonetheless exemplarily, pitting Jauss against Adorno may strike us as lacking counterparts on our critical scene. It would appear at first sight that Jauss's reception among us, already mediated by the publication of some of his essays in translation by Ralph Cohen in *New Literary History* and Michael Riffaterre in *Romanic Review*, will take place in the general space that we have recently taken to call "theory," and, within it, the subdivision known as "reader's response theory" presently cultivated in varying degree and orientation by the likes of Norman Holland, Stanley Fish, and David Bleich, and already prepared for Jauss's arrival by the earlier welcome accorded to his Constance colleague and fellow *Rezeptionsästhetiker* Wolfgang Iser. There is little doubt that students of this area will constitute a sizable portion of Jauss's readership, and, given the nature of his contribution and the importance of their concerns, the publication of the present translation would be amply justified. But it would be a pity, in my view, if Jauss were to be read only by such groups, for he is a thinker whose scope of vision extends beyond the boundaries of a specific research question. Rather, he is good for those treks which step off the trodden paths and set out into the wilderness, the present roaming ground of criticism as Geoffrey Hartman reminds us.[10] Since reader's response theoreticians and practitioners will approach Jauss from their special vantage point and with their interests, they need no guidance, whereas Jauss's qualifications for a walk through the desert require a few comments.

Jauss's critical endeavors arose, I suggested, out of the sense of crisis that had befallen German higher education in the sixties, and especially the humanities and social sciences. That we are presently in a state of crisis ourselves in the same areas is too much of a commonplace to bear reiterating, although it is far from clear that we have a sense of the transformation that we are undergoing. In many ways our crisis is unlike the German one: theirs was one of growth, ours one of retrenchment; theirs had to do with the rapid development of the mass media, ours does not; theirs took place in a heavily politicized milieu, whereas our campuses are perceived as more apolitical than ever. Such comparisons are not particularly enlightening. What is perhaps more important is to trace the shifts that are occurring in the organization of knowledge. If we take the discipline English as an example, the dimensions of the crisis become clearer and Jauss's concerns more pertinent.

We have been told, within the universities and without, that there is a "literacy" crisis abroad in the land, that students can neither read nor write, that they no longer comprehend what they read, and that employers view our graduates with distaste, or at least, apprehension.

Since we live in a society that demands rapid solutions to newly discovered problems, we have invested a tremendous amount of resources,
financial and human, over the past ten years, in writing programs,
whether they be called that or rhetoric, composition, or communication. This is not the place to undertake an evaluation or a critique of
such efforts, nor even to wonder at the wisdom, let alone the efficacy,
of implementing on a massive scale the results of one of the least re-
searched areas in our field. Suffice it to consider the effect upon departments of English: in nearly all instances, faculty have been reassigned to the teaching of writing; more important, the bulk if not the
totality of new appointments is made in this area at the expense of
more established parts of the curriculum. Since the teaching of writing
has traditionally been held in low esteem and generally been delegated
to junior faculty and teaching assistants, the present shift in resource
allocation has begun to produce resentment among senior faculty who
see their traditional departmental strengths and disciplinary profile
erode. As a result, at a large number of universities an adversary relationship has begun to develop between the central administrators
who, feeling that they are responding to societal pressure, want more
writing programs, and senior faculty in English who fear that whenever one of their ranks retires or leaves for another position, a traditional appointment in, let us say the eighteenth-century novel, will
give way to an assistant professorship in composition. The senior
faculty becomes more possessive of those positions which it values
and is generally prepared to argue for them on the basis of their importance as specialty fields. Slowly English departments take on a
rather new configuration: a service component teaching writing and
employing large numbers of graduate assistants, and a specialist component offering pregraduate and graduate training for those who intend to enter the profession, however bleak the prospects of employment might appear. In this respect, English departments are rapidly
becoming like foreign language departments which have traditionally
kept their language-teaching function quite separate from their graduate training and research. But English as a discipline was never meant
to be like French or German in English-speaking universities: whereas
those departments rely upon exotica or special interests for their appeal, English has been the department of choice for all those who have
wanted to study, and reflect upon, their own culture. The aspiring
writer, the future critic, the student generally desirous of acquiring a
well-rounded education which would prepare him or her for a broad
array of professional endeavors, all came to English, for if it were not
quite F. R. Leavis's "discipline of thought"[11] it came closer to that

ideal than any other segment of the curriculum. But today, the student is faced instead with an English department that is in the business of basic or remedial literacy at one end and intent upon reproducing itself—training future practitioners of its specialty—at the other. To literate students, the choice appears to be purely professional and, not surprisingly, they opt for those preprofessional programs which hold a greater promise of gainful employment. Should the current realignment of English departments along the structural model of foreign language departments continue, the broad sphere of cultural concerns will progressively diminish and disappear, first from the university and then from public life as well. This is at once the real nature of our crisis and the dimension of our wilderness. The risk is that we will be left with the increasingly strident cries of traditionalists nostalgic for a unity that never was and confident of the universality of their own pursuits, and an array of fragmentary discourses locked away in their specialized concerns and technical terminologies.

The work of Jauss may help us to recover this lost space of cultural criticism, but it is not an enterprise free of dangers. Since my exposition has proceeded through exemplary figurae (Jauss, Adorno, English), let me invoke a last one: Lionel Trilling. It is at once obvious that Trilling occupied eminently the space whose parceling we are presently observing. It would indeed be tempting to date the beginning of this process from his death, but I fear that would make better narrative than judgment, for some of the roots of our predicament are already in Trilling.

It is striking to note that Jauss's masterful discussion of aesthetic pleasure contained in this book has no recent antecedent in English unless we return to a text Trilling published in 1963 in *Partisan Review*, "The Fate of Pleasure."[12] This essay, whose translation into European languages would dispel the widely held view on the Continent that there is no aesthetic thought in English, examines a paradigmatic shift in the nature of pleasure and its consequences for our conception of art that occurred between the Enlightenment and Romanticism. Trilling begins with the puzzling statement in Wordsworth's Preface to *Lyrical Ballads* that "the grand elementary principle of pleasure" constitutes "the naked and native dignity of man." From its inception, then, Trilling's reflection upon pleasure is framed by the question of human nature: the dignity of man and the role played by pleasure in its achievement. Wordsworth's notion of pleasure is austere to be sure, but it is not unrelated to certain historical considerations, especially the eudaemonic thrust of Enlightenment political theory, best exemplified in the French Revolution's promise of universal happiness.

Trilling shows very carefully that the notion of dignity derived from a certain level of material well-being, characterized by the possession of luxurious goods. By contrast to Wordsworth, who is made to play, rather aptly, the role of *a moraliste des Lumières*, Keats is ambivalent about pleasure, or more precisely, discovers the specific dialectic of pleasure. Not content with the confinement of pleasure to the higher intellectual pursuits, though constantly mindful, in Wordsworth's sillion, of its cognitive power, Keats proceeded to affirm the principle of pleasure most boldly, discovering in this manner that it required the greatest scrutiny. As Trilling reminds us, in "the country of La Belle Dame sans Merci, the scene of erotic pleasure . . . leads to devastation" (p. 58). Keats does something that Wordsworth did not consider: he separates the experience of pleasure, which continues to be described in the most approving terms, from its effects, which are incalculable and therefore most unreliable. In "Sleep and Poetry," Keats draws upon this distinction in order to show that poetry, through the pleasure that it procures, can "soothe the cares, and lift the thoughts of man," thereby articulating what Trilling calls the "essence of Philistinism" (p. 60). Trilling takes Keat's distinction and sees it at the root of the dichotomy of politics and art today, where the first seeks to satisfy the principle of pleasure by increasing material influence, whereas the latter looks at such a goal with considerable disdain.

Since it is already apparent in Keats that aesthetic pleasure, just as much as erotic pleasure, may serve illusion as easily as cognition, that, in other words, pleasure is cognitively unreliable, modern art is forced to seek a firmer cognitive ground by abandoning the pleasure principle and cultivating what Trilling calls "the negative transcendence of the human, a condition which is to be achieved by freeing the self from its thralldom to pleasure" (p. 71). Trilling's best examples come from Dostoevski's *Notes from Underground* and its theme of the search for a greater intensity of life, and from Augustine's wonderment in the *Confessions* at his own perversity in stealing pears that he neither needed nor desired. The juxtaposition of the two examples results in a curious conflation of the historical dimension in the essay. Until the invocation of Augustine's sin, the phenomenon described had firm historical boundaries, corresponding to the emergence and hegemony of the bourgeoisie, which is in the business of purveying reified experience, "specious good" (p. 66). But a historical inquiry of this sort leads, in Trilling's mind, to an impasse: if his analysis is correct, the modern tilt toward a negativity of pleasure must be seen in its historical relativity, and modernity abandoned. But for what? Will it have to be "an idiot literature, [with] 'positive heroes' who know how to get the good out of life and who have "affirmative" emotions about their success in doing so?" (p. 69). Trilling has already precluded social change ("the impulse to destroy specious good would be as readily directed against the most benign socialist society, which, by modern definition, serves the principle of pleasure," (p. 67) and is left therefore with a strategy that will greatly alter the status of history in his inquiry. By showing that the negativity characteristic of modernity already obtains in Augustine, and is therefore prebourgeois, he can argue that it is a permanent feature of the human psyche, a solution already foreseeable in the decision to frame the analysis within the question of human nature. Not unexpectedly, Freud is invoked to give the stamp of scientific approval to the notion that negativity is part and parcel of humanity. The only historical question left is that of the changing equilibria between the pleasure principle and its beyond. This final gesture of Trilling's neatly removes the historical phenomenon of negativity from its contingency and relativizes history itself. Appropriately enough, the essay is collected in a volume entitled *Beyond Culture*, a space which is meant to be that of unchanging human nature and therefore "not within the purview of ordinary democratic progressivism" (p. 74).

Once historical considerations are removed, the realm of cultural criticism is set adrift for it no longer has a function. Either the critic can argue from the perspective of an atemporal human nature and denounce the present or the past dogmatically, that is, uncritically with respect to his/her own position, or s/he can cultivate specialized subfields which, by virtue of their technicity, appear to be beyond the judgment of value. It would be easy to speculate upon the historical coincidence of such a choice with the political upheavals of the sixties and early seventies, but it is more to the point here to observe that for all the similarities of concern, Jauss's problematic is diametrically opposed to Trilling's: it seeks to restore the historical consciousness of criticism after a period of painful repression, and even the presumed universality of aesthetic response is shown to fluctuate historically. The very vigor of Jauss's historical inquiry ought to help us to return from Trilling's 'beyond', to a realm of culture. It is for this long march through the wilderness that Jauss can be our guide.

III

The reopening of the cultural realm for criticism will not represent an advance, though, as long as the possibiltiy of Trilling's solution remains. We must recognize that his notion of culture rested upon an anthropology that is derived from Freudian ego-psychology. Jauss's notion of culture oscillates between a historically attentive view and one derived from the Kantian model of intersubjectivity, which ultimately relies upon the consciousness of the assembled community for its reality principle, i.e., its locus of cognitive determinacy. The recourse to anthropological models always carries with it the question of human nature with the consequences we have seen in Trilling and in English departments. In "The Fate of Pleasure" Trilling had come close to seeing another possibility, but by then he was already committed to the concept of 'beyond culture'. When he first sets out to find evidence of negativity, even before Dostoevski's *Notes from Underground*, he comes upon Keats's "On Sitting Down to Read *King Lear* Once Again." Here, Trilling writes, Keats "dismisses all thought of pleasure and prepares himself for the pain he is duty bound to undergo" (p. 62). It is of course in connection with Shakespeare that Keats had developed the notion of Negative Capability, so that it is logical to seek evidence of negativity in this poem which considers the very act of reading with its anticipations, reflecting on past readerly experience of *King Lear*.

There is little here of the Aristotelian expectation that a regenerating cleansing will occur. The experience will be painful, of that Keats is certain, but even more gravely, it may well not, through any catharsis, lead to the kind of emotional balance that would make him productive; rather, it may leave him to "wander in a barren dream," that is, threaten his very creative powers by closing him off from any principle of reality (wandering in dream), so that his only recourse is to pray that he can be saved from the experience. This experience, derived from past readings, is entirely caught in the metaphor of consumption by fire:

> 5   Adieu! for, once again, the fierce dispute
> 6   Betwixt damnation and impassioned clay
> 7   Must I burn through, . . .

and

> 12   Let me not wander in a barren dream
> 13   But, when I am consumèd in the fire,
> 14   Give me new Phoenix wings to fly at my desire.

The initial choice is not very appealing: the eternal fire of damnation, by definition, concludes history and is on the far side of any possible redemption; "impassioned clay," that is, clay fired by passion, achieves the solidity of brick, or a form already fixed once and for all. To leave romance for Shakespeare, then, is to risk either the permanent loss of the self or its imprisonment in a form that admits of no further modification. Cognitively, both possibilities are distressing, and so Keats launches an appeal to Shakespeare, rather surprisingly since *he* seems to be the cause of the present difficulty, and to the "clouds of Albion," a vague addressee to say the least. But the very recourse to apostrophe is here to indicate that the move about to be made is more rhetorical than cognitive, so that the invocation of the clouds and of Shakespeare participates more in a textual economy than a semantic one. For the poem does offer a solution: in the code of fires, there is always a third possibility, that of the phoenix who, though consumed by the fire, does not lose himself in it as do the damned, nor change state, as does the clay, but is reborn as a newer and better version of the self.

This solution, though, is wholly linguistic and textual. To the predicament posed by the reading of *King Lear*, and against two phenomenologically based possibilities, it opposes but another text, that of the legend of the phoenix, which it must temporarily treat as if it were unproblematic in its own reading. The reading of *King Lear* is framed by romance at one end and by the myth of the phoenix at the other. It remains quite obscure why the phoenix legend should prove cognitively more satisfactory than *King Lear* or indeed than romance, especially since it figures in classical romances and is indeed part of the universe of classical texts which had also been discussed with the injunction in lines 2–4:

> Fair plumèd Syren, Queen of far-away!
> Leave melodizing on this wintry day,
> Shut up thine olden pages, and be mute:

In her "melodizing" guise, we tend to think of the siren as a mermaid, and of her habitat as aquatic, but here she is explicitly qualified as "Fair-plumed" and must therefore be the teratological version of half woman-half flying snake who hails from Arabia, which just happens to be the phoenix's original home. The reception of *King Lear*, itself traversed by negativity, is mediated by the sublation of a prior negativity: the rejection of the classical legend is itself negated, and, in its return, the classical text relieves the negativity of the Shakespearean text.

Here culture is not an intersubjective paradigm, a structure which could be abstracted, formulated, and offered up for reading itself. It is rather a set of textual operations which must be read, which inscribe our historicity in relation to its own. At their best, Jauss's readings of the meanderings of our aesthetic experience recognize this dimension of culture and guide us through its discovery. Against the reaffirmation of sameness and against the new vocationalism, Jauss proposes the ideal of a critical literacy.

A Note on the Translation

Unless otherwise attributed, English translations of quoted material were done by the translator, Michael Shaw. Translations of the passages from Latin were done by Professor Stephen Nimis. "La maison de Silvie" by Théophile de Viau was translated by Professor Tamara Root. Translations from the modern French and Provençal represent a collaboration by the translator and series editor Professor Wlad Godzich.

Quotations from the primary literature are from the relevant editions and indicated as follows: large roman numerals (book/act); small roman numerals (chapter/scene); arabic numerals (verse/page).

Preface

What does aesthetic experience mean; how has it manifested itself in the history of art; what interest can it have for the present theory of art? For a long time, these questions were peripheral to aesthetic theory and literary hermeneutics. In all reflection on the theory of art both before and after aesthetics became an autonomous discipline, such questions were overshadowed by problems which Platonic ontology and the metaphysics of the beautiful had bequeathed to it. The polarity of art and nature, the attribution of the beautiful to the true and the good, the inseparability of form and content, structure and meaning, the relationship of imitation and creation, were the canonic problems when aesthetic reflection was at its height. Wherever the truth which art brings into being is accorded priority over the experience of art in which aesthetic activity objectifies itself as man's work, the often-unavowed Platonic legacy still makes itself felt in the philosophy of art of our time. For this reason, the question concerning aesthetic praxis which has underlain all art as productive, receptive, and communicative activity remains unclarified and deserves to be asked anew.

This is already testified to by its place in the tradition: of the effects of art, it is principally rhetoric which is discussed, as happened for a time in the church fathers' polemics against art, occasionally in the doctrine of affects of moral philosophy, later in the psychology of taste, then in the sociology of art, and recently most often in the study of the media. The significant exception in the philosophical tradition is the Aristotelian poetics in antiquity and Kant's *Critique of Judgment* in the modern period. But neither the Aristotelian doctrine nor Kant's transcendental illumination of aesthetic effects gave rise to a comprehensive and tradition-creating theory of the aesthetic experience. What militated against such a development was expressed by Goethe in his famous statement that rejected the very question about effects as alien to art; thus Kant's aesthetics was also reproached for subjectivism, and in the nineteenth century, his approach to a theory of aesthetic experience that reduced the beautiful to the consensus of reflective judgment fell under the shadow of the more influential Hegelian aesthetics which defined the beautiful as the sensuous appearance of the idea and thereby showed the historical-philosophical theories of art the path to follow.

Since then, aesthetics has been oriented toward the representational function of art, and the history of the arts has seen itself as the history of works and their authors. Of the functions of art in the world of everyday life, only the productive, rarely the receptive, and hardly ever the communicative efficacy and achievement of aesthetic experience were examined. Since historicism, scholarly research in the arts has indefatigably instructed us about the tradition of works and their interpretations, about their objective and subjective genesis, so that today it is easier to reconstruct the place of a work of art in its time, to determine its originality as compared to its sources and predecessors, and even to uncover its ideological function than it is to learn of the experience of those who in productive, receptive, and communicative activity developed historical and social praxis in actu, a praxis whose already reified result the histories of literature and art pass on to us.

This volume covers questions about aesthetic praxis, its historical manifestations in the three fundamental categories of poiesis, aesthesis, and catharsis (as I call the productive, receptive, and communicative activities in a backward glance at the poetological tradition), about aesthetic pleasure as the underlying attitude peculiar to the three functions, and about the contiguous relationship between aesthetic experience and other provinces of meaning in the world of everyday reality. It contains an elaboration of approaches which I first formulated in my *Kleine Apologie der ästhetischen Erfahrung* (1972), an expanded version of which I later submitted for discussion at the sixth colloquium of *Poetik und Hermeneutik*.[1] A planned second volume will attempt to demonstrate the task of literary hermeneutics not so much in another theory of understanding and explaining as in application, i.e., in the mediation of present and past experience of art. How the differentiation and fusion of horizons of present and past aesthetic experience can be achieved in a methodologically controlled fashion and how the relation of question and answer can be employed as a hermeneutic instrument (but also be shown as the sequentiality of problem and solution in literary processes) are the central problems here. The studies in the field of aesthetic experience presented in this book have their unavoidable limitations in the competence of the literary scholar. Even where they include testimonials from the history of the other arts and make use of findings in the history of philosophy and of ideas, they do not disavow the fact that the author acquired his experience principally in studies of medieval and modern French and German literature and formed his hermeneutic reflection in the praxis of literary interpretation. But the conjunction of "aesthetic experience" and "literary hermeneutics" in the title also means to signal his conviction that experience in the commerce with art is no privilege of a specialized discipline and that reflection on the conditions of such experience is not the esoteric concern of philosophical or theological hermeneutics, which may perhaps make dispensible the customary apology for dilettantism where unavoidable incursions into other fields occurred.

The division of this work into two volumes is further justified by a *fundamentum in re*: the phenomenological distinction between understanding and cognition, primary experience and the act of reflection in which consciousness returns to the meaning and constitution of its experience is also present in the distinction between assimilation and interpretation in the reception of texts and aesthetic objects. Aesthetic experience occurs before there is cognition and interpretation of the significance of a work, and certainly before all reconstruction of an author's intent. The primary experience of a work of art takes place in the orientation to its aesthetic effect, in an understanding that is pleasure, and a pleasure that is cognitive. Interpretation that bypasses this primary aesthetic experience is the arrogance of a philologist who subscribes to the error that the text was not created for readers but for him, to be interpreted by such as he. This sets literary hermeneutics the twofold task of methodologically distinguishing between the two kinds of reception, which means that it must on the one hand shed light on the actual process through which the effect and significance of the text concretizes itself for the present reader, and on the other reconstruct the historical process in which readers have received and interpreted the text at different times and in varying ways. Application must then be the demand to measure the present effect of a work of art against the earlier history of its experience and to form the aesthetic judgment on the basis of effect and reception.

If this means the recurrence of questions that I developed in my first lecture at Constance in 1967 because I wished to take a position on the crisis in the philosophical disciplines, I am perfectly aware that this beginning of my theory of reception cannot simply be extended and elaborated today. In the past ten years, not only the scholarly and the university situation but also the social function and thus the aesthetic experience of our present time have undergone a perceptible change. It was the decade of university reform which involved the literary scholars at Constance especially in a process that was generally characterized by a linkage of reform efforts at three levels: the democratization of the university as an institution; the restructuring of an education in the historical disciplines into the training for a profession, and the revision of scholarly and theoretical self-understanding. The forward movement, stagnation, and decline of this reform[2] were the background before and against which this book was written, a situation which was not propitious to the working out of a coherent theory. Nor is such a claim made for the essays that have been brought together in this volume. The earlier pieces (B, C, D, E) are intended to supplement the sketch (A) that precedes them (most of which was not completed until 1976/77 and which embodies current findings).[3]

Concerning the revision of scholarly and theoretical self-understanding, the philologists called to Constance were acting in their own behalf when they set up the German *Fachbereich* for literature and turned to the aesthetics of the effect of literary works, a movement which was introduced by my "Literary History as a Challenge to Literary Theory" (originally delivered in German as *Literaturgeschichte als Provokation* [1967]), and Wolfgang Iser's *Die Appellstruktur der Texte* (1970). Retrospectively, I would say that the "challenge" lay less in an attack on venerable philological conventions than in the unexpected form of an apology. When, in view of the worldwide successes of linguistic structuralism and the most recent triumph of structural anthropology, a turning away from the paradigms of historical understanding first became apparent in the old human sciences, it became similarly apparent that the best chance for success for a new theory of literature would come not by transcending history but in utilizing the insight into historicity which is peculiar to art. Not the panacea of perfected taxonomies, closed systems of signs, and formalistic descriptive models but a historical investigation that did justice to the dynamic process of production and reception, of author, work, and public, by availing itself of the hermeneutics of question and answer was to renew the study of literature and lead it out of the blind alleys of a literary history that was running aground in positivism, the sort of interpretation that had stopped serving anything other than itself or the metaphysics of an *écriture* or, finally, a comparative literature for which comparison had become an end in itself.

Beyond the so-called Constance school, the theory of reception subsequently enjoyed unexpected success. It encountered a latent interest which the general dissatisfaction with the traditional canon of philological training had nourished during the sixties[4] and which had been made more acute by the criticism the student protest movement launched against the "bourgeois idea of scholarship." Reception theory soon found itself in the cross fire of debate between ideology critique and hermeneutics. More important, it called forth a new research interest which found expression in an abundance of studies in the fields of the history of reception, the sociology of literature, and empirical reception analyses. Another reason for the success of the change in paradigm was the circumstance that it was not confined to Germany. My approaches to a new historical study of literature and art which had the hermeneutic priority of reception as their starting point had been preceded by the Prague structuralism which was in turn a further development of Russian formalism whose still not fully utilized results have meanwhile been made available to Western research by the editions and presentations of a group of scholars (*Forschungsgruppe*) in Constance.[5] Jan Mukarovsky's semiology of art and Felix Vodicka's theory of concretization had already overcome the dogma that synchronics and diachronics, system and process, are irreconcilable when scholars in the West also turned to the task of conceiving of structure as process and began to introduce the subject into the self-sufficient linguistic universe. In France, Paul Ricoeur had already pointed to the common root of a hermeneutics of demystification and a hermeneutics of the recovery-of-meaning when the Habermas-Gadamer debate in Germany was still pitting ideology critique and hermeneutics against each other. But both of these hostile brothers have opposed the objectivism and logical empiricism of so-called unitary science and decisively contributed to a revalidation of the linguistic nature of man's experience of the world, and thus to communication as the condition for the understanding of meaning.

Since it has been described by a variety of authors and is also adequately dealt with in this book,[6] it is unnecessary here to go into the history of the internal German debate which the two camps of "bourgeois" and "materialist" literary theory carried on about the basis and the application of reception theory. I consider the dispute about the "idealist" and the "materialist" points of view in the fields of literary theory, aesthetics, and hermeneutics to be closed. Discussion has clarified what annoyed each about the other—the idealist implications of the materialist,[7] and the materialist desiderata of bourgeois-idealist theory—and undogmatic representatives from both camps must now address themselves to the task of applying the theory of reception to a new history of literature and the arts.

The criticism of my "Literary History as a Challenge to Literary Theory" yields the following program for an elaboration of the positions developed there: In the analysis of the experience of the reader or the "community of readers" of a given historical period, both sides of the text-reader relation (i.e., effect as the element that is conditioned by the text and reception as the element of concretization of meaning that is conditioned by the addressee) must be distinguished, worked out, and mediated if one wishes to see how expectation and experience mesh and whether an element of new significance emerges. These two horizons are the literary one, the one the work brings with it on the one hand, and that of his everyday world which the reader of a given society brings with him on the other. Because it is derivable from the work itself, the construction of the literary horizon of expectation is less problematic than is that of the social one which, as the context of a historical life-world, is not being thematized. As long as the psychology of reception processes has been clarified as little as the role and efficacy of aesthetic experience in the system of the structures of action in a historical life-world, there is little point in expecting salvation from class-specific analyses of reader attitudes, or in looking for the most telling expression of economic relationships and veiled ruling-class interests in that latest fad, popular and pulp fiction.

The approaches toward a definition of interaction patterns of identification with the hero (B) and the essay on why the comic hero amuses (C) are devoted to the problem of how the emotional process of literary reception and communication is to be understood under the conditions of the aesthetic attitude. In the cross-sectional analysis of the lyric in 1857 (E), I hope to have shown how the structure of a historical life-world can be made transparent in the medium of a literary system of communication and how the aesthetic function can be described in actu. Essay E developed from an attempt to apply the sociology of knowledge and ultimately confirms once again that popular literature cannot be defined in its aesthetic and social function unless it is seen with reference to the highest levels of literary art.

Aesthetic practice is not yet being understood in its totality if one equates the productive and the receptive aesthetic activities with the economic dialectic of production and consumption but ignores communicative activity as the mediating third element of the aesthetic experience.[8] This mediating element is not absent from the circulation model in the *Introduction to the Critique of Political Economy* by Karl Marx to which the new Marxist reception theory could resort when it proposed to legitimate going beyond the mimesis model.[9] There, a third element which can be distinguished as *distribution* and *exchange* mediates between production and consumption. This element stands for the area of interaction but characteristically does no more than permit one to grasp communicative action in the stunted form of economically reified relations, and the intersubjectivity of communication merely in the abstract vis-à-vis of society and individual.

If it were to become the foundation for a new theory of aesthetic praxis, Marx's circulation model would first have to be completed by a revaluation of interaction. Otherwise, that theory would become subject to the criticism Jürgen Habermas has brought against the most weighty one-sidedness of Marxist social theory, i.e., the fact that it equates praxis and *techné* and therefore "does not really explicate the connection between interaction and work but reduces one to the other under the specific title of social praxis, i.e., communicative action to instrumental action."[10] To agree with this criticism does not mean that one need base all one's hopes for a new social praxis that would give greater priority to communicative than to instrumental action, and thus restore balance to the triadic relationship of *techné*, communication, and world view, on the ideal of a domination-free discourse. This hope can be more easily justified when the achievements of the three functions of human action are first demonstrated, where in aesthetic activity *techné* becomes transparent as poiesis, communication as catharsis, and world view as aesthesis—in that experience of art which maintains the autonomy of human action throughout the historical succession of changing relations of domination.

Since aesthetic experience does not yet have a canonized history and hence no relevant collection of sources is available,[11] an undertaking such as the one begun here depends more heavily on bordering disciplines and is not infrequently obliged to adopt their findings and interpretations or to construe them anew. There is no intent to create the impression that only my own research and discoveries made the tradition that emerges through my historical perspectives accessible to the reader. I therefore attempted to identify my borrowings where I believed that, lacking competence, I could rely on the findings of others. If this means that time and again, I quoted or discussed research that is not my own, I request exoneration from the author's I "appropriated."

To specifically call attention to these related studies also seems imperative because in their totality they made available a theoretical and historical foundation on which further research in the field of aesthetic experience may be based. Under interdisciplinary perspectives, this entire area of research is a permanent part of the themes and discussions of the research group *Poetik und Hermeneutik*. I found the richest body of earlier studies in the published volumes (I-VII: 1964–76). Hans Blumenberg's *Der Prozess der theoretischen Neugierde* (1973) is an essential addition to the history of aesthetic experience because it casts light on the interrelation of the theoretical and the aesthetic from classical antiquity to the moment of their dissociation in the early modern period. Ernst Bloch's *Das Prinzip Hoffnung* (1959) views aesthetic experience in categories of "showing forth" and thus extends Freud's one-sided theory of ideal formation. In *L'Oeil vivant* (I: 1961; II: 1970), Jean Starobinski brought new insights from the history of medicine to the study of the imagination and made them utilizable in paradigms of hermeneutical interpretation. Jean-Paul Sartre's *What Is Literature?* (1948) pioneered the rehabilitation of the reader and retains its significance as a theory of the dialectics of reading and writing. His phenomenological study *Psychology of the Imagination* (1953) distinguishes between the achievements of the imagining consciousness and perception. For further research in this field, we now have Mikel Dufrenne's *Phénoménologie de l'expérience esthétique* (1967) which sees itself as a transcendental analysis of the contemplative act and its "affective a prioris" and deals with several of the arts. With his *The Act of Reading* (1976), Wolfgang Iser complemented the theory of reception with a theory of aesthetic effect that leads from processes of assimilation to the constitution of meaning by the reader and describes fiction as a communicative structure. Jurij M. Lotman's *The Structure of the Artistic Text* (1977) is a semiotics which is also aesthetically competent and which expands the concept of the text to "suprainformation" and "modeling system." *Phenomenology of the Social World* by Alfred Schütz and Thomas Luckmann (1975) provides the indispensable foundation for dealing with the problem of setting off the aesthetic from other provinces of meaning of human activity. Odo Marquard has repeatedly defined the aesthetic historically and systematically by its compensatory achievements and given the impetus for a new interpretation of modern art which would make it the corrective of the contemporary loss of the telos. Dieter Wellershoff's *Die Auflösung des Kunstbegriffs* (1976), the most recent analysis of contemporary phenomena and expansions of the aesthetic sphere, extends its considerations beyond the temporal frame of my study.

I am not reluctant to admit that this overview reflects the canon my own experience created and that it omits a good many names. But it seemed pointless to me to engage in polemics with representatives of other positions where a prior decision for a work-immanent interpretation is openly declared or the communicative achievement of aesthetic experience is not examined at all. The theories of the so-called Paris semiotics and the Tel Quel group come under this heading. It is against the latter that Sartre raised the well-known and hitherto unrefuted objection that it posited the work as *écriture*, as an absolute, ignored the reader, and forgot that literature is communication.[12] And the fact that in defining the achievements of aesthetic experience I gave priority to the historical and hermeneutic method did not seem to me to require that I restart the old quarrel with structural linguistics, poetics, and communications theory. The mutual results will decide what the varying but perfectly reconcilable methods contribute to solving the problem of literary communication, and where they can supplement each other.

What I owe to the authors whom I progressively came to recognize and appreciate as my predecessors in the course of these studies may well be often obscured because their theories had to be summarized in positions from which the problem could be developed further. In the thirties, John Dewey's *Art as Experience* initiated the turn from the work aesthetics, and the same is true of Jan Mukarovsky's *Aesthetic Function, Norm, and Value as Social Facts* (1936). The former defined aesthetic experience as the inherent "quality" of all fulfilled experience, the latter as the "contentless," i.e., transparent, principle of the aesthetic function which can take hold of all other activities and dynamize them. The subjective presuppositions in the aesthetic attitude and the demarcation of aesthetic experience from other provinces of meaning of the everyday world remained open and made it possible to raise questions that furthered research.

Walter Benjamin's *Kunstwerk* essay (1936) and Herbert Marcuse's *Critique of the Affirmative Character of Culture* (1937) opened discussion about the end of autonomous art at the same time. Benjamin defined aesthetic experience by the concept of aura, anticipated Malraux's thesis of the *Musée imaginaire* (1951)[13] with the analysis of the consequence of the aura's deritualization in the age of the mechanical reproducibility of art, and attributed to technicized art the revolutionary significance that it would make the masses the subject of a politicized aesthetic praxis. Marcuse attacked the idealist culture of the bourgeois era, suspected all previous aesthetic experience of the affirmation of things as they are, and based the hope for a better order on a "liberation from the ideal" which would come about through the emancipation of the sensuous experience of the beautiful. In aesthetic experience which here threatens to fall victim to ideology critique, Marcuse later saw the "decisive dimension of freedom" and derived the "promise of possible liberation" from the "subversive truth of art."[14] But this also makes it necessary to demonstrate in the history of its experience this subversive potential of art which transcends every class content nonviolently. Or, with a view to Benjamin's theology of history and idea of saving criticism, it means that one expects the saving of the past not only from the "true moments" of a coincidence of politics and prophecy but also from the continuity of the practical, never wholly suppressible aesthetic activity of man.

Hans-Georg Gadamer's philosophical hermeneutics *Truth and Method* (1960) and Theodor W. Adorno's posthumous *Ästhetische Theorie* (1970) were the immediate impetus for this book. Gadamer's theory of hermeneutic experience, its historical unfolding in the history of humanistic guiding concepts, his principle of seeing in historical impact the access to all historical understanding, and the clarification of the controllable process of the "fusion of horizons" are the indisputable methodological presuppositions without which my undertaking would have been unthinkable. What does appear disputable to me is Gadamer's "saving of the past" by the classical to which, in the "eminent text," there allegedly accrues a "superiority of origin" and a "freedom of origin" as compared with all other tradition.[15] But how is such superiority of origin of the classical work to be reconciled with the principle of a progressive concretization of meaning, and how can the "identity of meaning" of the original question, "which has always already mediated the distance between origin and present,"[16] be harmonized with the productive attitude of understanding in hermeneutic application? I therefore believe I can invoke Gadamer against Gadamer when I follow his principle of application and understand literary hermeneutics as the task of interpreting the tension between text and present as a process in which the dialogue between author, reader, and new author deals with the temporal distance in the back-and-forth of question and answer, of original answer, present question, and new solution, and concretizes meaning in ever different ways, and therefore more richly.

A second disputable point, it seems to me, is Gadamer's critique of the "abstraction of the aesthetic consciousness."[17] Although it applies to the decadent forms of nineteenth-century aesthetic education, it leaves the achievements of aesthetic experience between the historic poles of the cultic ("aesthetic non-differentiation") and the imaginary museum ("aesthetic differentiation") unexplained.[18] In Adorno's *Ästhetische Theorie*, these achievements and the entire aesthetic practice of preautonomous art are subjected to a dialectic of affirmation and negativity. In view of a bad praxis which, in the circle of the manipulated satisfaction of needs, threatens to degrade all aesthetic experience to the level of consumerism, it is only the monadic work of art with its negativity and its solitary, reflective viewer who has renounced all aesthetic pleasure that can destroy the all-enclosing web of bedazzlement. In Adorno's aesthetic of negativity, the avant-gardist literature and art of the sixties was given its most inclusive theory and its strongest legitimation. I devote a more detailed criticism to it (chap. 2) because Adorno is the adversary who provoked me into attempting to play the unwonted role of apologist for the discredited aesthetic experience. I will close by briefly explaining the *parti pris* of my apologetic intent and how it relates to our contemporary situation.

The uncritical talk about the "commodity character" of contemporary art makes one forget that even the products of the "culture industry" remain commodities sui generis and that the categories of use- and surplus value can no more deal with their character of art than their circulation can be understood by relations of supply and demand.[19] There are limits to the manipulation of aesthetic need because even under the conditions of industrial society, the production and reproduction of art cannot determine reception. The reception of art is not simply passive consumption; it is aesthetic activity which depends on assent and rejection[20] and which therefore cannot be planned by market research. Hannelore Schlaffer, to whom we owe the most telling critique of the successful cliché about the work of art as commodity, has also shed light on how this ideology-critical aesthetics abruptly turns into a fundamentally conservative cultural pessimism: to escape the alleged total "bedazzlement" of contemporary aesthetic praxis, the work of art, its aura, and its solitary contemplation are unavowedly being revalidated as the aesthetic measure of a lost authenticity so that the materialist critique ultimately slides back into the idealist understanding of art characteristic of the "bourgeois aesthetics" against which it had waged its fight.[21]

Adorno's theory of the machinery of the culture industry and its total effect of an "anti-Enlightenment"[22] has elsewhere developed into the prejudice that the art of a shrinking educated elite finds itself in hopeless retreat before the culture industry of a growing mass of consumers. The contrast between an avant-gardist art which must be reflected, and the production of the mass media which can only be consumed, does not do justice to our present situation, however. It remains to be shown that the expansion of the aesthetic sphere by the unsuspected possibilities of poietic and aesthetic activity will necessarily be overtaken by the "dialectic of Enlightenment" and that aesthetic experience through contemporary as through past art (which the new media can now present to a previously unreached number of addressees rather than to an educated upper class alone) will unfailingly degenerate into affirmative consumer behavior. At least Brecht's remark about the effect movies have might be adduced against such a prognosis: "everyone agrees that film, even the most artistic, is a commodity. . . . Almost without exception, people deplore that fact. It doesn't seem to occur to anyone that getting into circulation that way might do something for a work of art."[23]

As more popular methods such as semiotics, information theory, and textual linguistics come into use, aesthetic theory is clearly being neglected. How can it, through its own competence and tradition, make a contribution to the question whether the so frequently prognosticated transformation of all communicative aesthetic experience into a merely ideological function is indeed the ineluctable destiny of contemporary art? Adorno's *Ästhetische Theorie* has only this puritanical answer: "refraining from praxis, art becomes the scheme of social praxis."[24] The ascesis that is thus being imposed on both the producer and the recipient of art is to free the nonautonomous consciousness of the individual from the denounced praxis of his consumer behavior. But it is not easy to see how the transition to a new scheme of social praxis is to be accomplished by recipes of pure negativity, which are also the best that materialist aesthetics of the kind the Tel Quel group subscribes to can come up with.[25] The thesis that it is precisely the autonomous work of art that articulates the most irreconcilable opposition to social domination inherits not only the revalidated *l'art pour l'art* principle but also the loss of praxis that resulted when art achieved its autonomy in the nineteenth century and was divided into areas of "high" (noninstrumental) and "low" (useful) art.[26] If a new Enlightenment through aesthetic expression is to counter the anti-Enlightenment of the culture industry, the aesthetics of negativity must stop denying the communicative character of art. It must rid itself of the abstract "either-or" of negativity or affirmation and attempt to turn the norm-breaking forms of avant-gardist art into norm-creating achievements of the aesthetic experience.

There are at least three good reasons in the history of aesthetic experience which suggest that even today the norm-creating function of aesthetic experience need not necessarily slide into ideologically manipulated adaptation and end in the mere affirmation of existing conditions. However hopeless the situation of the arts under the hold and impenetrable manipulation of the new mass media may appear to ideology-critical puritans, it is nonetheless true that in the history of the arts, there have been times of servitude for the arts which more nearly justified the prognosis of their decline than does our period. The ban on images, for example, which was periodically revived under the rule of the Church, was certainly no less dangerous to aesthetic praxis than is the flood of images to which our mass media subject us. Yet so far, aesthetic experience has always emerged in unexpectedly new forms from every phase of hostility to art and has accomplished this by circumventing bans, reinterpreting the canon, or inventing new expressive means, a matter to which I will return (chap. A4). This fundamental refractoriness of the aesthetic experience also manifests itself in a freedom it often demands and which, once granted, is difficult to revoke, a freedom to ask impertinent questions or to suggest such questions in the guise of fiction where a system of binding answers and authorized questions confirms and legitimates the sway of a given explanation of the world. This transgressive function of question and answer can be found on both the byways of fictional literature and the royal way of literary processes such as the reception of myths which—as the history of Amphytrion shows[27]—leave all "superiority of origin" far behind and are perfectly capable of competing with philosophical thought as vehicles of emancipation.

Concerning the question how art can negate what exists and yet create norms, in other words, how it can provide yet not impose norms that will guide practical action so that their bindingness arises only from the consensus of their recipients, there is the recipe of an eighteenth-century philosopher whose authority is indisputable. It is contained in Kant's explanation of the judgment of taste: "The judgment of taste itself does not postulate the agreement of everyone (for it is only competent for a logically universal judgment to do this, in that it is able to bring forward reasons); it only *imputes* this agreement to everyone, as an instance of the rule in respect of which it looks for confirmation, not from concepts, but from the concurrences of others."[28] It is thus not only with regard to production that the aesthetic experience is distinguished by being a "production through freedom" (§43), its reception is also one "in freedom." To the extent that aesthetic judgment is both the model of a disinterested judgment that nothing extorts (§5) and that of a "concurrence that is not determined by concepts or principles" (§8), aesthetic behavior also acquires mediate import for the practice of action. It is the exemplary which Kant distinguished as "following" from the mere mechanism of imitation, and mediates between theoretical and practical reason, the logical generality of rule and instance and the a priori validity of the moral law, and can thus build a bridge from the aesthetic to the moral.[29] What might at first seem a defect in the aesthetic judgment, that it is merely exemplary but not logically necessary, proves to be its special distinction: the dependence of the aesthetic judgment on the assent of others makes possible participation in a norm as it is being formed, and also constitutes sociability. For in the necessarily pluralistic judgment of taste, Kant also saw the capacity to judge all those things through which one can even communicate one's feelings to everyone else. And although merely in passing, he traced this empirical interest in the beautiful to a memorable analogue to Rousseau's *Social Contract*. The aesthetic judgment that requires that universal communicability be heeded satisfies a supreme interest. Aesthetically, it redeems something of the original social contract: "A regard to universal communicability is a thing every one expects and requires from every one else, just as if it were part of an original compact dictated by humanity itself." (§41).

Aesthetic Experience and Literary Hermeneutics

A. Sketch of a Theory and History of Aesthetic Experience

1. What does aesthetic experience mean?

The following explanation is intended to convey a preliminary idea of the area of research that this question opens up. The forms in which aesthetic experience presents itself are less amply documented in historical sources than are other functions of everyday life such as religious or theoretical ones. In an effort to present the greatest number of facets of the problematic, the following examples are taken from widely scattered sources, chosen from a variety of periods, and not presented in chronological order.

At a time when the symbolic representation of nature began to flourish on the capitals of Romanesque cathedrals, Bernard of Clairvaux complained in a letter to Abbot William that monks now preferred reading "in marmoribus" to reading "in codicibus" and would rather spend the whole day marveling at the incredible profusion of animals and fabulous beasts than meditate on God's own text, the Bible.[1] It was no justification for the monks he was criticizing that what they had before them were not only fabulous beasts like the ancient centaurs but also and principally the hallowed animal symbols of the *Physiologus* which Christian tradition had long since put to use in the typological interpretation of the history of salvation. The orthodox Bernard ignores their spiritual significance and applies the same standard to them as to those grotesque figures which are surely demons. He finds that his brethren are being led astray because they are curious, and he accounts for that curiosity by their amazement at the abundance of figures and the variety of forms. What Bernard rejects here is, from the point of view of a devout rigorism, an illegitimate form of curiosity which, along with the symbolic object, also enjoys its sensuous appearance which ensnares. This criticism makes clear that even religious art can never wholly guard against eliciting an aesthetic attitude that will be more encompassing than dogma allows. Historically speaking, theological symbolism in the twelfth century was in fact accompanied by a discovery of visible nature in the fine arts.[2] It is only unwittingly and indirectly, of course, that this passage testifies to the fact that aesthetic interest can be more than ordinary curiosity, more than the mere gawking at the new, that it can be a new kind of seeing which functions as discovery. From the point of view of religious authority, aesthetic experience is always and necessarily suspected of refractoriness: where it is employed to bring to mind a suprasensible significance, it also perfects the sensuous appearance and creates the pleasure of a fulfilled present.

The refractoriness of aesthetic experience as characterized here is marked by a curious ambivalence: in a reversal of direction, its transgressive function may also serve to transfigure social conditions by idealizing them. To induce obliviousness to the actual suffering in society, ruling authorities can avail themselves of the power aesthetic experience has over the imagination and thus provide the satisfactions that aesthetic pleasure also gives to those who do not content themselves with the consolations of religion. In his treatise *De musica*, Jean de Grouchy, another figure from the High Middle Ages, thus recommends the chanson de geste as the kind of epic that is principally suited for "ordinary or old people among the working population" during their leisure hours so that, hearing of the troubles and changes in fortune of highly placed persons, "they might put up all the more readily with their own misery and return more cheerfully to their work."[3] In this testimony of a rare frankness concerning the use to which poetry may be put and which today would be called "ideological," the point is also made that the recital of epics not only brings relief from daily suffering but also furthers commitment on behalf of the national community (*ad conservationen civitatis*). In this medieval variant of the Aristotelian catharsis, aesthetic pleasure links relief from the pressure of the everyday and solidarization for future action in a perfectly matter-of-fact manner, and this precisely not because the simple public discovers a transfiguration of its own situation in the poetry but because that poetry acts contrastively and thus gives access to a wishful world of heroic acts, as Daniel Poirion has observed: "But if the knights dream of shepherdesses, the little people can dream of battles, especially if the author can interest them in the fate of heroes that act in the name of the community."[4]

A public that could only escape the closed horizons of a world that was saddled with illiteracy and ordered by immutable doctrine if it listened to poetry or music or gazed at the illustrations of the "picture Bible of the cathedrals" must have felt with special intensity the fascination an imaginary heroic universe exerts. But even in our time, the disclosure of another world beyond everyday reality is the most obvious door to aesthetic experience. It would be difficult to document this more beautifully than by an anecdote Giraudoux tells: "They took my father to the gymnasium when he was eight years old. There was a real piano on the stage. He was so disappointed, he screamed."[5] In contrast to the mimetic or realist aesthetic, expectation in the prereflective aesthetic attitude is directed toward something that does not resemble the ordinary world but points beyond everyday experience. For this reason, the real piano on the stage disconcerts aesthetic expectation just as the wolf in the zoo disconcerts the naive fairy-tale conception of the child, should it be ignorant of the well-known argument that the wolf with its red hood has nothing in common with the wolf in the zoo.

It is only at the reflective level of aesthetic experience that, to the extent he consciously adopts the role of observer and also enjoys it, a person will aesthetically enjoy and understand with enjoyment the real-life situations that he recognizes or that concern him. A verse by Wilhelm Busch expresses this aspect of reflected aesthetic experience in this way: "What vexes us in life/is relished when portrayed."[6] This is the aesthetic variant of that everyday behavior known as "role distance" in the sociology of knowledge. For man in all societies, the possibility of distancing himself from his actions lies in the fact that even in his naive everyday life, he can choose alternative forms of conduct, that his roles can relativize each other, and that he can experience himself in the discontinuity between the everyday and other provinces of meaning (such as the dream, religion, science) as a role-independent self.[7] Beyond these possibilities, the aesthetic attitude can take him to a point where he faces his role, and this frees him of the constraints and the routine of his normal role performance. This inner distance originates in the aesthetic attitude of play, the ability to do of one's own free will what one must otherwise do in all earnestness, an attitude which a Rilke verse conveys in ecstatic intensification: "and we transcend awhile our limitations and act our lives unthinking of applause."[8]

The aesthetic experience of role distance can be intensified and become aestheticism when it is taken up in a real-life situation where the conventions of morality or tact demand a wholly serious involvement. When, for example, a work such as the Isenheim altar is perceived and interpreted solely as a carrier of aesthetic qualities and abstraction is made from everything that makes the representation of the martyrdom shocking, cruel, and thereby exemplary, it is not only a devout sensibility that will be offended. Such an attitude is also inappropriate to the understanding the object itself demands.[9] In the figure of his unheroic hero in the *Sentimental Education*, Flaubert embodied the provocative utilization of aesthetic role distance which his contemporary Kierkegaard discredited as aestheticism. Drawn from pure curiosity into the street battles at the height of the 1848 revolution, Frédéric Moreau nonetheless retains the attitude of the "flaneur": "The drums beat the charge. Shrill cries could be heard, and shouts of triumph. The crowd rocked in a continuous surge. Frédéric, wedged between two dense masses, stayed where he was. Fascinated, he was enjoying himself hugely. The wounded falling, and the dead lying stretched out, did not look as if they were really wounded or dead. He felt as though he were watching a play."[10] This episode is literary only in its pointedness, not by virtue of the conduct it portrays. For it is a common experience (one need only think of the comic aspects of a funeral) that the seriousness of any role turns into play the moment one either voluntarily or involuntarily adopts the aesthetic attitude of the spectator. The episode in Flaubert's novel that turns the bloody seriousness of history into mere spectacle for the "flaneur" is part of a historically significant context. In Frédéric's aesthetic stance and in the political acts of his friends, Flaubert's cryptic irony points up a second-hand experience of history: just as the aesthete copies a passé romanticism, the revolutionaries imitate the larger-than-life-size 1789 model. The literary interpretation of the failure of 1848 thus shows a curious congruence with Karl Marx's analysis in the *Eighteenth Brumaire of Louis Napoleon*!

In view of the irrecoverable distance from reality, the aesthetic experience here becomes tangible only as a decaying second-hand experience. But it may also be looked for where it precedes concrete experience and conveys norms and contents for the practice of life first hand. In his autobiographical novella *Novembre*, the young Flaubert expresses the sentimental education passed on by bourgeois reading material: "It is in books that I studied the passions that I would have wanted to feel."[11] And Rousseau sums up his report on the excessive night-time reading of father and son in the same manner: "I had no idea of things in themselves, although all the feelings of actual life were already known to me."[12] Erasmus's so much earlier formulation "lectio transit in mores" already presupposes the anterior orientation aesthetic experience can provide. According to the motto of humanistic education, the imaginative power of poetry was to be preferred to the logical conceptualization of philosophy when patterns of correct speech and action were to be conveyed.[13] In conclusion, here is one more example from the Middle Ages which most charmingly condenses the transition from reading to manners. Floire and Blancheflor, the romance of the same name tells us, already loved each other in tender childhood, as early as nature permitted. But it was not nature but culture in the form of eagerly read "heathen books" which taught them, sharpened their senses, and made them find the joys of love on their way home from school.[14]

The reversal of these patterns, in which expectations derived from reading encounter an alien reality and the pure sentiments and higher passions of poetry fail to materialize in life and can only be maintained in opposition to everyday experience in the fantasy worlds of the daydream, is a pathological reverse of the aesthetic experience. Some of the peak achievements of the novel took this phenomenon as their model. In this context, one need only mention *Don Quixote* and *Madame Bovary*, the two most famous instances of a pathology of novel reading. What is common to their protagonists is the fundamental aesthetic attitude that they must realize in a prosaic reality the ideals of an outdated world of meaning which is fed only by their imagination. They differ in that the "last knight of La Mancha" comically resolves the contradiction between literature and life by a tenacious reinterpretation whereas the belated romantic whom Baudelaire admired for her dandyism perishes—solitary and uncomprehended—in trivial surroundings. In the *Sorrows of Young Werther*, Goethe shows, in contrast, how the communicative power of reading may precede its pathological effect. Werther and Lotte discover the mutuality of their sentiments through a literary pattern as they observe a thunderstorm: "she looked up at the sky and at me, I saw her eyes full of tears, she placed her hand in mine and said—Klopstock!" And toward the end, the sentimental pair, again prompted by a reading of Ossian, allows itself the single embrace that seals the sorrowful end. It is a return of the moment that spells the doom of Dante's Francesca and Paolo as they read about Lancelot. What later caused the epidemiclike Werther fever to become a public scandal was not merely due to the rebellion of individual feeling. The unexpectedly strong effect this literature had on life was also fed by a transformation of a religious into an aesthetic pattern of identification: "And you, good soul, who feels the same urge as he did, console yourself with his suffering and let this little book be your friend, should your fate or your own failure not allow you to find a closer one."[15]

The seductive power of aesthetic identification was criticized by both the orthodox and the enlightened critics of the secular *Trostbüchlein* (book of consolation). For not only did it offer a pattern of conduct to an undefined aesthetic perception that ran counter to the bourgeois order: "every young man longs to love like that. Every young girl longs to be loved like that." It also consoled the unrealizability of the expectations thus aroused: "Let this little book be your friend," a consolation which up to that time had been the prerogative of religious edification. The naive identification Goethe himself warned against in the second edition ("be a man and do not follow after me") would have remained trivial, however, and would not have been taken up on all levels of literary reception, had it not promoted the irruption of an experience that only poetry can express. Even in the trivial forms of naive identification with the loving and suffering hero, aesthetic experience is also effective as a revelatory power for it shows the reader in exemplary fashion that human passion is a distinctive characteristic of individuality. This accords with Helmuth Plessner's view that neither biology nor empirical psychology is qualified to deal with passion for a human being or a cause as a motive unique to man in his eccentric position, that even psychoanalysis provides no more than a rudimentary understanding of it, and that it is a phenomenon whose causes and nature only poetry can set forth.[16] The aesthetic experience discloses and conveys the individuated form of the *passions de l'âme*. It therefore goes far beyond the aesthetic identification of the daydreamer Sigmund Freud describes, that person who, at a safe distance from the imaginary fate of the hero, there finds what life denied him. Nor is identification "upward" the only possible direction the aesthetic experience can take, as has been shown by André Jolles's example of the masked ball. The aesthetic experience of play that teaches us "to place next to our life another life, next to our world another world"[17] leads, in the case of the masked ball, to a preference being accorded to three categories of roles, those of the knight, the shepherd, and the jester. "Some of our guests look for what appears to stand above or below society, others for what lies outside it."[18] Three important genres of the literary tradition are rooted in these three directions of aesthetic identification, the heroic, the bucolic, and the picaresque. They answer the deep need to be someone else and are therefore superior to the arbitrary disguise in roles that do not lead into a desirable world, a world into which one also cannot take any part of one's old self.[19]

Ernst Bloch saw the disclosing quality of aesthetic experience as a utopian harbinger and distinguished it as the "anticipation of the power of the imagination" from the merely illusory quality of Freud's daydream. His examples are Brentano's *Vaduz* and Mörike's *Orplid* — ideal poetic landscapes which were already encountered in the dreams of childhood as lying beyond the known world and which can pass from the waking dream into poetry because they carry the "seriousness of a harbinger of possible reality" and give linguistic expression to something hoped for.[20] The anticipatory aesthetic experience takes on literary form in the "love through the portrait" motif whose most famous instance is the musical sublimation of the aria "this painting is enchantingly beautiful," which in Mozart's *Magic Flute* draws Tamino to Pamina, the beloved he has never seen in the flesh. To Bloch's interpretation of the Turandot motif may be added the medieval variant in which the dream image of the beloved arises from nothing more than the hearing of her praise and her name. It is the *amor de lonh*, the "love from afar" which inspires Jaufre Rudel to become the poet of that purest longing which finds its fulfillment in nonfulfillment. The poetic legend goes beyond this paradox of longing by having Jaufre finally voyage across the sea to Tripoli where, as he dies, the incarnation of his longing advances toward him to embrace him for the first and final time.[21]

In its paradoxical quality, this romantic *Urbild* of Troubadour poetry is the purest expression of an aesthetic experience that has tacitly adopted the Paulinian formula for the use of God's grace, "tamquam nihil habentes, et omnia possidentes" (as having nothing, and yet possessing all things, II Corinthians 6, 10). It unfolds its secular "as if" to the point where it is only *in extremis* that the perfection of anticipation can coincide with the real but must otherwise infallibly be disappointed by it. Don Quixote's love for Dulcinea remains perfect because he never finds her. In Proust's *Remembrance of Things Past*, love always dies anew when what was expected finds fulfillment and revives when jealousy imagines the beloved as another's possession. Proust's *recherche* is therefore also the place where the direction of expectation of the aesthestic experience reverses itself: the anticipation of the imagination which is foiled by the irreparable inadequacy of the actual present can fulfill itself in what is past when the purifying power of recollection makes it possible to recover in aesthetic perfection what was experienced deficiently. In a manner of speaking, aesthetic experience is effective both in utopian foreshadowing and in retrospective recognition. It perfects the imperfect world not merely by projecting future experience but also by preserving past experience which would continue unrecovered along the path of mankind, were it not for the luminosity of a poetry and art which transfigures and monumentalizes it.

This introductory examination has shown us some structural properties of the aesthetic experience which presented themselves principally as aspects of a communicative and receptive attitude. Before turning to the productive side of the aesthetic experience, the result of our initial inventory should be briefly summarized. On the receptive side, the aesthetic experience differs from other functions in the world of the everyday by a temporality peculiar to it: it permits us to "see anew" and offers through this function of discovery the pleasure of a fulfilled present. It takes us into other worlds of the imagination and thereby abolishes the constraint of time in time. It anticipates future experience and thus discloses the scope of possible action. It allows recognition of what is past or suppressed and thus makes possible both the curious role distance of the beholder and the playful identification with what he ought or would like to be: it permits the enjoyment of what may be unattainable or difficult to bear in life; it provides the exemplary frame of reference for situations and roles that may be adopted in naive imitation but also in freely elected emulation. It offers, finally, in a detachment from roles and situations, the chance to understand the realization of one's self as a process of aesthetic education.

Admiration for the productive capacity of art is most abundantly documented in the history of aesthetic experience. The measure of such admiration is the perfect skill by virtue of which the freely producing artist becomes superior to the craftsman who must obey rules.[22] It can also be the poet's ability to give perfect expression to all the things that the demands and conventions of daily existence would otherwise cause to remain mute, suppressed, or unrecognized. Goethe's famous motto from the *Trilogy of the Passions* indicates this: "And if man in his torment falls silent, a God gave me to say what I suffer." Here, the productive capacity of the aesthetic experience and its cathartic effect coincide: in the joy at the perfection of his work, the poet who transforms his experience into literature also finds a liberation of his mind which his addressee can share. The lyric poetry of experience of the nineteenth century made this aesthetic experience the paradigm of artistic greatness.[23] But it is older than its subjective institution by the aesthetics of genius and has its counterpart in the Platonic doctrine concerning the artist's "mania," which explained the creative act of the poet and "diviner" objectively, as a stepping out of oneself, a being filled by divine inspiration.

But from the very beginning, the aesthetic experience of the productive capacity of man was also the experience of a limit and resistance which the creative artist and poet encountered. Prior to the aesthetics of genius, the product of man's art also always gave rise to an experience of nature as limit and ideal norm which the artist cannot exhaust, let alone surpass, but only imitate or, at most, perfect where nature has left an incomplete model. To document this experience of the limit of man's aesthetic production, Galileo's judgment of Michelangelo is apposite: "The art of discovering a magnificent statue in a block of marble has placed Buonarotti's genius high above ordinary minds. And yet such a work is nothing other than a superficial imitation of a single pose of the body and of positions of the parts of an unmoving human being such as nature created it, a body in which there are so many external and internal organs, such a multitude of muscles, sinews, nerves, and bones which make possible so many diverse movements. Besides, there are the senses and, finally, the mind. Would we not then be justified in saying that the making of a statue is immeasurably less than the creation of a living human being, indeed of the most despicable worm?"[24] After the advent of the aesthetics of subjectivity (when aesthetic activity is neither any longer experienced as a creation *according* to nature nor—in Poe's and Baudelaire's antiromantic turn—as a production *like* nature's), aesthetic reflection which accompanies modern lyric poetry up to Valéry understands the artist's creation as a creation *against* the resistance and opacity of nature. It was Valéry who, in his Leonardo essays, most profoundly probed the antinaturalism of this modern period, and it is in his *Eupalinos* (1921) that he poetically thematized it. Here, the predicates by which Galileo characterized the ideality of nature are ajudged negatively and downgraded to the level of a range of external conditions of aesthetic production: nature, like Michelangelo's block of marble, becomes a mere materiality. Through the human process of abstraction, the countless properties of its material are brought into a new, constructive order whose totality is less complex than its parts. And as he confronts the unending development of nature which excludes neither blindness nor chance, the artist experiences his work as a blissful seizing of the possibilities of his own, finite world.[25]

Subsequent to the breakthrough of the autonomous aesthetic of genius, creative aesthetic experience refers not merely to a production in subjective freedom, without rules or model, or to the creation of possible worlds beyond the known; it also means the capacity of the genius to restore its pristine state and plenitude of meaning to that *one* world which is familiar, which he has always known but which has become alien. "But genius is simply childhood recovered at will, childhood now endowed, in order to express itself, with virile organs and with an analytical mind that enables it to order and arrange all the materials accumulated involuntarily."[26] The concept of the naive as encountered in the philosophy of history—the childhood of both individual and historical life (i.e., Greek civilization)—which is meant to counter the alienation of modern society[27] is linked in Baudelaire's definition of genius with the fresh perception of the child: "everything the child sees is new; he is in a constant state of rapture."[28] But it is not only owing to its freshness and plenitude of meaning that the child's perception becomes the ideal yardstick of aesthetic experience. What the child sees freshly because for the first time also permits the adult to rediscover what already lies within him as past experience and can be recalled; the poet whose conscious aesthetic activity can undo the alienation of reality and re-create the world in its original newness returns to our consciousness a forgotten or suppressed reality. Baudelaire's theory of aesthetic experience anticipates what is common to Freud's and Proust's aesthetics: the sharpened perception of the new or the surprising representation of another world are not enough. What is required as an additional and concurrent element is the opening of the door to the rediscovery of buried experience,[29] the lost time that has become recoverable. Only this constitutes the entire depth of aesthetic experience.

The poet of the modern period who thus conjoins the renewal of perception and the recognition of suppressed experience makes the totalizing power of memory the ultimate authority of aesthetic production. In contrast to the Platonic anamnesis, the atemporal essence of the absolutely beautiful no longer antedates the work. In the act of recollection itself, the aesthetic activity produces the telos that perfects and makes eternal the imperfect world and ephemeral experience. In addition to the two possibilities, that aesthetic production re-creates an already given telos or itself institutes the telos that fulfills itself in the work, there is the third: that aesthetic activity has only its own movement for its goal. In its result which can now carry the appearance of perfection, it thus disavows the effort that goes into the making of art. Valéry's poetics was not the first to recognize and describe the specific achievement of the aesthetic experience. On the threshold of modern times, Montaigne, his manner of writing, and the experience of himself that accrues in the act of composition already impressively testify to this. The incomplete enterprise of his essays describes a search that, in a progressive unmasking, tests and rejects one guarantee of identity after another: the offices and honors of public life, the retreat from the world, the stoic turning inward, the authenticity in the face of death, the fideist skepticism, and, finally, the return to *paraître* as the truth of natural life. Throughout the phases of this process, there occurs the discovery that an aesthetic identity, the abiding possibility of narrating himself, can take the place of an abandoned search for personal identity: "I have no more made my book than my book has made me—a book consubstantial with its author, concerned with my own self, an integral part of my life."[30]

Time and again, the initial phenomenological inventory of what may be called aesthetic experience has taken us to a limit where the aesthetic attitude detaches itself from the area of meaning of religious experience. Whether one understands this transition anthropologically, sociologically, or by way of the philosophy of history, it presupposes a peculiarity of the aesthetic experience which has not been brought out so far but which was an element in all attempts at definition, namely, the fact that the understanding of aesthetic meaning is a voluntary act.[31] The very circumstance that art cannot impose its validity, that its truth can be neither refuted by dogma nor "falsified" by logic is the grounds for the emancipatory chance its refractoriness provides, and explains why those in authority are interested in making its powers of seduction and transfiguration serve their ends. Art, as Jurij Lotman has said, could thus always rise again and outlive its oppressors, not because its existence contributes to the satisfaction of material wants but because it meets a need which the play character of aesthetic experience fulfills: "Ritual is obligatory, the round dance—optional."[32]

2. Critique of Adorno's aesthetics of negativity

The concept and categories of negativity enjoy an unmistakable and still growing vogue in more recent aesthetic theory. Not the least important reason for this is that negativity can define the work of art in its constitution and historicity, as both structure and event. Negativity characterizes the literary work and the productions of the fine arts as irreal objects which—for the purpose of aesthetic perception—must negate the real as an anterior reality if they are to turn it into image. Through this act, according to Sartre's phenomenology of the imaginary, they constitute "world" ("depasser le réel en le constituant comme monde").[1] But to the extent that it transcends the familiar horizon of a tradition, changes established relationships to the world, or breaks through prevailing social norms, negativity also characterizes the work of art in the historical process of its production and reception.[2] Finally, negativity marks both the subjective and the objective aspects of aesthetic experience. It is contained in Kant's "disinterestedness of aesthetic satisfaction," a formula of negation that gets at the "distance between self and object, that hiatus in the life of pleasure which is referred to as aesthetic distance or the moment of contemplation."[3] On the other hand, it also manifests itself in the relationships of art and society insofar as the work of art—though social product—always "contravenes reality through the element of form." It is precisely when art has achieved autonomy and refuses to bow to the norms of the socially useful that it recovers an eminently social function through its opposition to society.[4] Yet all their apparent fruitfulness for aesthetic theory notwithstanding, one may doubt that the categories of negativity adequately describe the achievement, the change of horizons, and the social function of aesthetic experience. It is this doubt that prompts the following reflections.

The aesthetics of negativity was probably given its most trenchant formulation in Theodor W. Adorno's posthumous *Ästhetische Theorie* (1970). According to it, the cognitive interest of art and therefore the philosophical rank of aesthetics derive from their place in the dialectic of enlightenment. Art, which participates in the process of social emanicpation on its path toward autonomy, is characterized by negativity in a twofold fashion: in its relation to the social reality which conditions it and in its historical origin which tradition determines: "there is no question that it is only by negating their origin that works of art became what they are. Having once retroactively destroyed what they derive from, the ignominy of their ancient dependence on hocus-pocus, service to those who rule, and divertissement cannot be held against them as a kind of original sin" (p. 12). It is not the traditional practical functions of art in cult, the establishment of norms governing ways of life, or the fellowship of play (to give more neutral terms to the "services" art performs) which are socially significant in Adorno's "aesthetic historiography" (p. 90). Only when art abandons all subservience and "opposes social domination and its extension into mores" (p. 334), separates itself from the empirical world as its other, and thus makes clear that "the world itself must change" (p. 264) is the social in art properly defined.

According to Adorno, it is not until it becomes autonomous that art attains its social rank. Precisely in negating all social ties does it become eminently social. It is true that owing to the law of aesthetic form, art remains mere appearance vis-à-vis social reality. But it is by virtue of this very fact that it can become the agency of a social truth before which the false appearance of the factual, the untrue, and the unreconciled in society's actual condition must reveal itself. The negativity of aesthetic appearance as here understood ultimately derives from the utopian figure of art: "what does not exist is promised because it appears" (p. 347). Art as portrayal of social truth is thus not mimesis but *promesse du bonheur*, although not in the sense Stendhal intended: *"Promesse du bonheur* means more than that all earlier praxis obstructed happiness: happiness would be above praxis. The force of negativity in the work of art measures the gulf between praxis and happiness" (p. 26).

Adorno's aesthetic of negativity did not have to hide its epochal origin—the bourgeois era from its zenith to its decline—and its polemical occasion—the rejection of the contemporary culture industry —behind a claim to theoretical generality which it cannot make good as regards all of preautonomous art. Given the total consumption-and-exchange society in the age of an administered world, the paradoxically pointed thesis that "refraining from praxis, art becomes the schema of social praxis" (p. 339) can clearly be vindicated. And Adorno's aesthetic theory is also the best conceivable instrument for doing away with those misleading antinomies, formalism and realism, *l'art pour l'art* and *littérature engagée* which are nineteenth-century legacies. But if one takes literally the principal element in this theory according to which what is social in art can only derive from the determinate negation of a determinate society, a dilemma is created which Adorno himself described in these terms: "This does not mean, of course, that all positive and affirmative works of art—almost the entire store of traditional works—are to be swept away or eagerly defended by the excessively abstract argument that they also are critical and negative because they abruptly contrast with empirical reality. Philosophical criticism of unreflected nominalism debars the simple claim that the course of progressive negativity—the negation of an objectively binding meaning—is the path of progress of art" (p. 239).

Adorno's aesthetic theory never resolved this dilemma for us. Under its premises, the sum of affirmative works of art remains a vexation that cannot be entirely removed by whatever circuitous account might be devised to make these works part of the path of progress. The history of art cannot be reduced to the common denominator of negativity even if, alongside the negative or critical works which count in the process of social emancipation, one sets off an incomparably larger number of positive or affirmative works whose natural tradition would simply have left behind the emancipatory "path of progressive negativity." This is so in part because negativity and positivity are not defined quantities in the social dialectic of art and society, and can even turn into their opposite since they are subject to a curious change of horizon in the historical process of reception. There is the further fact that the path of progressive negativity as a categorial frame is inappropriately one-sided in its emphasis on what is social in art, for it leaves out communicative functions. With older art, these cannot simply be dismissed by the mere counterconcept of affirmation, nor can they be ignored in modern and contemporary art.

On the first point: to the extent that they become "classical" by attaining public significance[5] through incorporation in institutions that confer cultural sanction and ultimately reaffirm, as cultural legacy, precisely those authoritative traditions whose validity they denied or infringed upon at the time of their appearance, even works of a negative character tend to lose their original negativity in the process of their reception. We are familiar with this phenomenon in modern art where expressions of protest, criticism, and revolt inevitably turn into the enjoyment of such negations when the provoked public absorbs the provocation and sees it at an aesthetic distance. But such neutralization occurred before it became "the social price of aesthetic autonomy" (p. 339). If one sees it in the larger perspective of its reception and interpretation, the history of the arts has always shown the swing of the pendulum between "transgressive function" and interpretive assimilation of works.[6] Older art also, which has come down to us with the halo of the classical, positive, and eternally ideal, as guaranteeing order and permanence, need by no means have merely affirmed and transfigured the state of a given society when it appeared. What may seem "affirmative" to the ideology-critical zeal of our times in Dante's *Divina commedia*, Lope de Vega's *Fuente Ovejuna*, Shakespeare's *King Richard III*, Racine's tragedies, or Molière's comedies, for example, may only have accrued to such works from the homogenizing power of tradition. To call them "system-stabilizing" blocks one's perception of their originally heteronomous intent, their norm-destroying or norm-creating effect. Not to mention the fact that neither the simple negation of a given society nor the pure innovation of form guarantee that a work of art will outlast its avant-gardist effect to then become classical and exemplary. Exemplariness clearly does not fit into Adorno's "path of progressive negativity." Precisely those works that have the historical power to transcend the canon of the customary and the horizon of what is expected are not immune from gradually losing their original negativity in the process of their cultural reception. The quality of being classical can be achieved only at the price of a second change of horizon which again annuls the negativity of the first change which a work of art may cause by its appearance.[7] The quality of being classical is the paradigm par excellence of the cooption of negativity in traditions of social affirmation. The classical as the "cunning of tradition" corresponds to the "cunning of reason" in Hegel's historical process. Through the change of horizon, cunning brings it about but also veils the fact that the path of the progressive negativity of art imperceptibly passes over into the progressive positivity of tradition.

Second: the social function of art on its earlier, preautonomous, and historical levels cannot be adequately understood by the pair of categories, negation and affirmation. This becomes clear in Adorno himself when he constantly reproaches affirmative works of art for the ignominy of subservience, the transfiguration of what exists, or false reconciliation,[8] and then attempts to save them again through the backdoor of negativity, as in the following passage: "All works of art, even the affirmative ones, are a priori polemical. The idea of a conservative work of art is contradictory. By emphatically distancing themselves from the empirical world, their other, they show that the latter itself must become other. They are unconscious schemata of its transformation" (p. 264). If one leaves undecided the question whether a merely "a priori polemical" polemic is not also contradictory, this curious negativity surely defines the work of art only as the object of theoretical reflection, not as a schema of primary aesthetic experience. Regarding the latter, polemics against what exists or the "negation of an objectively binding meaning" (p. 239) is not the only legitimate social function of art. This does not mean that the affirmative in the practice of the experience of art therefore deserves the taint of a conservative mentality, of the transfiguration of existing relations of domination. If one does not simply propose to deny the character of art to a literature of such indisputable social effect as heroic poetry, as Adorno's thesis would require, one must not start out by seeing and recognizing the social function of art in *negation* but in the *creation* of an objectively binding meaning.

In this as in other practical functions, art as symbolic or communicative action can clearly not be defined by Adorno's negative catalog of affirmation. "Affirmative portrayal" (p. 386), "consolatory Sunday exercises" (p. 10), communication as "adaptation of the mind to what is useful" (p. 115), "subjective identification with objectively reproduced humiliation" (p. 356), and similar formulas of rejection of all "transfiguring art" and its "appearance of reconciliation" describe nothing of the role that aesthetic experience has played in the formation, justification, sublimation, and transformation of social norms. If we take an example from an area Adorno so vigorously vilifies, "service to those who rule," namely the literature of courtly love, it will readily be seen that here, with the affirmative transfiguration of the aristocratic mistress, it is precisely not a condition of dependence which is being eternalized. Instead, what became possible was the enacted identification with a newly developing love ethic. Sociohistorically, its contribution to the emancipation of sentiment and the forms of communication between the sexes was so considerable, it is difficult to overestimate it. Already in this phase of aesthetic experience, a moment of negativity, i.e., the unexpressed negation of ecclesiastical norms governing marriage and ascesis, can admittedly be discovered. But for the twelfth-century public, this implicit negativity did not exclude but encompassed affirmation or, rather, the communicative identification with a developing social norm and lifestyle.

From what has been elucidated, our critical question can be answered as follows: As long as it remains within the categorial frame of negation and affirmation and the constitutive negativity of the work of art is not mediated with identification as its reception-aesthetic counterconcept, the aesthetic experience is divested of its primary social function.

Identification is one of those phenomena of aesthetic experience that clearly cause Adorno's aesthetic theory some embarrassment. For example: "Aesthetic experience first of all creates distance between the observer and the object. This is present in the idea of disinterested contemplation. Philistines are people whose relation to works of art is determined by whether and to what extent they can put themselves into the place of the characters. All branches of the culture industry are based on this and confirm their customers in this habit" (p. 514). The number of those chastised for philistinism here is larger than Adorno may have judged. If he were right, the aristocratic public of the heroic epic would already have been philistine, for we know that in the twelfth century, they often baptized their sons "Roland" or "Olivier." But even Diderot and Lessing would not escape the stigma of that appellation. As theoreticians of the bourgeois play, they demanded that the modern dramatist portray his hero as being like everyone else because only the sameness of hero and audience could arouse our compassion along with our fear.[9] As still called for here in the name of the bourgeois ideal of equality and as contrasted with the remoteness of the perfect hero of classical tragedy, identification seems to have sunk to the level of an exchange of need and satisfaction or, worse still, of meeting "an unstilled need by substitute satisfactions" (p. 362) in our time. But to conclude with Adorno that catharsis is "a cleansing action which is directed against the affects and consents to repression" and was always intended to safeguard the interests of the rulers (p. 354) is to pour out the child with the bathwater and to misunderstand the communicative achievement of art at the level of primary identifications such as admiration, emotion, laughing, and crying with the hero which only aesthetic snobbery will consider vulgar. For it is in such identifications and only secondarily in the aesthetic reflection that detaches itself from them that aesthetic experience turns into symbolic or communicative action. This is not to say that negativity must be abandoned as the fundamental characteristic in the experience of the aesthetic object, as will become apparent when we ask how aesthetic distance and communicative identification are mediated in the experience of catharsis (see below, chap. 7).

The strength and indispensability of Adorno's aesthetic theory—the reaffirmation of aesthetic autonomy in the form of the dialectical negativity of art which must prove its critical rank vis-à-vis a praxis that has become untrue or "activity as the cryptogram of rule" (p. 358)—has been purchased at the price of a derogation of all communicative functions. Communication here is suspected of an "adaptation of the mind to the useful by which it becomes one commodity among others. And what is called meaning today participates in this abomination" (p. 115). Along with the communicative competence of art, the entire sphere of its reception and concretization is also being sacrificed to modernism in Adorno's aesthetics of negativity (p. 339). This purism has the weighty result that Adorno must ignore the dialogic process between work, public, and author and therefore occasionally resubstantialize the history of art in spite of himself. And this in opposition to his passionate rejection of Platonism and the idea of an atemporal beauty (p. 49). The work of art that comes out of society only because of society's productive forces and then remains separate from it (p. 339) and which, as a "windowless monad," must represent what it is not (p. 15), must be given an autonomous historical movement, a life *sui generis*: "The significant ones constantly reveal new layers, age, grow cold, die" (p. 14). Authentic works of art "churn" (p. 339). They are answers to questions they themselves raise (p. 17); merely through "historical development, through correspondence with what comes later . . . they can actualize themselves" (p. 47). As if without the receptive, understanding, interpretive, and critically evaluating interaction between those to which it is addressed over successive generations, a work of art could out of its own substance constantly reactualize significance and thereby realize its historical, not atemporal, essence!

If the monadlike work of art thus threatens to move into the substantialist path of an "immanent historicity" (p. 15; 262ff.), its addressee on the other hand is sent into the solitude of his experience where "the recipient forgets himself and disappears in the work" (p. 363). Adorno describes this experience as "perplexity" or "shock" in order to contrast it with the customary concept of experience or of the enjoyment of art. But even as a "breakthrough of objectivity in subjective consciousness" (p. 364), this "memento of the liquidation of the self which in its shock becomes aware of its own limitation and finiteness" (p. 364) (and which is not so different from the previously rejected catharsis) is incapable of crossing the line from contemplative acceptance to dialogic interaction. Although it is admitted that for art, "its own social being is veiled and only to be apprehended through its interpretation" (p. 345), the active share in the formation and reformation of meaning by which a work lives historically is denied the interpreter and all receiving agencies of society in Adorno's aesthetic theory, which is undialectic to this extent.

The communicative function Adorno denies to contemporary art in the social sphere will only accrue to the liberated mankind of the future. Surprisingly, it is the beautiful in nature that becomes the paradigm for the "reconciled reality and . . . the restored truth about the past which the great works await" (pp. 66ff.). In opposition to Hegel, aesthetic theory is to be redirected toward this beauty (p. 99). For "the beautiful in nature is the trace of the nonidentical in things under the spell of universal identity" (p. 114). Behind this, there lies the intent to restore the "dignity of nature" as authority against the misused rule of "what is of the autonomous subject's own making" (p. 114). But Adorno succeeds here only by according a futuristic meaning to the beautiful in nature, a meaning which no longer has any connection with previous definitions and metaphors of the concept of nature: "The line against the fetishism of nature, the pantheistic escape which would be nothing other than an affirmative cover for an endless doom, is drawn because nature as it stirs tenderly and mortally in its beauty has not yet come to be. Modesty before what is beautiful in nature means that one might injure what is not yet by seizing what is. The dignity of nature is that of a not-yet-being which rejects intentional humanization by its expression" (p. 115). It seems that this new nature shares nothing other than dignity with the old. Here, the aesthetics of negativity has clearly abolished the concept of nature by simply making it historical and by thus promoting being that cannot be made, that cannot be disposed of, and that has always existed, to being that may be hoped for, that may someday be reconciled, but that is not as yet. In spite of this *promesse du bonheur* in his theory, those ready to adopt Adorno's opposition to Hegel's "theodic of the real" (p. 116) and to carry on his criticism of the circle of art and consumption will miss an answer to the question how the "gulf between praxis and happiness" is not just "measured" (p. 26) by the force of negativity in the work of art, but how it can be bridged again by aesthetic praxis.

My criticism of Adorno's aesthetic was meant to introduce the attempt to justify aesthetic experience vis-à-vis a theoretical claim that neglects or suppresses the primary modes of this experience, especially its communicative efficacy, in favor of the higher level of aesthetic reflection. The purity of reflection to which the solitary subject is to rise as he confronts the work of art is played off by Adorno against the sensory experience and communicative interaction of art with grandiose one-sidedness, but this is not just prompted by his sociocritical position. Here also, Adorno is heir to a tradition in the philosophy of art that withdrew to the ontology of the aesthetic *object* and that tended to abandon the question concerning the practice of aesthetic *experience* to normative poetics or to the psychology of affects. The rejection of all responses to art that have not reached the position of its classical autonomy becomes especially clear where Adorno's therapy of negativity against the seductions of the culture industry climaxes in the admonition: "Artistic experience is autonomous only where it rids itself of taste and its pleasures" (p. 26). One may feel that this therapy pours out the child with the bathwater. My thesis opposes this aesthetic purism: that attitude of enjoyment which art creates and makes possible is the aesthetic experience par excellence which underlies both preautonomous and autonomous art. It must again become the object of theoretical reflection where renewed meaning is to be given to the aesthetic practice of a productive, receptive, and communicative attitude for our time.

3. Aesthetic pleasure and the fundamental experiences of poiesis, aesthesis, and catharsis

If anyone in our time still had the courage to use the term *enjoy* as it occurs in the well-known Faust passage "And what to all of mankind is apportioned I mean to savor in my own self's core" (l. 1770)[1] to characterize his attitude toward art, he would risk being called a philistine. Worse yet, he would be chastised for satisfying mere consumption- and kitsch needs. Until recently, the enjoyment of art was considered a privilege of the much-maligned *Bildungsbürgertum* and tabooed as such, and this may still be true today. The older, basic meaning of *enjoy*, i.e., "to have the use or benefit of a thing," is perceived only in obsolete or technical usage at present. (Who among those that address each other as *Genosse* [comrade] still knows or cares to hear that *Genosse* comes from *geniessen* [enjoy] and originally referred to the person who grazes his cattle on the same pasture?) But even the lofty heights of meaning to which the word rose until the time of German classicism would now probably strike us as curious.[2] The meaning "participation and appropriation" which inheres only in the German word, and the specific sense "to delight in something," combined oddly during this epoch. In the religious poetry of the seventeenth century, "to enjoy" could substitute for "to partake of God." In pietism, both meanings, "pleasure" and "participation," combined in one act in which the believer directly assured himself of God's presence. Kopstock's poetry leads to "reflective pleasure"; Herder's concept of intellectual pleasure grounds self-certainty as a primary "having-oneself" which discloses a "having-of-world" (existence as pleasure). In Goethe's *Faust*, finally, the concept is used to refer to all levels of experience up to the highest desire for cognition (from enjoyment of life, of acts, enjoyment with consciousness, all the way up to the enjoyment of creation).

What does the unhappily still unwritten history of the concept "pleasure" teach us about the fundamental aesthetic experience?[3] The prestige that the meaning of aesthetic pleasure acquired during the classical period of German art was preceded by a process in which cognition and pleasure, i.e., the theoretical and the aesthetic attitude, were hardly differentiated. Aesthetic pleasure was given a definition of its own because it became necessary to justify it before philosophy and religion. But even modern reflection about the attitude of enjoyment which the production and reception of art may cause remained subordinate to rhetorical and moralistic argumentation for a long time. The following retrospective can only attempt to provide an initial orientation.

A key passage in Aristotle's *Poetics* which was to play a significant role in the history of its reception is the fourth chapter in which the reason for the pleasure taken in the portrayal of ugly objects is discussed (1448b). Aristotle traces this enjoyment to a twofold root of the pleasure in imitation: it may be due to the admiration of a perfect technique of imitation but also to the pleasure that comes from recognizing the model in the imitation. In this explanation of aesthetic reception, a completely sensuous and a highly intellectual affect thus come together in aesthetic enjoyment.[4] But there is more to the aesthetic experience than apprehension by sight (aesthesis) and a vision that apprehends (anamnesis): the beholder can be affected by what is portrayed, he may identify with the acting persons, give rein to his own aroused passions, and feel pleasurably relieved by their release, as if he had experienced a catharsis. This discovery and justification of cathartic pleasure by which Aristotle corrected the "straightline mechanism" on which Plato had based his condemnation of art[5] is probably the most provocative inheritance of classical poetic theory. Of it, one could say that "until today, it has given us the only conclusive answer to the question why the contemplation of the most saddening event gives us the most profound pleasure,"[6] a finding which has now also been confirmed by psychoanalytic aesthetics.

A second event of considerable import for the crystallization and self-assertion of aesthetic experience is the Augustinian distinction between *use* and *enjoyment*, *uti* and *frui*. Hans Blumenberg tells us that Augustine saw "the fundamental character of the world in its 'utilitas' as the instrumentality 'ad salutem' while a full and fulfilling relation to being could be expected only in a 'fruitio' that is turned toward God."[7] Chapters 33 to 35 of Book X of the *Confessions* bear this out.[8] The catalog of examples of "lust of the eyes" (*concupiscentia oculorum*) distinguishes between the use of the senses for pleasure (*voluptas*) and for curiosity (*curiositas*). The former refers to the "beautiful, the melodious, the fragrant, the savory, the soft," i.e., positive sensations of the five senses, whereas the latter also refers to their opposite, as is explained by the examples of a mangled carcass or even a lizard catching flies and the fascination these exert. Concerning both directions of the aesthetic experience, Augustine draws a new line between the good use of sensual pleasures, which is solely directed toward God, and the bad, which turns toward the world. The auditory pleasure during the singing in church can help the mind experience a more intense devotion; the pleasure of the eyes may call attention to the beauty of divine creation. But this *fruitio*, the sole legitimate one, is constantly in danger of sliding into naive sensual pleasure and abandoning itself to the aesthetic attraction of a sensuous experience that is heightened by the means of the arts. And *curiositas* which can paradoxically delight in unpleasant and even disgusting things is judged by Augustine to be the reverse of aesthetic pleasure and rejected because "it does not enjoy its objects as such but only *itself* and that because the ability to know is being confirmed through them."[9]

For the history of aesthetic experience, this introduction of self-enjoyment is no less significant than the application *per negationem* of the distinction between use and enjoyment to intersubjective experience. In *De doctrina Christiana* (I, 20), Augustine asks the "weighty question" whether the new commandment "as I have loved you, that ye also love one another" (John 13, 34) is to be understood as a relationship of *frui* or *uti*, and whether man must love man for his own sake. His answer again reserves *fruitio* of the other to God's love because "only that can be loved for its own sake which assures man a happy life."[10] This reservation has time and again led *fruitio* between two human beings in friendship or love to be claimed as a this-worldly possibility of the *vita beata*. Examples would be Abelard and Heloise (God knows that in you I never searched for anything but you), Montaigne and La Boétie ("because it was he, because it was I"), and the dramatic entanglement of Don Rodrigue and Dona Prohèze with Don Camille as the unloved third in Claudel's *Soulier de Satin*.[11] But this does not mean that love of another for his own sake is being claimed as an intrinsically aesthetic experience. If the Augustinian reservation downgrades it to an enjoyment of oneself in the other, the autonomous I-you relationship evinces a recognition of the other as both a physical and moral person and thus abolishes the distinction between *uti* and *frui* altogether. The productive side of aesthetic pleasure also falls victim to the Augustinian criticism of the self-enjoyment of *curiositas*; the self-affirmation man can derive from his own work, Augustine claims, causes him to miss that inwardness which is the only access to salvation in a contemplation of God that is oblivious to the self.[12]

A third point of departure for the question concerning the genesis of aesthetic experience is the famous eulogy the sophist Gorgias wrote in justification of Helena. With the discovery of the sensuous aspect of language and his theory of the effect speech could have—"it may banish fear and suffering, arouse joy and compassion"—Gorgias went back to the aesthetic enjoyment of one's own affects when aroused by speech and poetry and employed, before Aristotle, the categories of *phobos* (shudder) and *eleos* (wailing) and the medical analogy of catharsis.[13] But whereas Aristotle was primarily looking at the state of the viewer of a tragedy and the liberation of his mind as its goal, Gorgias was interested in the "preparation" of the listener of a speech and the transformation of his passionate interest into a new conviction[14] which "irresistibly forms his soul as it pleases." The rhetorical tradition that sets in here accentuates the communicative function of the cathartic effect: the aesthetic enjoyment of one's own affects as they are stimulated by speech or poetry is the lure to let oneself be persuaded as one is swept along by pathos and then becomes ethically calm (*excitare et remittere*, *movere et conciliare* in later terminology). The examples by which Gorgias illustrates the curious persuasive power a speech can attain through pathos and ethos and by creating cathartic pleasure show the ambivalence of the aesthetic lure: rhetoric can "present the unbelievable and unknown" and change a person's beliefs. In trials, it can sway many "even if it is not truthful," can affect the soul as poison can the body, be well-intentioned and charm the listener but also lead him into evil.

In its secular quarrel with philosophy and theology, rhetoric has always been charged with this ambivalence of its aesthetic means, as is well known. Even in the most recent debate between hermeneutics and ideology critique, the two aspects "prevailing on" and "talking into" turned up as "consensus" and "manipulation." For our purposes, it is important that the history of reception of the classical doctrine of cathartic pleasure usually had only its psychagogic side in view. The neglected communicative side must therefore be traced in the rhetorical tradition. On the basis of the doctrine regarding the role of affect in making something believable, the rhetorical tradition since the Renaissance has never failed to vindicate the legitimacy of the logic of the *sensus communis* (*logica probabilium*) as against demonstrative logic (*logica veritatis*), as Klaus Dockhorn has shown in his indispensable addendum to Gadamer's hermeneutics.[15] Luther also made use of the rhetorical principle of *movere et conciliare* when he described what took place in the "hearer of the word" and where that most difficult of all things was involved, the *rhetoricari* of the Holy Spirit: "Belief occurs in affect and must occur in affect because reason is incapable of making present the past and the future."[16] The doctrine of affects in rhetoric fundamentally shaped the newer aesthetics in particular and "was not just a theoretical complement of the culture during the Enlightenment but actually evoked it."[17] Even the romantic aesthetic of experience (*Erlebnisästhetik*), which took up a position that was antagonistic to the culture of reason of the *bel esprit* and the alleged artificiality of all rhetorical education, had to deny that its program of a new genuineness and immediacy was rooted in the old rhetorical demand that the speaker himself be passionately aroused if he is to move his audience.[18] As the new ideal of aesthetic pleasure, self-enjoying subjectivity abandoned the *sensus communis* as the expression of a sociable sympathy at the same moment the aesthetics of genius finally replaced the aesthetics of rhetoric.[19]

It is here that the history of the decline of all pleasurable experience of art begins. Now shorn of its cognitive and communicative efficacy, aesthetic pleasure appears either as the sentimental or utopian opposite of alienation in the three-phase models of the philosophy of history or, in contemporary aesthetic theory, as the essence of an attitude that is considered philistine when adopted toward classical art and simply excluded vis-à-vis modern art. A starting point of all historico-philosophical definitions of the modern antithesis of pleasure and alienation including the materialist is to be found in the sixth letter of Schiller's *On the Aesthetic Education of Man* (1793–94). Far in advance of its historical manifestation, the alienation of industrial society and the consequences its division of labor would have are grasped here in a way that makes it possible to read corresponding passages in Marx's *German Ideology* (1845–46) as a historical concretization: "state and church, the laws and customs, were now torn asunder; enjoyment was separated from work, the means from the end, effort from reward."[20] For Schiller, the separation of pleasure and work is tantamount to the loss of a totality once represented by a sentimentally perceived Greek civilization. It is true that the task of restoring that lost totality confers on the aesthetic, i.e., the enjoyment of genuine beauty, a privileged role because only the aesthetic state brings with it "a disposition which removes all limits from the totality of human nature" (twenty-second letter). But since such a purely aesthetic effect is not to be found in reality (where we "enjoy the pleasures of the senses simply as individuals . . . the pleasures of knowledge simply as a race," whereas it is "the Beautiful [alone] that we enjoy at the same time as individual and as race" but that Beautiful has its home in the realm of aesthetic appearance), the realization of the aesthetic state which would permit the ideal of equality to be fulfilled remains utopian (twenty-seventh letter). However the much discussed passage about the realm of freedom in *Capital* may be interpreted, it is part and parcel of the materialist consequence of the idealist philosophy of history that, alienation in Marx's utopia of the realized communist society having been abolished, the measure of fulfilled happiness would be found not in the abolition of work or in pure leisure but in the enjoyment of work as the first vital need and as the means toward self-realization.[21] Later Marxist aesthetics has held as decisively to the future-oriented character of aesthetic pleasure as has psychoanalytic aesthetics to its opposite, i.e., that aesthetic pleasure relates to the past, that it is a return of what has been repressed. To document the former, we will quote one of Brecht's *Geschichten vom Herrn Keuner* (stories about Mr. Keuner): "Mr. K. saw an old chair of great beauty of workmanship somewhere and bought it. He said: 'I hope to get a few ideas as I reflect what kind of life it must be where a chair such as this would not be conspicuous and the pleasure taken in it be neither disgraceful nor make one stand out.'"[22] Here, expectation of a utopian state of nonalienated work can absolve the pleasure taken in the beautiful of the taint of its origin in hidden suppression, whereas aesthetic pleasure in Freud acquires its deeper meaning first as a "release of greater pleasure from deeper psychical sources," i.e., from the recognition of past experience: "A strong experience in the present awakens in the creative writer a memory of an earlier experience (usually belonging to his childhood) from which there now proceeds a wish which finds its fulfillment in the creative work. The work itself exhibits elements of the recent provoking occasion as well as of the old memory."[23]

In contemporary usage, little remains of the lofty meaning pleasure once had. Although pleasure as a way of grasping the world and securing self-certainty and then as a historical-philosophical and psychoanalytic concept once justified involvement with art, there are many today who consider aesthetic experience genuine only when it has left all enjoyment behind and risen to the level of aesthetic reflection. The sharpest criticism of all pleasurable experience of art is again found in Adorno. Those who look for and find enjoyment in works of art are philistines: "Expressions like a 'treat for the ears' give them away." Those who cannot rid themselves of relishing art deal with it as they deal with the products of the kitchen or pornography. Taking pleasure in art is ultimately merely a bourgeois reaction to the intellectualization of art and thus the precondition for the culture industry of our time which serves hidden ruling interests in a circle of manipulated need and aesthetic substitute gratification. Succinctly: "The bourgeois wants art to be sumptous, life ascetic. The other way around would be better." (pp. 26–27). After the Second World War, avant-garde painting and literature undoubtedly contributed their share to counter the sumptuousness of the world of consumption by making it ascetic once again, and thus displeasing to the bourgeois. One need only recall such tendentially related and contemporary phenomena as Jackson Pollock's or Barnett Newman's abstract sublime and the new style of Beckett's plays or novels.[24] In this context, ascetic art and the aesthetics of negativity acquire the lonely pathos of their legitimation through their opposition to the consumer art of the modern mass media. But Adorno, the most outspoken pioneer of the aesthetics of negativity, saw the limit of all ascetic experience of art quite clearly when he observed: "but if the last trace of pleasure be extirpated, the question why there should be works of art at all would be difficult to answer" (p. 27). His aesthetic theory provides none, nor do the currently leading theories of art, hermeneutics, and aesthetics.

In the field of the fine arts, the kind of experience considered deserving of theoretical formulation today usually sets in beyond the contemplative or enjoying attitude which—as the subjective side of the experience of art—can be left to a largely uninterested psychology or denounced as the false consciousness of a late-capitalist consumer culture.[25] Before the First World War, the problem of aesthetic pleasure was a principal theme of psychological aesthetics and the general field of the fine arts, and Moritz Geiger wrote the clarifying phenomenological postscript on it.[26] Current hermeneutic philosophy as represented by Hans-Georg Gadamer is interested in this problem only under the aspect of a criticism of the abstraction of the aesthetic consciousness, especially of the imaginary museum of a self-enjoying subjectivity whose addiction is contrasted with the process of an experiencing understanding, the purpose being to "defend that experience of truth which comes to us through the work of art against that aesthetic theory which lets itself be restricted to a scientific concept of truth."[27] The social no more than the ontological truth of art requires mediation through aesthetic pleasure. From Plekhanov to Lukacs, when Marxist literary theory was restricted to mirroring, i.e., the mimesis ideal of bourgeois realism, a recognition of objective reality was expected on the part of the perceiving subject. Only since Brecht can we say that the effect of literature is being considered. But this is done with the intent to counter the subject's tendency to pleasurable empathy and aesthetic identification and to train him in a thinking and critical attitude. And finally, it should be mentioned that the reception aesthetics I have advocated since 1967 has so far dealt with this problem only in the case of popular literature or the change of horizon from the original negativity to pleasurable familiarity with the classics, but has otherwise presupposed aesthetic reflection as the basis of all reception and thus participated in the surprisingly unanimous ascesis that aesthetics imposed on itself vis-à-vis the primary aesthetic experience.

Soon after the appearance of my *Kleine Apologie der ästhetischen Erfahrung* (1972) and independently of it, Roland Barthes also advocated the rehabilitation of aesthetic pleasure in his *The Pleasure of the Text* (1973). Here, he turns against the panideological suspicion that aesthetic pleasure is nothing other than an instrument of the class in power at a given time: "Pleasure, however, is not an *element* of the text, it is not a naive residue; it does not depend on a logic of understanding and on sensation; it is a drift, something both revolutionary and asocial, and it cannot be taken over by any collectivity, any mentality, any ideolect."[28] Barthes believes that the time has come to sketch a modern aesthetics that will examine the "pleasure of the consumer." For this undertaking, he offers a dichotomy of *plaisir* and *jouissance*, of affirmative pleasure and negative aesthetic "bliss" which one might view as the French counterpart to Adorno's aesthetics in certain respects. It is up to the reader to share in or to oppose the "profound hedonism of all culture": "he enjoys the consistency of his selfhood (that is his pleasure) and seeks its loss (that is his bliss). He is a subject split twice over, doubly perverse" (p. 14). This contrast is carried further in additional pairs of concepts such as "sayable:unsayable," "seduction:force," "the familiar:the tabu-breaking new." Increasingly, they tend to assign a higher rank to the "atopie" of *jouissance* as the authentic than to the "ubiquity" of *plaisir* as the inauthentic aesthetic attitude. Barthes's approach thus also slips into the circle of negativity and affirmation: the mystified element of "rupture" divides literature undialectically into a double canon, assigns the master works of the past to the merely self-affirming *plaisir*, and omits what should have made up the subversive canon of *jouissance* (hardly more than the name of George Bataille appears here). Since Barthes one-sidedly emphasizes the "insular character" of solitary reading and the anarchic aspect of aesthetic "bliss," generally denies any dialogue between reader and text, and thus brackets the macrostructure of the communicative reading situation so that "lecture" reduces itself to the perception of microstructures, all that is left to the reader is a passive, purely receptive role, and his imagining, testing, and meaning-creating activity never figures as a source of pleasure. This goes so far that the text recovers the initially surrendered ontological priority and can even become an *objet-fetich* (p. 45). "The text you write must prove to me *that it desires me*. This proof exists: it is writing. Writing is: the science of the various blisses of language, its Kama Sutra" (p. 6). It is no accident that

Barthes's apology reduces aesthetic pleasure to the pleasure that lies in the commerce with language ("encore un autre mot, encore une autre fête": one more word, one more celebration). Since he fails to open the self-sufficient linguistic universe with enough decisiveness toward the world of aesthetic practice, his highest happiness ultimately remains the rediscovered eros of the contemplative philologist and his undisturbed preserve: "the paradise of words."

But what does the primary aesthetic experience consist in? How does aesthetic pleasure differ from sensual pleasure generally? What is the relationship between the aesthetic function of pleasure and other functions in the world of everyday reality? In contemporary linguistic usage, pleasure is opposed to work and also differentiated from cognition and action. Pleasure and work do indeed constitute an old opposition which has been part of the concept of aesthetic experience since antiquity. To the extent that aesthetic pleasure frees one from the practical compulsion of work and the natural needs of the everyday world, it grounds a social function which has characterized aesthetic experience from the very beginning. But aesthetic experience has not always been the opposite of cognition and action. In contrast to the secular validity of the Horacian doctrine of the twofold purpose of poetry (*delectare et prodesse*) which, together with the rhetorical trichotomy *docere-delectare-movere*, justified all aesthetic practice from antiquity to the later modern period and was felt to be permissive rather than restrictive of what could be portrayed, the separation of *delectare et prodesse* —the *l'art pour l'art* principle—seems an episode in the history of art. The cognitive efficacy of aesthetic pleasure which Goethe's *Faust* still plays off against abstract, conceptual knowledge did not become a dead issue until the nineteenth century, as art became progressively autonomous. And to the older, preautonomous art which conveys norms of action in multiple ways, the communicative function was still perfectly natural even though today it is often mindlessly suspected of affirming ruling interests, misunderstood as the mere transfiguration of existing conditions, and rigorously rejected.

In aesthic theory, the question concerning the difference between aesthetic pleasure and ordinary enjoyment, i.e., the direct sensuous surrender of the self to an object, is answered almost unanimously by reference to Kant's doctrine of disinterested pleasure and definitions of aesthetic distance. Whereas the self is wholly absorbed in elementary pleasure and this pleasure is sufficient unto itself as long as it lasts and has no reference to the rest of life, aesthetic satisfaction requires an additional element, the taking up of a position that brackets the existence of the object and thereby makes it an aesthetic one. In his critical continuation of Moritz Geiger's phenomenology of aesthetic pleasure, Ludwig Giesz has shown and described this in some detail: "Pleasure refers to the object of pleasure which is enjoyed in isolation. Aesthetic pleasure abolishes this isolation of pleasure in a certain sense since now a position is being adopted and satisfaction is found in the object of pleasure. There thus occurs that hiatus in the life of pleasure which is referred to as aesthetic distance or as the moment of contemplation."[29] By this, Geiger means "the creation of distance between self and object," Giesz informs us, but this does not suffice to distinguish aesthetic enjoyment from the theoretical stance since the latter also involves distance. The aesthetic attitude demands that the distanced object be not merely contemplated disinterestedly, the viewer should also participate in producing it as an imaginary object—like the world of play into which one enters as a fellow player. The distancing act in the aesthetic experience is at the same time a form-creating act of the imagining consciousness, as Jean Paul Sartre has shown in his phenomenological analysis of the imaginary. The imagining consciousness must negate the already existing world of objects in order to produce through its own activity and according to the aesthetic signs or schemata of a linguistic, optical, or musical text the verbal, pictorial, or acoustic form of the irreal aesthetic object.[30] The real—and this includes nature or a landscape—is never beautiful in itself: "Beauty is a value which applies only to the imaginary and which entails the negation of the world in its essential structure."[31] But if the beautiful is necessarily imaginary, the contemplative act of the viewer is always required to constitute the aesthetic object. The reverse, that the imaginary is beautiful per se, or that the act of imagination necessarily calls forth aesthetic pleasure, does not follow. Sartre's analysis elucidates the fundamental difference between perception and idea and their contradictory relationship to a given or absent object but not the question of the additional ingredient that would be needed if the idea of something absent is to bring aesthetic pleasure.

Giesz has defined this higher interest which goes beyond the filling in of the "mold" of an idea and the surrender to a concrete object of pleasure as a dialectical form of enjoyment: "for I also enjoy the state of balance into which I have brought the primary pleasure and its object."[32] It can be deduced from this definition that aesthetic distance cannot be a one-way, merely contemplative, or wholly disinterested relation to a "distanced" object. In the enjoyment of the aesthetic object, there occurs an interplay between subject and object whereby we "acquire an interest in our disinterestedness."[33] This aesthetic interest is most easily explained by the fact that as the subject makes use of the freedom it has to adopt a position vis-à-vis the irreal aesthetic object, it can increasingly enjoy both the object which its satisfaction progressively discloses and its own self which in this activity feels released from its daily existence. Accordingly, aesthetic enjoyment always occurs in the dialectical relationships of self-enjoyment in the enjoyment of something other. I have chosen the formulation "self-enjoyment in the enjoyment of something other" in order to characterize the state of balance Giesz brings out as a pendulum movement in which the self enjoys not only its real object, the aesthetic object, but also its correlate, the equally irrealized subject which has been released from its always already given reality.[34] If this state of balance is lost and a shift occurs toward one or the other of the poles, aesthetic enjoyment lapses either into what is probably already a mystical enjoyment of the object[35] or into a form of sentimental self-enjoyment in which, according to Giesz, "the person who merely enjoys (i.e. not aesthetically or 'in play') enjoys himself as someone who enjoys."[36]

Accordingly, the definition of aesthetic pleasure as enjoyment of self in the enjoyment of what is other presupposes the primary unity of understanding enjoyment and enjoying understanding and restores the meaning of participation and appropriation which originally characterized German usage. In aesthetic behavior, the subject always enjoys more than itself. It experiences itself as it appropriates an experience of the meaning of world which both its own productive activity and the reception of the experience of others can disclose, and the assent of third parties can confirm. Aesthetic enjoyment that thus occurs in a state of balance between disinterested contemplation and testing participation is a mode of experiencing oneself in a possible being other which the aesthetic attitude opens up.

The anthropological model of inner distance by which Hans Blumenberg has explained the possibility of aesthetically enjoying objective negativities which initially seem "nonenjoyable" (such as the ugly, the horrible, the cruel, or the deformed) must be distinguished from the aforementioned decadent forms.[37] Here, aesthetic pleasure can occur if it is not the objects in their shocking negativity but the pure function of the subject's own faculties as they are affected by them that is being enjoyed. This presupposes that the subject opens up to its affects in a "heightened consciousness of its own unconcern." This inner distancing eliminates not only the immediate relation to the presented object but also the immediacy of sentimental self-enjoyment. In the sense of my formulation, the affected faculties themselves become something alien here in which the subject, unconcerned in its core, can take aesthetic pleasure because it is free. It is obvious that Blumenberg's model of distancing oneself from one's own affects also describes the most dependable defense mechanism against tragic emotions: the spectator can escape all impact if he succeeds in confining his reflective enjoyment to the functions of his own affected faculties.

On various occasions, Sigmund Freud described aesthetic pleasure in a context that connects self-enjoyment and the enjoyment of what is other.[38] The paradigm he uses to explain the anthropological need for the hero of daydreams and literature traces the aesthetic pleasure of identification to the relief and protection aesthetic distance provides, but also to a deeper interest in the activity of the imagination. The spectator in the theater or the reader of a novel may "enjoy being a great man" and can surrender unhesitatingly to normally repressed feelings because his pleasure is predicated on aesthetic illusion, i.e., "his suffering is mitigated by the certainty that, firstly, it is someone other than himself who is acting and suffering on the stage, and, secondly, that after all it is only a game, which can threaten no damage to his personal security."[39] In this way, the aesthetic pleasure of identification releases possibilities of experiencing what is other which the "poor wretch" would never consider himself capable of in his everyday reality. But in Freud's theory, aesthetic self-enjoyment in the enjoyment of what is other amounts to more than a psychoanalytic restatement of Aristotelian catharsis. The effect of poetry here is not confined to the awakening of one's affects, the aesthetic pleasure of identifying with others' actions or suffering, and the relief afforded by a thorough purging. Freud shows the present relevance of the traditional doctrine of cathartic pleasure. But he also goes beyond it with the new insight that in the psychic economy, purely aesthetic pleasure has a farther-reaching function which is that of "fore-pleasure" or an "incentive bonus" designed to "make possible the release of still greater pleasure arising from deeper psychical sources."[40] It is the shocklike aesthetic experience of the return of the repressed: the recovery of expectations and wishes formulated in childish play, i.e., the blissful recognition of forgotten experiences and lost time. It is clear, and most impressively confirmed by a reading of Proust, that aesthetic enjoyment as here defined can take on an aura of incomparable luminosity when the inner distance from a self that has become alien is abolished in a catharsis which derives from the pleasure of the work of remembrance and which, in a manner of speaking, brings back the Platonic anamnesis to an earthly beyond.[41]

A not yet fully utilized advantage of Freud's aesthetic is that it permits the development of the productive and receptive efficacy of the aesthetic experience from a concept of aesthetic pleasure that underlies both and which can easily be supplemented on the inter-subjective side which is missing in Freud's theory, and that is the communicative function of aesthetic experience. For the three afore-mentioned fundamental categories of the attitude of aesthetic enjoy-ment, we can now introduce three concepts of the aesthetic tradition which we have encountered time and again in our backward glance at the history of aesthetic pleasure. They are poiesis, aesthesis, and catharsis.

Poiesis in the Aristotelian sense of the faculty to make something names that pleasure in one's own work which Augustine still consid-ered God's prerogative and which, since the Renaissance, has been in-creasingly claimed as the distinguishing characteristic of autonomous artistic activity. As the fundamental productive aesthetic experience, poiesis thus corresponds to Hegel's definition of art[42] according to which man satisfies his general need to be at home in the world by producing art. He "strips the external world of its inflexible foreign-ness," makes it into his own product, and by this activity acquires a knowledge that differs from the conceptual knowledge of science and the instrumental practice of self-reproducing craft.

Aesthesis may name that aesthetic pleasure of cognizing seeing and seeing recognition which Aristotle explained through the twofold root of the pleasure taken in imitation: the word *aesthesis*, it is true, is not specifically used for this purpose in the Aristotelian aesthetic. But with a basic meaning of sensory perception and feeling, it can be found at the beginning of that special science of aesthetics which Baumgarten founded. Aesthesis as the fundamental receptive aes-thetic experience thus corresponds to various definitions of art as "pure visibility" (Konrad Fiedler) which understand the pleasurable reception of the aesthetic object as an enhanced, deconceptualized seeing achieved by "defamiliarization" (Victor Shklovskij), a "dis-interested contemplation of the object in its plenitude" (Moritz Geiger), the experience of the "density of being" (J. P. Sartre), in short as "complex, clearly delineated, succinct perception" (Dieter Henrich), and which vindicate sensory cognition vis-à-vis the priority accorded cognition through concepts.

If one combines Gorgias's and Aristotle's definitions, *catharsis* names the pleasure produced by one's own affects when they are stimulated by oratory or poetry and which can change the listener's — and liberate the spectator's — mind. Catharsis as the fundamental communicative aesthetic experience thus corresponds to the practical employment of the arts for the social functions of conveying, inaugurating, and justifying norms of action. Catharsis also corresponds to the ideal object of all autonomous art which is to free the viewer from the practical interests and entanglements of his everyday reality and to give him aesthetic freedom of judgment by affording him self-enjoyment through the enjoyment of what is other.

I summarize the above in the following thesis: the attitude of aesthetic enjoyment that frees both *from* and *for* something can occur in three functions: for the producing consciousness, in the production of world as its own work (poiesis); for the receiving consciousness, in the seizing of the possibility of renewing one's perception of outer and inner reality (aesthesis), and finally — and here subjective opens up toward intersubjective experience — in the assent to a judgment demanded by the work, or in the identification with sketched and further-to-be-defined norms of action.

As the three fundamental categories of aesthetic experience, poiesis, aesthesis, and catharsis are not to be conceived hierarchically, as a structure of layers but as a nexus of independent functions. They cannot be reduced to, but may variously succeed, each other. The creative artist can adopt the role of observer or reader toward his own work. The fact that he cannot produce and absorb, write and read at one and the same time, will make him experience the shift of attitude from poiesis to aesthesis. In the reception of a text by the contemporary reader and later generations, the gap between it and poiesis appears in the circumstance that the author cannot tie the reception to the intention with which he produced his work: in its progressive aesthesis and interpretation, the finished work unfolds a plenitude of meaning which far transcends the horizon of its creation. The sequence from poiesis to catharsis may regard the addressee who is to be changed or taught by the structure of the text or it may turn back on the producer: the poet can thematize the making of poetry as if the liberation of his mind were an effect of poietic activity—"cantando il duol si disacerba" (as one sings, suffering loses its sting), to quote the famous Petrarchan verse[43] in which the fiction has abolished the hiatus between emotion and the distance of the author as he creates.

The cathartic function is not the only channel for the communicative efficacy of the aesthetic experience. It can also result from aesthesis. In the contemplative act which renews perception, the viewer may understand what he has perceived as a communication about the world of the other or adopt through an aesthetic judgment a norm of action. But aesthesis can also pass over into poiesis. The observer may consider an aesthetic object to be incomplete, abandon his contemplative attitude, and become a cocreator of the work by completing the concretization of its form and significance. And finally, aesthetic experience can be included in the process of the aesthetic creation of identity if the reader accompanies his receptive activity by reflection on his own development: "The validity of texts does not derive from the author's authority, whatever its reasons, but from the confrontation with our life history. Here *we* are the author, for everyone is the author of his life history."[44]

In all its uses, literary communication retains the character of an aesthetic experience only as long as poietic, aesthetic, or cathartic activity does not sacrifice enjoyment. This state of balance between pure sensuous pleasure and mere reflection has probably never been described as concisely as in a Goethe aphorism which also already anticipates the turning of the receptive into a productive act and thus comes closest to modern theories of art: "There are three kinds of reader: one, which enjoys without judgment, a third, which judges without enjoyment, and the one in the middle which judges as it enjoys and enjoys as it judges. This latter kind really reproduces the work of art anew."[45]

4. The ambiguity and the refractoriness of the beautiful — a backward glance at a Platonic legacy

An apology of art that goes back to poiesis, aesthesis, and catharsis in order to ground the peculiarity and efficacy of the aesthetic experience would remain one-sided if it failed to mention that these three fundamental determinations describe only one side of the coin. The other, the negative side, appears when one begins to realize why the great puritans in the long tradition of the philosophy of art—a sequence which includes such illustrious names as Plato, Augustine, Rousseau, and Kierkegaard—saw the experience of art in another, questionable or dangerous light and therefore suppressed or trimmed its cognitive or ethical claim. It is no accident that aesthetics was not established as an autonomous discipline until the eighteenth-century enlightenment. A history of aesthetic experience, to which this attempt is merely an introduction, would have to search for the aesthetic practice of productive, receptive, and communicative action in a tradition that usually either ignored or obscured it. Platonism casts a powerful spell on the tradition of theoretical reflection which accompanies Western art on the road toward its autonomy. It is the authoritative legacy from which and against which aesthetic experience developed in the history of European education. If someone could state that "the history of aesthetics is one long quarrel with the ancient doctrine that poets lie,"[1] it is equally remarkable that in spite of (or perhaps because of) the contradictions within the Platonic doctrine of beauty to which it originally belonged, this notion has had so powerful an effect.

Regarding the history and the theory of the arts, Platonism furnished the European tradition with a double orientation which proved extremely ambiguous. For the appeal to Plato could confer the highest dignity on commerce with the beautiful but could also bring it into disrepute.[2] *Dignity* because of the transmittal of the suprasensible since according to Plato, the contemplation of earthly beauty kindles recollection of the lost, transcendent beauty and truth. There is also a negative element, however, for the sensuous is indispensable: the perception of the beautiful may feel no need to go beyond the pleasure it takes in sensuous appearance or mere play. Those who enjoy the beautiful are not necessarily referred back to a transcendent perfection at home in the ideal. It is true that, for Plato, the dignity of commerce with the beautiful is subordinate to the *theoria* of philosophizing. But in the *Phaedrus*, it is assigned a higher rank than the other three kinds of "madness," the "inspiration of the Prophet . . . that of the mystic . . . that of the poet," and is ascribed to Aphrodite and Eros.[3] If the desire for the beautiful is honored and justified in the *Phaedrus* as a mediation between the human and the divine, it is obvious that Plato did not have the beautiful in the arts in mind. "Here as elsewhere, the relation of participation . . . remained closed to the sphere of artistic production although it could easily have been subsumed under the 'beautiful activities.' Plato reserved such production for the declaration of ontological nullity which the 10th book of the *Republic* pronounces."[4] In view of the disproportionately severe taboos and sanctions Plato there imposes on art, the inference cannot be rejected that he judged the sensuous power of the beautiful when unsublimated by recollection (anamnesis) as rather dangerous to his ideal of the perfect—and to us rather authoritarian—state.

It may be objected that insofar as the beautiful is concerned, Plato did not always clearly distinguish between sensory experience and suprasensible cognition so that one could also see a progression here.

It may also be said that the ontological criticism of art as a second-order imitation is countered by the myth of the demiurge in the *Timaeus* which could enhance the dignity of imitative art. In the reception process of Platonism, it is precisely this shifting evaluation of the aesthetic experience in major Platonic dialogues which further deepened the ambiguity in the use to which the beautiful can be put. From this ambiguity, both the highest dignity and the most serious defect were deduced. Either art could be justified by a cosmological function—as mediation between the practice of sensory experience and theoretical contemplation; or it could be denied all cognitive use and all ethical seriousness and be roundly condemned when the negative functions of mimesis—second-order imitation, deception through sensuous appearance, pleasure in amoral objects—were adduced.

Since the inception of the Christian era, the resulting inconsistent orientation of the aesthetic experience has manifested itself time and again. The Platonic legacy gave the early church fathers' hostility to art the best weapon with which to condemn the old belief as they criticized the untruth of pagan art and poetry. Its fictions became the instrument of the devil, the "father of art," the "liar from the very beginning," and the secret purpose of the artistically beautiful an enticement to sin.[5] But it is also true that the Christian church of the fourth and fifth centuries used Neoplatonism as an apology of the beautiful because it had to defend itself against the Manichean heresy which had adopted Platonic theorems on art and especially the condemnation of the body as the prison of the soul.[6] The Plotinian progression toward God's intelligible beauty justified the beauty and order of created things and returned to the creative artist a direct relationship to the idea. The historical role that fell to protean Platonism in the process which led by way of the utilization of the aesthetic experience to the progressive recognition of the fine arts is difficult to trace through history. So far, especially the evolution and history of the highly effective popularization of the Platonic doctrine of the triadic unity of the beautiful, the true, and the good has remained obscure. For this reason, only the historical frame for the modern development can be sketched here.

On the one hand, Renaissance humanism reinterpreted Platonic ideas and thereby freed artistic activity of the taint of bad mimesis. Panofsky has shown that art theory now fastened on the doctrine of ideas and, supported by the interpretation in Cicero's *Orator*, discovered the perfection of the idea in the inner contemplation of the human spirit. Since it is preeminently in artistic activity that the idea reveals itself, there occurs in the accounts of painting and sculpture the paradoxical inversion "that it is now the Platonic concept of ideas that serves to give the lie to the Platonic conception of art."[7] The humanist religion of art originated in the newfound dignity of the beautiful. The defense of ancient mythology by the Platonic academy in Florence, where poetry was raised to the level of an autonomous *theologia poetica*, is one climax of this process. Another is that, in line with the new dignity of human creation, Scaliger elevates the poet as a privileged creator above all other artists because he alone, as *alter deus*, can found a *natura altera*, a view which is already close to the mimesis principle.[8] As the fine arts begin to achieve self-subsistence, they become distinct from the merely useful ones. This involves a progressive loss of praxis on the part of aesthetic experience, a phenomenon which characterizes art as it detaches itself from cult and didactics and moves toward autonomy.

The claim of the arts to autonomy, on the other hand, provoked the opposition of Christian and social authorities, and even of an enlightened morality. This opposition could derive its arguments both from Plato's criticism of art and from the arsenal of Christian condemnations of the theater which extend in a secular tradition from Augustine and the church fathers to Bossuet and Bourdalou, the critics of French classicism, and which Rousseau carried even further in his *Letter to D'Alembert*. The polemics against the classical theater which climaxed in the Tartuffe scandal identify the negative effects of mimesis and employ arguments that had hardly changed since Tertullian's *De Spectaculis* (On spectacles) and the third-century Carthaginian dispute over the theater.[9] It was maintained that the portrayal of manners and morals on the stage did not lead to the moral purification that the poets promised the audience. What did happen was that the spectators identified with the passions of the characters on the stage.[10] The irredeemable claim that a mere holding up of a mirror could improve manners (*corriger les moeurs*) betrayed an illegitimate arrogance of the theater to be a public agency of moral judgment.[11] Worse than the furtherance of imagined passions is the practical uselessness of the seriously intended morality of Molière's comedy: "He has shown our century the fruit one may expect from the morality of the theater which attacks only what is ridiculous in the world but leaves it all its corruption."[12]

This Christian and dogmatic criticism in the name of enlightened reason was not simply adopted by Rousseau. He gave it greater depth and sharpness with additional arguments which merit renewed interest today: in an astonishing manner, they anticipate something for which the culture industry and the mass media are being attacked today, i.e., manipulation. They thus make manifest the unavowed puritanical derivation of materialist "commodity aesthetics" and ideology critique. Practical reason must reject the stage which merely mirrors prevailing manners, says Rousseau, for it will inevitably lead its public to an endorsement of the existing, undesirable state of society.[13] It promotes useless pleasure rather than the joys that come from the true needs of human nature.[14] The seductive power of curiosity removes the spectator to a distance from which he can savor and which makes him forget his most immediate duties over an imaginary fate.[15] Aesthetic experience leads to identification with the passions of the figures on the stage. It also contains a subliminal power which undermines our moral sensibility. For curiosity takes the spectator to the point where the natural horror of evil with which he reacts to a Phaedra or Medea at the beginning of the tragedy gradually weakens and imperceptibly changes into sympathy.[16] The audience of comedies is similarly induced to laugh at the absurdity in the virtue of an honorable misanthrope which means that the hidden vice which lies behind the pleasure it takes in the comic is being addressed.[17]

The ambivalence of the dignity and the deficiency of the beautiful returns in a different form during the period of German classicism. Along with the establishment of aesthetics as an autonomous discipline, German idealism made a large claim for the dignity of aesthetic experience when it assigned to it the cosmological function philosophy had surrendered. Art and aesthetic judgment now undertook to return to subjective sensibility the *whole* of nature which the Copernican revolution had barred to direct perception—and to do so by aesthetic mediation.[18] For it was Kant who raised the aesthetic to an authority of mediation between nature and freedom, sensuousness and reason, yet also denied any and all cognitive function to the subjective aesthetic judgment. The ambivalence of the dignity and the deficiency of the beautiful thus manifests itself at this level of aesthetic experience in an opposition which the theory and history of nineteenth-century art deepened until a gulf developed between aesthetic autonomy and an ethically serious existence and the choices it must make. A further stage was to lead to the total loss of praxis characteristic of the disinterested art of the *l'art pour l'art* movement.

A late form of the Platonic ambivalence of the beautiful can probably be seen in the fundamental contrast between the experience of art as "truth event" on the one hand and "aesthetic consciousness" as self-enjoying subjectivity on the other, an opposition which Gadamer has used to elaborate Heidegger's philosophy of art into a hermeneutic ontology. And even Adorno, who saw himself as a pronounced antagonist of Plato, gave unwitting testimony to the persistance of the Platonic legacy of the ambivalent power of beauty. For we have already shown that Adorno's aesthetics considers that art has the power to restore the "dignity of nature" in opposition to the misused rule of the autonomous subject, yet also denies it the communicative function which would be required, were the "reconciled reality" which announces itself in "natural beauty" to be actualized.

But Gadamer's and Adorno's positions appear in a different light when one glances at the materialist aesthetics and the ideology critique of the recent past. They issued in an abundance of attempts designed to show that the slogan "the ruling literature is the literature of the rulers" is correct and proceeded to do this either by unmasking hidden interests of the ruling culture industry or by claiming that the products of "subcultures" were the real art of the suppressed.[19] In view of the extreme puritanical ascesis and the abstract idealism that characterize this trend at different levels, Adorno's dialectical aesthetics of negativity can now almost be invoked as counterauthority to the materialist reduction of his *Dialectic of Enlightenment*, as can Gadamer's hermeneutics of the dialogue to the panideological reduction of his rehabilitation of prejudice. What is common to the aesthetic theories of these camps is that they recognize nothing but the veiling or the repression of ruling interests in the ambiguous power of the beautiful and believe they can escape the vicious circle of "false consciousness" only if they set aside for "true consciousness" a place beyond the seductions of the economically subservient arts and all the manipulations of distorted communication. This new expulsion of the arts from the state, their suspension in a corrupt society with the purpose of ushering in their purity in a state of nondomination, was the hidden motive behind the provocative, recent obituaries for literature, for "bourgeois" art, and for aesthetics generally.[20] The unavowed Platonic legacy thus asserts itself in new opposites, i.e., the authenticity and inauthenticity of the aesthetic experience.

But the historical manifestation of art shows how aesthetic experience has always transcended the limitations that were developed from premises of the Platonic metaphysics of the beautiful. This already applies to the Greek experience of art. While Plato's doctrine of ideas provides "the best understanding" of late classical art, both that art and the theory occupy a counterposition to the preceding rich style.[21] To that extent, the Platonic doctrine of the beautiful—which did not specifically refer to art in the *Phaedrus* and which continued to carry the ambivalence that the beautiful manifests itself ("shines forth") and yet is merely meant to recall something higher and other—can hardly be a key to the phases of reception of Greek classicism. The Platonic justification of the beautiful as a reflection of something transcendent is probably rather to be understood as the philosophical answer to the refractoriness of the beautiful and thus as an attempt to make art that fulfills itself in the portrayal of earthly perfection amenable to philosophical theory.

Regarding the literature of the Middle Ages, I have elucidated elsewhere[22] the refractoriness of the aesthetic experience which, in contrast to the Platonic canon of transcendence, also found ways of asserting the immanence of the beautiful during the older art periods. Since the middle of the twelfth century, the courtly *roman* and soon thereafter allegorical poetry showed the ambition of secular poets to go counter to the moral canon of Christian exegesis and its demand for a radical change in the natural attitude toward life, and this by making the life of the individual aesthetically consistent and exemplary. In contrast to the *vita* of the saint, it is by the telos of a this-worldly search and a perfection of nature that the paths of the adventurous knight and that of the lover are raised to the level of a model. The animal epic as represented by the old French *Roman de Renart*, on the other hand, violates the canon of perfection binding for heroic poetry when its authors, protected by the fiction that they are writing of animals, begin describing human nature as beyond good and evil and in a variety of everyday characters and thereby create the possibility of an account of individual, i.e., no longer exemplary, life. In the Middle Ages, the description of the biographical and historical individuality found itself confronted by a Christian canon that limited all self-portrayal to the fulfilling of general norms (such as *confessio laudis* and *confessio peccati*). It was Dante who went farthest beyond this limit. In formal obedience to the canon of transcendence, he made this world as reflected in the supernatural order, and the historical existence of singular persons in the ultimate destiny of the damned, the penitent, and the blessed, the subject of poetry.

That the rigorism of a prevailing canon usually provokes a new license of aesthetic experience is true even where political or church authorities are in a position to regulate the development of the arts. The barriers erected against a genre that seemed dangerous brought it about that aesthetic activity was shifted to other areas or compensated for when the very authority that had issued the ban officially adopted it for its own purposes. The resultant preferential treatment had consequences that had hardly been anticipated. The first church fathers already exempted heathen poets from the general ban when they recounted exempla in word and deed. For centuries, not only the collection, recording, and transmittal of the most heterogeneous narrative material was justified by the appeal to the exemplary meaning, a practice which was authoritatively vindicated by Basil.[23] This appeal also permitted the dissemination of fiction for purposes of a practical moral application which normally introduced every novel in the Middle Ages and which could even shield the frivolous or scatological tale. Especially sculpture as heathen cult images and the invention of demon-possessed human beings had fallen victim to the iconoclasm of the early Christian church which revives again in the *Libri Carolini* of the Carolingian Renaissance. But after Alcuin's theoretical treatise had merely admitted a "primerlike aid to memory" for the fine arts and the illustration of the doctrine was initially restricted to the relief, "its confinement to the wall," transparent glass painting—the most extreme contrast to sculpture—began to develop into the most curious creation of the new Christian art.[24] Concurrent with the reformation of belief, Protestantism also renewed the old polemics against iconolatry and instituted a new canon against the world-affirming and world-transfiguring poetry and art of the humanists. The same Luther who measured poetry by its parabolic function and praised the "simple fables and fairy tales" in Aesop's manner above all else also excepted a higher, nonmimetic art from all polemics —and this not without invoking the Platonic doctrine concerning music as the expression of divine law, that noble music which, beginning with the four-part Protestant chorus, was thus set free to embark on the lofty path that was to lead to its classical form.[25]

In the experience of art of the modern era, the emancipation of the aesthetic experience occurs in the explicit turning away from the Platonic metaphysics of the beautiful. The complete break shows most clearly in the French tradition, in Baudelaire. In his *Homage à Théophile Gautiers* (1859), the famous doctrine of the indissoluble unity of the beautiful, the true, and the good which had characterized classical aesthetics postromantic modernity now consigned to the irrevocable past. During the time of Victor Cousin, the last exponent of a Platonizing philosophy of art, it had been a heresy to doubt that the beautiful was grounded in the true and that it permitted the perception of the good. Now, the person who expects from the work of art what only science or morality can give becomes guilty of a heresy toward the new religion of art.[26] It is not only in the meaning of their anti-Platonic title that the *Fleurs du Mal* conform to this provocative theory. Through the expression of a new lyric experience, they also realize practically what Diderot, a pioneer of this modernity, had considered unthinkable a hundred years earlier. His criticism of Hutchinson had climaxed in this hypothesis: man has been endowed with an inner sense for the beautiful but can discover it only in things that harm him. The order of the world has preserved us from so great a calamity for we generally experience the beautiful in things also as the good.[27] In its still intact idealist conviction of an indissoluble unity of the beautiful and the good which was already being questioned in the German tradition at this time, Diderot's hypothesis rejects Hutchinson's theory of the sense of beauty.

In that German tradition, the rise of philosophical aesthetics is part of a process in which the beautiful in art is separated from the truth of the sciences and the good of practical action on the one hand and where, on the other, aesthetic experience as *cognitio sensitiva* is played off against the rationalism of conceptual cognition and logic. Baumgarten defines beauty as the perfection of sensitive cognition and assigns it the task of making beauty "present to the mind as the perfection of the world."[28] Kant, who distinguishes between the beautiful and "the normal idea,"[29] also extends aesthetic experience beyond the fine arts when he contrasts the positive pleasure in the beautiful and the negative pleasure in the sublime. With respect to the element of freedom, the sublime is superior to the beautiful both through its object (limitlessness rather than limitation) and through the mode of its experience: whereas "the beautiful is directly attended with a feeling of the furtherance of life" (§ 23), the negative pleasure in the sublime "gives us courage to be able to measure ourselves against the seeming omnipotence of nature" (§ 28). As art attains autonomy in bourgeois culture, the emancipatory process of aesthetic experience reaches a climax where German idealism saw its "realm of freedom" realized. On this historical summit of the period of classical German art, the ambivalence of the beautiful manifested itself in a new form. In his critique of the affirmative character of culture, Herbert Marcuse has given the most thorough analysis of its problematics.[30] Precisely because I share his intention to revalidate aesthetic enjoyment in the face of a secular devaluation of sensuous aesthetic experience, I will consider his theses before turning to the historical manifestations of poiesis, aesthesis, and catharsis.

In the three-phase historical and philosophical aesthetics of Marcuse, the decisive event is Aristotle's severance of the practical and the necessary from the beautiful and from pleasure. For the materialism of bourgeois praxis (which consigned the enjoyment of the true, the good, and the beautiful and thus the happiness of a free humane existence to the spiritual preserve of culture) is also based on the separation of work and leisure. Beyond everyday reality that imposes its acceptance and where the reproduction of material life takes place under the rule of the commodity form, culture detaches itself from civilization as a more ideal world. Along with the idealist culture of the bourgeois world and its "realm of the soul" which becomes the escape route from an increasingly reified world for the self-liberating individual, all aesthetic experience falls under the suspicion of being idealistically corrupted. Since the separation of work and leisure, the attitude toward art has undergone the same process as the by no means initially affirmative but rather sociocritical idealism, according to Marcuse. This process is nothing other than the imperceptible adjustment to what exists. Only with the "liberation from the ideal" can the beautiful and its desensualized pleasure be freed of the taint of affirmative culture. A new form of work and pleasure must appear in which mankind has become the subject, has mastered matter, and has found the space and time of human happiness in material praxis itself.

But if one moves back from canonical aesthetics to the latent aesthetic experience, it can be shown that idealism and affirmative culture are not the sole and exclusive province of the production and reception of the beautiful, either initially or during the bourgeois epoch. The ambivalence of the sensory experience of the beautiful (its distance-creating, liberating, and norm-setting power on the one hand, and its seductive, sublimation- or fascination-weaving spell on the other) was not first brought into existence by that fall in the history of society that is the separation of work and leisure. To the extent that it provides relief and functions cognitively and communicatively, the attitude of enjoyment toward art always presupposes that the beautiful is appearance. To wish to substitute the direct enjoyment of sensuous happiness for this "happiness through appearance" means that one no longer needs art. It is therefore only consistent when Marcuse expects that returning culture to the material life process will create a new social condition in which beauty and its enjoyment will "sustain fulfillment itself and no longer merely desire" and will thus no longer revert to art.[31] As long as Plato's utopia of the state from which the poets are rigorously excluded, and Marcuse's utopia of a third age in which, conversely, sensuousness has been liberated and art as such has become objectless, are equally distant from where we find ourselves, aesthetic experience retains a productive role. To accord it the merely resignful function of keeping alive the desire for a happier life is to misapprehend the genuinely social achievements of aesthetic praxis which are often realized in opposition to philosophical idealism and affirmative culture. It is to these achievements that we now turn.

5. Poiesis: the productive side of aesthetic experience *(construire et connaître)*

Historically, the productive aspect of the aesthetic experience can be described as a process during which aesthetic practice frees itself step by step from restrictions that were imposed on productive activity in both the classical and the biblical tradition. If one understands this process as the realization of the idea of creative man,[1] it is principally art which actualizes this idea to the extent that first, when the poietic capacity is still one and undivided, it asserts itself subliminally and later, in the competition between technical and artistic creation, it explicitly claims to be a production of a special kind. It is in the history of the concepts *labor* and *work*[2] that the restrictions become most palpable. In Greek tradition, all producing *(poiesis)* remains subordinate to practical action *(praxis)*. As the activity of slaves who are rigorously excluded from the exercise of the virtues, it occupies the lowest rank in social life. In the Christian tradition, handiwork is cursed, which means that it is only by the effort he makes that man is meant to maintain himself against a resistant nature ("cursed is the ground for thy sake," Gen. 3, 17) and that salvation can only be found beyond his activity in this world. But in both the classical and the Christian conceptual field relating to labor, we already encounter ambivalent definitions which could introduce and justify an upward revaluation of man's labor.

According to the Aristotelian conception, the subordination of poiesis to practice corresponded to a ranking of knowledge in which the activity of the craftsman or artist as *techne* was distinguished from the labor of slaves, which was merely the following of orders. What such poietic capacity has in common with ethical action is that it presupposes subordinate work in the form of physical services and assistance (the slave is no more than an instrument of action, *Politics*, 1254a 5-8). The technical skill of the craftsman who can make an object according to a model is a knowledge that can be acquired and thus ranks below moral knowledge *(phronesis)* which, as self-knowledge without anterior certainty, is directed toward the right life as a whole and can only define itself in its application.[3] Theoretical knowledge *(episteme)* occupies a higher rank because it is no longer grounded in the changing sphere of action. In contrast to moral insight, poietic capacity characteristically can have degrees of perfection: "Wisdom in the arts we ascribe to their most finished exponents, e.g. to Phidias as a sculptor and to Polyclitus as a maker of portrait-statues, and here we mean nothing by wisdom except excellence in art" *(Ethics*, 1141a). As the highest attainable form of *techne*, the work of art here falls outside the dogmatic juxtaposition of work and virtue. The product of artistic work points in a direction that leads to philosophical wisdom through the perfect skill of the masters. It is nonetheless far from being recognized as a "medium of self-knowledge and self-activation for man": as long as technical and aesthetic work can only reproduce what nature sets before him as exemplary, binding, and essentially perfect, man cannot understand his activity as creative, as the elaboration of as yet unrealized ideas.[4] What had to happen to transcend the limiting conditions of the *imitatio naturae* has been elucidated by Hans Blumenberg. The process in which aesthetic experience discovers art as the sphere of creative originality and as the paradigm of the creation of a human world has the second, no less significant source of its legitimation in the history of creation in the Bible.

The Old Testament myth of creation conferred high dignity on making, which man's activity, in spite of the curse that weighs on his work, could never wholly forfeit. Adamitic man has a share in God's creation: he is placed in the garden of Eden "to dress it and to keep it" (Gen. 2, 15) and called on "to have dominion" over nature and all its creatures. The contamination of two textual traditions in Genesis led to an ambiguous twofold definition of man's activity and position in God-created nature. Man's work could be understood as the task of participating in the work of God's creation, the latter as a *creatio perpetua*, and man—created in God's image—as the fellow creator on whom it was incumbent to complete God's work. But the Christian *homo sapiens* who would immediately have come into existence as *homo artifex* can also interpret his office according to Genesis 1, 26 as a mission to take up dominion over nature and to transform it into a human world by his work.[5] Work as service and as domination are both present in the biblical history of creation. The polarity of humble service to God's work and the rule and disposition over nature is not abolished as a result of the fall with which the work of history begins for man. Much earlier than the triumphant progress technique has made since the industrial revolution, medieval man's attitude toward his world already showed the change from service to dominion according to the inference from the Christian story of creation that the world of nature is there for man.[6] And the Christian curb, which may be compared to the classical mimesis concept and according to which human work is subordinate to God's, is dismantled by the process of aesthetic experience to the extent that *homo artifex* understands his activity as a second creation and the poet, as *alter deus*, lays claim to the concept of *creatio*, which the authority of the Bible had reserved for God alone, as properly applying to art as man's authentic work.

Although artistic poiesis in the Middle Ages continued to be judged by the criterion of craftsmanship, there is no lack of records in which the names and self-revelations of artists emerge from anonymity and the obligatory *humilitas*. How aesthetic practice outruns theory, even within the sphere of influence of the medieval church, becomes especially noticeable in the twelfth century. In the most developed meditation on the concept of creation, the reception of Plato's *Timaeus* in the school of Chartres, human art still occupies the lowest rung of creation. The *opus creatoris* which was created out of nothingness lasts forever; the *opus naturae* which produces beings of similar type has permanence in the species; the *opus hominis* arisen from a deficiency (instead of from an overflowing) and through the reshaping of matter, is ephemeral ("nec in se remanet nec aliquid ex se gignit," neither does anything remain in itself nor beget from itself).[7] But Meyer Schapiro could show for the same period that in various areas of the fine arts such as the sculpture on romanesque capitals, ornamental initials, the use of color in textiles and glass windows, the beginnings of a nonfunctional art were developing on the periphery of religious symbolism, as it were. This is matched on the side of the maker where we find the first testimonials of an artistic self-awareness or the recognition of individual achievement.[8] From the abundance of works that, in defiance of the modest status of the craftsman, already bear the signature of their creator, the inscription over the gate of the chapter house of Toulouse cathedral deserves mention: "Gilabertus vir non incertus."[9] This sort of proud self-declaration (*incertus* means both "certain" in the sense of perfect or infallible and also "well-known") can also be found in a poem of the first known troubadour, William IX of Acquitaine: "Qu'ieu ai nom maistre certa" (VI, v. 36).

Among the genres of the Middle Ages, the poetry of the troubadours is the most autonomous. It could be said of it that it was the first to make the joy of production, the "singing of singing," a theme.[10] It appears directly in the "I" form which, while excluding the expression of what is individual, openly proclaims pride in the *opus hominis*. It is true that we find the formula *maistre certa* in a poem that brags, and its deliberate ambiguity refers to both artistic and erotic "mastery." But this context does nothing to temper the provocative claim to perfection of craft in an author who elsewhere also showed no lack of self-esteem.[11] For his most famous poem[12] begins with a verse that is usually translated: "I will make a poem *about* nothing" but which one is equally justified in rendering as follows:

> I will make a poem *out of* nothing at all
> it will not speak of me or others
> of love or of youth
> or of anything else
> for it was composed
> while I was riding a horse, asleep.

Being a "creation out of nothing," William's poem can have no object, no theme to which it refers. The time of its creation also is absolute "while I was riding a horse, asleep." It points to no before. The female friend who can be replaced at will "by an even nobler and more beautiful one" (verse v/vi) accords with this. Thus William IX competes most subtly with the divine *creatio ex nihilo* (creation out of nothing)! As a human *creatio ex nihilo*, his poem bypasses all objectification since what comes into being at the end of the inconclusible string of negations is the beautiful as a structure which points to nothing other than its own movement—the poem of the poem as a lonely peak of lyric poiesis.

Following C. S. Lewis, one can define the exceptional position of this paradigm in the "world model" and also vis-à-vis the later lyrical convention of the Middle Ages as meaning that the lyric *creatio ex nihilo* breaks out of the "devolutionary scheme" according to whose Christian and Platonic version "all perfect things are prior to all imperfect things."[13] Just as the change from a devolutionary to an evolutionary world model lies between medieval cosmology and modern biology (where what is at the beginning has lost its ontological priority over what developed from it), we also have a change from the medieval to the modern understanding of artistic poiesis: it is the change from a making which the perfect antedates as a model to be imitated, to a creation which itself produces the perfect (or, expressed differently, the beautiful appearance of perfection). A history of the concept *perfectio* would show how, in this process, the plural tantum of the temporally and individually perfect increasingly replaces the singular tantum of an atemporal and universally binding perfection.[14] Concerning the productive side of aesthetic experience, one would have to trace how in his progressive praxis, *homo faber* frees himself of the ties to the Platonic eidos, or god-created nature, and successively comes to see technical invention, the work of art, mathematics, and finally history as a whole as a creation of man. The stages of this process require a new historical analysis.[15] Here, we can only highlight the development by which the fine arts came to be excluded from the general theory and practice of the poietic faculty.

Jürgen Mittelstrass introduced the concept of poietic capacity to show the modern discovery of progress as a "result of a revolution in scientific thought" and to thereby dispense with theories that explain the break in continuity between the Middle Ages and the modern period by a secular recasting of Christian positions. To accomplish this, he employs an Aristotelian distinction: "While theoretical ability consists in constructing true sentences and practical ability in judging actions as better or worse, poietic ability tells us what can be *made*." Understood in this way, the poietic capacity transcends the limiting condition of the imitation of nature in all those cases where it becomes apparent "that what can be made always goes beyond the present state of theory and practice.[16] During the early modern period, this is shown not only in the technical know-how of the "New Science," which Mittelstrass traces back to origins in the tradition of the northern Italian workshops, but also in the aesthetic capacity, which sharply broke with medieval tradition in all art forms but which in its theory continued to subscribe to humanist doctrine whereby all innovation was understood as the return of a perfect past.

The process of a separation of the fine from the mechanical arts was thus initiated and provided fresh fuel to the old competition between technical and aesthetic capacity. In the dialogue *De mente* (1450) by Nicolaus of Cusa, for example, the layman boasts to the philosopher and the rhetorician that his product, a spoon carved from wood, differs from the painter's and the sculptor's work in having no need of a model in nature and coming into existence "sola humana arte." The value of his testimonial in which "the whole pathos of the creative individual is expressed and the break with the principle of imitation made manifest in the work of *technical*, not *artistic* man" becomes even greater because declarations concerning poietic capacity in the technical sphere have remained rare, according to H. Blumenberg.[17] But they had always been expressed in poetry and art, which is also shown by the new concept through which the creative self-understanding that frees itself from creation according to models was to express itself: *genius* as the quintessence of competencies that set poietic capacity above creation according to patterns and learnable rules was named and characterized in the aesthetic sphere before it was attributed to the scientific discoverer and technical inventor and subsequently also to the major political and military figure.[18]

On the threshhold of the modern age, technical and aesthetic capacity also differ in that the former sets in beyond the pale of any and all theories and academic traditions whereas the latter begins to actualize its unrealized possibilities in a constant struggle with the predominant legacy of ancient aesthetics and especially the newly received Aristotelian poetics. The new form of independence which attempts to articulate itself in the tradition of the workshops is "no longer seen in superior scholarship but in a technical competence which helps change the world." Leonardo da Vinci, for example, who belongs to this tradition and presents for both his contemporaries and posterity the prototype of the *homo universale*, has left the most variegated achievement though it cannot escape the blame of a "total lack of theoretical architectonics."[19] Yet it is possible to speak of the implicit theory of his poietic praxis. It becomes most tangible in the reception by a modern poet, Paul Valéry, who went back to Leonardo and, in a twofold attack on the mythicized creativity of poets and the conceptual knowledge and language blindness of philosophers, developed his own aesthetic theory which he later called *poiétique*. The *Introduction to the Method of Leonardo da Vinci* shows the break between the classical and the modern conception of poietic capacity under a double aspect: first, that of the *productive* aesthetic experience which utilizes the cognitive function of *construire* in a combination of artistic and scientific practice which is represented by Leonardo but which became one-sided because of the later separation of "arts et sciences." Second, the *receptive* aesthetic experience which revalidates a perception that has been renewed by the means of art ("voir par les yeux") as against the traditional priority of cognition through concepts ("voir par l'intellect"). What fascinated Valéry in Leonardo's method and what he tries to explain as the common root of the "entreprises de la connaissance et les opérations de l'art" was the imaginative logic of construction, i.e., of that form of praxis which obeys the principle of "faire dépendre le savoir du pouvoir."[20] Leonardo, quintessence of creative capacity and of the universality of the human spirit, symbolizes the change from the classical to the modern concept of cognition. For *construire* presupposes a knowledge that is more than a turning back to the contemplation of preexisting truth: it is a cognition dependent on what one can do, on a form of action that tries and tests so that understanding and producing can become one.

The equating of producing with comprehending, which gives man access to truth through his poietic capacity, gave rise to enthusiastic declarations on the experience of creativity during the period of Leonardo. The idea of man as a second creator, which was derived from poetry and hermetic writings, caused mathematics to be understood as a man-made conceptual world ("scientia mentis, quae res facit," science of the mind which makes things).[21] Pico della Mirandola defined man as "sui ipsius quasi—plastes et fictor" (a sort of molder

and fashioner of his own self) who, in an intermediate position between divine perfection and animal limitation, intellect and sensuality, is himself to produce the form of his life.[22] And Scaliger elevated the poet above all other artists because, as a second god, he
could create a second nature, in a manner of speaking: "poeta et
naturam alteram et fortunas plures etiam ac demum sese isthoc
perinde ac Deum alterum efficiet" (The poet fashions a second nature
and many fortunes, even to the point of making himself in this way
a second God, Poet. I, 1). But these declarations of a new creative
consciousness encountered ontological barriers which were not removed by philosophy until Leibniz.[23] For the boldly seized possibility of poiesis searching for truth where man produced it by his
own work must ultimately be qualified by an insight that counsels
modesty because it tells us that the first creator withholds the ultimate truths of his work from man as the second one. According to
Scaliger poetry, as a second nature created by man, could bring together in a work the perfection that lay scattered about in the world
and produce a semblance of things that do not exist in reality. But
though in this fashion human poiesis portrays "what exists in reality
as more beautiful than it is," it ultimately remains within the limits
of the *one* existing world which it idealizes and with which its product can compete (I, 1.3), but with which it dare not yet contrast another world which does not already exist.

Renaissance poetics did not take this final expectable step toward
autonomous art which would have required a complete break with
the *imitatio naturae*. The claim that poietic production can create
more than just a second, more beautiful nature, i.e., a different, heretofore unrealized world, will not be made until the literary revolution of the eighteenth century. It thus made good in the area of aesthetic experience what Vico in his turn against Cartesian rationalism
had claimed at the same time for a "New Science" of the *mondo
civile*: "history cannot be more certain than when he who creates the
things also narrates them. Now, as geometry, when it constructs the
world of quantity out of its elements, or contemplates that world, is
creating it for itself, just so does our Science create for itself the
world of nations, but with a reality greater by just so much as the institutions having to do with human affairs are more real than points,
lines, surfaces, and figures."[24] With Vico's interpretation of the
phrase "verum et factum convertuntur" (truth and action are altered),
the history of the concept of poiesis reaches its ultimate meaning. The
dictum that it was not God who made history but that men produced
their historical world themselves does not refer to aesthetic experience

and historical action in the same way, however. Ferdinand Fellmann
has shown that Vico was far from maintaining that history could be
made or that political action could be rationalized, as the later autonomy thesis of the idealist philosophy of history understood it. The
original meaning of the Vico axiom was rather: "it is not as actors
but as intellectually creative individuals that men 'make' their history."[25] The greater certainty that derives from equating producing
with understanding relates to technical and aesthetic capacity but
not to history as a total process for which man in his historical reality
is responsible as subject without being able to direct it.[26] In political
life, man constantly encounters the contradiction between intent and
result of his acts: here, the efficacy of his will is tied to an order that
is beyond him and which Vico attempts to justify as the providence
that holds sway in the cycles of culture. In the sphere of poietic capacity, the productivity of the spirit, on the other hand, where ideas
(quite un-Platonically) mediate between production and cognition,
man is the autonomous creator of his works.

Raising intellectual history to the level of a "new science" resulted
in further insights which gave the history of poiesis a new turn. Where
rationalism proposes to derive the progress of history from a new
methodological beginning, Vico sees the origins of history and thus
man's history-making power in his sensuous productivity, i.e., in the
aesthetic truths of myths and the primacy of the practical arts. With
this revaluation of the myth-making imagination as a form of mastery
over nature, Vico, whose effect remains so curiously obscure in the
nineteenth century, anticipates the new science of aesthetics which
Baumgarten had also grounded in sensory cognition. As Vico thus
sees the beginnings of the sciences as grounded in the world of the
arts, he simultaneously "breaks with the traditional conviction that
theory had sprung from the leisure of certain individuals": the *Nova
Scienza* places practical ahead of theoretical curiosity, the public
character of *facere* ahead of the solitary reflection of *invenire*."[27] This
revaluation, which now assigns to Hercules rather than Prometheus
the highest rank in the heroes' gallery of poiesis,[28] points ahead to a
phase in the history of poiesis where the contraposition of free poietic
capacity and unoriginal because merely reproductive work is abolished
and where finally "all of so-called world history" is understood "as
man's product through man's work."[29]

Since Hegel's interpretation of history as the "labor of the concept," German idealism has given this understanding of poiesis its
highest expression. But it also initiated a process whereby the concept of economic work detached itself from that of communicative

praxis and was gradually given a higher rank until the total reversal of the classical relationships between these values appeared in Marx: here, work, *concrete activity*, is the true productive activity and placed above all theory and all political and communicative action. In this process, the relationship between technical and aesthetic production was also revaluated. Kant's distinction between "free" and "industrial art" is based on the contrast between "making" (*facere*) and "acting and operating in general" (*agere*) and distinguishes art as "play, i.e. an occupation which is agreeable on its own account" from labor "which on its own account is disagreeable (drudgery) and is only attractive by means of what it results in (e.g. pay)."[30] Play as an activity for its own sake thus becomes determinative of artistic production and replaces *leisure* which, as the contemplative attitude and the condition of *theoria*, had constituted the opposite of unfree work or the making of something in the Aristotelian tradition of praxis.[31] This definition of aesthetic activity through play, which is its own end and which is so characteristic of German idealism, is not wholly lost even in its materialist inversion.

When practice had long since become so pervasively economic as to give concrete making (*facere* as producing) the unconditional priority over communicative action (*facere* in Vico's sense), the young Marx recurred to the idealist definition of aesthetic capacity in a passage of the *Economic and Political Manuscripts*, which have become famous only in our time, and characterized work as the properly human activity, albeit one that is alienated by the egoism of possession. The passage distinguishes man from the animal that produces only for its immediate need and according to the "standards and needs of the species it belongs to." "[M]an produces free from physical need and only truly produces when he is thus free . . . and knows how to produce according to the measure of every species and knows everywhere how to apply its inherent standard to the object; thus man also fashions things according to the laws of beauty."[32] Here, Kant's production in freedom has not just been extended from artistic production to the productive activity of all human labor. Along with that, the young Marx elevates productive or concrete doing to the level of aesthetic activity, in other words, he interprets technical production according to the "inherent standard" of artistic production. The fashioning of beauty in labor is to fulfill that general human need "to be at home in the world" which, in Hegle's *Aesthetics*, could be satisfied only by art.[33] For the young Marx, labor is the true "resurrection of nature" whenever it humanizes nature as it produces beauty and through its products makes the poietically appropriated nature appear to man as his work and his reality.[34] This abolition of the distinction or separation between technical and aesthetic poiesis can be interpreted as the goal or as the still utopian final state in Marx's 1844 philosophy of history. But the function of aesthetic experience (i.e., the fashioning according to the laws of beauty) in the dialectics of the appropriation of nature could also be taken to mean that artistic production is less subject to becoming alienated through possession (i.e., through private property) than is work, so that even during the history of alienation, art continues to provide the possibility of nonalienated work. Doesn't the attitude toward art permit a "having as if you did not have" (to use Paulinian theology in support of the aesthetic approach of the young Marx)? For it is certainly true in the case of the work of art that here man "can freely confront his product." This applies to the producer for whom the product of his work in the work of art cannot become an alien power as it does to the recipient since it is in aesthetic experience that need or enjoyment most obviously lose their egoistic nature.[35] Understood in this way, the work of art could serve as a paradigm of nonalienated labor in a materialist aesthetics which could preserve the idea of free productivity and of a receptivity that can change people's minds during phases of alienated material labor. But as it fell under the spell of economic reductionism, such approaches were eclipsed in a Marxist aesthetics which now merely saw one aspect of exploitation in the history of poiesis. They did not revive until a materialist aesthetics that had been revitalized by Benjamin, Adorno, Bloch, and Marcuse set out to rediscover in art the *promesse du bonheur* and thus the chance to abolish the alienation of all work.

The changed meaning of poiesis which has accompanied the avant-gardism of the emancipated arts and the schools in their ever-more-rapid succession can again be sketched in terms of Valéry's aesthetic theory. His essay *Leonardo and the Philosophers* (1929) completes the poietic theory of *construire* and shows the horizon of possibilities which opens up to modern art once it has transcended the final positions of classical aesthetics: "Beauty is a sort of corpse. It has been supplanted by novelty, intensity, strangeness, all the *shock values*. Raw excitement is the sovereign mistress of recent minds, and works of art are at present designed to tear us away from the contemplative state, the motionless delight, an image of which was at one time intimately connected with the general notion of the Beautiful. . . . Seldom do we encounter anything produced by a desire for 'perfection.' "[36] Having abandoned the perfect form of the esthetic object with the metaphysics of the timelessly beautiful, the imitation of the artist with the preexistent truth of the idea, and the noninvolvement of the observer with the ideal of calm contemplation, art finds itself on a new course. It frees itself of the eternal substantiality of the beautiful by "making the indefinable the essential characteristic of the beautiful."[37] And it frees itself of the model of the theoretical cognition of the true, the *connaître* of the philosophers, by disputing the precedence of meaning over form in the process of aesthetic production. Here, Valéry completes Edgar Allan Poe's *Philosophy of Composition*[38] (1846); "It is hard for a philosopher to understand that the artist passes almost without distinction from form to content and from content to form; that a form may occur to him before the meaning he will assign to it; or that the idea of a form means as much to him as the idea that asks to be given a form."[39] And it frees aesthetic reception from its contemplative passivity by making the viewer share in the constitution of the aesthetic object: poiesis now means a process whereby the recipient becomes a participant creator of the work. This is also the simple meaning of the provocative, hermeneutically unjustifiably controversial phrase: *"mes vers ont le sens qu'on leur prête"* (my poetry has the meaning one gives it, Pleiade, I, 1509).

In his *Eupalinos ou l'architect*, Valéry had already sketched this turn in the history of poiesis. In a modern "dialogue of the dead," he has Socrates advance the reasons why, given the chance for another life, he would prefer the productive work of the architect to the contemplative knowledge of the philosopher. In an authoritative interpretation, Hans Blumenberg has shown how the traditional, Platonic ontology of the aesthetic object is being dismantled here step by step.[40] I will reproduce his interpretation of the *objet ambigu* because it can help illuminate the poietic activity which the observer is to perform as he confronts the fine arts of the twentieth century. The "ambiguous object" in Valéry's dialogue is something that the sea has thrown up on the beach: "a white thing of the most pure whiteness; polished and hard and smooth and light."[41] Finding this object sets off a train of thought in the young Socrates which he cannot bring to a conclusion: "it is an object which cannot be interpreted within a Platonic ontology. Socrates sees this immediately—it is an object which recalls nothing and yet is not amorphous."[42] The question concerning the natural or artificial origin which can always be decided in ancient ontology cannot be answered here. In view of the equivocalness of this object which negates the borderline between art and nature, Socrates must decide whether his attitude toward his find should be one of inquiry or of pleasure, theoretical or aesthetic. The aesthetic attitude "can always . . . content itself with a solution which is not a resolution of what is given but can deliberately ignore the remaining indeterminacy of other possibilities. The theoretical hypothesis, on the other hand, is burdened with the possibility of other, better solutions none of which can ever definitively exclude the chance that its verification will fail."[43] Valéry's Socrates throws the object back into the sea, thereby becomes a philosopher, and now attempts to solve the question how the poiesis of nature differs from that of art by advancing a theory that defines the work of nature as a form that is perfect at any given moment whereas the work of art is merely a possible solution before an unending task.[44] It is with reference to a new historical question which must be asked in connection with Valéry that the "ambiguous object" is of interest here: what is its significance for the contemporary development of the fine arts where we encounter it at every step, though under new conditions which illuminate the most recent phase of the history of poiesis?

This historical perspective takes on concreteness when one remembers that the Dada movement used such "ambiguous objects" as Marcel Duchamp's *Bicycle Wheel* (1913), pop art Jasper Johns's *Flag*, optical art Victor Vasarely's quivering screen (1951, beginning of the kinetic period) to constantly shock the observer anew, i.e., to confront him with a range of different "ambiguous objects" which no longer negated the distinction between art and nature but that between art and reality. This development of the modern arts cannot be adequately understood by the traditional aesthetics of representation. Their comprehension demands the elaboration of an aesthetics of reception which goes beyond the traditional definitions of the contemplative attitude and which can formulate the aesthetic activity demanded of the viewer through new definitions of the poiesis of the receiving subject. The history of aesthetic experience (which the colloquium *Poetik und Hermeneutik III* discussed as a "process which extends the sphere of what can be art"[45] when it considered the changing spectrum of the "beautiful and no longer beautiful arts") took a turn toward deconcretization during the period following Hegel's famous or infamous prognosis concerning the "end of art." The result was that along with the beautiful which had been the ultimate goal of the classical ideal of art, the boundary line between the work of art and extra-artistic reality was finally done away with altogether.[46] Deconcretization having become total, the aesthetic status itself becomes a problem and the viewer is time and again placed into a situation where, confronted with an ambiguous object, he must ask himself and is called upon to decide whether this can *still* or *also* claim to be art.

When the Dada movement first presents an object belonging to extra-artistic reality—Duchamp's *Bicycle Wheel*—as a work of art, the artist's aesthetic activity is reduced to the nearly momentary poietic act of choosing a front wheel (and mounting it on a stool) while a disproportionate effort is demanded of the viewer: only if—and to the extent that—he can summon up the earlier canon of art as beautiful appearance so that he might be able to deal with the provocation of the antiart work, and only as he looks for the questions conferring meaning on an object that is indifferent in itself, will he be able to aesthetically enjoy this ambiguous object. This questioning reflection and reflective enjoyment cannot end. It does not lead to a definite meaning, let alone a reassuring definition of what is going to be called artistic quality (*Kunstcharacter*) from now on. All that is aesthetically enjoyable here is the poietic activity of the viewer, not the object itself of which Duchamp said that it never had the opportunity to "become beautiful, pretty, agreeable to look at, or ugly."[47] The relationship between the theoretical and the aesthetic attitude as Valéry had defined it in his *Eupalinos* is thus inverted: since the viewer cannot accept the indefiniteness of the ready-made as such but only enjoy it when he yields to the provocative stimulus of questioning, defining, and rejecting, he adopts the Socratic role and the theoretical attitude turns into the aesthetic. It is not decisive here whether he decides in favor of the solution Duchamp probably intended, a "re-instauration of the object in a new domain," a solution which, according to Max Imdahl, would be a "reflection on the mere thinghood of the thing."[48] For even with this solution, the question concerning the relationship of art and reality does not come to rest; even the experience of the "thinghood of the thing" cannot confer a characteristic status on the ready-made since that experience has always been accessible to philosophical reflection and also part of a Platonizing aesthetic tradition. The abolition of art as beautiful appearance shifts the reality presented in the ready-made into an indefinableness where appearance and being become interchangeable. Duchamp's ambiguous object confronts aesthetic activity with an incompletable task because in its contingency, it remains aesthetically indifferent and thus holds open the possibility that a new *objet trouvé* will ask in different terms under what conditions an isolated object can become art and the aesthetic therefore an event in this case as well.

"Is it a flag or is it a painting?" It is with this question, which can be formulated in a great many different ways, that Jasper Johns later carried the poietic paradox of the ambiguous object to a much-discussed "identity crisis."[49] With the choice of the American flag, the best-known emblem and first "commonplace" of the public world, the artistic act becomes anonymous along with the object. "By letting compositional qualities pass into object qualities and by sublating the former in the latter," the manner of presentation becomes as banal as the object itself. As the edges of the painting and the border of the flag become one, there occurs the paradoxical identity of work and reality which places the actual poietic effort on the viewer.[50] He in turn becomes entangled in a *circulus vitiosus* of questions which cannot simply be answered "yes" or "no." And this is true whether he explains this new ambiguous object as a historically informed observer and with the help of a theory as an overcoming (action painting) or as a fulfillment (*art concrete*) of earlier theories[51] or whether he wants to understand it in the sense of the later pop art as a monumentalized quotation which refers to our prefabricated environment in order either to praise it as "second nature" or to question it in its matter-of-factness. The last alternative revives a problem well-known in the history of poiesis. For it is no accident that the pop demonstration should remind the informed observer of a similar demonstration of the ambiguous object, the grapes of Zeuxis, about which a perfectly comparable discussion was carried on in the eighteenth century. Its most famous exponents were Diderot and Goethe.

The discussion was set off by Diderot's proposal for a modern play which was to attain as perfect an illusion of reality as possible in order to break through the beautiful appearance of the classical stage. As a philosopher of the Enlightenment, Diderot sought to do away with the gulf separating the true-to-nature and the beautiful in art which the classicist Goethe, appealing to the Zeuxis anecdote, considered essential.[52] Only the wholly uninformed observer, Goethe wrote, could take a work of art for a work of nature. The true admirer "sees not only the truth of the imitation, but also the excellence of the selection, the refinement of the composition, the superiority of the little world of art." Goethe resolved the paradox of the appearance of the true by justifying the beautiful appearance the composition creates, an appearance which has the function of conveying the illusion of a higher reality along with what is true to nature. Diderot, on the other hand, traced the appearance of truth to nature in the work of art to the truth of what is imitated, i.e., to the latent harmony of the "système de la nature" which the great artist knows how to make manifest in the reality all of us share. Diderot believed he could solve the paradox of the appearance of the true in the other direction because for him, the nature of things already included that higher reality which, according to Goethe, only the artist could produce as a "second nature." The pop demonstration would have had Diderot's approval if one understands its goal as an "innovation of the obvious."[53] which calls on the viewer to discover in the "commonplace of our environment" the hidden harmony or potential artistic beauty of a world of consumption which man has created.

What is new for a history of poiesis in the pop demonstration is therefore not the abolition of the line dividing art object from object of the environment (this was also attempted by the *trompe-l'oeil* of classical painting) but rather the call on the viewer of an esthetically indifferent ambiguous object to switch from a theoretical to an aesthetic attitude. As a condition of the poietic activity of the viewer, this switch supplements the formulation in which H. Blumenberg summarized the pop art discussion: "But the pop demonstration did not show that everything *is* art already but that when a certain point of opposition to the canon of art has been reached, everything can *become* art, and this by isolating it from the context of reality which is thus thrown back on itself. It is also true, however, that the trick of isolating it does not set the fiction of an object but the fiction of its aesthetic quality against the reality concept of the context. The aesthetic attitude does not encounter the evidence of an object but the absurdity of a function that is claimed in spite of the object."[54] For the aesthetically indifferent object to fulfill an aesthetic function, the viewer himself must create the horizon of conditions of a new genesis of art, regardless of whether the *objet ambigu* demands for this the context of an existing reality, the canon of the earlier art, or merely the opposition between a new and an old theory of art, according to the axiom: "Whatever else it may be, all great art is about art."

Recently, Tom Wolfe used this famous statement of Leo Steinberg's as a key to reconstruct through an overarching principle the development that sets in with Fauvism, Cubism, and Dada (about 1900) and extends down to the most recent experimental schools of Conceptual Art and Photo Realism. His paradoxical thesis informs us that modern art set out by renouncing every academic, realist, or concrete credo. But then, and without being aware of it, it replaced the abandoned "literary" character of traditional art by the "painted word," i.e., works created for the sake of a theory: "Modern Art has become completely literary, the paintings and other works exist only to illustrate the text."[55] If one looks at the poietic process of art in the modern period in the light of this ironic description, it can be made to include tendencies such as naive painting which run in the opposite direction and whose origination at about the same time was not a matter of chance. They contradict the theory-related reflectivity of the work by a demonstrative renunciation of all theory, including the techniques of painting since the Renaissance. But by preferring subjects that embody a global world view (be it rural, exotic, or paradisiacal), they also contradict the "partial character" of modern art (D. Henrich). The switch from the theoretical to the aesthetic attitude is matched by poietic activity's turning back to the atheoretical attitude. Poiesis and aesthesis enter into an interaction, and this applies not only to the phase just described but already characterizes the entire development of the arts since the turn from the nineteenth to the twentieth century. For this reason, our backward glance at the history of aesthetic experience which isolated the perspective of poiesis for reasons of economy can best be concluded by a comment by Valéry on the *plaisir esthétique*. Valéry describes the interaction of poiesis and aesthesis with respect to the modern turn from the contemplative to the poietic observer as follows: Aesthetic pleasure perfectly typifies "the confusion or interdependence between the observer and the thing observed, which is driving theoretical physicists to despair . . . a pleasure that can stimulate the strange need to produce or reproduce the things, event, object, or state to which it seems attached, and which thus becomes a source of activity *without any definite* end . . ."[56]

6. Aesthesis: the receptive side of aesthetic experience
(voir plus de choses qu'on n'en sait)

"Media are not mediations." The new mass media of contemporary art have not merely unsettled the old reading culture of the bourgeois era. With the preeminence of the sign over the word, with their shock effect and plethora of stimuli which supplant the understanding enjoyment of reading, with the manipulative power of information which can merely be stored but hardly integrated any longer in personal recollection, they also threaten the growth of aesthetic experience in the traditional sense. It is not the oracularly invoked "end of art" which has been heard again in the recent past but rather the questioning of the classical achievements of aesthesis which characterizes the present situation of aesthetic experience, as Geoffrey H. Hartman showed impressively in *The Fate of Reading*.[1] That modern techniques and media of reproduction would not only bring destruction of the aura and of the solitary contemplation of the classical work of art but also lead to a perfectly positive turn, a "secular illumination of a materialist, anthropological inspiration" in the form of a new, no longer esoteric experience of art which would be open to the masses and pass over into political praxis—these are hopes which Walter Benjamin wished to derive some forty years ago from the abolition of autonomous art, but they have clearly gone unfulfilled.[2] A sharpened "sense for the universal equality of things" probably did come from the destruction of the aura and accrued to an unfettered mass art and the collective reception of art.[3] But a new sensory and simultaneously communicative experience which did not continually have to maintain itself against the constraints of adaptation to the world of consumption did not come into existence.

The screen, which brings the variety of distant events into close range as reproduced phenomena, did not merely turn Benjamin's concept of aura ("the unique phenomenon of a distance, however close it may be") into its opposite. It also rendered ambiguous whatever art value the documentary may have: "Indeed, the copy or fake may now be sharper than the original. So the image on the screen, undimmed by memory or the confusion of life, revives a simulacrum of the past brighter in photographic brilliance than the actual happening could have been."[4] Under the new conditions of technological change, which opened to human perception undreamed-of areas of experience, the ambivalence of aesthetic experience, so familiar from an old tradition, takes on a new form. On the one hand, photography, whose camera eye makes it possible to experience the optically unconscious by arresting the momentary and uncovering the accidental,[5] and the motion picture, which uses techniques such as the close-up and slow motion to take in unknown dimensions and sensory realms of space and movement, have extended the scope of aesthetic experience beyond all the limits that a secular tradition considered naturally given. But this undreamed-of emancipation of the senses has also made palpable that it is "a different nature (which) opens itself to the camera than opens to the naked eye."[6] And with the discovery of hitherto unsuspected realities, there also grew the possibility of subliminally "manipulating" the perceiving consciousness with new stimuli of seduction.

This also explains why the enjoying and the critically reflective attitude of the contemporary public diverge more than ever before. The blossoming of popular fiction which already began in the nineteenth century, of kitsch and of forms of art intended for immediate consumption (a search for which in the aesthetic praxis of more remote epochs only leads, as is well known, to nonspecific analogies), is a counterphenomenon to l'art pour l'art and is to be explained historically and sociologically, as a result of, or answer to, the beginning "culture industry." (One of the earliest pieces of evidence for art industriel is Sainte-Beuve's article on the feuilleton novel of 1839).[7]

Whereas it is only in peripheral products that preautonomous art can be separated into purely entertaining and purely aesthetic functions, the growing opposition between a merely consumable art and one that can be thought about is central to aesthetic practice after the "end of the period of art" (*Kunstperiode*). It is in the differing evaluations of this opposition that the exoteric and the esoteric modern aesthetics of W. Benjamin and T. W. Adorno diverge most sharply. How the gulf between mass art and esoteric avant-gardism might be bridged again has been a central problem of aesthetic theory ever since. In view of this most recent crisis of aesthesis in which all art threatens either to fall victim to ideology critique or to survive only as a place of refuge for the "happy few," aesthetics has principally developed theories that amount to utopias of a future art or that recommend a turning back to the solitary experience of the aura of art.

Dieter Henrich has countered this alternative with a different diagnosis of modern art. On the one hand, he carries further the undeveloped beginnings of the psychological aesthetics rooted in Aristotelianism. On the other, he elaborates, from a critical revision of Hegelian aesthetics, the categories of partiality and reflectivity which do greater justice to the most recent developments in the arts. According to D. Henrich, contemporary art "must be newly understood without recourse to the suspect schemata of progressive decay and the anticipation of progress" and should be seen as the effort "to make bearable, familiar and the basis of an expanding life feeling (*Lebensgefühl*) the world of machinery, of technically produced materials and the floods of information which are conveyed in all languages and deform all of them, and to which traditional ways of life cannot stand up."[8] The possibility of such an interpretation of modern art is also to be served by the following backward glance at the history of aesthesis. For it reveals that human sensory perception is not an anthropological constant but subject to change over time and that it has always been one of the functions of art to discover new modes of experience in a changing reality or to propose alternatives to it. In extending contemplative aesthesis to include the poietic activity of the receipient as discussed in the last chapter, we therefore probably already see a new mode of experience by which the arts in the twentieth century answer the challenge of a technicized world. In the following retrospective sketch, the historical change in the receptive aesthetic experience will be illuminated by a number of textual interpretations. The poiesis chapter with its predominantly theoretical and historical orientation will thus be complemented by a perspective on aesthetic practice.[9]

The attempt to provide exemplary descriptions of the historical change of aesthesis through its poetic realizations comes up against the hermeneutic difficulty that aesthetic perception in poetry and the arts has always already concretized itself and has only rarely been thematized. For this reason, reconstructing aesthetic perception through an analysis of the constitution of the aesthetic structure has its limits. Such an analysis will take into account the history of interpretation of a text but go beyond mere interpretation because it must ask how the aesthetic object successively constitutes itself, becomes a whole for the viewer, and thus discloses a perspective on, or a province of meaning in, the world. Whether the mode of experience of the past viewer, the contemporary of the text, can be de facto recovered in this fashion could only be confirmed by (usually lacking) documents detailing the specific sensory perception of past periods. Nonetheless, what we can still find out about the past and the historical change of human sensory perception is most easily discovered in the medium of aesthetic experience. A given text demands a particular perception of the aesthetic object. As the later observer becomes aware of its nature in the process of his appropriation, he will usually, as the view of a represented world discloses itself in its otherness, encounter a mode of experience that is no longer natural to him. One's own and the alien mode of perception can be mediated by aesthesis: to one's own manner of seeing, which abandons itself to aesthetic perception as it is led along by the text, there opens up, along with an alien manner of seeing, the horizon of experience of a differently viewed world. This hermeneutic function of aesthesis is due to the fact that the human glance is interested by its very nature. It is not satisfied with what directly presents itself, is lured by what is absent, and reaches out for what is still hidden. It is, in short, "an appetite to see more,"[10] as Jean Starobinski has shown in *Le Voile de Popée*. Myths such as Poppaea whose beauty requires a veil to make it irresistible, or other myths such as Orpheus, Narcissus, Oedipus, Psyche, or Medusa testify to this energy of the fascinated glance and take to the point of blindness and ruin the lure of the hidden in what is at hand and tangibly close, yet elusive. Aesthetic perception vitalizes this energy of the glance, sublimates the desire to see and be seen to a "poetics of the glance," and thus sustains the process that led artistic aesthesis from discovery to discovery.[11]

The description of the shield in the *Iliad* (18, 478ff.) can serve as our first example.[12] The question concerning the successive creation of the aesthetic object becomes easier here because through Hephaestus' work, Homer lets the shield of Achilles come into existence before our eyes. The poiesis of the skilled god guides the aesthesis of the human beholder: "First of all he forged a shield that was huge and heavy, elaborating it about . . ." Our glance is first directed toward the cosmos as a whole: "He made the earth upon it, and the sky, and the sea's water." The spheres of human life follow in contrasting scenes, and here again, it is the highest values that are set forth first: war and peace which are symbolized by two cities. There follow rural life, properly constituted by field, vineyard, and pasture which are articulated in turn according to such activities as plowing, mowing, the harvesting of grapes, and the herding of cattle and sheep, and finally the Cretan dance so that at the end, the sphere of free play comes to lie like a garland around the activities of life. The view of the world that constitutes itself on the shield in concentric circles in this fashion is of a perfect order. Every part offers itself to aesthetic perception as clearly defined and equally illuminated. And through the harmony of opposites, heaven and earth, war and peace, town and country, work and play, the relationship of part to whole becomes immediately understandable and meaningful and hardly requires interpretation.

If one pays attention to the hermeneutic difference, however, one observes that this admirable prospect is not what we see when our glance takes in the spatial and temporal concreteness to which we are accustomed. K. Reinhardt ignored this when he wrote: "The human life which the god of craftsmen portrays in concentric circles, between heaven in the center and the Ocean River at the periphery, is a sublime, 'beautiful' life."[13] For in the center field, there is not just heaven but also earth and the sea and thus the entire cosmos, first portrayed by itself and then a second time but now successively and through the scenes of human existence which at the end the sea again encircles so that the latter figures twice, along the edge of the shield and in center field. The Homeric aesthesis clearly induced a nonperspectivist view of an all-encompassing totality. Both what is closest and what is farthest away appear equally perfect and present on Achilles' shield. This also applies to events whose temporal sequence is abolished in Homeric description as epic succession is transposed into visibility. Sowing and reaping can occur side by side. A single tableau seems to extend one process through several phases (the driving out to pasture of the cattle, the attack of two lions, the beginning pursuit) and to arrest it at the climax (the shrinking back of the dogs before the cornered beasts); the description of a state (such as the gathering of the multitude on the marketplace) passes unexpectedly into the narration of an event (such as the trial involving the quarrel over a fine) which makes the modern beholder forget that he is supposed to be able to see at a single glance on a shield what is being told piece by piece.

In contrast to the medieval aesthesis in which the simultaneous stage, for example, permits what is chronologically distinct to be perceived in such a fashion that events of varying temporal remoteness appear next to each other and can thus portray a chronological or figural order, it is precisely the failure to distinguish between the earlier and the later that is characteristic of the Homeric aesthesis. The earlier does not have less plenitude of being than the later; the beginning is no less perfect than the middle or the end. To put matters differently: whatever is seized by the glance which is guided by the description of the shield appears perfect in its here and now and fulfills the meaning of *kalos* ("what thrives, what manifests itself in the greatest plenitude of being").[14] What shows itself in such aesthesis does not require representation to be beautiful, does not become beautiful only as the product of the skilled Hephaestus but is beautiful in itself, as it were. By their handsome disposition on Achilles' shield as by virtue of the aristocratic standard, the absence of all menial services, for example, and the choice of the ideal moment, the scenes of human existence are an expression of an "exalted life." "From scene to scene, life regularly culminates in a moment: in the drink offered the plowmen, in the meal for the reapers, the presentation of the scepter to the judging geronts, the clash of the two armies, in the Linos song which the boy sings during the vintage, in the singer who plays for the dance."[15]

What the modern perspective experiences as alien in the Homeric aesthesis emerges even more sharply when it is contrasted with the narrative style of the Old Testament, as Erich Auerbach has shown.[16] The well-ordered description of the Homeric epic, which gives its due to every detail, which knows no opaqueness, no background, and which fully translates every affect into well-turned speech even where the action seems to press ahead, forces the modern reader to curb his eager expectation and to pause at every point of the movement. The "technique of epic retardation" goes so far as to expect us to put out of our mind what might precede or follow as we enjoy what is there at every moment: "What he narrates is for the time being the only present, and fills both the stage and the reader's mind completely."[17] At the critical moment when the old housekeeper Eurykleia washes his feet, Ulysses' scar threatens to betray his identity. How the wound came about requires more than seventy lines to tell and is no interpolation in the sense of a perspectivist flashback but a self-fulfilled present that excludes all else and is to be enjoyed for its own sake.

This is even more true of the description of the shield in the *Iliad*: unlike the shield in Vergil's *Aeneid* (8, 608ff.), it does not point to the future but discloses, precisely because it has no connection with Achilles' nature and deeds, a general context of meaning, the "view of the continuity of life which is tied to no time, which remains nameless, which is part of no past or legend, which outlasts heroic catastrophies."[18] As the pleasurable lingering in the presence of a perfect manifestation, aesthesis here expresses its highest concept.

If aesthesis as the enjoyment of a fulfilled present corresponds to the ancient concept of reality as a "reality of momentary evidence,"[19] Auerbach's stylistic analysis, on the other hand, allows one to infer that the narrative form of the Old Testament texts such as Isaac's sacrifice does not ground an opposing type of aesthesis but runs counter to all aesthetic experience. The lack of any description for its own sake, the unexpressed, merely guessable intentions and affects, the fragmentariness of events, the opaqueness of the action—all these things demand an interpretation of what is not said and presuppose a claim to truth which derives its evidence not in the momentary but in the hidden nexus between past and future. For this concept of a reality that is not visible but merely guaranteed by faith,[20] a corresponding form of aesthesis emerges only at the moment a new Christian poetry and art begins to body forth the invisible realities and agencies of belief. But antiquity has passed on a second paradigm of aesthetic experience which prefigures the discovery function of aesthesis, namely the Odyssean myth of the sirens whose irresistible song lures those sailing past to destruction:

> Bring your ship in, so you may listen to our voice
> No one ever yet sped past this place in a black ship
> Before he listened to the honey-toned voice from our mouths
> And when he went off delighted and knowing more things.
> For we know all . . .[21]

Ulysses, who has himself tied to the mast in order to be able to enjoy the "sweet song" of the sirens without risking his life, takes a position in the context of the Homeric epic where the desire for pleasure and that for knowledge—aesthetic and theoretical curiosity—are not yet distinct. The sirens, originally vampirelike ghosts, were clearly given greater beauty by Homer and elevated to the duality of erotic enticement and divine knowledge.[22] As symbol of the highest aesthetic pleasure, the sirens' song also promises a knowledge which is the prerogative of the gods and therefore fatal to man. This mythological heightening of aesthesis also reveals an ambivalence of the beautiful, of which the modern reader finds a surprising echo in a celebrated and obscure Rilke verse: "For Beauty's nothing but beginning of Terror."[23]

Wily Ulysses, who knows how to restrict his freedom and therefore emerges cognizant from the experience of the beautiful, has been interpreted as predominantly ethical in the abundant Christian reception, as proof of the value of Christian virtue which will not let itself be deterred from "returning home," but also as the "mystery of the purifying danger which the life of grace must undergo," or even as the prefiguration of Christ allowing himself to be crucified. The history of reception changed with Clemens of Alexandria who extolled Ulysses at the mast as a "model of the humanist openness of the Christian to Hellenic wisdom."[24] The step toward aesthetic interpretation by which theoretical curiosity replaced this primordial image of discovering aesthesis is exemplarily represented by Montaigne's return to the "truth of phenomena" and the correlative affirmation of the aesthetic desire which the senses cannot satisfy: "there is already happiness in knowing desire as desire." This sentiment runs counter to a secular moral wisdom which teaches that one should not desire what lures and also remains unattainable. Montaigne wants "the sirens to sing" precisely because the pleasure which is not fulfilled in, and unavoidably fades through, possession permits the world of the senses to be discovered as the sphere of unlimited aesthetic reflection.[25]

If one wished to establish a threshold leading from the classical to the Christian canon of aesthesis in the history of the experience of art, it would probably be the famous though retrospective judgment in Jean Paul's *Vorschule der Ästhetik*: "Like a day of final judgment, Christianity abolished the entire world of the senses with all its charms, compressed it to a burial mound, turned it into a ladder leading to heaven, and replaced it with a new spirit world. Demonology became the true mythology of the physical world, and devils as seducers went to inhabit men and the statues of the gods. The present substance of the world thinned into a heavenly future. And what remained to the poetic spirit after this collapse of the external world? The world into which it collapsed, the inner!"[26] The Christian rejection of the classical cult of images also included the pleasurable surrender to the fictions of the arts and the "lies of the poets," but there accrued to them a new task which exempted them from the condemnation of all "lust of the eyes": to convey the contents of the Christian faith which demanded the representation of "invisible past and future things."[27] The negation of the entire world of the senses thus produced the gradual representation of the suprasensible spheres of the Christian world order, and from the negation of the present substance of the world there followed anticipatory hints of an as yet invisible future. The collapse of the outer world, finally, led to the discovery of the inner which from the abstract motif of the psychomachia unfolded more and more into the visible new landscapes of the soul. Under the title of a "poetry of the invisible," I have interpreted this process elsewhere[28] and recalled why the allegorical *modus dicendi* of ancient rhetoric (*aliud in verbis, aliud in sensu ostendit*) gave rise, in the Middle Ages, to allegory as the dominant mode which, in an unexpected abundance of forms, put its stamp on the epoch and extended to all genres. Since, for Christian poetry, the truth of what was to be portrayed lay in the three spheres of the invisible—the hidden beauty of God's kingdom to which the world of the senses and everything it contained referred as signs; the transcendent intermediate world of religious agencies between heaven and earth; and the transcendent inner world of the soul's struggle—allegorical (or typological) speech was required in order to also and always preserve their difference in the correspondence between figure (or event) and meaning. For the person addressed, this difference between figure and meaning included the appeal that he imagine what transcends the evidence of the sayable. Such a formulation underlines the difference between medieval aesthesis and its classical counterpart most strongly. In literary practice, however, the allegorical difference was frequently leveled out: where the sign- or imagelike form does more than objectify already known meanings, there develops that curious play with personified concepts, chains of *distinctiones*, or proliferating paronomasias which even today's philologically trained reader will find difficult to enjoy aesthetically as "mannerism," let alone understand as the expression of a religious experience.

As an example of the aesthesis that corresponds to the allegorical *modus dicendi*, I have chosen a passage from the "paradisology" of the Christian Middle Ages which Reinhold R. Grimm has saved from undeserved oblivion.[29] Among the themes taken up by the new poetry of the invisible, the allegory of paradise occupies the highest rank. The necessity of interpreting the *paradisus voluptatis* of Genesis 2, 8ff. justified recourse to the inventory of motifs of classical "places of pleasure" (*Lustorte*) and led to a fusion of the exegetical and poetic traditions. Especially since the twelfth century, this gave rise to a flowering of works in which religion and secular poets competed in filling the place "the collapse of the classical world of the senses had left empty," to quote Jean Paul, with a vision of a happy world.[30]

Works such as the *Navigatio Sancti Brendani* (which takes literally and describes as a path the search and discovery of the lost paradise of the first human couple—a paradise which, according to medieval belief, still exists somewhere on this earth), or the first *Roman de la Rose* (which first gave concrete expression to the *paradisus amoris* which had been hinted at in poetry but only abstractly designated through personification such as "Joy" or "Joven" [youth]) are less characteristic for our inquiry than the Bible poetry that developed directly from exegesis.

There, one encounters the paradox of an aesthesis of the suprasensible which demands of allegorism that it make accessible to the human senses what transcends their present experience. If, because of the fall, man has lost the subtlety and abundance of sensory experience, how can he have any idea of the perfection of the lost paradise? For it was perfect not only through the outward splendor of the place but also, as *paradisus corporalis*, by the as yet unspoiled, still virginal senses through which the first human couple could enjoy its beatitude. "Integris illis et virginibus sensibus quibus pura utebatur natura" (those whole and untainted senses which a nature pure makes use of)[31] is the Christian correlate of the classical concept of aesthesis as fulfilled present. But since the Augustinian speculation about paradise, the aesthesis of Christian allegorical interpretation had stood under the premise of an aesthetic negativity: since the paradisiacal state of man is irrecoverable, the perfect cannot simply be described and narrated but only be made approximately imaginable in the difference between sensory experience and suprasensible significance.[32] Ernaldus, abbot of Bonneval and friend of Bernard of Clairvaux, extricated himself from this dilemma in his Hexaemeron commentary by taking the five senses themselves as guide for the allegorism of life in paradise:[33]

In the middle of paradise, there was a transparent source which watered and moistened the roots of all vegetation, yet did not rise very high but watered the entire garden in its subterraenean course. Extensive foliage on slender trees shaded the grass growing below. The moisture of the earth and the moderate temperature above nourished an eternally green grass. A southern wind swept away vapor, if there was any. Snow and hail were unknown, and an even, eternal spring made it pleasant. The fruits and bushes scattered spices, and succulent herbs grew from the trunks. Fragrant bushes trickled and the liquid of the balsam which came from the bark adequately moistened the earth's crust. Fragrant, ointment-like nard oil flowed through the meadows. The entire region was filled everywhere with the countless fragrances of dripping rubber trees without the force of a press being necessary. Nothing was melancholy there, nothing spoilt that would have disturbed the rest for all the plants of that garden diffused the fragrance of the perfection of their planter and delivered sermons on the grace of heavenly glory. The trees exuded fat, the love of the saints produced purity, and the fragrance of that loveliness makes us understand the dignity of the sermon and the drunkenness of everlasting bliss. The fragrance representing the bodily senses was a kind of ecstasy though not one which brings profound slumber or keeps man from fulfilling his obligations but one which sharpened and purified the acuity and freedom of the spirit for every kind of work and for study. Myrrhs of various kinds, aromatic plants, spicate plants and medicinal herbs which grew in abundance fattened the fertile earth and though nature provided all that was needed, the still more liberal grace did its part. Although fever did not yet exist, there was already a cure for it. As yet, nature had no flaws, yet remedies for infirmities already grew.

Looked at from the tradition of biblical exegesis, this text shows the moment when allegorism must become poetic to fulfill its didactic purpose: the sensory perfection of the *paradisus voluptatis* can become imaginable for the reader only through the senses. For this reason, Ernaldus does not proceed in the traditional fashion of interpreting the sacred text word for word to discover its hidden meaning. For that would mean dissolving the sensuous experience in suprasensible significance. Instead, he uses the meanings that have collected in the exegetical tradition, the *proprietates* of things with their allegorical and etymological correspondences. By a procedure of "allegorizing the allegorism," he retranslates them back to the literal plane as it were,[34] allows them to be absorbed in his interpretive description, and tries to come close to the aesthesis of the suprasensible through their new plenitude. How far he goes beyond the biblical description becomes immediately apparent when one looks at the spare correspondence in the Vulgate: "sed fons ascendebat e terra, irrigans universam superficiem terrae" (2, 6); "Plantaverat autem Deus Paradisum voluptatis principio" (2, 8); "Produxitque Dominus Deus de humo omne lignum pulchrum visu, et ad vescendum suave" (2, 9) (but a spring rose from the earth, watering the whole face of the earth (2, 6); then God planted a garden of pleasure eastward (2, 8); and the Lord God brought forth from the ground every tree beautiful for seeing and sweet for eating (2, 9). From the one source in Paradise and the planting of the garden of Eden with "all kinds of trees which are pleasant to look at and good to eat" (in Luther's translation), there arises an entire landscape that incorporates the place of pleasure of classical pastoral poetry and the fragrant flowers of the late-classical epithalamia and far surpasses them in lushness. But the perception of this blissful world unfolds in a way that differs from that of the account of the shield in which the cosmic order is clearly articulated in its totality and its detail, presented in its harmony and contrasts, and could be drawn without difficulty according to the motto *ut pictura poesis*. After the first few sentences, it becomes clear that this description of paradise does not fit into the perceivable order of an overall view. For the modern reader who tries to visualize what is not meant for an aesthesis through sight, the imaginative effort becomes increasingly frustrating.

True, Ernaldus also begins with the center, the source. But his description does not extend concentrically and horizontally but vertically, to the foliage "above," the moist ground "below," and the eternally green grass in between. The freshness of this green leads to an interpretation of climate and time which climaxes in the bucolic state of an eternal spring. Everything that now follows is no longer spatially articulated: the fruit and the shrubbery, the meadows that are not localized, and finally the variety of herbs do not appear as elements of a landscape but as sources of countless fragrances. When he comes to the odd because neither metaphorically nor hyperbolically intended sentence: "Fragrant, ointment-like nard oil flowed through the meadows," the modern reader can no longer fail to recognize that it is not the customary concreteness but a hitherto unheard-of aesthesis through the sense of smell that determines the order of what is to be perceived. Many previously inconsistent details are thus brought together on a level of meaning where they are meant to make comprehensible for the reader the ecstasy of paradisiacal bliss in the perfect relaxation of *sensus* and *deliciae*. But the aesthesis of Christian allegorism does not reach a contemplative resting point in this pure sensory fullness ("Nothing was melancholy there, nothing spoilt"). Ernaldus permits his reader to linger in the perfect present only to refer him to a higher level of meaning in the midst of this evocation, from the "fragrance of perfection" to its creator. The following sentence accomplishes the switch from sensory experience to suprasensible significance through a stylistic break which strikes one as abstruse: "The trees exuded fat, the love of the saints produced purity . . ." There follows a switch in levels through an allegorical inference: if first it was the bodily senses through which the ecstasy of life in paradise could be experienced, it is now the fragrance of the garden of paradise that represents those bodily senses ("deliniens sensus carnis.")! Ernaldus does in fact see man before the fall as microcosm in the macrocosm,[35] the earthly paradise as the "material conformance of his distinctive nature which is to be God's image."[36] But the remainder of man's highest dignity—"magna hominis dignitas, cujus factor Deus, consors angelus, minister mundus, regio paradisus"[37] (the great dignity of man, whose maker is God, whose consort is the angel, who is minister of the world and king of paradise) — is inevitably followed by the hint of his fall and the possibility of his salvation. Ernaldus concludes this piece of his poietic allegorism with an image that shows this ecstatically experienced present pointing toward a menacing future: although fever does not yet exist, there is already a cure for it. As yet, nature has no flaws, yet remedies for infirmities already grow.

It is well known that Petrarch stylized the beginning of a new aesthetic curiosity about the world and a sensory experience of nature in an event which he dated April 26, 1336. The ascent of Mount Ventoux would remain an occasion in the history of aesthesis even if Petrarch had merely invented it. For a literary fiction could only enhance the significance of this crossing of the boundary line of aesthetic curiosity, and its subsequent retraction. If Petrarch specifically made up the account to demonstrate how a hitherto unheard-of temptation to see something forbidden[38] had prompted an Augustinian turning inward, it becomes all the more justifiable to infer the great strength of the barrier erected against an experience of nature which, in its aesthetic manifestation as landscape, has become so natural for us through the work of Claude Lorrain, Poussin, or Constable and, in literature, through romanticism. The gradual dismantling of this barrier would give us an excellent sense of the process by which aesthetic perception freed itself from the Christian ascetic priority of the inner world and the concern for salvation, and discovered a new experience of inwardness which permitted to sublate the opposition of world and soul aesthetically, in the "correspondences" of outside and inside. Here, it must suffice to explicate the beginning and the climax of this phase in the modern history of aesthesis through Petrarch and Rousseau.[39]

We begin with the experience of the prospect which unfolds for Petrarch on Mount Ventoux before he opens his copy of Augustine's *Confessions*. Having reached the peak which is described as a small area (line 124ff.), the long yearned-for moment arrives: "Primum omnium spiritu quodam aeris insolito et spectaculo liberiore permotus, stupenti simili steti" (At first I stood there nearly benumbed, overwhelmed by a wind such as I had never felt before and by the unusually open and wide view). The first reaction is neither satisfaction over the success of the enterprise, nor astonishment at what has never been seen and now opens up before his eyes, but a paralysis of all his senses. Yet even the experience which then follows and which Petrarch tries to explain to his spiritual mentor is not yet an unencumbered enjoyment of the view "from above," let alone that admiring discovery of the beauty of the sublimity of nature which will characterize the aesthetic experience of nature as "landscape" only at a much later date. From all Petrarch sees and takes in, he always turns away again in order to abandon himself to recollection or meditation. The glance downward where clouds block the view produces a learned reminiscence: in the future, he will find reports about the classical mountains Athos and Olympus less unbelievable. The view eastward where the Alps rise rigidly, wildly, and snow-covered, evokes the memory of Hannibal's violent crossing ("ferus ille quondam hostis romani nominis," the fierce enemy of the Roman name) and stirs the longing —already no longer prompted by what he sees—("animo potius quam oculo," in the mind rather than in the eye) to return again to his friendlier Italian fatherland. With this sensation, his attention is wholly drawn from the spatial expanse into the depths of time ("a locis traduxit ad tempora," he crossed from places to times): he observes that the tenth anniversary of his "childish studies" is approaching and takes himself to task for the time he has wasted. Already regretting the arrogance that took him to this place, he turns westward where a richly articulated landscape stretches from the Rhone almost to the Pyrenees. He has seen enough now, and the body which carried him to these heights admonishes him to also direct his soul to higher things. His glance falls on the edition of Augustine and providentially on the famous passage from the tenth book: "And men go abroad to admire the heights of mountains, the mighty billows of the sea, the broad tides of rivers, the compass of the ocean, and the circuits of the stars, and pass themselves by" (X, viii, 15). All of external nature, however astounding the prospect from this newly reached height, cannot stand up to the inner world of the soul which alone is admirable ("nihil praeter animum esse mirabile," that nothing is more wondrous than the mind). It shrinks to the measure of "hardly an elbow" when man turns inward where in his *memoria*, which Augustine praises as a "boundless chamber," as "that great receptacle of my mind, stored with the images of things so many and so great" (X, viii, 14–15), he finds not only all of external nature but also himself and God. The outward look, toward newly opening horizons of sensory experience, must again serve a turning back and inward: the bold ascent to the "peak of arrogance" ("cacumen insolentiae") was merely a detour to the height of human contemplation ("altitudo contemplationis humanae"), the spiritual experience of the true self.

The effect of this analysis on the history of aesthesis was that the aesthetic interest in the world which newly manifests itself in Petrarch remained tied to the Augustinian-medieval understanding of the world in a twofold respect. External nature as it presents itself to the eye is not yet experienced aesthetically, as "landscape" in the correspondence of world and soul, and the turning inward discovers memory initially as "world inner space," not yet as a world-appropriating faculty. It is true, however, that Petrarch's vernacular poetry goes beyond the Augustinian scheme in that the lyrical persona reflects itself in the phenomena of external nature and thematizes its loneliness as spatial and temporal distance from the beloved. And with the "inner landscapes" of its turning inward, it opens up a new, secular dimension for *memoria*. Petrarch's *Canzoniere* is the beginning of modern lyric poetry. It presented the lyric subject as poet and clothed the lyric theme of "pleasure through pain" in sublimated language that would endure for centuries. But it is still characteristic of this poetry that it also makes recognizable the barriers that Christian *humilitas* put up against modern aesthesis.

If medieval aesthesis is understood as the poetry of the invisible, Petrarch's cycle of sonnets which removes the mistress into spatial distance and makes her an object of memory presents itself as a poetry of absence which sublimates and interiorizes the lyric of the troubadours. This is how I would summarize the poetic peculiarities of the *Canzoniere* which Hugo Friedrich has already studied at some length and contrasted with the spiritual ideas of earlier poets.[40] It is precisely the only two events with which the Laura legend could connect later in the history of reception, the first encounter and the death of the beloved, which, as seemingly concrete memories of the poet's life, correspond with Christ's passion, as the symbolic dating, the sixth of April in each case, is meant to indicate (the Good Friday of the beginning in canzone #3 already prefigures calendrically the earthly end of this love in canzone #267). Recollection as the lyric medium of absence as discovered by Petrarch, which sublimates the concrete person and sensuous presence of the mistress by making it the unique manifestation of a distance, reaches the highest level of such sublimation with Laura's death—the "turn" between the first and the second phase of the love in the sonnet sequence: "only the departed is the truly present."[41] In the painful recognition of the places where the poet thought of her when she was still alive, recollection can now become "recollection of recollection,"[42] and the dead beloved can emerge from her sacral unapproachability and take on, as dream appearance, the features of a mother or a wife (#285).

Along with temporal removal, spatial distance as the lyric medium of absence also acquires new meaning in Petrarch. The remoteness of the beloved is the ultimate source of the inner movement in which the lover experiences and enjoys himself in his abandonment as he faces alien nature. Before the reader's eyes, new kinds of impressions of the world of the senses thus give rise to the aesthetic structure of an "inner landscape" in whose creation—as Friedrich also showed— "visibility and dematerialization of the visible combine in such a manner that at the end nothing is being reproduced and a place such as Vaucluse becomes like any other, yet subjective experience unmistakably manifests itself.[43] Lyric aesthesis can seize phenomena of external nature such as the times of the day or the seasons in newly perceived shadings which then become integral parts of a whole that has its center in the name of Laura and often gets its significance only through the symbolism of that name:

> Zephyr returns, fair weather in his train
> and flowers and grass, and all his gentle brood,
> and Procne's chirp and Philomel's sad strain,
> and spring in scarlet and in white renewed;
>
> the sky grows clear and smiling is the plain,
> Jove on his daughter looks in happy mood,
> love fills the water, air, and earth again,
> and every creature finds love's counsel good.
>
> To me, alas, return more heavy sighs,
> drawn from the heart in that profound distress
> by one who took its keys to paradise;
>
> and birdsong and the hillside's flowered dress
> and ladies in their motion sweet and wise
> seem savage beasts that roam a wilderness.[44]

This typical sonnet, which varies a theme with a long tradition—spring as the time of desire of all of nature—by mingling mythological reminiscences and new sense impressions ("spring in scarlet and in white"; "ladies in their motion sweet and wise"), switches into the dissonant opposite tonality and thus repeats in a sense the Mount Ventoux experience. In both cases, "the soul would become less aware of itself if it did not look at nature."[45] But doesn't the lyrical persona look at nature only to then turn away from its sensory appearance and to express the ambivalent experience of its inner nature, "beautiful pain?" Yet the lyrical experience in the *Canzoniere* certainly does not stay within the confines of the Augustinian scheme. Petrarch only makes use of patterns of behavior and images of Christian self-examination such as remorse and repentance, meditation, pilgrimage, suffering, and the return to heaven in order to rediscover and spiritualize his profane love within the horizon of religious self-analysis. The theme of remorse at the youthful madness of love and poetry in the first sonnet does not lead to penitence and self-transformation but grounds a wholly aesthetic experience. In it, the Christian-medieval understanding of the world and the "beginning of the modern period" intersect in a peculiar manner: although Petrarch does not yet have at his command aesthetic perception as a world-appropriating understanding, the inwardly turned lyrical experience of the *Canzoniere* already transcends the sphere of Christian *humilitas*. For the poet who knows how to free himself of his suffering in the medium of beautiful verse ("cantando il duol si disacerba," singing consoles grief, #23, v. 4), poiesis includes its own catharsis: "the text invents a suffering and stills it in art."[46]

If one agrees with Joachim Ritter and sees the modern history of aesthesis as the movement "in which the aesthetic sense tries to make nature itself, as the unseen and unsaid, shine forth in ever new landscapes,"[47] the aesthetic discovery of mountains is of a late date and therefore especially instructive in our context. True, Arno Borst has traced a change in the understanding of nature in the five recorded instances of mountain climbs which are all that have come down to us from the Middle Ages. The fear of demons in the mountain wilderness was a barrier which could be conquered by strangers if not by indigenous residents where the ascesis of monks established settlements in an inhospitable solitude and closeness to heaven or where a sovereign's desire for glory—Charles VIII of France during his Italian campaign (1492)—brought it about that a peak such as Mount Aiguille which was considered out of reach could be conquered by what was already a technically planned expedition.[48] But this change of motivation from medieval closeness to God to the modern concept of nature is still far from the attitude that wants to experience aesthetically a mountain world untouched by man, as a landscape where inside and outside harmonize. This is confirmed by a glance at the history of landscape painting.

In the overall development of the arts, painting is certainly ahead of poetry in the aesthetic discovery of ever new views of nature appearing as landscape. In their aesthetic fullness, the idyllic or heroic ideal landscapes of the French and Italian painters surpass both the bucolic and the heroic novels of the seventeenth century as much as the prosaic everyday landscapes of the Dutch surpass the comparable picaresque tales. And when the great parks replaced the French gardens in eighteenth-century England, it was the model of Claude Lorrain,

Poussain, and Constable according to which the new form of the "aesthetic gardens" was created.[49] But Werner Hofmann has shown that in this process, the experience of nature and the experience of the self only very gradually entered into an aesthetic relation.[50]

In his treatise on painting (before 1518), Leonardo, who already saw landscape segments with topographical precision and was interested in the spectacle of natural catastrophies, also included the view of the unlimited landscape which Petrarch had discovered *per negationem* as an example of the *imitatio naturae* where painters surpass all other artists: "As he sees the bottoms of valleys or looks down from high mountain tops on the extensive fields spread out before him and, behind them, the horizon of the sea, he is their master."[51] Similar to the contemporary report about the expedition to Mount Aiguille in this respect, Leonardo's vision also discovers a part of previously unseen nature as an object to which sovereign man can extend his rule. And in Renaissance painting, nature as landscape appears in a vis-à-vis which places acting man into the foreground: "autonomous man becomes the center, the world his accompaniment. From this comes the relation of dependence which has marked landscape painting from the beginning."[52] Landscape as beautiful, idyllic, or heroic nature forms the background for the representation of motifs from mythology or the history of salvation whose higher dignity first justifies the aesthetic presentation of landscapes: "the higher, worthier intellectual content is accorded the ideal form for what is involved there is spiritual elevation. Landscape merely satisfies the sensory perception of the viewer."[53] This is the reason that, after Alberti, "landscape" originally lay below the level of the sublime and that the Renaissance ranked historical higher than landscape painting. Even Claude Lorrain's heroic landscape which Goethe experienced as a liberation "from the intrusive, disturbing world" does not aim at a subjective experience but complements the exemplary appearance of acting man as a "great, beautiful and significant world in which a human tribe of few wants and noble sentiments seemed to dwell."[54] It is not until the eighteenth century that along with the discovery of a new mode of experience of aesthesis, the sublime, that nature as landscape is brought into a direct connection with the *viewing* subject: "The sight of unlimited distances, and heights lost to view, the vast ocean at his feet and the vaster ocean above him, pluck his spirit out of the narrow sphere of the actual and out of the oppressive bondage of physical life. A mightier measure of esteem is exemplified for him by the simple majesty of nature, and surrounded by her massive forms he can no longer tolerate pettiness in his thought."[55]

It is no accident that in Schiller's definition of the sublime (around 1793/94), there should be a return of the view of external nature which Petrarch had negated. The prospect from the mountain, the expansion of the horizon, and the "witty disorder of a natural landscape," which is how the virginal mountain world presents itself, fulfills most adequately the concept of the sublime which the viewer can enjoy in an elevation of his spirit and without the mediation of the rules of beauty of the prevailing classicism. Edmund Burke (1757)[56] and Rousseau (1761) had pioneered this liberation of aesthesis from the traditional canon of the beautiful. This was followed by the discovery of the English mountains and lakes and of the Swiss Alps in painting. The enormous success of the *Nouvelle Héloise* also made public the aesthetic discovery of the Wallis mountains by Rousseau whose literary document became the twenty-third letter of his novel. A more detailed interpretation of this letter is called for at this time.

By a quotation that interprets the climbing of the mountain symbolically, as a rising from the physical to the nonphysical ("Levan di terra al Ciel nostr'intelletto"),[57] Rousseau himself recalls Petrarch to the reader's mind. But that the Petrarchan scheme is being inverted immediately becomes apparent because here aesthetic experience moves from inside to outside: "I wanted to dream but was always distracted by some unexpected sight." Saint-Preux, on whom Julie has imposed a separation after the first proof of his love, wants to abandon himself on the mountain path to the mood of yearning of his "coeur sensible" and is constantly kept from this by unexpected natural sights. What he sees no longer fits into a field of meaning where every natural phenomenon speaks symbolically of the absent beloved, nor does it refer to a recognizable vanishing point: "Sometimes immense rocks hung in ruins above my head. Sometimes tall and noisy waterfalls deluged me with their heavy mist. Sometimes an eternal torrent opened up an abyss at my side whose depth my eyes did not dare to measure. Sometimes I lost my way in the obscurity of a dense forest. And occasionally, as I emerged from a ravine, a pleasant meadow suddenly delighted me." The quickly changing sights reveal neither a hidden harmony of opposites nor a "beautiful disorder." They are the same phenomena that travelers had hitherto experienced as the threats of the mountain world but which now become a spectacle for the wanderer. This means that, in Kant's words, they can arouse his "pleasure but a pleasure mixed with dread" if he is susceptible to the "sense of the sublime."[58]

The final sight produces the unexpected switch from wild to civilized nature, and the following description shows what the hand of man could produce even here: ("excellent fruits on the rocks, and fields among the precipices"). The specifically thematized contrast between natural state and human labor, however, appears as merely one among other "bizarre" contrasts in this newly perceived nature. As the wanderer moves on, the never suspected, time-and-space-comprehending totality of nature is revealed to him: "In the East, the flowers of spring, in the South, the fruits of autumn, in the North, the ice of winter: it united all the seasons at the same moment, and all the climates in the same place." Rousseau's new hero, who leaves the restricted realm of his daily duties, not only discovers in the hitherto unseen mountains the unlimited prospect of nature but also raises himself in the unhampered and pleasurable contemplation of it to a view of the whole which life "in the plain" (which here also symbolizes his social existence and the humiliations of his life as private tutor) had denied him: "for since the perspective of the mountains is vertical, it strikes the eyes all at once and much more powerfully than that of the plains which one only sees obliquely, and where every object hides another." Like religious ecstasy or philosophical *theoria*, the rapture of the wanderer also involves an elevation to a blissful life ("a quiet pleasure which has nothing bitter or sensual about it"). Like classical theater formerly, the ever new "spectacle of nature"[59] induces a catharsis. The purity of the air seems to purify the passions ("It is in such fashion that a happy climate makes the passions which elsewhere cause his torment serve the felicity of man"), and in this harmony of inside and outside, the observer enjoys the happiness of a pure existence which no longer needs a transcendent home because it has discovered its "new world" in "another nature."[60]

It is not merely incidentally that Rousseau sharply contrasts the new aesthetic experience of nature with philosophy and its hollow ideal of the sage who allegedly rises above his passions though no one knows how.[61] The epochal turn in the history of aesthesis which the twenty-third letter of the *Nouvelle Héloise* signals, anticipates the shift of function from philosophy to aesthetics which Joachim Ritter elucidated in drawing on Kant: "After the science of nature had embarked on a certain path by restricting itself to 'spelling out' the phenomena with which it deals in the field of possible experience only, the aesthetic imagination takes on the task of making present to the mind nature in its totality and as the representation of the idea of the suprasensible which we can no longer recognize in the 'concept of worlds'. . . . Where the heaven and earth of human existence are no longer known and expressed in the sciences as they were in the ancient world in the concept of philosophy, poetry and art assume the task of conveying them aesthetically, as landscape."[62] With the document interpreted here, Rousseau stands at the beginning of this turn where the discovery of the correspondence between landscape and subjectivity still occurs in the nexus between subjective and social experience; as subject of the landscape, the wanderer discovers at the end of his walk a mountain village where the state of nature is realized socially, in the community of a happy and hospitable tribe characterized by simple customs, the joy it takes in its work, and a high degree of equality. This nostalgic *Urbild* of an achieved *contrat social* is certainly the germ of that romantic Rousseauism to which German idealism's most impressive answer was Schiller's poem "Der Spaziergang" of 1795 and its insight that it was precisely "the rupture between man and an originally peaceful, surrounding nature" which constituted the necessary condition of freedom.[63] The fact remains that in Rousseau, romanticism did not make the philosopher of the *Contrat social* but the *promeneur solitaire* and the author of the *Rêveries* the paradigm of solitary subjectivity. Rousseau's aesthetic legacy to romanticism which culminates in the fifth *promenade* could not be summarized better than in this sentence by Schelling: "The highest relationship between nature and art is attained when nature makes art the medium through which it makes manifest its soul."[64] To this romantic conception of aesthesis, there corresponds most closely in landscape painting that motif made famous by Caspar David Friedrich where one or several figures, their backs turned toward the viewer of the painting, look into the landscape (as in *Mondaufgang am Meer* or *Der Morgen im Gebirge*); acting man, for whom the heroic landscape is merely background, has been replaced by the viewer of nature whose glance is absorbed by what he sees, just as what is being seen seems significant only because he looks at it.

With this, a point in the history of aesthesis has been reached where the specifically modern experience of nature as landscape completes the reversal of the Augustinian scheme which began with Petrarch; not the world-negating inward but the world-seizing outward turn is the movement that allows the viewer to find his true self in the correspondence of landscape and soul. The modern subjectivity, however, no longer grasps external nature as animated landscape in the unmediated enjoyment of what is at hand. According to Schiller, romantic aesthesis is the sentimental feeling for the lost naive or, according to Goethe, "a calm perception of the sublime in the form of the past or, what amounts to the same thing, of loneliness, absence, remoteness."[65] Romantic aesthesis presupposes the emancipation of the theoretical and the aesthetic which had been polemically asserted by Rousseau and systematized and perfected by Kant. But if the aesthetic world concept now takes the place of the speculative one and art assumes the cosmological function abandoned by philosophy, aesthetic experience on its own can also no longer make present the whole of nature in its classical sensuous fullness. It can, however, return it to the modern sensibility in the medium of recollection. The beautiful, which romantic subjectivity attempts to preserve as man becomes reified in bourgeois society and its division of labor, is the beautiful as something past: it originates in an attitude "which looks for the truth of a past nature in the remoteness of history and, in the nearness of surrounding nature, for the absent totality, the lost childhood of man."[66] With romantic art which interiorizes the alien external world as landscape, there sets in the discovery of the aesthetic capacity of recollection, and the prelude to that process is the *Confessions* in which Rousseau undertook to totalize the contingency of his life history.

Before Rousseau's autobiographical writings, one will hardly find historical evidence of the process of this discovery. It presupposes a new attention to what has been involuntarily or unconsciously experienced and which eludes enlightened reason and sanctioned morality but can be discovered in and behind the rationalizations and idealizations of past life if an emancipated aesthetic experience now also begins to take charge of the examination of conscience. Remembrance as the aesthetic faculty that looks for the lost truth of the past in the precipitate of the affective, unobserved life because it mistrusts the interested selectivity of the historian and the idealizing memory of the memorialist comes to light only retrospectively. The discovery of the *poésie de la mémoire* in the nineteenth century could be recognized as a historical phenomenon only after Proust had fathomed it, elucidated it in predecessors such as Nerval, Baudelaire, and Ruskin, developed it in his theory of the *souvenir involuntaire*, and poetically realized that theory in the retrospective fable of his *Remembrance of Things Past*. As early as 1929, Walter Benjamin had already recognized in Baudelaire's lyric the effort to restore the lost aura to things through remembrance because in the denatured existence of urban civilization, the capacity for experience was withering. Remembrance being involuntary, it had a rejuvenating power, Benjamin believed, and for that reason, the *Fleurs du Mal* had to be seen as part of the prehistory of Proust's *Recherche*. But this remained a historically undeveloped thesis which came to naught in Benjamin's violent attempt to bring dialectical materialism to bear on the *Fleurs du Mal.*[67] The aesthetic efficacy of remembrance and its significance for the constitution of a modern poetics was the subject of my earlier studies of Proust and Baudelaire, the results of which I summarize here.[68]

Regarding the question of Baudelaire's place in the history of aesthesis, my interpretation of his *Le Cygne* shows that it is not only the changed experience of society during a period of abruptly growing industrialization—"the productive power of man alienated from himself"[69]—that is inscribed in the *Fleurs du Mal*. Baudelaire's swan poem is also exemplary for the new form of aesthesis which, in view of the crisis of perception in the progressively technicized world, was first developed in lyric poetry. The aesthesis of modern lyric poetry has its antiromantic starting point in the *Fleurs du Mal*. Here, Baudelaire accomplishes the aesthetic revaluation of nature. Along with it, the reassurance of the Platonic aesthetic, which the concept of the symbol in romantic poetry still implied, was lost. In "Andromaque, je pense à toi," any trace of a predestined harmony between man and nature, or a hidden analogy between sensible appearance and suprasensible meaning, is gone. The expectation that behind the chaotic realities of a city (half destroyed by Haussmann's renovations), the familiar horizon of a higher and more beautiful reality might still reveal itself to confer meaning on the alien "landscape of ennui" is foiled. The Platonic horizon that has vanished here is constitutive of the lyric aesthesis of the older tradition of *poésie descriptive*, as is shown by my analysis of the swan poem by Theophile de Viau with its similar motif. There, the baroque technique of a continuing metaphorical or mythological transformation of the field of vision serves to estrange a concrete landscape, park, and pond of Chantilly. But this is not yet the object of this poetry. Rather, the seemingly "modern" dematerialization merely serves the intent to retranslate the singular quality of the Parc of Chantilly and the special situation of the persecuted poet into the imaginary space of an idyllic-mythological landscape and to thus direct the reader's perception through the manneristic alienation toward a higher, spiritual reality. This Platonic horizon of a "ciel antérieur où fleurit la beauté" (Mallarmé) is evoked only *ex negativo* in Baudelaire's poem: in view of its "empty ideality," it is meant to introduce a movement of aesthesis which takes the opposite direction. But to demonstrate the dissonance between spleen and ideal, the reified chaos of the metropolis and the worldless exile of the mythical swan is not Baudelaire's ultimate object. From the ruins of the familiar nature of old Paris, his poem gives rise to a new counterworld of the beautiful which derives neither from the correspondence with "natural nature" nor from the transparency of a more beautiful, Platonic ideality. Here also, in the poem itself and before the eye of the reader, there takes place a retransformation of the world of objects which has become alien and frozen in allegory. But now it is only remembrance from which the counterimage of the new and the beautiful ("Un monde nouveau, la sensation du neuf") arises in a solemn procession of evocations. The harmonizing and idealizing power of remembrance is the newly discovered aesthetic capacity which can replace the extinct correspondence of soul and timeless nature by the coincidence of present existence and prehistory, modernity and antiquity, historical now and mythical past.

When he noted that there were no longer any simultaneous correspondences in Baudelaire, Benjamin defined the poetological turn very preceisely: "the correspondences are data of remembrance— not historical data, but data of prehistory. What makes festive days great and significant is the encounter with an earlier life."[70] But this is a far cry from Benjamin's statement elsewhere that the "fundamental paradox" in Baudelaire's aesthetics lies in a "contradiction between the theory of natural correspondences and the rejection of nature."[71] Remembrance as the modern form of aesthesis presupposes that there has been a break with that anthropocentric understanding of nature which had lain at the base of the romantic experience of landscape as the harmony of inwardness and a nature far from civilization. Even in its polemics, Baudelaire's rejection of "natural" nature which he occasionally stylized as hatred of all growing and green life testifies both to the melancholy of an irrevocably lost natural understanding of the world and to the discovery of a modern concept of the beautiful, that version of the fleeting beauty (*beau fugitif*) of the moment that does not return, a beauty which, being gone, leaves behind its own *antiquité*. In this way, Baudelaire created the new poetry of the artificial metropolitan landscape where the nature produced by man triumphs as the testimonial of a productivity that is his alone, and then disintegrates again. In the *Tableaux Parisiens* and the prose poems of the *Spleen de Paris*, the new landscapes of ennui and ecstasy[72] often contrast as violently with each other as do the shock experience of the *beauté fugitive* and the correspondences of the "data of remembrance." In Baudelaire, remembrance as a capacity of aesthesis cannot yet mediate such opposites. It is merely evoked here as a poetic force to counter the destruction of the natural aura and cannot demonstrate its totalizing efficacy until Proust uses the more suitable epic form to poetically restore the cosmological horizon with his fable of lost time and recovered world.

Of course, the step from Baudelaire to Proust represents only *one* path of aesthetic experience along which modern poetry tries to deal with the crisis of perception during the epoch of progressive industrialization and technicalization. Another emerged during the second half of the nineteenth century in the development of a language-critical function of aesthesis which has its correlate in modern painting, in the theories and programs of the new vision, i.e., a kind of vision which has been renewed by art. In analogy to the original situation of aesthetics in the eighteenth century, the justification of cognition through the senses (*cognitio sensitiva*) is taken up again and developed further, this time as a protest against the ideology of positivism and its vulgar-aesthetic correlates, i.e., naturalism and industrial art (*art industriel*) which made its appearance at the first world fair. The epochal nexus of the statements that characterize this phase of aesthetic experience has not yet been comprehensively described in the history of art and aesthetics.[73] The following phenomena belong here: in literature, Flaubert's step from an aesthetics of representation to one of perception which arose from his redefinition of style as an absolute mode of seeing (*manière absolue de voir les choses*); in painting, the "deconceptualization of the world," and the making over of the eye into an organ of unreflected seeing by French impressionism;[74] the theory of art as pure visibility which was elaborated by Konrad Fiedler during the eighties and which, through the work of Adolf Hildebrand, Alois Riegel, Heinrich Wölfflin, and Richard Hamann, has remained—and continues to be—relevant in the contemporary discussion of aesthetics.[75] Almost concurrently with Fiedler, there was Valéry's first Leonardo essay (1894) which countered the conceptual hypotheses of philosophers and the expectation clichés of everyday perception by a sight that had been renewed through art; and finally, the aesthetic theory as developed by Viktor Shklovsky and the Russian formalists according to which the "automatism of perception" is to be dealt with by a method of "defamiliarization," a "forcing us to notice," a theory Shklovsky developed by an analysis of Tolstoi[76] and which, as alienation, had an incalculable effect on the theory of drama through Bertolt Brecht.

For Valéry, the principle of pure seeing ("seeing more than one knows") was primarily opposed to the concept of nature. Led astray by both poets and philosophers, we see nature in the mirror of anthropocentric concepts such as cruelty, kindness, economy, as if we could not bear its immemorial aspect: "the vision of a green, vague, and continuous eruption; of some great elemental work as opposed to everything human; of a monotonous quantity that will some day cover us . . . ." Valéry's criticism continues the tradition of the radical aesthetic revaluation of nature previously carried out by Baudelaire. Here, it climaxes in the demand that cognition through sight of the nature surrounding us can be had only by observing "any corner whatever of that which exists" ("un coin quelconque de ce qui est") which does not allow the illusion of nature's suitability for man's purposes to arise. This arbitrary corner also occurs in Zola's famous formulation about the "coin de la nature vu à travers un tempérament," except that here, the programmatic naturalism obscures again the polemics implied in the notion of the "arbitrary," a polemics directed against the anthropocentric concept of nature in romanticism. The antinaturalist practice of indifference toward motifs corresponds to this arbitrariness that theory calls for. Parallels could easily be found in lyric poetry since Mallarmé and in the painting during the same period.

In the twentieth-century novel, the two modes of aesthetic experience, the language-critical and the cosmological function of aesthesis, climax in the contrasting positions of Beckett and Proust. In his Proust essay of 1931 and in his later novel *Malone Dies* (1951) which alludes to Proust's situation, Beckett proclaimed the "death of the subject," inveighed against the search for identity in the medium of remembrance, and introduced a form of writing without aesthetic distance in order to negate all aesthesis for being a literary positing.[77] This defines a turning point after which hardly anyone continued to follow Proust's example. Carried to its ultimate aporias, Beckett's doubt in the competence of the writer to grasp social and individual life with the teleological forms of narration without falling victim to the "lie of representation" and the deception of an opaque manipulation of language has since come into vogue[78] and stamped the *Nouveau roman* and the prose of the Tel Quel group in particular. These writers decisively reject the realistic portrayal of individuals in the tradition of Balzac, "this objectifying rounded view whose principal parameters were character, milieu and fable."[79] and continue the critical function of Flaubert's aesthetics of perception by dismantling those remaining narrative functions that carry meaning. The result is that the hiatus between perceived world and perceiving subject becomes unbridgeable for the reader. Flaubert's procedure of dissolving the fable as the precedent, meaning-creating unit of apperception already led to the cognition of unfamiliar reality by a perception that was made more difficult because no longer centered in the narrator; through the perspectivism of the interior monologue, the reader is made aware that the clichés of language govern experience, and the phenomenalization of events makes him realize that the tele-ology of historical succession is mere appearance. He is thus deprived of the positivist confidence in the causal transparency of his world.

The contrasting neutrality of things which Flaubert sets against the preoriented perception of his ordinary characters which has be-come second nature for them recurs as a structural element in Robbe-Grillet's novels. What Flaubert not infrequently raises to the novum of a "poetry of objects" which confronts the disillusioning purposes and desires of man as alien and in indifferent beauty is reified by Robbe-Grillet in the litanylike descriptions of the plantation in *La Jalousie* and becomes the extreme form of a quasi-mathemtical view of objects which imposes on the reader a wholly uncustomary ascesis of perception that issues in boredom. Hans Koppe has shown that in this way, the technique of defamiliarization can again lose its critical function and a "materialist scientism" can finally stylize nonpur-posive instrumentality as its own fictitious salvation.[80] Here, we see a provocative overextension of the poietic role of the reader who has been encouraged to imagine and reflect on his own in the most re-cent history of aesthesis. The avant-gardism of modern *écriture* as practiced by Philippe Sollers (which absolutizes the "writing of writing," which uses what remains of narrative elements merely to admit and show that they have been invented and are not binding, which makes permanent reflection about narrative functions and structual problems the only remaining "moral of the story," and which therefore can expect no more from the mocked reader than a theoretical and philological interest in a reference-less language game) not only robs itself of what is, paradoxically, a nonetheless expected ideology-critical or "consciousness-changing" effect. Without being aware of it, it surrenders the cognitive and communicative efficacy of aesthesis along with the aesthetic pleasure it denies and thus cannot really escape the serious objection D. Wellershoff has raised: "Is this sensitive attention to processes of consciousness still an enlargement of the terrain, or does it merely take hold of the fine-grained trickle of substanceless modulations which always occur but which, having no structure, only express the passage of the moments of life and no longer produce any experience, any insight which calls forth others and to which one might relate?"[81]

Since *Remembrance of Things Past*, which was published between 1913 and 1927, the world in which we live has certainly been stan-dardized and instrumentalized to a degree Proust could hardly have anticipated. It seems to me, nonetheless, that his theory of aesthesis and the poetics of remembrance inscribed in his novels retain a paradigmatic significance for contemporary aesthetics which, on the literary scene, can be described as a swinging back of the pendulum toward narration, the autobiographical, and the documentary. Anyone who has passed through the ascetic aesthetics and the powerfully reflective art of negativity and wishes to retire it certainly cannot simply reinstate the narrator who has been declared dead, or bring back the naive confidence in language and the realistic "imitation of reality." Against such nostalgic inclinations, Adorno was right to demand as early as 1954 that for the contemporary novel to remain faithful to its inherently realistic heritage, it would have to take a stand against the lie of representation, take seriously the universal alienation and self-alienation, destroy the superficial connection by the elimination of aesthetic distance, and institute such resistance against opinion as the "second alienation of an alienated world" to bring about its restoration.[82] Such demands, the last of which is raised in Adorno's Proust essay, charge the contemporary novel with the paradoxical task of fulfilling the representative function of aesthesis without using the traditional means of narrative mimesis.

Where we invariably view the familiar world through a network of already known significances and unconscious valuations, and do not truly see things but merely recognize them, the déjà vu of deficient daily perception blocks all realistic mirroring. Aesthetic perception which "will make the stone stony" again,[83] which is to reconstitute the sensory perception of the world in its alienated reality, cannot be won through, but only in, a struggle against the recognition of what is already familiar. The formalist theory of aesthesis which uncovered the realistic circle of mimesis and anamnesis—the unavowed Platonic legacy of materialist aesthetics—too one-sidedly emphasized the innovative achievement of techniques of alienation as the highest aesthetic value. But that aesthetic perception which can free us of the automatism of alienated language and world experience does not completely coincide with the innovation by which it counters the old and familiar with a new view of the world. The demand of the aesthetics of the "new seeing" that the object be described "as if it were being seen for the first time, and an incident as if it occurred for the first time"[84] also includes the discovering or confirmatory seeing of what need not be new but could have remained hidden or repressed in previous experience.

Proust's theory of the aesthetic capacity of remembrance is exemplary in the sense that, by the rejection of all narrative realism, his criticism of the déjà vu of the routine experience of the world led to the aesthetic restitution of a kind of recognition that ran counter to all mimetic tradition and that employed the cognitive function of anamnesis to turn upon Platonizing aesthetics. His point of departure was the observation that ordinary perception loses its object, a belief which the narrator of *Remembrance* intensifies to a point where it becomes extreme doubt that present reality can be known at all: "Whether it be that the faith which creates has ceased to exist in me, or that reality will take shape in the memory alone, the flowers that people shew me nowadays for the first time never seem to me to be true flowers"[85] The epistemological agnosticism Proust has frequently been charged with can, in our context, be understood as his attempt to overcome the deficiency of *connaissance* in the everyday world by a new, aesthetic experience of *reconnaissance*. What we immediately perceive eludes cognition. Submerged by purposes and habits and prey to the "error of indifference,"[86] reality can, however, disclose itself to consciousness in the medium of art, once it has been filtered through remembrance. In Proust's method, the critical function of pure seeing is conferred on remembrance. There is added the more stringent condition that the capacity to discover the truth is tied to what was experienced involuntarily, what remains inaccessible to the vagaries of the observing intelligence and the memory that is subservient to it (*memoire volontaire*).[87] In remembrance, aesthetic experience thus discovers the capacity to inquire into what lies below the surface of the perceivable world and furnishes artistic aesthesis the opportunity to bring to light in the temporal process of remembrance how "what appears becomes thing."[88]

But for Proust, remembrance is not only the precision instrument of aesthetic cognition. It is also the real, the sole remaining sphere of origin of the beautiful. At first glance, this looks like nothing so much as an unavowed Platonism, and that was certainly the view of E. R. Curtius, whose pioneering essay culminates in an interpretation of the famous page on the death of Bergotte where he praises the breakthrough to the metaphysical, to a Platonic spirituality as the resolution of all dissonance and as the morality of his art.[89] But in his novel, Proust did not return to that Platonism of Ruskinian derivation which his Ruskin studies show him to have left behind.[90] Recollection, in *Remembrance*, refers to the immanence of an experience which needs the déjà vu, the lived temporal distance between an original, lost perception, and a later re-cognition. Recovered time therefore only seems to point to a transcendent home and an atemporal existence but points in fact to an earthly beyond: the former world of the narrating self which has become perceivable through remembrance and communicable through art. The aura surrounding Proust's art is an imperishable something that has been created in the process of remembrance itself and occupies the vacated place of timeless Platonic beauty.

In the affinity of Proust's and Baudelaire's positions, W. Benjamin recognized the nexus between aura and remembrance and praised Proust's novel as the heroic effort of a work in which the gain that lies in having involuntary memory return their lost aura to things had to be purchased at the price of abandoning experience to what is chance in temporal existence. Later, the "seamless success of the ultimate intent," i.e., the unified form of "recovered time," seemed problematical to him.[91] Does this mean that the aesthetic solution of *Remembrance* is no more than a hopeless private performance, designed to save subjectivity? Lacking negativity because it is ultimately a fable — the story of a vocation whose nature discloses itself only retrospectively — is *Remembrance of Things Past* no longer at the level of our literary situation which Adorno defined in the paradox: "story-telling is no longer possible, yet the form of the novel demands it." (1954)?[92]

Proust did in fact affirm until the end that his novel contained nothing merely invented, although he nowhere described anything and had never written a sentence patterned after the realistic cliché: "the marquise went out at five o'clock." But it was also Adorno who saw how Proust's experience had satisfied the paradoxical demand he had made on the contemporary novel. For this new demand, *Remembrance* is exemplary not only because, through an inextricable interweaving of commentary and action, Proust allows the aesthetic distance to decrease.[93] In the compositional figure of the "search for lost time," his novel also contains a genuine solution to the paradox of narration. His way of writing avoids the "lies of representation" by a specific form of negativity: no element of the objective world or of the factual life story may be described or told in the light of something directly or objectively given. In contrast to the reified milieu of naturalism or the concretized past of memoirs, things and events of preexistent reality can enter the world of the novel only in the avowed form of their mediation, just as the remembered world can enter only in the specifically portrayed, temporal process of remembrance, the commenting reflections only in the imperfect generalization of the remembering self in search of its identity. We thus have the paradox of a way of writing in which, as Benjamin unforgetably formulated it, all action and the identity of the person merely form the "reverse of the continuum of memory" and must be inferred by the reader from the "pattern on the back side of the tapestry."[94]

If Proust compensated for this negativity in a hidden compositional figure that only appears at the end and that allows the contingent search for lost time to give rise to the monumental architectonics (image of the cathedral!) of recovered time, this crowning solution of his poetics of remembrance is certainly not predicated on a composed conclusion of a fulfilled search for identity and an aesthetic distance thereby restored. For the subject of *Remembrance* and its reader along with it can recognize only *post festum* that the contingent, never surveyable path of the remembered self with its forever vain attempts "to start writing tomorrow" is in fact already the story of his vocation that was hidden from him. The search itself is thus nothing other than the work of art that merely needs to be written "now." That this "now," the expectable identification of remembered self and writing subject, does not occur at the end is more than a mere device. For in this way, the retrospective insight of the "Matinée Guermantes" only mediately restores to the subject lost in contingency the searched-for identity with his past. It is not the identity of the present with a past self which lights up, lightninglike, in the *souvenir involontaire* (for that identity is a gift owed to the negativity of chance), it is the identification set for the writer and which he alone can attain that is the final compositional figure of the work: the insight which derives from aesthetic experience that lost time since its distant beginning can not only be preserved in the work of art but be made palpable in a beauty that comes from remembrance alone and therefore does not fall to paradises until they are lost. And this is Proust's turnabout of the remark about art as *promesse du Bonheur*.[95]

The reader, on the other hand, for whom the aesthetic distance remains suspended in the horizon of his first reading, can perceive in the light of the retrospective fable, behind the contingent appearance of lost time, the totality of a unique past and recovered world that imperceptibly grew from it. True, it is a world which must negate the horizon of future happiness if it is to save what is past. But as Proust curtails its cosmological function, he also grounds the communicative efficacy of his "poetry of remembrance," i.e., to "see the universe with the eyes of another."[96] to let us recognize how different the world—seemingly the same for all—may appear to someone else, a world whose otherness in the eyes of remembrance only aesthetic experience can uncover, only art can make communicable.

So far, our examination has shown that since the middle of the nineteenth century, both the productive and the receptive aesthetic experience had a share in the recovery of the cognitive function of art. This is to be set against Gadamer's criticism of the "abstraction of the aesthetic consciousness"[97] which may apply to the historical form of "aesthetic education" that emerged in Germany from the neohumanism of Weimar but which does not consider the reverse process sketched here. In this process aesthetic experience at the level of aesthesis took on a task vis-à-vis the growing alienation of social existence which had never previously been set for it in the history of the arts: to counter the shrunk experience and subservient language of the culture industry by the language-critical and creative function of aesthetic perception. In view of the pluralism of social roles and scientific perspectives, such perception was also to preserve the experience of world others have and thus to safeguard a common horizon which, the cosmological whole being gone, art can most readily sustain.

7. Catharsis: the communicative efficacy of aesthetic experience *(movere et conciliare)*

The third and final step in my attempt to uncover the forms of efficacy of aesthetic experience which have been misjudged by ontological art theory and the aesthetics of negativity addresses itself to its communicative function. If, with a view toward the largely implicit theory of aesthetic practice, the productive and receptive functions could be set forth historically by using the concepts of poiesis and aesthesis as our guide and be traced back to their origin in the attitude of aesthetic pleasure, the communicative function of the aesthetic experience can be grasped under the concept of catharsis only when one includes these three phenomena: the Aristotelian understanding of cathartic pleasure, the Augustinian criticism of the enjoyment of *curiositas*, and the power the affects have in making a speech more persuasive, a phenomenon first explained by Gorgias. In section 3, I derived the communicative efficacy of the aesthetic experience from this threefold root and defined catharsis as the enjoyment of affects as stirred by speech or poetry which can bring about both a change in belief and the liberation of his mind in the listener or spectator. This definition presupposes the dialectical interplay or self-enjoyment through the enjoyment of what is other and makes the receipient an active participant in the constitution of the imaginary, something which is denied him as long as aesthetic distance is understood according to traditional theory as one-directional, as a purely contemplative and disinterested relationship to an object at a certain remove. But my definition of catharsis also includes the possibility that the state of suspension characteristic of the attitude of aesthetic pleasure becomes one-sided and either a distance-less enjoyment of the object or sentimental self-enjoyment, that cathartic experience thus runs the risk of being used for ideological purposes or of becoming prefabricated consumption, thereby losing its genuinely communicative function.

With this result of my third section, I hope to have modified my earlier position concerning the nexus between catharsis, identification, and communication sufficiently to meet the objections raised against it in the *Poetik und Hermeneutik IV* discussion. What proved especially unsatisfactory was my attempt to view aesthetic identification with what is represented, and which is implicit in all catharsis, as an essential characteristic of the primary, i.e., prereflective aesthetic experience. D. Henrich's argument has convinced me that the aesthetic attitude—be it as polymorphous as in the older art, or as explicitly adopted as in the modern period—cannot be defined by offers to identify because role paradigms that lack aesthetic mediation can also persuade one to do so. It is true, however, that the aesthetic attitude is fundamentally one of openness to offers of identity because there is an objective correspondence between the structure of perception of the aesthetic attitude and the representation of models and patterns of a humane conduct of life.[1] Just as the aesthetic attitude can be more closely described as "complex, succinct perception," so "every development toward an evolved personality is identical with one toward a specific, clearly defined and simultaneously complex motivational structure."[2] According to D. Henrich, this affinity explains why art in the medium of the aesthetic attitude is especially receptive to offers of identification even though additional reasons are necessary to activate this disposition. Such additional reasons which explain what the aesthetic attitude contributes when it conveys an offer of identification become recognizable when one extends Henrich's definition of "complex, succinct perception" from the object of aesthetic perception to the perceiving subject and understands aesthetic enjoyment as self-enjoyment in the enjoyment of what is other, as I propose. In that case, the specific openness of the aesthetic attitude to offers of identification is explained not only by the affinity between the succinctness of perception and personal differentiation but also through the cathartic pleasure that is released in the identification of spectator and hero.

The aesthetic attitude disposes the individual more strongly to adopt a model than does a model set by religion, tradition, education, or a life pattern called for by the abstract affirmation of morality, because in the former case, self-enjoyment through the enjoyment of the other functions as an incentive bonus. The psychagogic effect of a genre such as tragedy, i.e., liberation of the mind through the pleasure taken in the imaginary destiny of the hero, conveys insight into what is exemplary in human action and suffering. The greater force of the aesthetic response to a literary model derives from the greater complexity of cathartic pleasure. This does not mean that aesthetic identification and passive adoption of an idealized pattern of behavior are one and the same. It occurs in a back-and-forth movement between the aesthetically freed observer and his irreal object in which the subject in its aesthetic enjoyment can run through the entire scale of attitudes such as astonishment, admiration, shock, compassion, sympathy, sympathetic laughter or tears, alienation, reflection. He can fit the offer of a model into his personal world, succumb to the fascination of mere curiosity, or fall into unfree imitation. The history of aesthetic experience offers an as yet unexhausted repertory of these primary attitudes of aesthetic identification which will be examined through the interaction pattern of the hero in essay B. Here, we are interested in the prior question concerning the historical manifestation of the relationships between psychagogic effect and communicative efficacy which thus disposes the aesthetic attitude in the cathartic genres to convey offers of identification. For the classical justification of aesthetic catharsis which claimed an ideal unity or necessary sequence of *delectare* and *docere* has been questioned before the most recent period of modern art which could be characterized by partiality and reflection. Rather, the conceptual history of "catharsis" appears as the ever renewed attempt to undermine the direct evidence of aesthetic identification and to impose on the recipient the effort of negation so that his aesthetic and moral reflection may be set free and not succumb to the fascination of the imaginary.

A historical investigation of the communicative function of the aesthetic experience which cannot be worked out here would have to trace the process of its emancipation and begin with the detachment of catharsis from cultic participation, go on to the various stages and modes of norm-creating identification, and then consider the refusal of communicative identification as it is practiced by the reflectivity of the contemporary experience of art. The theoretical reflection which accompanies this process of emancipation would become most palpable in the history of the reception of Aristotle. But it remains obscure where aesthetic theory is more concerned with the dignity of the work of art than with its effect on the viewer, as in the Platonism of the Renaissance and the aesthetics of German idealism, or where the point of view of autonomous art and its adversary, materialist orthodoxy, are obliged to dismiss as psychologism or mere sociology of taste the question concerning the mode of reception or the concretization of subjective experience and the public meaning of works of art. But even Adorno's *Ästhetische Theorie* is as severe in this regard as anyone might wish. Here, the aesthetic experience which "creates distance between viewer and object" is contrasted with the philistinism of an identification with portrayed individuals, and the Aristotelian tradition of catharsis is bluntly blamed for having fostered a principle "which is ultimately taken over and administered by the culture industry" (pp. 354, 514). What is meant here is the principle of aesthetic sublimation which follows catharsis and which, as "substitute gratification," can only serve the affirmation of ruling interests, as is true of any aesthetic behavior that seeks identification and thereby remains under the spell of practical purposes, of self-preservation and the pleasure principle.

Adorno overlooks here that the Aristotelian account of the effect of tragedy on the spectator already presupposes that specific efficacy of the aesthetic experience which he ascribes exclusively to modern, autonomous art, i.e., that aesthetic experience can break the "spell of obdurate self-preservation" and thereby become the "model of a state of consciousness in which the self no longer finds its happiness in its interests, and ultimately in its reproduction" (p. 515). The classical concept of aesthetic catharsis already implies a distancing on the part of the spectator which can be described as a twofold, outer and inner, liberation. On the one hand, emotional identification with the hero of tragedy liberates the spectator from his practical concerns and his own affective entanglements. To the extent that he negates the concrete interests of his everyday world and adopts the aesthetic attitude toward the tragic action, pity and fear, the conditions for identification of spectator and hero, enter into play. But the spectator who thus puts himself into the hero's place is *also* to be "purged" of the purer affects, i.e., those the tragedy has aroused. Through the tragic emotion, a "desirable composure" is to be induced.[3] As aesthetic experience is being set free in this fashion, the imaginary status of its objects takes on a role that cannot be overlooked.

Just as the Platonic concept of mimesis already called for an imaginative performance (*phantasia*) so that the copy of the copy (*homoioma*) can come about, so the Aristotelian concept of catharsis also presupposes the fiction of a true or probable object through which the desired "purging" must occur. It is precisely the relation of the aesthetic experience to the imaginary that brings about the liberation of the mind, as Starobinski, in elaborating on S. H. Butcher, has recently explained: "For on the one hand, the imaginary retains the power reality has to rouse our passions, to reverberate in the depths of our bodies. But on the other hand, the event represents nothing real, and the emotion it gives rise to can therefore expend itself purely (as 'pure loss'), which accounts for the effect of purgation, of catharsis."[4] If, according to Plato, art is corrupted because, as *mimesis phantasmatos*, it can only induce an illusion of the sensory phenomenon, only a copy of the copy, this ontological weakness seems to conversely ground the advantage of aesthetic experience in the case of Aristotelian catharsis, i.e., the creation of the "disinterested interest" peculiar to it. It is precisely the imaginary object of the tragedy, its action which is remote from the practical purposes of life, which free the spectator so that in the identification with the hero, his emotion can be sparked more uninhibitedly than in everyday life and consume itself more purely. There is thus no contradiction whatever between catharsis as the antithesis to the practical conduct of life, and the identification of the spectator with the tragic hero or the listener with patterns of action that the orator suggests to him. Rather, catharsis involves such offers of identification and patterns of behavior as a communicative frame within which the imagination, stirred by affects and set free, can act. As a communicative frame for possible action, the aesthetic identification of spectator and listener who enjoy themselves in and through another's fate or uncommon model can pass on or create patterns of behavior; it can also question or break through customary behavioral norms. But this social function of catharsis has a reverse which deserves equal consideration. Cathartic identification can also let the observer find a purely private satisfaction in the solitary liberation of his mind, or cause him to remain in a state of mere curiosity. The observer, freed by the "pleasure in the tragic object," can adopt through identification what is exemplary in the action. But he can also cushion and aesthetically neutralize the experience of identification if he does not go beyond a naive amazement at the deeds of a "hero."

The fundamental ambivalence of the aesthetic experience which catharsis induces is this: it may break the hold of the real world but in so doing, it can either bring the spectator to a free, moral identification with an exemplary action or let him remain in a state of pure curiosity. And finally, it can draw him into manipulated collective behavior through his emotional identification. This fundamental ambivalence can be seen as the price that must be paid: liberating catharsis is purchased through the mediation of the imaginary. It is an ambivalence which, in the history of aesthetic experience, has time and again become the target of a polemics carried on in the name of religious authority, social morality, or practical reason, and waged against the uncontrollable effects of art. Concerning the communicative efficacy of aesthetic experience, the different orientation of Christian literature and art was of particular significance. For to the degree that it took control of the conduct of life, the authority of the Christian church and doctrine did not content itself with adopting the Platonic criticism of poets for their mendacity. For purposes of instruction and preaching and to maintain religious belief among the laity, it gradually developed or sanctioned its own expressive forms of aesthetic experience whose rationale ran counter to the aesthetic canon of pagan antiquity: elation in worship and edification is set up against the aesthetic-contemplative distance; compassion that leads to action, against cathartic cleansing; the productive power of the exemplary, against the issueless enjoyment of the imaginary; the hortative principle of *imitatio*, against the aesthetic pleasure of mimesis.

In this contrastive expansion and revaluation of the aesthetic experience, the historical dividing line between the classical and the Christian canon of what is worthy of representation becomes more clearly visible than in a Christian aesthetic. For such an aesthetic can only be postulated, there is no independent testimony for it in medieval art and poetry, it did not emerge without notable delay—until toward the end of the predominance of the Christian religion, on the threshold between the Enlightenment and romanticism—and was developed in historical retrospection by Hamann, Schelling, Chateaubriand, Jean Paul, and Hegel.[5] Genuine phenomena of the Christian literature of the Middle Ages such as the "creatural realism" (Erich Auerbach) which derived from the figural understanding of history and the mixture of styles of the *sermo humilis*, or allegorical poetry which blossomed into the "poetry of the invisible,"[6] gave rise to no autonomous Christian aesthetics. As regards their theory, the art and poetry of the Middle Ages remained under the control of theological dogma; in their practice, they were overshadowed by a rigorous "canon of transcendence" which had its historical roots in the Platonic-stoic and Neoplatonic doctrines of the beautiful.[7] Yet even during the age of the total dominance of the Christian faith, this subservience is counterbalanced by an aesthetic praxis of Christian authors which, in opposition to the "aesthetic," i.e., the enchantment through the beautiful appearance of secular art and poetry, developed new expressive forms of a poietic, receptive, and cathartic experience. They redefined the scope of aesthetic experience and incorporated its communicative efficacy into the horizon of faith of the Christian public. What becomes noticeable here time and again is a process in which an attitude of moral identification such as edification, compassion, or *imitatio* which first inserts itself heteronomously in the canon of the aesthetic itself becomes progressively poeticized as the aesthetic forms of expression and communication are appropriated. Moral identification, initially intended to break through the contemplative aesthetic distance, seems increasingly mediated by the aesthetic attitude. Along this path, morality can gradually be objectified aesthetically and ultimately disintegrate in the degenerate forms of sentimental self-enjoyment and consumer behavior.

None of these attitudes of the Christian reinterpretation of the cathartic experience suffered more from this reversal than edification. As a norm-affirming and norm-fulfilling identification, edification in our time is confined to the lower depth of the hackneyed, the merely entertaining, and the demagogic; it makes its appearance in dime store novels, Harlequin romances, devotional objects, in the lyrics of pop tunes, and in political lyrics. The popularity of Johann Peter Hebel's *Kalendergeschichten* only seems to indicate the opposite. Here, we have a case of aesthetic pleasure due to historical distance: today's educated reader can again enjoy the enlightened edification of the "wise family friend" nostalgically. It is the experience of another time, when stories could still be told with an easy mind and when one had a right to believe that they might teach something of value for one's personal life, or that good intentions could produce good literature. Afterward, the dictum: "c'est avec les bons sentiments qu'on fait la mauvaise littérature" attained such undisputed currency that it amounted to a provocation when, in his *Vocabulaire esthétique* (1946), Roger Caillois uncovered the old confusion between morality and conformism, denounced the new conformism of immorality, and asserted: "edification is as indispensable in literature and in life as it is in architecture," thus recalling the forgotten historical origin of the word *aedificatio*.[8]

Today, as we are being flooded by commercialized art, edification is seen primarily as a degenerate form of aesthetic experience and placed first in the catalog of vices of ideological accommodation and system-affirming reception. Once, it was the first justification of Christian poetry and, far into the Enlightenment, the principal spur to a great literature of religious inwardness whose potential the secular poetry of experience has been appropriating since the *Sorrows of Young Werther*. The religious pattern of spiritual uplift which Goethe's *Trostbüchlein* utilized aesthetically—a circumstance which conferred on the new literary cult of autonomous feeling a provocative justification—did not become an expressive form of conscious subjectivity and solitary inwardness until late. *Aedificatio* originally meant the preparation for the imitation of Christ which was to be achieved by a depersonalization whereby the individual as part of the community becomes an "edifice of belief" through a movement of his soul. What the term emphatically did not mean was a turning back to subjective inwardness. The cathartic movement of edification does not simply cause the devout soul to fuse with the object of its devotion. It sets in on a ground which not itself but a *sapiens architectus* has laid (1 Corinthians, 3, 10). In the paradoxical image of the *lapides vivi*, it has the Christian work simultaneously on himself and on the *domus spiritualis* of the religious community of faith: "Ye also, as lively stones, are built up a spiritual house, an holy priesthood, to offer up spiritual sacrifices, acceptable to God by Jesus Christ" (I Peter 2, 5).

As the documentary evidence in the New Testament shows, edification, as a heteronomous aesthetic experience, originally presupposed the reflective distance which it has lost in its modern degenerate forms. In the movement of the soul, the implied meditative attitude makes possible both a devout dwelling on the moment of portrayed suffering and a meditative perception of the horrible and the shocking elements of the *gloria passionis*.[9] Only the progressive poetization of what is edifying leads to experiences of aesthetic identification with what is portrayed where the contemplating subject could discover the inwardness of his feeling but also encountered the dangers of "empathy" and mystical self-enjoyment. The first phase of this process becomes very apparent in the material that Reinhart Herzog brought to light from late-classical bible poetry and which he was the first to make available to reception-aesthetic research.[10] In this new perspective on the first great tradition of Christian epic poetry, edification turns out to be the motor of an initially heteronomous aesthetic attitude which made possible for Christian authors the reception of the means and patterns of pagan poetry. The curious deformation of the biblical text in the meditative paraphrases, the mutilation of the classical models for purposes of their integration, and the abandonment of narration for its own sake are findings which Herzog can explain both by the new needs of devotion and by its edifying satisfaction. Contrary to the customary aesthetic pleasure in the story line, the edifying intent shows in phenomena such as the "deformation through devout and excessive conscientiousness" when the plot is arrested to create an image of devotion by means of classical ekphrasis, often with hyper-realistic elaboration which can be intensified to become "devout disgust," or by an early instance of the use of "slow motion." But the affective involvement of the reader can also be directed toward an "indignant devotion" when an event is not concretely described but viewed with the force of the contrasting feeling.[11] In these interpretations, late classical and medieval edification offers an amazingly nuanced gradation of psychagogic and presentational intensification; characteristically, it stops this side of the direct expression of subjective emotion. An "unfulfilled ardor" (*ardor inexpletus*) "as a feeling which abounds in a variety of manifestations, which is constantly searching for the appropriate expression,"[12] the emotion of author and reader, and the excitement of the portrayed biblical figures who encounter the divine always remain an objectified edification, indeed one that becomes incarnate: "here also, the final point is an executed picture of devotion where the extra points at the principal figure and thereby creates a deeply felt distance between himself and it."[13]

If we now inquire into the Christian reception and revaluation of the classical doctrine concerning purgation through catharasis, the threshold in the history of aesthetic experience is most brightly illuminated when one juxtaposes the Augustinian critique of the cathartic "pleasure in pain" with the (newly formed!) concept of *compassio* which names the attitude the medieval passion play—the first form of a Christian "tragedy"—demands from the spectator. Augustine's criticism of the "sheer delight of poetic imaginings" appears in the first book of the *Confessions* (I, xiii). His account of the aesthetic effect Vergil's *Aeneid* had on the student of Latin first uncovers the fascination of a merely imaginary fate ("the wanderings of Aeneas— whoever he was"), and then the paradoxical pleasure in the grief over the suicide of Dido, and thus aims at the essential flaw in the enjoyment of secular poetry from the Christian perspective—forgetfulness of self: "I was forced to memorize the wanderings of Aeneas, forgetful of my own, and to weep for dead Dido because she killed herself for love the while, with dry eyes, I endured my miserable self dying among these things, far from thee, O God, my life" (*Confessions*, I, xiii). Here, Augustine takes up the Platonic criticism of the harmful effects of poetry. He denies that the cathartic pleasure cleanses the stirred passions and gives greater depth to the attack on unreasonable "pleasure in pain" by equating its self-sufficiency with missing the only true experience of self, the one that is open to the Thou of his God.

But whether he wants to or not, Augustine can only confirm the power of cathartic pleasure in his retrospective self-accusation. Between the new experience of the Christian faith which lets man search for and find his true self in the alien yet also close Thou of his God, and the enjoyment of self in the enjoyment of the other which the aesthetic experience yields, there exists a hidden analogy. In the fact that the "pleasure in pain" could also enrich the audience through sympathy "because of the happiness and misfortune that befall strangers and attend events, the soul in a certain manner acquires experience through words."[14] Gorgias had already seen the other achievement of the cathartic experience which Augustine's zealous faith denies. Why then should the strong effect of cathartic pleasure not be placed in the service of Christian teaching, why should the self-sufficient identification with the imaginary fate of strangers not be redirected toward the suffering of the true heroes of the faith and, through *compassio*, toward the imitation of Christ, considering that the new truth of the history of salvation had won out over the old "lies of the poets?"

The religious play of the Christian Middle Ages which developed in the twelfth century without any tie whatever to forgotten classical tragedy can indeed be understood as stemming from the interest in a Christian appropriation of the cathartic experience. More than a merely contemplative attitude of enjoyment is expected from the spectator of a religious play: he is to be shaken and moved to tears by the biblical action being presented to him. And this all the more so since he is no mere spectator who is separated from the scene by curtain and apron but someone who is drawn into an action that brings the biblical protagonists together as dramatis personae and the biblical people as participating witnesses in one and the same scene. Not an admiring looking-up to the perfection of a hero or martyr, not the cathartic cleansing of the soul to achieve freedom of judgment, but a "heart full of compassion" is the attitude to which the public is called as it views the "great suffering that has gained us our salvation."[15] The cathartic experience demanded here is not purgation but the transformation of the stirred affects into the readiness to imitate Christ.

This movement of *compassio* is explained in medieval documents as a mystical sequence of steps but also as a process of reflecting oneself in the other. The theology of the passion tractate demands a participation intended to lead the person from contemplation (*meditatio*) through compassion (*compassio*) to imitation (*imitato*).[16] The author of the previously quoted *Mystère de la Passion* seeks to grasp the inner process of compassion with the help of the mystical mirror metaphor: Christ's passion is given to the *compassio* of the beholder like a mirror in which he can recognize not only his own suffering but also himself in the suffering of the other ("chascun sa fourme y entrevoit") and where he can finally see the essence of the everlasting splendor of Christ.[17] The mirror metaphor replaces the purgation metaphor and thereby eliminates the absurdity which, for the Christian, attaches to the Aristotelian understanding of catharsis as "homeopathic cure": "One can be cleansed of hardness of heart but not of compassion."[18] But the document also shows why *compassio* cannot yet be understood as subjective empathy. What is involved is the back-and-forth movement of a reciprocal reflection through which the individual in an almost physical compassion is to also recognize and take on something else, the model (*sa fourme*) of his *imitatio*, which means that he is not to lose himself in an *unio mystica*.

But the elimination of the aesthetic-contemplative distance of the viewer through the stirring up of his soul and the moral identification of compassion (*imitatio Christi*) also involved a risk within Christian poetry for which the Church fathers had blamed its pagan counterpart. The *repraesentatio* of a sacred, biblical, or hagiographic action meant that like all imagery, the represented event might be perceived only in its obvious appearance but not understood as having an evocative, demonstrative, or admonitory reference. Even the doctrinal intent of the religious play could not prevent the joy of recognizing a pictured event from turning into aesthetic pleasure in what was being imitated. Instead of following the *sensus moralis* pointed to or the *conversio morum* that was being demanded,[19] the spectator could satisfy his idle curiosity or lapse into self-sufficient emotionalism. Worse still: even the Christian audience of a religious play could be drawn into the collective identity of archaic rituals by which a heretical and dualistic popular piety subconsciously rebelled against the rule of the nominalist God and monotheist dogma, as Rainer Warning has shown.[20] The use of aesthetic and rhetorical means to body forth truths of the faith, and the dangers of aesthetic indentification which the Old Testament ban on images already implied, create a dilemma which has preoccupied Church authorities time and again. John of Salisbury, who lived at the time of the greatest flowering of the courtly lyric, left a subtle appreciation and criticism of the effects and dangers of music in the first book of his *Policraticus* which denounces the amusements of courtly society. This art of sounds which man himself created and whose magic power surpasses anything that nature—and be it the nightingale itself—can produce can lift the devout soul toward God but, like the siren's song, it can also lead it astray through a "tenderness which is related to sensuality" (*voluptati cognata mollities*). It does not suffice to trust the judgment of one's ears and to believe that the critical distinction of artful modulations could protect one from succumbing to the seduction of so much "sweetness." When music goes beyond the bounds imposed on it as the medium of participation in suprasensible delight and bliss, it will quickly produce an "itching of the loins" rather than a feeling that liberates from earthly cares and lifts the listener toward God and the *societas angelorum*.[21] In both a positive and a negative sense, there hardly exists a more appealing testimonial to the Christian understanding of the cathartic experience of music. The question concerning the communicative function of the cathartic experience and the dangers of the "lust of ears and eyes" was dealt with especially in instructions on how to sermonize.

On the one hand, it is a topos in the instructions for the clergy that the Christian teaching of laymen should avail itself of rhetorical and aesthetic means for purposes of illustration because truths of the faiths also can be conveyed more persuasively through the senses than through reasons ("laicis autem oportet quasi ad oculum et sensibilitatem omnia demonstrare simplice enim melius inducuntur repraesentationibus quam rationibus," "It is, moreover, fitting to present all things to laymen as if to the eyes and the other senses, for the commons are better swayed by representations than reasons).[22] Religious painting can thus be justified by the argument which also applies to the religious play, i.e., that an action which is presented visually, "quasi in presenti geri videatur" (let it seem to be manifest as if present), moves the spirit more than when it is heard, for then it must always be recalled to memory.[23] This argument corresponds to an Aristotelian tradition according to which the eye ranks above the other sense organs in regard to cognition.[24] But there is also a tradition which goes back to Augustine and which prefers the ear as the higher organ because it attains insight immediately (*aures quidem ponuntur pro intellectu, quoniam auribus audiendo intelligimus*, the ears were given for the sake of understanding, since we know by hearing with our ears) and because faith also rests on what is heard (*fides ex auditu est*, trust is from hearing).[25] Using the example of seduction through sight, Augustine had explained the negative side of sympathetic identification: the chained consciousness, spellbound by what it sees.

The one example is the famous account in which Alypius attends a gladiatorial contest against his will, first closes his eyes because he does not care to see what is going on, but then, overwhelmed by curiosity, opens them as the crowd wildly cries out, can no longer look away, and is inflamed by bloodlust: "For so soon as he saw that blood, he therewith drank down savageness; nor turned away, but fixed his eye, drinking in frenzy, unawares" (*Confessions*, VI, 8). Through curiosity, the sympathetic identification the compassionate spectator feels with the seriously wounded gladiator degenerates into the collective identity of cruel voluptuousness. The perversion of a "game" in which life and death are at stake destroys not only the aesthetic attitude but also the moral freedom of the observer (he . . . was stricken with a deeper wound in the soul than the man whom he had opened his eyes to see got in the body"). In his criticism of the passion for the theater, Augustine described another degenerate form of sympathetic identification as a false because self-sufficient, absorbed pleasure in imaginary pain: "But how can the unreal sufferings of the stage possibly move pity? The spectator is not moved to aid the sufferer but merely to be sorry for him, and the more the author of these fictions makes the audience grieve, the better they like him" (*Confessions*, II, 2). The true *compassio* (Augustine still uses the term *misericordia*) with which Christian poetry wants to break through the "Pleasure in pain," i.e., the aesthetic objectivation of a sympathetically enjoying attitude, must prove itself as readiness for *imitatio*.

The modern crisis of the cathartic experience of art, whose outstanding testimonial one may consider to be Rousseau's *Letter to M. d'Alembert* (1758), and Brecht's writings on the epic theater (1933–48) renew the Augustinian arguments but also make apparent how much the form of compassion has changed in modern times: "I hear it said that tragedy leads to pity through fear. So it does, but what is this pity? A fleeting and vain emotion which lasts no longer than the illusion which produced it; a vestige of natural sentiment soon stifled by the passions; a sterile pity which feeds on a few tears and which has never produced the slightest act of humanity."[26] This traditional reproach is now given a new social point. For Rousseau's critique does not aim at compassion as such but decisively disputes the claim of the stage that it restores through the artificial mediation of the imagination that "natural sentiment" which may lead to active solidarity with the suffering of others. In his *Discourse on the Origin of Inequality*, Rousseau had already made the ethical demand of Christian compassion so much his own that he had ascribed pity (*la pitié*) to man in the "state of nature" as the only required "natural virtue." Hobbes, who denied that man had any virtues sanctified by tradition, had not understood that it was precisely "natural Man" as a "deficient being," who needed pity to compensate for his natural weakness, that pity was that natural disposition which could be found even among animals: "an innate dislike of seeing his fellow men suffer."[27] Prior to the use of reason, pity for his like could alone counterbalance the principle of self-preservation (*amour de soi-même*) and guarantee the preservation of the species. This truly universal virtue sufficed to derive all "social virtues" developed during the course of human history from a common root and to dispense with the hypothesis of a *sociabilité naturelle*.[28] In view of the alienation which has become man's second nature in a historical development for which he alone is responsible, Rousseau sees in the cathartic capacity of art the most unsuitable means to reawaken the withered sympathy with the suffering of his contemporaries as the first social virtue: far from promoting insight into the necessity of transforming society, the effects of the theater are limited to confirming existing conditions, prejudices, and private inclinations, indeed to deepening them ("it seems that, its effect being limited to intensifying and not changing the established morals (manners), the drama would be good for the good and bad for the vicious").[29] Rousseau's conclusion can therefore be nothing other than the old recipe that the city of Geneva reject the project of a stage — as Plato had demanded for the ideal state — that it dispense with art altogether and promote instead among its citizens the simple and natural joys that come from work, the family, and the communal spirit.

There exists an illustrious model for this, the simple, artless, and sublime life of the old Spartans and their festivities without ostentatiousness and luxury, which Rousseau contraposes to all modern seductions of the imagination in the final pages of his condemnation of the theater.[30] But the seduction to which he secretly succumbs, though he be a puritan and hostile to art, is itself an aesthetic attitude: the sentimental relationship to antiquity which, in its nostalgia for the lost "simple life," already ushers in romanticism.

Brecht drew the opposite conclusion from the modern crisis of the cathartic experience. He developed the idea of a non-Aristotelian drama which was to counter the alienation of social life through a second alienation, i.e., through the new techniques of the "epic theater" where the "place of illusions" would once again become a "place of experience."[31] From our perspective, Brecht's critique of Aristotelian catharsis is interesting because he reduces it to "empathy with the individuals represented," i.e., to the unreflected adoption of their norms of action or world pictures. In opposition to the enjoyment that lies in such empathy, techniques of alienation will be used to convey events "in their remarkableness and strangeness" so that the spectator will be shown the world in such a way "that it becomes subject to control."[32] To provoke his critical reflection, the spectator is deprived of his familiar identification with the characters but is also to find pleasure in the "learning-plays" so that the old problem returns: how can the new theater be both entertaining and instructive?[33]

The open question of the earlier *Non-Aristotelian Dramaturgy* (1933–41): "is the enjoyment of art possible at all without empathy or at least on a basis other than empathy?" leads, in the later *Short Organom for the Theatre* (1948), to the attempt to recover this emotional basis in the "special pleasures . . . of our own age."[34] Brecht's spectator whom the alienation effects of the epic theater have given the critical distance of the "new view" or, in other words, whom they have purged of all empathetic identification, will ultimately find the reward for his puritanical-materialist catharsis in the old cathartic pleasure!

If one sees in Brecht's conception of a non-Aristotelian dramaturgy not so much a renouncement as a dialectical reception of the Aristotelian doctrine of the cathartic effect of art, it also becomes more understandable that his equation of catharsis and empathy which was unjustly aimed at classical tragedy actually referred to the bourgeois theater with its cult of the great individual and the deceptiveness of the naturalistic illusion: "Empathy with changeable individuals, with avoidable actions, superfluous pain, etc., is no longer possible. As long as it is in his breast that we find the stars of King Lear's fate, as long as he is taken as unchangeable, and his actions are presented as determined by nature, altogether unpreventable, fated, in other words, we can emphathize. Any discussion of his conduct is . . . impossible."[35] But Shakespeare's theater aimed as little at such empathy as the religious play of the Middle Ages or Greek tragedy. Counter to the tendency that "the spectator could never see more than the hero with whom he empathized,"[36] an information gap between the spectator and the actors was already created in different ways in the earlier periods of European theater. The purpose was to make problematical the conduct of the protagonists, to make "discussable" the ambiguity of fate. In this connection, we need only remind the reader of the function of the classical chorus, the medieval speaker of the prologue, the ironic commentary of Shakespeare's fools and Molière's servants.

It is certainly true that neither the Aristotelian drama of classical antiquity and humanism nor the Christian theater had Brecht's large pretention: "the theater now presents to him the world so that he can take hold of it."[37] The excessive expectation that the epic theater need merely estrange what it presents in order to make the spectator believe that the seemingly unchangeable world can in fact be changed, however, required more than the mere appeal to reasonable insight if it was to be fulfilled. And that is the motive for the progressive rehabilitation of the oldest and "most noble function" of the theater as "a place of entertainment."[38] In this process, the "special entertainments" of the present, scientific age are being examined: "They must be entertained with the wisdom that comes from the solution of problems, with the anger that is a practical expression of sympathy with the underdog, with the respect due to those who respect humanity, or rather whatever is kind to humanity, in short, with whatever delights those who are producing something."[39] One may doubt whether all this would suffice "to make dialectics enjoyable."[40] Brecht's "Lehrstücke" certainly also had simple means at their command "to make their moral lesson enjoyable, and enjoyable to the senses at that . . ."[41] Thus Brecht rediscovered the psychagogic effect of the cathartic experience in the "aesthetics" of his *Short Organon for the Theatre* and enriched it by his own techniques, but he did not exhaust the communicative efficacy of that experience. The problem was not just how the theater could again become both entertaining and instructive, how alienation could bring pleasure, but also how the solitary spectator could be motivated to pass from critical reflection to solidary action, and this means how norms of action could be suggested to him without their being overtly or covertly imposed. The "positive hero" of socialist realism was certainly the opposite of a solution for Brecht. That such a solution was already searched for before him is shown by the history of the concept of the exemplary to which we will devote a final backward glance.

In the Christian conduct of life, the exemplary differentiates itself from the ambivalent power of the imaginary even more markedly than does the communicative emotion of compassion. For its suggestiveness rests primarily on the demonstrative power of an action that has actually taken place so that an *imitabile* is presented which, because it appeals to insight, does not seduce through the senses. The standard set by exemplary action derived a new legitimation from the Christian-typological understanding of history, as the writings of the Church fathers widely attest. This may explain why as Christian teaching spread, the exemplum acquired new value and literary rank and why it flowered from the instruction of the laity during the High Middle Ages to the Renaissance understanding of history. The principal reason for its communicative effect can already be inferred from the first theoretical statement concerning its use by Christians. Ambrose recommended it as a means of proof principally suited for laymen "quia cui verba satis non faciunt, solent exempla suadere" (since him to whom words are not enough, they are accustomed to persuade with examples).[42] Like the fable and other forms of the example, the exemplum draws on the aesthetic evidence of what is concretely set forth but through the greater power of the factual, as a model that actually exists, it is superior to the invented example. What was exemplary in the Christian sense could thus be defined as norm-creating identification and therefore distinguished from the means of pagan rhetoric which Christian preachers and poets criticized for casting a spell over the soul by invented speech and thus never expressing the true but only the verisimilar.[43] In a norm-creating function, the Christian exemplum could also be played off against theoretical reason and its claim that insight into the true was exclusively reserved to conceptual thought and its logical means.[44] Behind the new claim of the exemplary, there lies the Christian conviction that greater weight must be attributed to what is historically documented than to what is mere thought, to the visible act as event than to mere doctrinal edifice. For corroboration, the preacher could invoke the norm-breaking example of all examples, Christ, who "taught by deeds more than by words": "Quia autem ad haec suggerenda et ingerenda et imprimenda in humanis cordibus maxime valent exempla, ideo summa Dei sapientia, Christus Jesus, primo docuit factis quam verbis et subtilitatem praedicationis et doctrinae grossam, quasi corpoream et visibilim reddidit, muniens et vestiens eam diversis similitudinibus, parabolis, miraculis et exemplis, ut eius doctrina citius caperetur" (Because examples are especially effective in suggesting, implanting, and impressing these things in human hearts, the greatest wisdom of God, Jesus Christ, taught mainly by deeds rather than by words both the subtlety of his message and the weight of doctrine, as if to render it corporeal and visible, fortifying and dressing it by various comparisons, parables, miracles, and examples, so that his doctrine would be more quickly grasped).[45] In the exemplary, negativity and identification are tied in such fashion that the extraordinary, which is also the authentic, breaks through the norm of the habitual conduct of life (*exemplis confundi*, to be mixed with examples)[46] in order to free consciousness for insight and conversion and to outline the frame of action within which the moral identification of *imitatio* is to prove itself.

There is no need here to document at length that in a history of aesthetic experience, the exemplary would have an especially significant place. Its norm-creating and communicative function is evident not only in the instruction of laymen by the Church and in religious communities or in the moralistic literature and practical philosophy which began emancipating themselves from theological tutelage at the beginning of the modern period. It is also apparent in the theory and practice of elementary education since Comenius and, last but not least, in the way history was experienced up to the epochal threshold of 1789), an experience which was always shaped by the example (*historia docet*). The reasons the humanists advanced for the practical significance of the exemplary (*lectio transit in mores*, the lesson passes into actions) were adopted by the authors and theoreticians of the novel from Huet to Blanckenburg because they wanted to make the authoritative power of what they read serve the emancipation of a bourgeois community.[47] If anywhere, it is here that the communicative function of art in the formation of an objectively binding meaning becomes palpable. The aesthetics of negativity misses this function where it considers all identification leading from the aesthetic to the moral as negative because merely adaptive, system-perpetuating social affirmation.

The threshold which Reinhart Koselleck recognized in the disintegration of the topos "historia magistra vitae" and ascribed to the historicism of the Enlightenment is an important one in the history of aesthetic experience. The new insight that it is in the recurring *histories* of nations, institutions, and their actors and through them that the irreversible process of the one *history* of mankind takes place rendered invalid the exemplary use of patterns and models of the past where questions concerning the beginning and goal of this singular and universal history and man as its responsible subject became the principal themes of philosophy and historical thought.[48] Karlheinz Stierle has enlarged upon this thesis by more closely defining Montaigne's position in this process. What is involved here is not simply the commonly mentioned skeptical use of history but "the suspension of judgment being made the very principle of presentation."[49] By setting traditional exempla against each other and thus problematizing the universal applicability of their moral maxims, he also opens up an area of reflection which compensated for the discredited "lessons history teaches" by a new discovery: "As Montaigne turns away from the 'exemples étranges et scholastique' (III, xiii), he discovers his own self as an inexhaustible source of 'exempla' which have the authority of experience. The self thus replaces 'historia' as the quintessence of authenticated stories."[50] It is decisive here and has often been overlooked that the "I" in the medium of the essays in no way discovers an atemporal substance as its "true self"; Montaigne's testing of himself does not elevate the solitary individual to a *magister vitae* but wants to be exemplary as an experience which, reflecting on others' inconsistent and contradictory conduct, attains to an insight into the perfectly ordinary yet indeterminate nature of its own self: "This long attention that I devote to studying myself trains me also to judge passably of others, and there are few things of which I speak more felicitously and excusably. . . . By training myself from my youth to see my own life mirrored in that of others, I have acquired a studious bent in that subject . . ." (III, xiii).

In the new literary form of the *essai* which Montaigne created, the exemplum is problematized in its twofold function as elucidation of moral maxims and as a means of proof in persuasion or dissuasion prior to a decision.[51] The *essai* also opens up a new experience of what can be exemplary for human life. Not only the extraordinary deeds of acting man which a secular historical tradition monumentalizes and presents one-sidedly in both its good or its bad effects but also what is ordinary in life and the inner states of any individual whatever are part of the *humaine capacité*: "I set forth a humble and inglorious life; that does not matter. You can tie up all moral philosophy with a common and private life just as well as with a life of richer stuff. Every man bears the entire form of man's estate" (III, ii). It is true that the classical moralistic tradition also observed that an insignificant event, "an expression or a jest" can often cast a more telling light on the exemplary quality of life than the most "glorious exploits" on the battlefield.[52] But this famous argument from Plutarch's "Parallel between Alexander and Caesar" refers to the biographies of two historical personages whereas Montaigne, rejecting the authority of the *"viri illustres,"* looks for the exemplary precisely at that point where Caesar's life can tell him no more than his own experience: "The life of Cesar has no more to show us than our own; an emperor's or an ordinary man's, it is a life subject to all human accidents" (III, xiii). It is precisely the extraordinary, historically authenticated acts which make it difficult to tell what was merit, what fortune's favor: "My actions would tell more about fortune than about me" (II, vi). The new form of the essay makes it possible to look for the exemplary in an experience that has not yet been externalized in the heteronomy of action: "What I chiefly portray is my cogitations, a shapeless subject that does not lend itself to expression in actions" (II, vi). But this exemplary quality of reflection about the self has the paradoxical function of being merely "an example of the particular, not the general."[53] It is an exemplariness that excludes *imitatio*.

In the case of the exemplary, the fundamental ambivalence of the aesthetic experience has always manifested itself in the fact that it includes two possibilities of *imitatio*: the free, learning comprehension by example, and the unfree, mechanical following of a rule. The moral identification of the exemplary occurs between the two opposite poles of free following and unfree imitation. This distinction was elaborated in the area of the Christian conduct of life (*imitatio Christi*), but it also has importance in moral philosophy and especially in Kant's doctrine of the example.[54] In the relevant discussion in the *Critique of Judgment*, example is distinguished from precept and following contrasted with the "mere mechanism of imitaton": "Following which has reference to a precedent, and not imitation, is the proper expression for all influence which the products of an exemplary author may exert upon others—and this means no more than going to the same sources for a creative work as those to which he went for his creations, and learning from one's predecessors no more than the mode of availing oneself of such sources" (§ 32).

The concept of the exemplary as here understood can bridge the gap between aesthetic judgment and moral praxis and make clear the transition from aesthetic to moral identification. The characteristic achievement of the exemplary in both the aesthetic and the moral realm lies in the fact that it breaks through the scheme of "rule and case": "what the exemplary refers to is 'indeterminate,' it has a dynamic character, i.e. every new concretion expands its definition." In the sphere of practical reason, the exemplary can therefore "overcome the aesthetic objectivation of morality" by the *vivid portrayal* of moral sentiment and create interest in the actions themselves.[55] To the extent that, according to Kant, the necessity of aesthetic judgment "can only be termed exemplary, i.e. a necessity of the assent of all to a judgment regarded as exemplifying a universal rule incapable of formulation" (§ 18), the exemplary in Kant's sense offers the pattern of an open, norm-creating consensus. It is on its basis that Herbart attempted to establish ethics as aesthetics.[56]

8. Aesthetic experience among the problems of everyday life: problems of delimitation

Our historical presentation of the three basic functions of poiesis, aesthesis, and catharsis has constantly touched on the relationship between aesthetic experience and other areas of meaning of our experience without specifically thematizing it. As might have been expected, it developed that the areas of religious, theoretical, and ethical (or political) experience were most closely related. As one looks back at the phenomena and events in the history of aesthetic experience as set forth here, there emerges the picture of a curious process: aesthetic experience does not seem to develop "organically," on a field of its own, but to progressively expand and maintain its area of meaning at the expense of bordering experiences of reality, and this by usurpations and compensations, the crossing of boundaries, the offer of competing solutions. Basing the history of aesthetic experience on such premises might lead to a productive renewal of the historiography of the arts. The present sketch should be seen as the groundwork for such an undertaking. Since a historical synthesis is not yet attainable, I will conclude this preliminary effort with three paradigms (the ridiculous and the comic, sociological and aesthetic role concept, autobiography and individuality) which are intended to illuminate how aesthetic experience borders on other areas of meaning. This leads us to the problem of the functional multiplicity of human action, to which behaviorism, structural aesthetics, the sociology of knowledge, and, more recently, the theory of speech acts have made significant contributions, though an exhaustive systematics has not yet been provided. To the extent that these theories illuminate the place and distinctness of aesthetic experience in everyday life, they will now be briefly recapitulated and discussed.

In *Art as Experience* by John Dewey, a pioneering achievement in the field of aesthetic experience, the aesthetic experience lies at the base of all higher functions in the development of human life. The life process, basically experienced as a constant fluctuation in the interaction with the environment, acquires an "aesthetic quality" with the moment of recovered unity. The connotations of this "recovery of union" are, for Dewey, "ordered change," form, and intensity: "The moment of passage from disturbance into harmony is that of intensest life."[1] Aesthetic quality not only characterizes the attitude toward art as a productive, receptive, and mediating activity but is already present in certain phenomena of daily life such as, for example, the "fire-engine rushing by; the machines excavating enormous holes . . . the tense grace of the ball-player . . . the delight of the housewife in tending her plants, the man who pokes the sticks of burning wood."[2] The artist merely makes conscious and art intensifies and idealizes what is already potential in certain life processes. Aesthetic experience in the more narrow sense of our attitude toward art is rooted in the aesthetic quality of the phenomena of the object world where a process attains a climax, an experience its fulfillment — a thesis whose converse is also true for Dewey: "that . . . no experience of whatever sort is a unity unless it has esthetic quality."[3]

To the extent that Dewey opens up the view on the aesthetic outside of art and describes its sphere as if it could be extended indefinitely, classicist definitions of the beautiful such as order, form, harmony, are imperceptibly turned into properties of an aestheticized world of objects and Aristotelian definitions of the unity of the epic fable into conditions of the possibility of experience as such.[4] But this surely means that in his attempt to grasp the aesthetic without recourse to a transcendent principle of beauty and to define it as a quality of life experiences of special intensity and meaning, Dewey assigns the traditional predicates of the beautiful in art to natural phenomena or those belonging to the world of objects. In other words, he projects them onto these phenomena to then demonstrate that they are everyday "sources" of aesthetic experience. This circle need not be a shortcoming of Dewey's theory, for it has always underlain the experience of what is beautiful in nature, as is shown in aesthetics from Kant's *Critique of Judgment* to Sartre's *L'imaginaire*. According to Kant, it must be possible to view beautiful nature also as art: "there is our admiration of nature which in her beautiful products displays herself as art, not as mere matter of chance, but, as it were, designedly, according to a law-directed arrangement, and as finality apart from any end" (§ 42). Nature, like all ambient reality, is not beautiful in itself; it only becomes so through the contemplative glance of the observer which, as Sartre showed, must negate from a certain point of view the complex plenitude of the given if the imaginary form of the beautiful is to be produced.[5] The shortcoming in Dewey's theory is rather that it maintains the illusion of the objectively beautiful without tracing the aesthetic quality of the objects and phenomena of the everyday world back to the attitude of the observer. But only when this is done does it become possible to set off Dewey's concept of aesthetic experience from other functions of the praxis of life.

That aesthetic experience and pragmatic experience border on each other becomes clear when one considers that not all the objects Dewey refers to as aesthetic have always produced pleasure when perceived. While those who worked were only aware of its inhospitableness and the traveler of its dangers, the natural beauty of mountain solitude did not exist. The aesthetic attitude toward the sublime which did not become general until the eighteenth century had to come into being before this object was accorded aesthetic quality. As regards the beauty of industrial production, early testimonals from the middle of the nineteenth century indicate that admiration for the "new art of the machines" did not come from objective, previously unknown qualities of such products but from the astonishment at the seemingly unlimited capacity of industrial production to surpass nature and, along with it, classical, i.e., merely imitative art, by technical constructs.[6] A new industrial product such as the locomotive may have clumsy, brutal, and even ugly forms. Only the person who can see the astonishing achievement of this *art industriel* as a victory over the old *imitatio naturae* concept will discover its aesthetic qualities.[7] Whereas such judgments were still those of an avant-garde at the time of the first world fair, the masses had so completely made them their own some eighty years later that Dewey could see the habitual aesthetic attitude toward technical production as an aesthetic quality that inheres in the object.

If such examples suggest that aesthetic aspects of our historical life world can often be traced to prior experience in the commerce with art, this is not intended to mean that in earlier times also, the aesthetic outside art was necessarily preceded by an experience of art. Antedating the autonomous and conscious production of aesthetic objects toward which an explicit aesthetic attitude must be adopted if they are to be appreciated in their quality as art, something like an unconscious manifestation of the aesthetic must certainly be assumed. The aesthetic self-representation of man through ornament, the ornamental stylization of objects and gifts, or the musical elaboration of rituals would suggest this. In such instances, an aesthetic attitude need not have been explicitly adopted. In Dieter Henrich's formulation, it can "also be an element in polymorphous forms of behavior without its being possible to distinguish it from them. Its presence must be assumed wherever there is competent use of predicates which can only be interpreted in the context of an aesthetic attitude. Such implicit aesthetic attitude may already be developed during illiterate epochs and in earlier times which have not yet originated purely symbolic acts."[8] The verification of the hypothesis regarding such an implicit aesthetic attitude is, for the present, a problem for anthropology. To answer it would require a theory of the evolution of the aesthetic toward which Dewey took no more than the initial steps.

My attempt (section 8a) to differentiate between the comic as an aesthetic attitude conveyed by the theater, and the manifestations of the ridiculous in everyday reality point in the same direction. The result could easily be fitted into the context of *Art as Experience*. For it was Dewey who paid tribute to the experience of art as the most universal language and the freest form of communication.[9] Time and again, his analyses invite the reader to delimit functions where he was the first to see the aesthetic experience as a whole. A case in point is the complementary unity of production and reception, those two aspects of the aesthetic activity which are distinguished in English by the labels "artistic" and "aesthetic" respectively. Dewey shows their complementariness first by pointing to the artist who must constantly shift from the productive to the receptive attitude in order to correct the work in progress. He also illustrates it from the other side, the perspective of the viewer, who must himself become creative and not receive the work passively, as a finished product, lest aesthetic perception degenerate into mere recognition.[10] Here, we have the anticipation of a premise of the later reception aesthetics, though from that theory's point of view, one would have to criticize Dewey for having claimed the "intimate union of doing and undergoing" for the aesthetic experience and failing to recognize the asymmetry which necessarily arises between its productive and receptive function.[11]

Regarding their content, poiesis and aesthesis are not complementarily dependent: the activity of the observer who concretizes the significance of the finished work from his perspective neither directly continues nor presupposes the experience that the artist gained in the course of his work. In all aesthetic experience, there is a gap between genesis and effect which even the creative artist cannot bridge. He cannot simultaneously create and reveal, write and read what has been written, as Sartre demonstrated in detail in connection with Valéry's aesthetic.[12] In his effort to anchor the fundamental unity of all functions of human action in the aesthetic, Dewey time and again failed to show what the constituents of the aesthetic experience are, and how its functions differ from others. But he did arrive at an insight that was being developed by structural aesthetics at the same time: the achievement of the aesthetic in living praxis can be recognized by its capacity to dynamically organize the experiences of reality and the interests of other provinces of meaning.[13]

Even more decisively than Dewey's theory, the theory of aesthetic function, which Jan Mukarovsky has been pioneering in various treatises since 1936, turns its back on any and all metaphysics of the beautiful.[14] The investigation of the aesthetic in its social function, as "an energetic component of human activity," is to render superfluous the question "whether the esthetic is a static property of things" and, ulitmately, the very concept of the beautiful itself.[15] With the introduction of the concept of aesthetic function, the presumably objective determinations of aesthetic quality are seen as flowing from human activity. The work of art loses its character as thing; as "aesthetic object," it requires the human consciousness to constitute it. Being a dynamic principle, the aesthetic function is potentially unlimited: "it can accompany every human act, and every object can manifest it."[16] Its limit lies in the fact that it derives from the dialectical negation of a practical or communicative function. And because the phenomena it produces in the constant renewal of the aesthetic experience are subject to societal judgment, i.e., must find public recognition before they can enter the tradition-creating process as aesthetic norms, there is a second, intersubjective limitation.[17] In contrast to Roman Jacobson's earlier definition of the poetic influence of language, the aesthetic function is not self-referential for Mukarovsky; it is more than a statement oriented toward expression for its own sake. Because the aesthetic function "changes everything that it touches into a sign,"[18] it becomes transparent for the thing or activity that it "sets . . . aside from practical associations." Precisely because the aesthetic function differs from all others (the noetic, the political, the pedagogic) in having no "concrete aim" and because it lacks "unequivocal content," it can take hold of the contents of other functions and give their expression the most effective form.[19]

The scholarly revolution that resulted from Mukarovsky's theory was assessed by R. Kalivoda in these terms: "What is involved is no longer the aesthetic content of the meaning but the aesthetic elaboration of an extra-aesthetic meaning. . . . The discovery of the 'contentlessness of the aesthetic' is the bridge across which aesthetics works its way toward the theoretical comprehension of art as a specific shaping of reality. It is the precondition for the demythologization of art and the humanization of reality."[20] For Marxists, Mukarovsky's theory of the aesthetic function has the special point that, lacking "unequivocal content," it appears to be wholly in consonance with the aesthetics of reflecting reality, though it covertly refutes it. For if the aesthetic lacks content, it is also "essentially classless" and an "instrument of humanization" for that very reason.[21] From the point of view of "bourgeois" reception aesthetics, Mukarovsky's theory has the shortcoming that it persists in setting aesthetic value as an objective, third element against the dialectic of aesthetic function and aesthetic norm which is immanent in history. And it leaves unexplained how the aesthetic function can be a dialectical negation of the communicative and emotional functions and yet convey something.

Mukarovsky himself has asked whether "the problem of aesthetic value has been exhausted by discussion of the aesthetic function (the force which creates value), and of the aesthetic norm (the rule by which it is measured)."[22] He believes he must anchor aesthetic value objectively, beyond the dialectics of aesthetic function and aesthetic norm, if he is to explain why high art is ultimately "the source of aesthetic norms . . . and that from such art they penetrate into other sectors of aesthetics."[23] This creative superiority of art which causes the aesthetic outside art to seem its mere residue must in fact have a *fundamentum in re*, i.e., its basis in the material artifact whose identity is also required, after all, if one is to recognize the concretization of one and the same work in the historically changing forms of reception of the aesthetic object. If Mukarovsky had contented himself with explaining this identity through the uniqueness of the structure of the artifact,[24] he would have avoided the contradictions in which he involved himself through his attempt to attach the identity of the work of art to the existence of an objective aesthetic value. The detailed demonstration of the variability of aesthetic value in his 1936 treatise (which has become a classic) is at odds with the claim that the aesthetic judgment has objective validity (i.e., independent of the perceiver).[25] If, on the other hand, Mukarovsky arrives at the result that changeability "belongs to the very basis of aesthetic value, which is a process and not a state, energeia and not ergon,"[26] it follows that aesthetic value cannot exist independently of the aesthetic judgment of the percipient. Rather, it must derive from the historically mutable canon, albeit a canon objectified by the growing *consensus omnium*, of what in this connection may be termed the "classical." The process-like character of aesthetic value which, according to Kant, is grounded in the merely exemplary character of aesthetic judgment precludes a definition of what is objectively present in the work except by its structure as it has been elaborated once and for all. And Mukarovsky has indeed turned the search for an invariant definition of the content of aesthetic value into a functional direction: what is the relationship between the aesthetic value of a work of art and the extraaesthetic values it contains? His answer will surprise no one: the aesthetic value relates no differently than the aesthetic function before: it "dominates over the others, but does not disturb them, only joining them into a whole."[27] With this formulation, aesthetic value has dissolved as an a priori quality. In its place, the consensus-shaping authority of aesthetic judgment as an element within the dialectic of the meaning-creating aesthetic function and the rule-creating aesthetic norm would have to be defined anew.

The second point of my critique concerns the concept of function itself. What precisely does the aesthetic function accomplish when it links up with other functions, organizes them dynamically, or dominates over them in the work of art? How does the character of a communication change when the aesthetic function "dominates" over the communicative one? So far, Mukarovsky has no clear answer to these questions. The reason for this is, first, that his concept of the aesthetic function derives primarily from one of the aesthetics of representation and must therefore be defined further in its communicative aspect if the aesthetic experience is to be differentiated from other functions of life praxis. Definitions such as distancing from reality, isolating a thing or activity from its practical context, making reality a unified totality through the sign function, all apply as much to the theoretical as they do the aesthetic function.[28] A clear demarcation emerges only in passing, when it is said that "another important feature of the aesthetic function is the pleasure which it evokes. Hence its ability to facilitate acts to which it belongs as a secondary function . . ."[29] In his typology of the functions (1942) which employs "practical" and "theoretical," "symbolic" and "aesthetic" as paired opposites, the emotional is consigned to the practical functions and it is asserted that "it [the aesthetic sign] cannot be the means for expressing emotion."[30] But this makes it impossible for Mukarovsky to get a grip on the cathartic achievement of aesthetic experience, though this would be necessary to provide his concept of aesthetic function with the missing anthropological basis.

It is well known that the irreconcilability of the aesthetic and the emotional is a dogma of *l'art pour l'art* aesthetics which Mukarovsky's theory of the transparency of reality in the aesthetic sign expressly contradicts elsewhere. Lev S. Vygotski has shown that an absolute hiatus between real and imaginary feelings cannot be stipulated. Just as any present feeling may become embodied in an idea, so even our fantastic experiences have a real emotional base.[31] Emotion and imagination participate in one and the same psychic process. Feeling or emotion in the aesthetic attitude is fed by the same instinctual energies and differs from real feeling only by its further destiny in aesthetic experience. There, it may be purged by a highly intensified activity of the imagination but also directed into contradictory affects, sublimated by postponement, or cathartically liberated by the ultimate resolution of conflicting emotions: "Aesthetic reaction is nothing other than catharsis, i.e. a complex transformation of feelings."[32] Vygotski's description of the complex transformations as feeling and imagination come together concretizes the achievement of the aesthetic function very well, whereas that function remains abstract in Mukarovsky's dynamically organizing principle. But this means that the mechanistic idea according to which the relationship of two functions is already clarified by the assertion that one "dominates" over the other must also be revised.

This can be shown by an example from Czech folk lyric which Mukarovsky quotes to demonstrate the predominance of the emotional over the aesthetic function in the "most modest of arts": "Anna, while scrubbing the floor, does not complain that she would like to spend a pleasant afternoon in the park, but rather that she longs only for the dark grave. . . . Basically Anna is not a deeply melancholy creature: on the contrary, one would say that she is a gossip and a giggler. Well then, if Anna wishes to rise to higher spheres (which is ultimately the most serious goal of poetry and music) she will attain the region of sad and inconsolable feelings; nothing ennobles her so much as the prospect that she will soon be in her coffin wearing a wreath on her brow."[33] When Mukarovsky states that the emotional norm here dominates over the aesthetic one whereas that relationship is reversed when such a popular song is received in the canon of *Kunstpoesie* (serious or high poetry) or is quoted in its context, it must first be noted that it is the aesthetic attitude which makes the bleak feeling that she will soon lie in her coffin palatable to Anna in the first place. In view of the complex connection of feeling and imagination in the internal structure (pleasure in grief, enjoyment of the imagined "beautiful death," satisfaction at the pain such a death would cause others) and in the pragmatic situation (contrast between drudgery and "deserved rest," rising from the everyday to the higher sphere of "poetry"), it becomes difficult to give objective reasons for the postulated priority of the emotional norm over the aesthetic function. Seen from the point of view of reception aesthetics, the singing person may prefer the emotional or the aesthetic attitude. Even in a sentimental identification with what she sings, she will not wholly lose the contrastive relation to the pragmatic situation, as Mukarovsky incorrectly assumes: "Emotional disturbances, not only as a direct reaction to reality, but also as a pure function of some thing (i.e. a song being performed), dominate in popular urban songs, and the emotional norm subordinates the aesthetic norm."[34] For the imaginary emotion as seized and dynamized by the aesthetic function does not simply set aside the contradiction that is the frame; the emotionally nourished imagination preserves something of the pragmatic reality which it negates dialectically: the negated world of daily drudgery, in this instance the floor that must be scrubbed forms, in the pragmatic context of the aesthetic experience, the horizon for the fiction of a more beautiful death.[35] Not only does the aesthetic experience organize the complex transformation of feelings in the imagination. Via negation, it also retains in consciousness everyday reality as that background against which the fiction can first unfold the "higher spheres of poetry." Aesthetic experience is more than is taken hold of by Mukarovsky's concept of the aesthetic function: its "transparency" is the condition of its specific capacity to thematize as "subuniverses" the experiences of the realities of life in the horizon of fiction.

We have reached the point where structural aesthetics finds its necessary complement in the sociology of knowledge and the theory of speech acts. The inadequacies of Mukarovsky's concept of function are that he derives the functions of human action abstractly, from the duality of subject and object, without also grasping as structured universes of consciousness the experiences of reality peculiar to those functions[36] and that he subsumes all conceivable activities (the noetic, political, pedagogic, religious, emotional, erotic, magical, etc.) under the "basic polyfunctionality of human activity and . . . the basic omnipresence of functions"[37] without examining their autonomy. Whether autonomy can be ascribed to any of these functions is decided by whether or not it can form the horizon of a specific reality or self-contained "subuniverse." After what has been said so far, one will hesitate, for example, to accord the emotional an autonomy comparable to that of the theoretical or the religious. The concept "subuniverse" comes from the sociology of knowledge which Alfred Schütz founded in 1932 with his *Der sinnhafte Aufbau der sozialen Welt*. His concluding but unfinished work was completed by Thomas Luckmann who published the first volume in 1975 and gave it the title *Strukturen der Lebenswelt*.[38] According to this theory, the shared, intersubjective world of everyday life can be grasped in various orders of reality into which subjective experience in all societies articulates itself.[39] Such subuniverses—the "world" of religion, of science, of the imagination, of the dream—thus do not constitute themselves through areas with objectively different contents but by virtue of the changing meaning an identical reality can have when it is experienced through a religious, a theoretical, an aesthetic, or some other attitude. Subuniverses have the structure of closed, internally layered provinces of meaning, which is to say above all that "all experiences which belong to a closed province of meaning manifest a characteristic style of experience and cognition. With reference to this style, they concord and are mutually compatible."[40] The constitutional analyses of the sociology of knowledge describe the style of experience and cognition of such provinces of meaning in the articulation of a structure that is grounded in the specific tension of consciousness (between complete wakefulness and dream), requires a particular epoché and dominant form of spontaneity, and rounds into shape in a subuniverse specific modes of spatial, temporal, and intersubjective experience.

There is no need here to elaborate further on the theory of the sociology of knowledge since I have already tried elsewhere in this volume and in other publications to show what significance it has for aesthetic and literary hermeneutics.[41] The discussion of "La douceur du foyer" in particular is meant to justify my thesis that thanks to its transparency, aesthetic experience can illuminate the structure of a historical life world, its official and implied interaction patterns and legitimations, and even its latent ideology. If one analyzes it from the *Fleurs du Mal* down to the most banal newspaper poem, the spectrum of lyric poetry written in 1857 makes palpable—as the horizon of fiction and even at this remove—what the historical and sociohistorical documents of the bourgeois life world of the Second Empire do not expressly record, or fail to mention. This relationship of contiguity of aesthetic and pragmatic experience raises the interesting problem whether the aesthetic can be accorded the status of a closed subuniverse at all. (The systematic elaboration of a typology of provinces of meaning is still a common desideratum of the disciplines involved.) The special status of the aesthetic experience in the life world derives from the peculiarity already mentioned by Mukarovsky, that art can compensate for other functions because "it preserves for a future period human products and institutions which have lost their original, practical function, so that they can again be used, this time in a different practical function."[42] The tradition-forming and tradition-renewing power of aesthetic experience presupposes that its province of meaning is not wholly contained in the here and now of a closed subuniverse. Its transcendent character also asserts itself vis-à-vis other subuniverses: if one reformulates the insights in Mukarovsky's analyses of the aesthetic function in terms of the sociology of knowledge, aesthetic experience can form a world of its own without therefore eliding the reference back to the suspended world of everyday life or one of its provinces of meaning. Rather, the aesthetic experience can enter into a communicative relation with the everyday world or any other reality and annul the polar opposition of fiction and reality: "instead of being its mere opposite, fiction tells us something about reality," as Wolfgang Iser formulated it.[43]

This thesis would certainly have to be nuanced with reference to the nonmimetic arts: more directly than poetry and painting, architecture and music make the viewer or listener part of a perfectly closed aesthetic subuniverse. But it is precisely through their own language that they can become the preferred medium for opening to us the horizon of other provinces of meaning, specifically that of religious experience. A. Schütz therefore did well to speak of "fantasy worlds" in the plural only and not to stipulate an autonomous province of meaning with its own structure of meaning for the aesthetic experience.[44] Unless a second, so far unpublished volume offers a solution to this matter, it remains uncertain how one should conceive of the transition from one province of meaning to another, and specifically of the relationship of contiguity of the aesthetic experience. That the transition here also can only be accomplished by a "leap [which] must be accompanied by a shock experience" hardly solves the problem.[45] It is true that as the curtain in the theater rises, or as one becomes "absorbed" in a painting, the natural attitude toward the world of everyday life breaks off. But the everyday reality thus being dismissed remains *per negationem* as the horizon of experience before which the fiction develops its theme and reveals the meaning of the suspended world. The fiction of the last knight—to take an example Schütz uses[46]—is the horizon against which Don Quixote must recognize the prosaic meaning of a changed world on his long journey of disillusion, and this recalcitrant, unideal world is in turn the horizon against which the ideality of knightly adventure is illuminated more sharply *per negationem* than could happen in the closed world of meaning of the naively received old knightly poetry. It might also be mentioned that Don Quixote, who re-creates this ideality according to the motto, "so much the worse for reality if it does not submit to my principles," also shows that the transition into another closed subuniverse does not always require a leap but can occur through persistent reinterpretation.

To bring this argument to a conclusion, I have adopted findings from the theory of speech acts by Karlheinz Stierle which is based on approaches in my reception aesthetics.[47] His analysis of the forms of literary reception, which articulates the act of reception of pragmatic and fictional texts on the levels of both the naive and the reflected use of language into a progression of language acts, is based on Husserl's distinction of inner and outer horizon and thus leads to the question concerning the life-world function of literary fiction. Stierle's proposed solution corrects the widespread conception of the self-referentiality of literary fiction which was also problematized by Iser. His thesis is: "The world of fiction and the real world provide each other's horizon: the world appears as the horizon of fiction, fiction appears as the horizon of the world."[48] The question left unanswered by Mukarovsky —how the aesthetic function can be a dialectical negation of the communicative and the emotional function and yet convey something— resolves itself in the relationship between fiction and reality as the dialectical relationship between theme and horizon. Fiction can make its world light up in the open horizon of possibilities which break through an established order of the social reality. But it can also provide the closed horizon of a seemingly unaltered order which negates change in the historical world and reduces all individual action to the role-playing of social behavior. My second paradigm (chap. 8b) explains this reversal through the fiction of the *theatrum mundi* which in various historical figures refers to the world of social behavior and even points ahead to the modern sociological concept of role. That fiction can be the horizon for experience of the world and vice versa ultimately also defines the relationship of contiguity of aesthetic experience and other provinces of meaning in the everyday world. I attempt to show this in my third paradigm (chap. 8c) through the history of autobiography. Here, Augustine's *Confessions* and the predicates of divine perfection, which make man conscious of his deficiency and dependence on the creator, provide the horizon of the subuniverse of Christian belief which the self-portrayal of modern man presupposes and transcends as—ostentatively through Rousseau—aesthetic experience appropriates the predicates of divine identity to stamp them into norms of the experience the *individuum ineffabile* has of himself.

a) Delimiting the ridiculous and the comic

In view of the manifestations of the ridiculous and the comic, can a line be drawn between life and art, pragmatic conduct and aesthetic attitude? Where does the specifically aesthetic experience begin? If the act of laughter is anterior to the aesthetic attitude, how can it be transformed by the aesthetic experience or brought about by aesthetic means? Questions such as these are old problems in the theory of aesthetic experience. With a distinction that seems to simply cut the Gordian knot but which proves at once faceted and seminal. E. Souriau has advanced furthest in their solution. He assigns the ridiculous to the world of everyday life, the comic to art. What exists contingently and occurs spontaneously in the former and often makes us flout all decency, morality, or taste with our laughter is aesthetically purified as an artificially created and presented comic, ethically justified, and raised to a communicative function in the latter (i.e., in art). The aesthetic efficacy inherent in the comic world would thus be a kind of filter which can turn the mere negativity and ethical inadequacy of laughter into something positive. Souriau describes this as a cathartic process. Laughter itself as an immediate reaction is not yet an "aesthetic value," any more than is fear or some other affect. Laughter and all other so-called basic feelings become specifically aesthetic only through the "long ascesis" of a transformation which Souriau sometimes refers to by such concepts as sublimation, refinement, "révision réflexive," or again explains as the accession of a positive factor which derives from art and which neutralizes coarse, aggressive, or amoral laughter.[1]

By explaining what is characteristic of the aesthetic experience as a change in attitude toward basic feelings (the tragic emotion thus appears as aesthetically purified fear, admiration of the perfect—my example—as aesthetically purified amazement), this captivating thesis has the advantage of exempting aesthetic theory from searching for primarily aesthetic feelings. Its weaknesses are partly a function of the tradition of French classicism in which Souriau is most at home, and can be remedied without detriment to his principal point. With the concept of the "aesthetic attitude," I have already corrected the antiquated notion that the aesthetic has to be defined as an "additional artistic element" and thus a "positive value." The transformation of fundamental states of feeling into aesthetic feelings which Souriau describes as phases of an "ascesis" certainly does not imply, especially in the comic catharsis, that the resultant aesthetic attitude is to be equated with the recognition and acceptance of positive, already established norms or value judgments.[2] But a similar moral narrowing also appears in the definition of what is basic in laughter as a "rire brut, le rire sans plus, le rire de simple négation, de simple refus, de simple auto-défense spontanée" (coarse laughter, simple laughter, the laughter of simple denial, of simple refusal, of spontaneous self-defense, p. 153). In this way, Souriau divests laughter of its paradoxical aspect, which is that it can be both an expression of joy and an aggressive discharge. Nor does he do justice to E. Dupréel's demand that a theory of laughter prove itself by explaining this paradoxical "nexus of joy and malice."[3] The original character of laughter as response, to which H. Plessner called attention, therefore also eludes Souriau. What Souriau sees merely as an act of spontaneous aggressiveness does not seem so unjustified from the laughing subject's point of view when the individual is faced with a boundary situation with which he can deal in no other way and recovers his "freedom of distance" by laughter, i.e., an answer the body gives in behalf of the person.[4] Laughter as a phenomenon in life is richer and more ambiguous than Souriau describes it. The line dividing it from the comic does not simply separate the negative from the positive, uncontrollable discharge of affect and liberating aesthetic judgment. Yet neither Dupréel nor Plessner inquired about this dividing line and neither discusses laughter as a form of aesthetic behavior. To combine their findings with Souriau's theory of the comic therefore demands that it first be explained whether and how its character as response changes when what is laughed at is no longer a boundary situation in real life but a comic event on the stage.

R. Warning's attempt to describe the comic "message" of the play and the "answering" laughter of the audience semiotically, as a process of communication, and to ground it in a pragmatics of the dramatic genres addresses itself to this matter. Compared with Souriau's, his thesis has the advantage of avoiding an idealist and therefore one-sided interpretation of the comic: the occasion for the response of laughter is the comical collision of two worlds, the real world of the audience and the fictional one of the stage, not the comic event or the comic figure itself. The collision is thus not tied to any hierarchy of values. To the extent that the message of the comedy is not comic in itself but from the perspective of the normal world which it violates, the spectator, being a participating addressee and having his own perspective or expectation, is more immediately involved here than in tragedy which demands an identification with the tragic hero. Comedy, on the other hand, keeps the spectator at a distance.[5]

But here the "message" of the comedy and the "answer" of its laughing addressee appear in a paradoxical light which makes greater demands on semiotics than that science can satisfy. For the "comic message" is no message with a decodable content; what the audience acknowledges by its laughter is the comic collision as such, the collapse of a normative understanding of the world as it comes into contact with the inconsequential counterworld of the comedy. And the answering laughter of the public is not really the decoding of a message, let alone its interpretation; anyone who merely reacts by laughter does not give the "sender" an answer of his own, and this irrespective of the fact that he may later reflect about the question whether the comic occasion for his laughter also conveyed a practical insight. The specific pleasure taken in the comic event on the stage cannot be explained semiotically but only hermeneutically, by drawing on J. Ritter's theory.[6] That this pleasure comes from a comic positivizing of what normative seriousness suppresses or ignores cannot be explained by a special rapport between spectator and comic role which is unique to comedy. True, the self-referential play keeps the spectator at a distance. But this distance can be utilized for both comic and tragic effects. (Anouilh's modern reworking of the classical *Antigone* is just one example among others.) It is true that the relationship between spectator and comic character is less direct than that between spectator and tragic hero. But this certainly does not preclude the possibility of admiring or sympathetic identification with a comic character, and this whether the laughing understanding be due to a laughter *with*, or *at* (*with* Scapin's role or *against* Tartuffe's, in Warnings' terminology). The aesthetic pleasure in comedy is guaranteed by the certain expectation that the answering laughter need merely affirm the "positivizing of negativity" being presented. For in contrast to the ridiculous in real life, the staged comic spares the laughing spectator the risk and the effort of reacting to a boundary situation or a catastrophe; the play on the stage has already accomplished the comic positivizing of the inconsequential which normative seriousness suppressed, and thereby ensured that "underlying lighthearted mood" which the participating spectator in a "congress of laughter" may expect.

Insofar as laughter about the comic in the world of comedy has the character of a response, Warning is right in emphasizing that what is involved is the laughing entente with a partner and therefore something essentially communicative. But the ridiculous in real life, which Ritter equates with the comic, is hardly such a partner, he tells us. It does not play, it assaults. Comedy does not assault but play. It portrays contrariety, invents counterworlds, inconsequential counterworlds from the point of view of the norm it violates, positive counterworlds for the pleasure it gives the audience.[7] In the interest of a theory of aesthetic experience, this thesis invites us to examine whether the comic is so wholly confined to the aesthetic attitude that even its appearance outside art would have to be explained as a turning of that attitude back toward life. On the other hand, one would also have to inquire whether the ridiculous inevitably resists any aesthetic and ethical expectation and can therefore enter art only in a sublimated or indirect form.

The history of concepts and contemporary usage testify to the need to distinguish between *ridiculum* and *vis comica*,[8] the refractoriness of the ridiculous and the purified power of the comic. When we say of someone "he made himself ridiculous," but cannot say "he made himself comic," or, "mon père riait rarement, n'avait nul sense du comique" (my father laughed rarely, he had no sense of humor), but not "il n'avait nul sense du 'ridicule'," this points to an old line which was most sharply drawn in the poetological tradition. The *ridiculum* attaches to a person though not as a permanent quality but as an occasional failing (Molière: "il n'est pas incompatible qu'une personne soit ridicule en de certaines choses, et honnête homme en d'autres," an individual may quite well be ridiculous in certain things, yet perfectly well-bred in others).[9] Being originally applied to a person who violates a social norm, the term enters into the set phrase that introduces a rebuke: "ridiculum est . . ." Clearly, *ridiculum* here cannot be replaced by *comicum*: a rebuke has no room for the comic which is obviously unsuited to promote the codification of human behavior. The *vis comica* originates in a situation that may involve one or more persons without its being possible to hold them responsible for it. This quality as event points back to the fundamental meaning of *comicus* as "belonging to comedy," i.e., to an event on the stage which is amusing or laughable for someone, the spectator. The shift of *comicus* from one context (technical term of stage language) to another (everyday life) in the sense of "as customary in comedies" is a late phenomenon in the development of Latin where we do not find it before Donatus and Hieronymus (authors of late antiquity).[10] Although it is a shift of considerable importance, we cannot trace how the use of the comic as a term in the world of the theater and the use of that term in everyday life overlap, for there is unfortunately no history of the word.

There is something else we can learn from the contrast between *ridiculous* and *comicus* in the poetological tradition. The limited area allowed between the humorous and the serious and the restrictions imposed on the use of the ridiculous in rhetoric permit the inference that its manifestation was considered threatening in the everyday world of classical antiquity. According to Aristotle (*Poetics* 5), comedy may imitate only those characters who are ridiculous by virtue of a defect or an ugliness but who remain protected from pain or injury in such ridiculousness. It can therefore be assumed that in the everyday of classical antiquity, the ridiculous was conceived of as a power that could cause pain, hurt, or even become ruinous for the person concerned. Because laughter, being refractory, does not spare what should deserve compassion or arouse disgust, it was also demanded of the orator that he confine use of the weapon of ridicule to the area between misericordia and odium.[11] Such domestications indicate how seriously the secret fear of the ridiculous was taken. This becomes clearest in the history of the word during the *Ancien Regime* in France which shows, according to F. Schalk, "to what extent the century had fallen under the dominion of a cruel criticism."[12] That one shrank back from the destructive power of a "ridicule" that humiliates the antagonist in his innermost self-esteem is shown by the example of La Bruyère, a writer who, in his *Caractères*, had all the nuances of mockery at his command: "la moquerie au contraire est de toutes les injures celle qui se pardonne le moins; elle est le langage du mepris . . . elle attaque l'homme dans son dernier retranchement, qui est l'opinion qu'il a de soi-meme, elle veut le rendre ridicule a ses propres yeux. . . . C'est une chose monstrueuse que le gout et al facilité qui est en nous de railler" (mockery, on the contrary, is that insult which is less easily forgiven than any other. It is the language of contempt and attacks man in his ultimate refuge, which is the opinion he has of himself. It aims at making him appear ridiculous in his own eyes. . . . Our inclination to mock others, and the ease with which we do it, is something monstrous).[13]

This extreme instance of the ridiculous in real life which is so savage that one no longer can or wants to laugh contrasts in French classicism with an aesthetic concept of the purely comic whose very object is to make "the wise and the virtuous" laugh. Again according to La Bruyère, this requires that the comic have no witty or obscene component and derive wholly from the "nature" of man. We would say that it has to come from the isolated comic instance or from the differences between manners and "characters" in which lie "la première source de tout le comique, je dis celui qui est epuré des pointes, des obscenités, des équivoques, qui est pris dans la nature, qui fait rire les sages et les vertueux" (the first source of all comic, I mean the comic that is free of mockery, obscenity, or the equivocal, the comic that is drawn from nature and which makes the wise and the virtuous laugh).[14] Like French classicism, German classicism, also considered the comic a higher concept than the merely ridiculous except that now subjectivity was discovered as the actual source of the comic. Criticizing Molière's characters, Hegel, in his *Aesthetics*, thus makes this distinction: "whether the folly and one-sidedness of the dramatis personae appears laughable to the audience only or to themselves as well, whether therefore the characters in the comedy can be mocked solely by the audience or by themselves also."[15]

This short retrospective examination of the switch in the use of the two contrasting terms *ridiculum* and *vis poetica* in the poetological tradition may suffice to explain in summary fashion under what conditions the comic can constitute itself by a redirection of the aesthetic attitude toward life. Understood as the boundary line between the ridiculous and the comic, the aesthetic attitude requires: (1) the leeway between the humorous and the serious (2) the contrariety of the comic, and (3) the receptivity of the spectator. If it is to amuse, the unseriousness of the comic conflict must be guaranteed, i.e., the seriousness of whatever could evoke compassion, contempt, or disgust must be excluded from the sphere of the comic. The deviation of a person or his speech from a prevailing norm is not yet properly comic in the aesthetic sense. What is required is a situation in which the violation of the norm takes on the form of a comic conflict for which the person involved is not responsible. The comic of such contrariety can only be felt by someone who has the *sens du comique*, who, as uninvolved observer, can see in the light of which norms the comic in the world can be discovered in a situation.

Applying these three conditions to the examples H. Plessner provides, it can easily be shown how the aesthetic attitude can make what is ridiculous in real life appear in a comic light.[16] As possible occasions where elemental laughter occurs before all aestheticization, the following are treated in Plessner's discussion of Bergson: (a) humorous natural phenomena (like certain cloud- or rock formations or the half-clipped dog Bergson mentions); (b) animals "which appear as grotesque exaggerations of a form, as nature's jokes" (p. 85) (like the hippopotamus, the sea cow, the rhinoceros hornbill); (c) contrariety between the living and the mechanical (the jumping jack, the snowball, the marionette); (d) the human body as carrier of comic qualities (like the overlong nose); (e) the ridiculous resemblance between two human beings, disguises, confusions. We can quickly dispatch case a because it clearly presupposes as much of an aesthetic attitude as is necessary to find comic or humorous natural sights in analogy to the form or sphere of man. Concerning case b, the humorous appearance of animals, Plessner writes that "there is no longer a question of anything human" but of norms and "natural" proportions of the animals themselves which are being contradicted by the caricatural in the appearance of the hippopotamus, for example. But "this opposition to the norm is only apparent," not truly comic, "because animals cannot be other than they are" (p. 86). It seems to me that his qualification ultimately amounts to saying that although the comic aspects of animals may not be due to the animals' "natural form" reflecting a human one, they do rest on the comic imputation that animals, like human beings, can contradict norms by their appearance although "norms can be required [only] of man as a free being" (p. 86).

With the snowball which, rolling over the snow, becomes something disproportionately different, Plessner introduces his concept of contrariety "which, nevertheless, presents itself, and seeks to be accepted as, unity" (p. 83). In this form, the still inauthentic comic of the world of objects comes closest to what is properly called comic, which Plessner ultimately restricts to the human sphere. The snowball whose expansive mechanism gives rise to laughter becomes comic the moment the aesthetic set discovers the paradox of rolling ball and growing avalanche, amusing play and threatening natural force. The comic quality of this contrariety, however, ultimately derives from the analogy to the sphere in which man himself is involved: "Only man is really comic because he belongs to several levels of existence at once" (p. 87). The threshold of the properly comic is crossed, in other words, where the aesthetic attitude discovers in the contrariety of a situation the comic conflict between two different levels of human experience. "The entwining of his individual in his social existence, of his moral person in psychophysically conditioned character and type, of his intellect in the body, opens ever and again new chances of collision with some norm or other" (p. 87). The overlong nose (case d) becomes comic to the extent that "the face is to be guided by it, so to speak" (p. 89). The merely ridiculous similarity of identically dressed persons (case e), presents itself in a comic light if it creates an undesired group identity as its unintentional effect (when among the passengers of a cable car, there appears a traveler with a dachshund who happens to be followed by a second, a third, etc). These examples show not only that there is such a thing as presocial laughter which is not tied to the dialogue of at least two individuals[17] (cases a through c) but also that the comic itself is "no social product"[18] but conditioned anthropologically, by man's "eccentric position," and to that extent also overlaps the social phenomenon of laughter as described by Dupréel.

In the last-mentioned case (e), Dupréel pointed to the solidarization effect which could result in both a *rire d'accueil* and a *rire d'exclusion*. Plessner's examples illuminate that both the welcoming and the excluding laughter between social groups is not comic in itself but can become so only as an "elementary reaction to what is disturbing in the comic conflict" (p. 87). The laughter with which a group welcomes a new member or excludes a stranger and the laughter with which those concerned can solidarize in a new group or form a splinter group arises on this side of the boundary of the comic. It can pass this boundary only where the aesthetic attitude discovers the contrariety of a comic conflict in a difference between groups. According to Dupréel, it is characteristic of social laughter that the excluded individual is always seen as a member of another group, i.e., he is not laughed at as a person but because of a typical otherness. This ridicule can in turn become comic through the contrariety of a merely assumed group identity, as when the person being laughed at is put into an abstract classification or placed out of bounds by assignment to a pseudo-group ("one could hardly maintain that all the mothers-in-law are a social group, or that the totality of misers is one," p. 239). A further example is a frequently observable instance of a reversal from the ridicule of the *rire d'exclusion* to the comic incongruity of the *rire d'accueil*. If the speaker before a polarized gathering can manage to make the antagonistic parties laugh about something, this may create a momentary solidarity which is comic in view of what were hardened fronts a moment before. The return to the seriousness of the debate is often accompanied by a reawakening annoyance, as if one had to be ashamed of having shared one's laughter with the opponent. The "contrariety which . . . presents itself, and seeks to be accepted as, unity" here constitutes the comic quality of the situation of the momentarily liberating laughter between two fronts. This is also true of humor, the highest level of social laughter, which Dupréel proposes to explain by an intimate fusion of the *rire d'accueil* and the *rire d'exclusion* (p. 253). But what can be the meaning of the obscure demand: "pour que la satire reste humoristique, il faut que l'exclusion se fasse à l'occasion d'un accueil" (for satire to remain humorous, exclusion has to occur at the moment of welcome, p. 253) except that comic figures such as Mr. Pickwick or Don Quixote whom we find both ridiculous (*rire d'exclusion*) and sympathetic (*rire d'accueil*) present themselves to us in the comic light of that contrariety which Freud so matchlessly described in the case of the humoristic hero as the comic conflict between the reality principle and narcissism, between the demands of a hostile reality and the victoriously maintained inviolability of the self?

At this point in the argument, J. Ritter's theory will be of help in making a somewhat sharper distinction between the contrariety of the comic and the character of laughter as response in Plessner's sense. Even where it relieves, the latter implies a physiologically conditioned necessity, whereas the former calls for and makes possible an element of freedom: the comic can amuse but does not necessarily provoke laughter. The situation to which we respond by laughter because we cannot deal with it in any other way is not comic for that reason but is a boundary situation that "has nothing to do with such alternatives as true-false, good-bad, beautiful-ugly" (p. 122). As soon as the aesthetic attitude discovers the contrariety of a comic conflict, it gains the freedom of a distance which allows us to deal with the threatening situation, at least on the aesthetic level. But the releasing force of the comic can really only spring from the contrariety of differing norms or levels of existence where these are not of equal rank and in serious conflict but take the unexpected turn of bringing into play the inconsequential which normative seriousness excludes, where they affirm it or—in Marquard's variant on Ritter's formulation—allow "the inconsequential to become apparent in what is officially sanctioned, and the sanctioned in what is inconsequential by general consensus."[19] Plessner's theory takes its stand on this side of the line which Souriau began to draw between the ridicule of everyday life and the comic of art, whereas Ritter's sets in on its far side. But as I tried to show in connection with all three approaches, this line can be crossed in both directions by the aesthetic attitude: by the sublimation of the ridiculous which yields the comic in the world of art and the stage, and by the aestheticization of laughter and its object in the real world.

The contrariety of the comic conflict and the aestheticization of the laughable certainly did not altogether escape Souriau. But he too quickly reduces the former to the collision between the "liberating values" of art and the oppressive power of everyday reality (p. 181) and too one-sidedly derives the latter from the special case that the aesthetic education of laughter can teach us to find the appearance of a natural object humorous as a pseudo-work of art or as the creative joke of a putative creator ("c'est que ce hasard fait si exactement ce que pourrait faire de plus ingénieux un habile artiste en comique," this chance achieves exactly the same thing as the most ingenious product of a clever comic artist could, p. 179). The buzzing bee that hits the window of a classroom may appear comic only because it collides with the instruction that is being experienced as moral repression; but here it is indispensable that the unexpected element of a provisional liberation be touched off by the comic provocation of something "inconsequential in what is officially sanctioned." In his investigation of the laughter at the person who falls because he is clumsy, Souriau was even able to show that Bergson was wrong and could demonstrate statistically that a person's fall is not in itself enough to make us laugh, that sympathetic laughter is much more common than censorious laughter in such a situation, and that, finally, two levels must always interact if the misfortune of another is to be found comic. The brutal mechanism of crashing on slippery ice seems comic when it is justified aesthetically as "involuntary acrobatics" (p. 170). Here, as in the opposite example of the clown whose lack of skill we know to be deliberate and thus an effect of his art ("de l'art qui reconstitue intentionellement une sorte de schéma stylisé du risible de base," an art that intentionally reconstitutes a sort of stylized schema of what is basically laughable, as Souriau aptly remarks, p. 178), the production-aesthetic explanation of comic interplay—the assumption of unintentional acrobatics in the one case, the engineered mishap in the other—clearly requires a reception-aesthetic premise. By this I mean the advance work of the aesthetic attitude which must first uncover such interplay and recognize that an official norm is involved in a banal event if the comic is to shine forth in the behavior of the falling person or the clumsiness of the clown. This advance work, the "sense of humor," can itself be creative, a fact which I cannot document more aptly than by an anecdote whose profound comic really stems from the creative comment which surpasses the event itself: one day, the well-known zoologist Heck slipped as he got off the street car and fell on his hat, a folding top hat, which promptly collapsed; a coachman who was driving by consoled him, "poor fellow, that sort of trick won't put any money in your pocket."

If, from here, we glance back at the much-discussed case of the proto-philosopher Thales, it becomes evident that the Thracian servant girl can hardly have been less witty than the Berlin coachman. For to simply laugh at Thales, no wit was needed. But it is indispensable if one is to discover here, though what may well have been the very first instance of the aesthetic attitude, that in the interplay of theory and practice an inexhaustible source of the comic was being tapped.

We must still ask what happens when the ridicule of daily life is brought into the sphere of art without the sublimation of the comic. How can the negativity of the ridiculous preserve its aggressive, unmasking, and norm-breaking force and yet be put in the service of art with whose inherently idealizing tendency it conflicts? The ridicule in this function is principally known from satire whose tradition and effect as a literary genre is distinctive in being constantly hedged by prescriptions and taboos which serve to keep the refractoriness of the ridiculous within bounds. This is shown not only in classicist demands of "purity" but in the command to generalize so that the individual might be spared,[20] as above all confining the comic to the achievement of moral purpose. Satire unquestionably adopts the point of view of what is to officially obtain; its ridiculum directly attacks what opposes it, draws a clearer line (*rire d'exclusion*), and is incapable of doing any justice whatever to the point of view of the excluded party. To find it merely comic that gay satire attacks human weaknesses and vices with the weapon of the facetum, or not to take seriously the tone of indignation which chastising satire demands, is to miss the intent and to misjudge the legitimation of the genre. Regarding the Russian scene in which the comic emigrates from the servitude of satire to the only apparently related grotesque, D. Tchizhevskij makes clear that the domesticated ridicule of satire has historically tended to be on the side of the old (or newly established) powers, that it served the oppression of the refractorily new or of those who did not toe the line, not the renewal or change of a social order.[21] The development during the French Enlightenment, on the other hand, crosses the classical bounds of satire in several respects, as J. Starobinski has shown in his interpretation of the *Neveu de Rameau*.[22] Diderot's satire, which prefigures the Hegelian theme of the "unhappy consciousness," uses the weapon of ridicule first to invert social hierarchies, as an "incentive bonus" to bring about the suppressed "*égalité foncière*," to invert the relationship between accuser and accused, and, finally, to invert the classical function of satiric unmasking: by posing as ridiculous, it is precisely the unworthy person, the previous object of satire, who now acquires the upper hand of criticism.

A glance at the problem of the boundary between the ridiculous and the comic allows the following formulation of our findings: at the height of Enlightenment satire, the weapon of ridicule strikes back at normative seriousness which subjected its refractory power to what was in force. The subliminal efficacy which makes possible this reversal, which can subversively come to the aid of the now submissive ridiculous against the overt power of what is in force and secure its rights to suppressed inconsequentiality is none other than the *vis comica*. Although the comic derived from an experience of art and presupposes the aesthetic attitude wherever it realizes itself, it is neither originally subservient to established power nor conservative. This rekindles the doubt whether laughter is justifiably suspected of being conservative and whether Warning's thesis that pleasure in the comic "only happens where all criticism remains subordinate to a fundamental assent to the given"[23] can be supported by new reasons.

b) Sociological and aesthetic role concept

For the literary historian, the boom that the sociological concept of role is presently enjoying and has been enjoying for some time is not a cause of annoyance but an occasion for quiet joy in the house of a theoretically underdeveloped, "poor relative." I do not mean the spiteful pleasure that lies in demonstrating to a neighboring discipline that it has been taken in by a metaphorical language it did not see through, that it is unaware that its concept of role has been shaped by the history of aesthetics. Like many aesthetic categories, role and play, scene and spectator, have the hermeneutic advantage of thematizing a form of behavior that can be derived from them so that what they accomplish need not first be inferred from hidden intentions. Satisfaction over the use, indeed the apparent indispensability, of the metaphoricalness of theoretical roles for the "stage of social action" should instead be an occasion for reciprocally illuminating aesthetic and pragmatic role behavior. That not all the components of the original sphere enter into the formation of the paradigm does not make such analogies specious. On the contrary, the elision involved in such cases shows in what direction the adoption tended, at what price it was had, and what idealization occurred in the process.

In our case, theatrical role performance has three components: the originator, the players, and the spectators. In the primary, aesthetic metamorphosis, a theocentric paradigm came into being: God became the originator, men his players (or puppets), the cosmos the stage, and a privileged group (angels, saints, or ultimately God himself) the spectators.[1] In the secondary, sociological metamorphosis, the positions were partly reassigned, partly omitted; society became the writer of the roles, individuals the carriers of interchangeable roles, the everyday world the scene of social action. Usually no one was cast for the role of spectator, presumably because the critical sociologist hesitated to occupy ex officio the still vacant spectator's seat and thus to take into account this hermeneutic condition of his analytical-empirical method. But another elision was probably even more consequential: whereas the theatrical actor must play a role that is usually determined down to the very words but which he paradoxically may and must interpret with subjective freedom, sociology for a long time was interested only in the normative achievement of role behavior. Just recently, sociology has begun discussing the function of "role distance" and thus moved closer to the problem of role interpretation. In differentiating between the sociological and the aesthetic role concept, it must finally be taken into consideration that in the creation of its role theory, it only looks as if sociology had an atemporal model of the theater in mind. Actually — and this is something the literary historian notes with some pleasure — it must have thought of very specific historical forms of the stage: the role concept of the *homo sociologicus*, which Ralf Dahrendorf popularized, presupposes the "great theater of the world" of medieval provenance,[2] just as the role playing of the everyday "presentation of self," according to Erving Goffman and his disciples, presupposes the naturalist drama with the old picture frame stage.

Through recourse to the aesthetic paradigm of the *theatrum mundi*, the theory of the *homo sociologicus* could idealize a historical life world in threefold fashion. Like the world of the stage which, being self-contained, evokes the idea of a total order articulated in a hierarchy of roles, and makes one forget that, de facto, it merely symbolizes a segment of a more complex, unordered, and mutable reality, social life on the stage of social action appears as a self-sufficient order of pronounced structure and without background. Here, no one can deviate from the repertory of existing roles, and he certainly cannot disappear behind the stage. Just as the "great theater of the world" ultimately serves the idea of a world tribunal before which all persons are judged according to the way they met their obligations and exercised the rights of their roles and where, at the end, when the masks must be taken off, they represent the equality of all before death, so the social stage also appears as a playing of roles where the observation of the rules is guaranteed by role expectations, customs, and laws. One's scope of action is thus largely determined by positive and negative sanctions even though the individual believes himself to be free.

Just as the unpredictably free behavior of individuals becomes predictable and transparent for the spectator when they must act as *dramatis personae* with status signs (the great theater of the world with its hierarchy of estates, professions, and conditions and the coincidence of status symbols and role attributes idealizes this reduction to the typical most perfectly), so sociological role enactment reduces the contingent entanglement of individual acts to a surveyable system of conditioned expectations which, thanks to their finality, can be deciphered like texts with stage directions and precisely described as perpetually repeated position- and role conflicts. The implicit hermeneutics of the aesthetic role concept thus makes possible the presumably purely analytical-empirical theory of socially conditioned forms of action!

There are only two points where the analogy of the *theatrum mundi* seems to break down. In it, the individual has only a single role, whereas sociology is interested in transforming this substantial unity of role and person into a cluster of position- and role segments which must be variously integrated.[3] And whereas the actor is permitted to *play* his role, i.e., to double himself in relation to his role, as it were, and to return from this aesthetic distance to the seriousness of everyday reality, *homo sociologicus* is expected not to let himself be misled into "seeing in his role-playing social personality something like an inauthentic individual who need merely drop his 'mask' to appear as he really is."[4] But how is he to do justice to his social role without "playing" it? How can he be husband or wife, father or mother, physician or teacher, "not in play but in all seriousness,"[5] since he must always, whether consciously or not, adhere to the specific role a particular situation calls for? To *play* his social role without taking it seriously would involve as many sanctions as the other extreme, the total identification with a position at the expense of all other role expectations. Like the theatrical role concept of the "as if" of the aesthetic attitude, the sociological concept clearly also calls for a specific attitude toward, or distance from, the role. And this all the more since *homo sociologicus* is defined by a whole cluster of roles in modern society; some remaining distance, the less than total absorption in whatever role is being played at the moment, first guarantees that the individual can satisfy a variety of role expectations, that he can do one thing, yet keep another in mind. Dahrendorf did not confront this problem. For this reason, his theory finally reverts to an idealist "paradox of the double individual" in which the causal determination of social behavior and the sphere of private freedom, man as the aggregate of roles and the autonomous individual, are juxtaposed without mediation, as if the latter had a home somewhere beyond all roles. And if the real self, or *individuum inef-fabile*, thus ultimately manifests itself again behind the interchange-able role player, the aesthetic paradigm of the *theatrum mundi* which lies behind this theory also returns in a final (unintentional?) metaphor: "it is a feeble consolation for the sociologist that 'homo sociologicus' and the free individual appear before the seat of judgment (!) of transcendental criticism as perfectly reconcilable persons."[6]

In his justly famous article "Soziale Rolle und menschliche Natur" (social role and human nature, 1960), Helmuth Plessner showed why the aesthetic paradigm of the *theatrum mundi* so brilliantly supports and covertly legitimizes the doubleness of the public and the private individual. Role and play serve to idealize forms of behavior "which society expects from man. He slips into his role and has to take care that he plays it well. Those who forget themselves and misbehave dis-turb society, make themselves impossible in both its lowest and its highest stratum."[7] Although the venerable great theater of the world is thus diminished by the loss of its cosmic dimension so that the im-manent scene of social action becomes its focus, even the reduced paradigm retains enough of its formerly theocentric functions to justi-fy the functionalism of the formal role concept and its consequence, the split into public and private existence. The social role play of the pervasively rationalized modern working society needs the old hope of the *theatrum mundi* where men and things still "testified to the success of a whole which could be inferred though not entirely derived from their efforts but rather underlay them as a plan."[8] Plessner's crit-icism is directed against this legitimation which "fits in with the square in front of Salzburg cathedral but no longer with today's open hori-zons"[9] and sets his anthropological concept of man's *doppelgängertum* against the idealist separation of alienated existence (social "appear-ance") and autonomous inwardness (consciousness of self as "being"). This concept precedes both the social and the theatrical role concept in the sense that in giving oneself up to a role, it is not self-alienation but the possibility of selfhood that is recognized: "in adopting a role and thus doubling himself, man is yet always first what he really is. Whatever he takes for his authentic being is also only his role which he plays to himself and for others."[10]

It seems to me that the implications of Plessner's thesis have not yet been fully unfolded for both sociological and aesthetic role the-ory. In its light, the difference between aesthetic and social role be-havior can be most sharply defined. In both modes of experience, man is called on to double himself by taking up an already existing role. This doubling in a role figure can occur on different levels of identification, between "deadly seriousness" and "cheerful play," and be prompted by varying motivations, ranging from routine and imitation to free interpretation. The threshold between social and aesthetic role behavior would always be crossed when the implicitly adopted role distance (which, in the case of social roles, is lost only in the repetition compulsion of pathological conduct) is made explicit through the "as if" of the aesthetic attitude. This means neither more nor less than that, through the distancing act of the aesthetic attitude, the actor reaches a position vis-à-vis his role which frees him—as though in a play—from the seriousness and motivational pressures of daily roles. This inner distance may be understood as an "enjoying oneself in the role" or a reflected adoption and thematization of the role as role. In either case, the distance derives from the aesthetic illusion of play, i.e., to be able to do freely what one must otherwise do in all seriousness. The aesthetic relationship to a role thus does not differ in kind from habitual or engaged behavior in a social role. It merely makes contrastively conscious the doubling that is inherent in all role behavior and makes it possible to enjoy oneself in the experience of a role (to quote Wilhelm Busch, "what vexes us in life/is relished when portrayed"). The aesthetic attitude is thus by no means a privilege of the actor who, according to Diderot's famous *Paradoxe sur le comédien*, achieves the strongest impact when he retains an inner distance from the affects whose portrayal moves the audience. The aesthetic attitude can be adopted in relation to any and all social roles. Its "as if" often remains unnoticed in social life and will only be penalized in situations where a demonstrative "aestheticism" offends against a serious ritual or what is considered tact in a community.

The aesthetic role concept not only thematizes role distance as man's possibility to experience his self through the doubling that role enactment occasions. It also thematizes the fundamental relationship of intersubjective role and selfhood in a sense that has hardly been considered by sociological role theory, as far as I can see. I am thinking of the latitude of interpretation that becomes available to man through the self-estrangement of role enactment, and which can make up for the inevitability of predetermined behavior. The sociological analysis of the face-to-face situation is a revealing example. Hans Peter Dreitzel informs us that like the everyday self-presentation in role figures as analyzed by Erving Goffmann, it is based on constitutive premises and rules which are familiar to the literary historian through the drama of the naturalistic, representational stage.[11] Role performance as the drama of the self-presentation of a social group shows a "public side of role behavior behind which the technique of staging is hidden"; "it allows a certain freedom which may not be stretched with impunity"; it thus ensures not merely unimpeded communication between the players but also controls information vis-à-vis outsiders.[12] In striking contrast to the great theater of the world, which appealed to the higher insight of the spectators or wanted to arouse their moral conscience as it confronted them with players wholly absorbed in their roles, there is, from the very beginning, "an understanding between spectators and actors" on this new sociological stage.[13] This means that the drama of social self-presentation so clearly and one-sidedly serves the preservation of the status quo of a "closed society" that—in spite of an appreciation of the many insights into the perfect staging of behavior which this theory uncovers in the role structure of families, businesses, hospitals—one would like to ask the sociologist how his analysis of man in society would change if he derived his role concept from our contemporary theater. For as is generally known, concealing the technique of staging from the spectator is the very thing that has not been done since Pirandello and Brecht, and this because the naturalistic illusion concerning social determinants was to be laid bare. Karl Löwith's interpretation of Pirandello's *Cosí è (se vi pare)* could serve as a paradigm for an analysis of the "public side of role behavior" where typified social role performance would be shown in the dialectics of self and being-for-others and the individual no longer be understood in his abstract opposition to social existence but *in the role of fellow human being.*[14]

Face-to-face communication represents an interesting borderline case of the functionalism of social roles because here "the personality of the interacting partners, their full subjectivity, is always present as an insecurity factor which must be controlled to insure predictable behavior."[15] From this, Dreitzel derives something like a categorical imperative of social behavior, the "demand to typify our conduct and that of the other."[16] Would it be a wholly unsociological thought to suggest that this postulate find its complement in the demand that the unavoidably prior mutual typification be undone again and is in fact frequently undone in face-to-face communication when social role behavior is no longer intended to exclude subjectivity as an "uncertainty factor" but to include the individual in the role of fellow human being? If it is true that we "typify others every time we interact with them,"[17] this does not mean that the other in the face-to-face situation remains in the objectivization of a "generalized vis-à-vis": "taking the role of the generalized other" (G. H. Mead) implies instead a process in which my role expectation can be constantly revised by the other so that a reciprocal interpretation of behavior is initiated in and toward the role that makes possible the discovery of the other as individual through his role. Not just modern drama furnishes an aesthetic paradigm here, as in *Amphitryon 38*, for example, where Giraudoux proceeds in anti-Kleistian fashion by eliminating the idealist separation of identity and role and by foiling Jupiter as transcendent authority because the human couple finds a historical identity in the affirmation of its conjugal roles.[18] Classical comedy since Marivaux has furthered the breakthrough of what was surely not just a literary form of dialogue in which reciprocal interpretations of speech bring to light others' unconscious intentions which lie hidden behind established roles and thereby reveal their individuality. The reciprocal role interpretation in the face-to-face situation does not already presuppose role distance as a given but shows its intersubjective genesis.

Indeed, role distance is not just a question of having room to maneuver in one's own role or a result of solitary reflection about one's role behavior. The distance to one's conduct, the suspension of the naiveté of customary role behavior also can be, and usually is, achieved through the reciprocal interpretation of the roles adopted during, and existing prior to, the exchange. It would probably not be difficult to make this intersubjective genesis part of the excursus in which Thomas Luckmann describes the formation of role distance as a process of triangulation.[19] According to this thesis, man in all societies can distance himself from his conduct because in unreflected everyday life also, he has alternatives of action available to him, because his roles can relativize each other, and because he can experience himself in the break between the everyday and other spheres of reality (such as the dream, religion, science) as a "relatively role-independent self." But in that case, wouldn't the reciprocal relativization of role realities in the face-to-face situation of two dialogue partners as the most common of all triangulation processes find its place at the lower end of the scale that, according to Luckmann, originates in the subuniverses or "provinces of meaning" of subjectively experienced reality on the one hand or in the socio-structural specialization of various institutional spheres with function-specific role definitions on the other and which extends all the way up to the role-integrating achievement of biography?

Why the "independent self," which can discover itself both in the crisislike inversion of the everyday and the simple triangulation of the transition from one role reality to another, must always be only a "relatively independent" one can then be explained by the primarily intersubjective genesis of role distance. The construction of an overall nexus of the ascribed and assumed roles in a biography which, in modern industrial society, is no longer understood as an antecedently existing schema but subjectively, as personal achievement, does not contradict this. For literary tradition shows that even after the secularization of confession, autobiography retains the function of a justification before others. It also shows that the autonomous subjectivity must double itself in the meta-role of the writer if it is to make its life as a role before others, retrospectively, part of a whole. In literature, on the other hand, the "I-you" relation of friendship or love is celebrated as a role-independent relationship. When Heloise refuses to marry her only love, Abelard, because she would rather remain his mistress than assume the role of wife ("ut me ei sola gratia conservaret, non vis aliqua vinculi nuptialis constringeret," so that I may be preserved for him by grace alone, and not constrained by the force of marital bonds), she applies a famous argument to the love between the sexes which, in Cicero, had applied to friendship alone.[20] Montaigne took it up again to explain his friendship with La Boétie: "If you press me to tell why I loved him, I feel that this cannot be expressed, except by answering: because it was he, because it was I."[21] The sociologist would probably view this ecstatically formulated friendship or love of the I-Thou relation as a purely literary or mystical mode of experience. But can we not also find a less demanding, intersubjective experience of reciprocal role distance behind this ecstatic formulation? Such an experience is perfectly well known to us from everyday life as that face-to-face situation of disburdening familiarity which can develop between friends, lovers, or marriage partners when, through mutual interpretation of the required roles or a conscious suspension of rolelike behavior, they encounter each other on the level of a relationship that need not necessarily be ecstatic to correspond to Montaigne's formulation, "because it was he, because it was I?"

It may certainly be objected that such a transcending of social roles must ultimately lead back to a reciprocal role relationship which, though initially a departure from the pattern, will unavoidably become habitual once more. An impressive example, driven to the point of aporia, would be George and Martha in *Who Is Afraid of Virginia Woolf*; they negate all social roles, invent their own, abandon them again, and, in a symmetric escalation, finally remain the prisoners of their own game.[22] But this objection implies a self-contradictory concept of the social role: if an "I-Thou" relationship produces its own game whose roles could be assumed by no third person, we have roles with noninterchangeable players. In what sense can these still be viewed as roles? As a singular "I-Thou" relationship is being entered here, is there a crossing of a threshold into a sphere which sociology readily leaves to the theory of aesthetic experience, conceding that, like all individual behavior, such role performance can only be portrayed and analyzed in literature? The question Thomas Luckmann raises ironically and leaves open[23] would therefore seem even more interesting to me if it were rephrased as follows: can one play the roles of "I" and "Thou" the way one plays "railroad conductor" or "critical sociologist?"

c) The religious origin and aesthetic emancipation of individuality

To the extent that it manifests itself in the history of autobiography as its genuine literary form, the discovery of individuality shows us whether and how the identity problem was prefigured in aesthetics.[1] If by individuality one means the professed totality of a life experience which a self can share with no one, its norm-setting beginning in Augustine shows that it was not originally an aesthetic category. Rather, the new self of the Christian that came into existence with *conversio* — the constitutive act of his faith — discovers his individuality in the turning to God as dependence on the creator and, simultaneously, in the turning back to his old self, as the dubiousness of his temporal life. It is its split that constitutes Christian subjectivity: vis-à-vis its creator, it experiences itself as "a particle of Thy creation . . ." (I, i), as a mere "trace of that most profound unity" (*vestigium secretissimae unitatis*, I, xx) which, in regard to its past, depends on the capacity of its memory which is equally deficient and can reach neither the origin nor the totality of its life. The First Book of the *Confessions* describes this situation of the Christian in a self-accusatory backward glance at childhood, and in the praise of divine providence and also probes in this "confessio peccati et laudis" (confession of sin and praise of God) what the individual self in its imperfect identity can experience only through the measure of the perfect identity of its creator. The dependence on the creator lays down for the creature as predicates of divine perfection all those identity concepts that make imperfect man in the state of heteronomy aware that in view of the plenitude of divine attributes, his individuality is a deficiency. But to the degree that man strives toward autonomy as his goal and begins to ground his true self in his own individuality instead of seeking it in the alien "Thou" of his creator, the aesthetic experience takes hold of the predicates of divine identity and turns them into norms of a self-experience which manifest themselves literarily in the forms and claims of modern autobiography. In what follows, Augustine and Rousseau will serve to substantiate and explain this thesis.

The first predicate of divine identity that makes the creature conscious of its dependence on its creator is all-embracing totality. It appears early in Book I as the whole from which everything comes ("ex quo omnia, per quem omnia, in quo omnia," "For of him, and through him, and to him, are all things," Romans 11, 36) and in which everything is contained though without any creature therefore being able to grasp it ("Do the heaven and earth then contain Thee, since Thou fillest them? or doest Thou fill them and yet overflow, since they do not contain Thee? I, iii). Of his integrity as part of an all-encompassing whole, even fallen man preserves a trace ("vestigium secretissimae unitatis"): the child, although from the very beginning not without sin, has been created in God's image, "with a pleasing shape and functioning senses."[2] In spite of his deficiency, man can thus retain an idea of his creaturely *incolumnitas*, and the need for its ultimate restitution can make itself felt even in his fallen state. Augustine describes this condition by a Neoplatonic concept of identity, the opposition between the unity of spiritual existence and the multiplicity of matter: "And in pouring Yourself out upon us, You do not come down to us but rather elevate us to You. You are not scattered over us, but we are gathered into one by You" (I, iii). The ontological relationship between God's unity, which simultaneously gives and preserves itself, and man's existence, scattered into multiplicity, becomes, in Augustine's *Confessions*, the dichotomous scheme of autobiographical portrayal. Its subject is the split Christian subjectivity: an atemporal and nonlocalized writing self which, after the turn from the inessential to the essential, accusingly confronts a self lost in time. Its subject matter is very sharply divided into the state preceding and following conversion. Augustine reports his wandering only up to the garden scene (Books I to IX) but says nothing about the twelve years of his ascent in the church hierarchy which lie between conversion and composition. It is only Augustine the individual in the inwardness of his faith, not the bishop as the bearer of social roles, who is to be worthy of the interest of his readers. The narrative form of the Augustinian confession is horizontally and vertically discontinuous. The episodes of his past life allow the contrast between "then" and "now," between the entanglement of the old and the insight of the new self, to emerge in ever varying formulations. And the life history as a whole does not conclude epically, in the circle of beginning and end, but is vertically broken in its middle: as if the step toward the essential could not but render inessential the further development of his self, a long meditation on *memoria* sets in after the conversion and Monika's death (Book X), and Augustine begins to write a commentary on the immemorial history of creation (Books XI to XIII). The norm-setting autobiography of the Christian era thus has its telos in its self-sublation: Augustine's reader is meant to recognize that the Christian can find his true self only when the recollection of what he was and has become is transcended and goes back to the beginning of all creatures, when speaking about himself finally yields to "God's own grammar" so that the creation of all things may be praised as God's poiesis.[3]

"Here is a portrait of man as painted exactly according to nature and in all its truth, the only one that exists and that probably ever will exist" (I, 3). In its extravagant claim, this very first sentence of Rousseau's *Confessions* refers back to a usurped divine predicate. The announced portrait of a man who owes his "entire truth" to nothing other than the transparency of *être soi*, i.e., of no longer being in the "image of God," is to be so unique as to render dispensable all that has ever been, or will ever be, said about him. Universal and individual at one and the same time (" . . . and that man myself. Myself alone! I know the feelings of my heart, and I know men. . . . If I am not better, at least I am different," p. 3)—it is to the autonomous self that the old paradox of God's embracing and embraced totality now applies. Knowing oneself through the new certainty of one's feeling is tantamount to knowing all men. The addressee of these confessions can only be mankind in its entirety; everyone is to discover something about himself. Since one has to read the heart of one's fellow to understand one's own, this book might serve as the hitherto lacking point of reference for the study of the human heart (I, 3). Thus Rousseau does not merely claim to confess both his own and others' sins as sanctimonious Catholics do.[4] His book (with whose composition the aesthetic attitude adopts the religious expressive form of confession) is to render transparent the most secret motives of the human heart and assigns that function to his fellowman's revelation which in Augustine's self-experience had been God's alone: "Let each reader imitate me, turn inward as I have done, and say to himself in his innermost conscience if he dares: 'I am better than that man was.'"[5]

A second predicate of divine identity by which the converted Christian recognizes his lost integrity after changing his life is the "Immutable who changes everything": "Suffering no change and changing all things: never new, never old, making all things new" (I, iv). In contrast, the convert experiences himself in the split identity of a new and an old self, and his confession appears in the discontinuity of "now" and "then." Far from recognizing retrospectively an unchanging self, let alone an individuality in the process of formation in the ever changing experience of life, the structure of the Augustinian *Confessions* constantly re-creates the gulf between former experience and present insight.[6] The identity of the new and the old self, though given in physical identity, is vainly searched for in the discontinuity of remembrance and must thus become a problem to which insight into the deficiency of a mutable heart is no sufficient solution. This contrasts with Rousseau's pretension to maintain counter to both the discontinuity of Christian individuality and the lack of focus of worldly existence the unity of his true self: "Everything holds together . . . everything is one in my character . . . and this bizarre and singular aggregate needs all the circumstances of my life to be properly unveiled."[7] The Augustinian figures of the "then" and "now," where the repentant attitude of confession understands and bemoans the wandering of the old self, is therefore replaced in Rousseau by the affirmation of the "then *as* now"—moments of insight that childhood experiences like the "sentimental education" of novel reading or the much-quoted "*fessée* by Mademoiselle Lambercier continue to have their effect to the present hour and indelibly mark his individuality.

Yet for Rousseau also, there is an event which he says irrupted vertically, as it were, into the consistency of his life story and gave an early turn to the development of his individuality which did not correspond to its original plan. It is the underserved punishment for breaking a comb, the child's cruel first experience of the injustice of the world which achieves epochal significance for the backward-looking Rousseau. Experienced as an expulsion from innocence and the unalloyed happiness of paradise, "we were there, as the first man is represented to us—still in the earthly paradise, but we no longer enjoyed it" (p. 19), this step out of childhood is the autobiography's equivalent of Adam's fall in the history of salvation and the loss of the "state of nature" in the history of society. Yoked between the nostalgia of a lost, and the expectation of a recoverable, innocence, the individual's personal fate henceforth falls under the sway of the law of Rousseau's philosophy of history and its three-step progression.[8]

One can also see here a provocative inversion of the Augustinian theology of history. Whereas in the latter, man alone is responsible for the loss of the bliss of paradise, the expulsion from the paradise of childhood and the loss of the natural state are the result of external events behind which Rousseau identifies the true culprit. The modern confession demonstrates the innocence of what was heretofore the sinner, and accuses the society that was presumptious enough to judge him. Rousseau has no doubts about what he might have become, had life been simple, and had external intervention not made him abandon the path of what he was meant to be: "I should have been a good Christian, a good citizen, a good father of a family, a good friend, a good workman, a good man in every relation of life" (p. 43). The insight by which he explains to himself the beginning of his misfortune here is the same that he ascribes to the ecstatic illumination on the road to Vincennes and which he considers the highest purpose of his writings, i.e., to show "that man is naturally good and that it is only through institutions that men become evil."[9] If one looks in Rousseau's *Confessions* for a counterpart to Augustine's garden scene, one will find that the account of this illumination is both formally and stylistically the closest. "From the moment I read these words, I beheld another world and became another man" (p. 361). The lightninglike irruption of the true, the turn toward a new self, the vision of another world, and the weighty consequences of this moment ("the misfortunes of the remainder of my life were the inevitable result of this moment of madness," p. 361)—all this evokes moments of the Augustinian conversion and simultaneously inverts its content. For in regard to his personal destiny and the history of mankind, Rousseau's illumination amounts to nothing other than the revision of the Augustinian premise that man is sinful from the very beginning. The new self which emerges from Rousseau's "conversion" proves its innocence to itself in the autobiography and charges in both *Discours* the whole of society with responsibility for its history.

A third predicate of divine identity through which the newly discovered Christian subjectivity experiences the "patchwork" of its physical and temporal existence is that God, in whom nothing dies, is eternal and placeless: " . . . in You nothing dies: for before the beginning of time, before anything that can even be called 'before,' You are . . ." (I, vi). This divine predicate set over against the insight that "my childhood has long since died while I am still alive" establishes the limit of that human capacity whose astonishing power Augustine first really probed and praised as the preeminent path toward the experience of God. The discovery of *memoria* as the immeasurable space of inwardness encounters paradoxes in the *Confessions* which, in contrast to the complete evidence of Platonic anamnesis, time and again make the searching spirit aware of the imperfection of his insight. Human memory does not reach back to the beginning of life; unaided, it finds no answer to the questions whence it came into this "dying life and living death" (I, vi), how it can feel the need for a blessed life as keenly as if it were a joy of memory when this feeling could hardly have come into memory from experience (X, xx–xxii), or how God can live in his memory though his "place" is everywhere for anyone who asks (X, xxvi). But memory can also guarantee no more than a fragmentary identity of the self because it is constantly in danger of forgetting, because it cannot explain why I can remember my forgetting (X, xvi), and because human experience in time can never attain to the *totum simul* of divine plenitude but only the subjectively perceived and therefore limited (if not distorted) past and future, as they present themselves from any given present: "For these three do exist in some sort, in the soul, but otherwise do I not see them: present of things past, memory; present of things present, sight; present of things future, expectation" (XI, xx).

In the Augustinian meditations on the power and limits of *memoria* (meditations which are the first to descry physical identity down to its unconscious processes, repressions, and sexual fantasies), the Christian individual probes his subjective temporality in a way that prods him not to resign himself to the discontinuity of the religious experience of self. The new religious experience of an identity split into a naive self and a self that has withdrawn from the world offered the aesthetic attitude the challenge of overcoming the heteronomy of the experience of the self and of making the "fragments of a great confession" the whole of a self-portrayal of the *individuum ineffabile*. And the history of the aesthetic experience does in fact show the process in the course of which poetry takes hold of the Augustinian scheme of the experience of self, secularizes memory as "world inner space" in love poetry, increasingly emphasizes the world-appropriating capacity of remembering aesthesis, utilizes, since Rousseau, its affective evidence to totalize the contingency of a life history; and climaxes in Proust's poetics of recovered time which his cycle of novels completes as an "edifice of the fourth dimension," i.e., as an imperishable thing that has been created in the process of remembrance itself.[10] I have sketched this process elsewhere[11] and would merely like to show here in a further comment how Rousseau believed he could redeem the claim that he was making his individuality and all it experienced and felt transparent for the reader, and how, in the arrogance of "saying all there is to say," he finally usurped the predicate of divine omniscience.

"Abandoning myself at one and the same time to the impression I received and the feelings I now experience, I will paint the state of my soul twice, that is, at the moment the event happened to me, and at the moment I described it" (I, 1154). For Rousseau, the discontinuity of autobiographical narrative as created by Augustine establishes the inverse possibility, i.e., the recovery and deepening of the truth of the past. Since affective recollection can renew a past experience in present feeling, it annuls the temporal distance between old and new self and can therefore achieve more than mere perception. "Since, as a rule, objects make less impression on me than the remembrance of them, and since all my ideas assume the form of the representations of objects in my mind, the first traits which have stamped themselves upon my mind remained, and those which have since imprinted themselves there have rather combined with them than obliterated them" (p. 180). As if the Augustinian formula of subjective temporality were being taken literally in an unexpected manner, Rousseau fuses present and past (*praesens de praeteritis*) and thus realizes the possibility of the *totum simul* of an experience of the self which reaches back to its own beginnings and makes present for itself in the "chain of the feelings which have marked the development of my being" (p. 284) the continuity of its becoming and having become! J. Starobinski has noted in commenting on the quoted passages that if his conception of the immediacy of the original language guarantees the transparency of his experience of the self, Rousseau may indeed consider the truth of his self-representation to be infallible. To the extent that in the act of writing, he wholly abandons himself to his inner experience as it reveals itself in the stream of remembering feeling, language can also again become a pure medium which makes the truth of experience expressible.[12] It is a truth, however, that cannot be judged by objective historical criteria for it is at home in the sphere of the authentic which remains true even when the writer calls on his imagination, makes factual errors, or draws certain features of his self-portrait incorrectly.[13] For as testimonials, the gaps in his memory have the same value as do the compensations of his imagination if in fact in the transparent language of self-awareness and in and through all experiences and errors, partisanship and wishful thinking, indeed cynicism and lies, only one and the same thing, the *individuum ineffabile*, forever displays itself.

This brings into play a fourth predicate of divine identity: the omniscience of "Him who has numbered the very hairs of your head" (Matthew 10, 30). Augustine quotes this line as he looks back on his school years and sees that to be compelled to learn was salutary for him though he did not understand this, and that those who forced him to learn did not act well because they thought only of worldly success as the highest goal (I, xii). Human knowledge is thus inadequate not merely because *memoria* has gaps and limitations. Its defectiveness must prove even more serious where man does not see through the secret motives of his acts, allows himself to yield to the pressure of present interests and concerns, and cannot gauge the significance an event may have for his life as a whole. Even the turn from the old to the new self does not suddenly make this nexus transparent; even after his conversion, much in his biography remains obscure to Augustine, like the moment, for example, when he wants to know from God the significance of the fact that his baptism was postponed (I, xi). Since only God sees and sees through the human soul and all its acts and aspirations, it would be pure vanity *"de se paindre soi-même,"* as Pascal still reproached Montaigne. All that remains for the Christian after confessing his sinful past is to fall silent about himself and to praise God's benevolence and justice in their unfathomable dispensations.

Nowhere does the total inversion of the Christian confession therefore emerge more sharply than in the provocative gesture with which Rousseau offers the work of his literary self-revelation to the enlightened reader: "Let the trumpet of the Day of Judgment sound when it will, I will present myself before the Sovereign Judge with this book in my hand, I will say boldly: 'This is what I have done, what I have thought, what I was. I have told the good and the bad, with equal frankness. . . . I have unveiled my inmost self even as Thou hast seen it . . ." (p. 3). In this opening of the *Confessions*, as famous as it is infamous, the entire Augustinian scheme with its metaphysical premises is evoked and dismissed in order to legitimate the enlightened individual's having come of age, and to demonstrate "ad oculos" all that is required to satisfy the claim of self-sufficiency ("se suffire à soi-même"). Here, the unity of feeling and remembrance as the new court of truth establishes not only the transparency of the portrayal of the self in both its good and its evil but the authenticity of the knowledge of its entire history as well; the autonomous self which understands itself through everything it has created, thought, and been, appropriates the history of salvation to resolve the question of its salvation and justification in the writing of its individual history.[14] In this fashion, the predicate of divine omniscience is being usurped in a number of ways, for God reserved unto Himself the knowledge of good and evil ("ye shall be as gods, knowing good and evil," Genesis 3, 5) and only God in His justice can judge the acts and aspirations of the human heart and may not wait until the end of time to pronounce judgment but do so here and now.

"Few men have done worse things than I, and no one ever said about his person what I will say about myself" (I, 1153). The literary self-revelation competes with Christian confession in being unreserved and "saying it all" and obliges the reader to listen to things he may not care to hear (I, 21). But that reader himself is to pronounce judgment now on Jean-Jacques's guilt or innocence, though he is to suspend that judgment until he has learned the entire story and thus the entire truth (I, 175). For Rousseau, however, the truth of his life story is manifest and complete at every moment; let them call him to judgment whenever they please. This judgment to which Rousseau appeals with the "book of his life" to obtain his acquittal is an ironic inversion of the biblical "Last Judgment!" For from now on, the reader as the representative of all of humanity ("the countless host of my fellowmen," p. 3) is to be sovereign judge while God is sent to the witness stand: "I have unveiled my inmost self as you have seen it." All the places in this apocalyptic scene are reassigned: the community which was the witness before which Augustine had made his "confessio peccati et laudis" is elevated to highest judge; the omniscient god and creator demoted to informed witness in the forum of mankind. The ledger on mankind kept at God's throne can be dispensed with for there is Rousseau's;[15] acquittal is not expected from an act of grace but from an appeal to the solidarity of all men.[16] Rousseau's self-judgment draws mankind into his trial so that it may become its own judge and sit in judgment on its problematic history in this paradigmatic case.

In the next great autobiography, no trace of Rousseau's moral tribunal can be found. Goethe's *Poetry and Truth* detaches autobiography from all moral problematics and places his self-revelation under a new principle which permits him to view the historical and social world as *material* or *store* for the education of a unique personality.[17] Even for this step in the history of autobiography, the Augustinian counterposition can be identified through a predicate of God's identity which Rousseau, stopping this side of the threshold of aesthetic autonomy, had not yet touched: "An quisquam se faciendi erit artifex?" (could any man be his own maker? I, vi). Since only God as the creator of all things can be conceived of as His own origin, the question Augustine asks is so absurd as to be its own negation. But it does anticipate the highest claim of the autonomous individual which is that, being a genius, it can, like god, create out of itself and "turn life itself into a work of art" in the process. Although this formulation may more properly apply to the one-sided development of aesthetic education in the nineteenth century than to *Dichtung und Wahrheit*, Goethe's autobiography nonetheless shows what price had to be paid for the aesthetic autonomy of the individual. For to omit Rousseau's moral tribunal from the portrayal of the self involved an implicit aestheticization, as Goethe's meditation on the demonic shows.

The mysterious power which, "if it be not opposed to the moral order of the world nevertheless does often . . . cross it" and whose awesome manifestation Goethe sees on the great stage of world history and often in one of its actors, also seems to work its will in the "littleness of my own life,"[18] though here it is beneficial rather than fear inspiring. Presumed to be that mysterious dispensation from which flow the accidental and inadequate in his life, the demonic seems concerned that all that happens to him should ultimately turn to the good. It thus confirms for his private path of salvation that curious but prodigious dictum with which Goethe appropriated a (cryptic) divine predicate for the aesthetic experience of the self: "Nemo contra deum nisi deus ipse" (no one should oppose God unless he be a god himself).[19]

B. Interaction Patterns of Identification with the Hero

Preliminary remarks

In its original version, the following study was discussed at the sixth colloquium of *Poetik und Hermeneutik* in 1972. The results prompted me to make a revision[1] which led to an improved frame for my suggestion that the interaction patterns of identification with the hero be studied on five levels of aesthetic experience. The most important addition was the definition of the boundaries of that frame. Identification is not inherently an aesthetic phenomenon, nor is the hero something only poiesis creates. Given the aesthetic attitude, heroic, religious, or ethical models can provide cathartic pleasure, which then becomes the "incentive bonus" that makes it possible to more effectively convey patterns of behavior to reader or spectator and to further his readiness to act when he is shown what is exemplary in human action and suffering. But the aesthetic attitude which thus disposes us to identify with the model is always in danger of aesthetically neutralizing the call for emulation or of lapsing into the mere "mechanism of imitation" (Kant). Identification in and through the aesthetic attitude is a state of balance where too much or too little distance can turn into uninterested detachment from the portrayed figure, or lead to an emotional fusion with it.

We are thus faced with the problem of defining this state of balance more closely both in its aesthetic constitution and as a "phase in a process of distancing."[2] For while the aesthetic attitude that results from the reception of a tragedy or a novel may fulfill itself in the admiration of a literary figure, it is also true that in the course of reception, the spectator or reader passes through a sequence of attitudes. Astonishment, admiration, being shaken or touched, sympathetic tears and laughter, or estrangement constitute the scale of such primary levels of aesthetic experience which the performance or the reading of a text brings with it. The spectator or reader may enter into these states but also disengage himself at any moment, take up the attitude of aesthetic reflection, and start in on his own interpretation which presupposes a further, retrospective or prospective, distancing. The relation between primary aesthetic experience and secondary aesthetic reflection thus takes us back again to the fundamental distinction between understanding and cognition, reception and interpretation.

Identification with the hero does not exhaust the possibilities of aesthetic identification. Identification with what is being portrayed may occur through other relevant figures or through a paradigmatic situation which characterizes especially a primary level of the lyrical experience. Yet even though he has long since fallen into disrepute and recently been pronounced dead once again, the literary hero is indispensable, at least for aesthetic theory. Concerning the problem of the functional relationship between the primary levels of the aesthetic experience, the interaction patterns of identification with the hero furnish an incomparable wealth of concrete material. That this material must be drawn from the past does not exhaust the historical interest in the paradigm of the hero. We will begin by discussing his significance for the history of aesthetic experience, especially since this was the point of departure of my investigation.

1. On the demarcation of the primary levels of aesthetic identification

Our retrospective look at the changes in the cathartic experience in the sphere of the Christian practice of life (chap. A7) showed us how original interaction patterns of religious experience set in heteronomously to the aesthetic canon of classical antiquity, progressively availed themselves of literary forms of expression, and thereby increasingly mediated the required moral identification at the levels of the hortatory, the edifying, the sympathetic, and the exemplary through the aesthetic attitude. As the interaction patterns thus became literary, they shed light on an entire spectrum of the social achievement of art which can no more be grasped by the formalist categories of innovation and reproduction than under the ideology-critical heading of the affirmation of existing governing interests. In the secular history of preautonomous art, the antithetical emancipatory and conservative effects of art do not exhaust the field of aesthetic experience. Between the extremes of the norm-breaking and the norm-fulfilling function, between the progressive change of horizon and the adaptation to a ruling ideology, there lies an entire range of frequently overlooked possibilities for the social effectiveness of art which can be referred to as communicative in the social sense. They include both the norm-creating (establishing, initiating, heightening, justifying) achievement of heroic art and the immense role didactic art had in the transmission, distribution, and elucidation of the knowledge of the daily praxis of life as it is passed on from one generation to the next.[3] In these processes of reception, one must distinguish between learning, i.e., the grasping of a norm by means of example, and the mechanical or unfree, i.e., norm-fulfilling following of a rule. This defines the various functions of the social effect of art which an interaction pattern can take on in the communicative process of aesthetic experience.

The communicative patterns of an aesthetically mediated identification can be typified by using the hero. They can be integrated in a heuristic model that includes the entire range of aesthetic experience, extending from cultic participation to aesthetic reflection.[4] It covers the same areas as Northrop Frye's typology of the hero, but its point of departure has nothing to do with degrees of the hero's "power of action" or modes but is based on the modalities of reception. These modalities can be articulated on five levels which can partly complement Frye's five stages on the receptive side but whose principal difference from his scale of heroes lies in the fact that no historical sequence is ascribed to my model. Frye's scale[5] includes divine being, half-god of romance, hero as leader, hero as "one of us," hero (in an ironic sense) and is intended to explain his theory of "displaced myth" according to which the archtypal myth returns in a historical displacement, is dismantled in a progressive approximation to everyday plausibility, and then pales to a transparent pattern until on a final level modern poetry in an inverse irony thematizes a return to myth. Although my five levels of reception are derived from an examination of historically attested interaction patterns, they are to be understood as a nexus of functions of the aesthetic experience which may appear side by side during a given period but which can also follow each other. Cultic participation can pass over into the associative identification of the game but also be touched off by irony and made the object of a purely aesthetic attitude. Admiring identification with a hero can be broken by compassion, sympathetic identification annulled by a cathartic freeing of the mind, aesthetic reflection undermined by an appeal to moral identification—in short, one can pass from any level of identification to any other so that our heuristic model is not to be conceived as a hierarchic sequence of steps but as a functional circle of possible primary attitudes of the aesthetic experience where the momentarily dominant identification can be described both in the phases of the reception process and in its result.[6]

In delimiting the five levels, I assigned the hero as "divine being" to cultic participation and therein differ from Frye. The aesthetic attitude would be as inappropriate to the myth of the dying god as it has come down to us in vegetation cults and later in major religions as would moral identification. On the side of reception, the myth demands the subject's surrender to the community of the cultic ritual. An aesthetic analogue to this cultic relinquishment of the self can be seen in the aesthetic experience of play, which requires that all participants renounce their subjectivity and adopt the new identity of a role in the play community. Whether it be the ceremonial of a festival, a secular ritual that originated in literary communication, or a form of sociability that derived from it—all these forms of play have in common what the religious drama of the Middle Ages reveals in its purest form: everyone participates and the vis-à-vis of work and viewer, actors and spectators, is therefore annulled. I find myself at odds with Gadamer here who wishes to see the cultic (or religious) act as a "genuine representation for the community" and this because he wants to establish a closer connection between the theatrical play as a "playful act that, of its nature, calls for an audience," and cultic play.[7] In so doing, he must ignore the fact that in both cultic and social play, the vis-à-vis of playful act and spectator is annulled. If a cultic act becomes a performance for a community, we have the beginning of a play for spectators and the cultic is no more (even social play would be disturbed by a nonparticipating spectator if it did not ignore him). If we call the assumption of a role in playful aesthetic behavior *associative identification*, the ambiguity of the imaginary becomes apparent in the fact that identification with the playing community can both attain to the pleasure of a freer existence (positive effect) or slide back into the unfreedom of collective identification with archaic rituals (negative effect).

The transition from cultic participation to associative identification can be explained through a historical threshold between religious and aesthetic experience. It has long been known and is documented in some detail how the religious play of the Middle Ages evolved from the liturgical celebration and the latter especially from the Introit of the Easter mass (from the Trope "quem queritis in sepulchro"). Rainer Warning's most recent research has now shown that between the liturgical celebration *intra muros* and the religious play *extra muros ecclesiae* there does not lie the homogenous process of a progressive secularization but a recasting which is of interest here.[8] The liturgical "drama" was not yet a "play" but a celebration. Its place is therefore on the far side of the threshold separating cultic participation and associative identification. As yet, its function is the same as that of the liturgy itself: celebration and commemoration, participation in the story of salvation, not its representation.[9] The step toward the associative identification of the biblical play is taken in the twelfth century. The *Jeu d'Adam* (1174) is no longer a celebration but the representation of a biblical event; the characters are no longer acolytes but participants in a play with which the spectators as people involved in what is set forth are to associate themselves. The stage directions for the *Jeu d'Adam* allow no doubt about this; the progress of the devil across the square in front of the church ("discursus diaboli per plateam") is a "path through the people" (*discursus per populum*) which ostentatiously implicates the gathered faithful in Adam's temptation and its consequences.[10]

But the vernacular play does more than move the sacred action from the *intra muros ecclesiae*, as Warning showed. As "mass on the marketplace," it generated its own ritual forms which could diverge from orthodox doctrine and ultimately even go against it. The vernacular tradition which begins here returns its rightful place to the devil as God's dualistic antagonist. In the Easter play, the arisen Christ can take on aspects of the reborn god of spring. The climax of this heteronomous development is the extravagant representation of the torments of Christ's crucifixion; in their drastic depiction, aspects of an archaic scapegoat ritual can hardly be overlooked. Warning explains this process as a remythicizing of the history of salvation where a dualistic and pagan popular piety expresses itself as protest against the monotheistic dogmatism of nominalist theology. His thesis is supported by previously unknown documents which show this regression of Christian plays to the collective identification with archaic rituals and make understandable for the first time why the performance of passion plays in the late Middle Ages was officially banned.[11]

Like Frye, one can start with the Aristotelian division of characters as one delimits the other four levels of primary aesthetic identification. According to Aristotle's scheme (*Poetics* 1148a), characters in poetry can be shown as either "better" or "worse" or "on the same level" as the rest of us. The fundamental distinction between *admiring* and *sympathetic* identification (which Max Kommerell discovered at a turning point in the reception of Aristotle, namely Lessing's critique of Corneille's aesthetic theory) corresponds with this contrast between "better" and "on the same level."[12] What was involved here was a moral reinterpretation of tragic pleasure whose goal in Corneille and Lessing is not the same. Corneille starts off with the spectator's own fear which is to be purged by way of the admiration he feels for heroes and martyrs who are perfect even in their suffering and which is to turn into the emulation of the virtue portrayed. Lessing, on the other hand, starts off with the pity for the other that results from empathy. The spectator is to identify with an imperfect hero of average quality through which process he will come to understand human situations and be roused to make moral decisions. What results is the fundamental antithesis of two primary aesthetic attitudes which can be found in the interaction patterns of all periods of the literary tradition: "Admiration is an affect which creates distance, pity one that annulls it. For I admire what is no longer possible for me, what transcends what I am."[13]

There is an alternative to admiring and sympathetic identification, and that is the possibility of making conscious the hiatus between aesthetic identification and moral praxis; for this hiatus disappears in the admiration we feel for a hero because his perfection is being demonstrated to us. It disappears as well in the empathetic pity for his situation which results from solidarization. The specific achievement of cathartic identification in the narrower sense of the classical interpretation is that although the spectator is also put into the situation of the suffering or beset hero, this is now done with the intent of liberating his heart and mind by tragic shock or comic relief so that he may form a judgment and act on whatever insight he has gained, and do this in free reflection, without didactic pressure or the suggestions of the imagination. This large demand has not prevented cathartic identification from causing the spectator to succumb to the magic power of the imagination, nor has it kept him from losing himself in a merely pleasurable identification with what is being presented, from having a pitiless ritual of laughter drown out the laughter of insight, from having aesthetic reflection immure itself in an objectification of morality. This ever threatening turn is counteracted by procedures that break through the spell of the imaginary and the self-sufficient aesthetic attitude by seemingly initiating but then refusing or ironizing the identification the spectator desires or expects. If I assign the negation of expectable identification patterns to a level of identification and speak of *ironic identification*, I must justify this paradoxical designation and lay claim to the right of using language that is itself ironic. In the spectrum of the social functions of the aesthetic experience, the level of ironic identification constitutes the norm-breaking interaction pattern par excellence. That even the negativity of ironic identification patterns can miss its objective and result in deficient aesthetic attitudes such as irritation, boredom, disgust, or indifference confirms the fundamental ambivalence that is a characteristic of all aesthetic experience, given its dependence on the imaginary. The accompanying table (which summarizes not only what has been established up to this point but also the results of the following historical explanation of the five levels of aesthetic identification) makes note of this ambivalence by assigning key terms to progressive and regressive behavioral norms.

I am perfectly aware of the fact that this model is provisional and that it has the specific weakness of lacking the foundation that a theory of the emotions would give it. But I hope that it will at least make clear the research interest in this aspect of the aesthetic experience and that, being a result of investigations in the history of literature, it may serve as a stimulus to further work by neighboring and interested disciplines. There can be no question that this entire field has been neglected and that the discrediting of aesthetic pleasure and of the hero who has been banished from modern literature has been at least a contributing cause. The interest literary scholarship has shown in the theory of affects of rhetoric and the poetological tradition has been almost wholly historical. Between the historically investigated "classical feelings" and the modern psychology of the emotions, there is a gap which even psychoanalysis has not bridged, particularly since the practitioners of that discipline feel that the problem of identification has been only inadequately solved and the question of identification under conditions of the aesthetic attitude barely touched upon. In the psychology of literature, the analysis of production is dominant, the theory of literary reception still in its beginnings. The fundamental approaches and interpretative models of Simon Lesser and Norman Holland are oriented more toward the psychic disposition of the reader and the forms of his fantasy in the reception process than they are interested in the communicative achievement and the interaction patterns of aesthetic experience.[14] It seems to me that empirical research in the psychology of literature has paid too little attention to them. Linguistic pragmatics and communications theory have hardly concerned themselves with the question involving the emotional conditions of fictional interaction patterns. In Karlheinz Stierle's theory of speech acts, which proved so fertile in dealing with the fusion of the horizons of fiction and pragmatic experience, one misses the level of the naive reception of fictional texts.[15] And a modern theory of "communicative action games" such as Siegfried J. Schmidt's continues to be exclusively interested in the reflective level of "aesthetic communication" and has use for aesthetic pleasure only if it comes from the recognition of the polysemy of an aesthetic text. It also denies that any of the primary identifications of my model refer to legitimate aesthetic experiences.[16]

Interaction Patterns of Identification with the Hero

Modality of Identification	Reference	Receptive Disposition	Norms of Behavior or Attitude (+ = progressive) (− = regressive)
associative	game/competition (celebration)	placing oneself into roles of all other participants	+ pleasure of free existence (pure sociability) − permitted excess (regression into archaic rituals)
admiring	the perfect hero (saint, sage)	admiration	+ *aemulatio* (emulation) − *imitatio* (imitation) + exemplariness − edification/entertainment by the extraordinary (need for escape)
sympathetic	the imperfect hero	compassion	+ moral interest (readiness to act) − sentimentality (enjoyment of pain) + solidarity for specific action − self-confirmation (tranquilization)
cathartic	the suffering hero	tragic emotion/liberation of heart and mind	+ disinterested interest/free reflection)
	the beset hero	sympathetic laughter/comic relief for heart and mind	− fascination (bewitchment) + free moral judgment − mocking laughter (ritual of laughter)
ironic	the vanished or anti-hero	alienation (provocation)	+ responding creativity − solipsism + refinement of perception − cultivated boredom + critical reflection − indifference

I hope to have dealt with Schmidt's criticism of a shortcoming in my earlier version, which did not adequately distinguish between identification and the added element which is the aesthetic attitude.[17] But I gladly avail myself of this opportunity to again make clear that in my view also, all aesthetic experience, including primary levels such as admiration or pity, demand an act of distancing. To that extent I fully agree with Wellershoff when he writes: "The reader who is being affected by a text wants to recognize himself and yet be able to make distinctions, which means he wants scope for alternatives. And this is guaranteed for the text is fictional; ending as it does on its last page, its reality can be dismissed."[18] In my opinion, this formulation is perfectly consonant with my definition of aesthetic pleasure as "enjoyment of the self in and through the enjoymnet of what is other." For neither mere absorption in an emotion nor the wholly detached reflection about it, but only the to-and-fro movement, the ever renewed disengagement of the self from a fictional experience, the testing of oneself against the portrayed fate of another, makes up the distinctive pleasure in the state of suspension of aesthetic identification. As long as "aesthetic communication" exists for Schmidt only beyond the emotional and is limited to a categorial frame of experience of self, experience of meaning, and experience of the work—where it is not by chance that the intersubjective correlate is absent—Schmidt misses the distancing which never breaks its connection with the offer of emotional identification.[19]

Wellershoff's formulation of the intersubjective correlate, the experience of self through the experience of the other, permits the justification of what is today so disreputable an undertaking, the attempt to show that the allegedly defunct hero is in fact an indispensable paradigm of aesthetic experience: "I distinguish between myself and the character and in this distinction, I live my possibilities through him."[20] Identification with the hero as an element in aesthetic theory was discredited in part because Freud's essay "Writers and Daydreaming" (1908) created the impression that "His Majesty the Ego," whom all literary figures do no more than confirm as the hero of his own daydreams, exhausted the psychoanalytic interest in the paradigm of the hero. What was overlooked was that this short essay with its turn from a production aesthetic to a reception aesthetic problematics already advances a new explanation for the fascination of popular fiction, and also contains the beginnings of a hermeneutics of the experience of great poetry which has hardly been developed.[21]

First, there is the insight into the function that shocklike recognition and rediscovery have for aesthetic experience, a matter which was already discussed in connection with the related positions of Proust and Freud.[22] The psychoanalytic explanation of aesthetic pleasure as "the release of still greater pleasure from deeper psychical sources" and the blissful return of the repressed or forgotten makes clear the one-sidedness of those aesthetic theories for which all experience of art is to be measured by the categories of innovation: the excitement of a constantly renewed form. The break between work and tradition, the negation of an objectively binding meaning, and the opposition of art to social reality.[23]

Second, there is also the possibility of viewing Freud's theory that aesthetic pleasure comes from the shocklike experience of recognition as a precondition for a theory of aesthetic sublimation, in which sublimation is understood as a process leading the subject to new insights insofar as he appropriates in self-enjoyment what is alien to him and expands his own experience through the otherness of the hero. Paul Ricoeur has already postulated that this sublation of the opposition between regression and sublimation can derive from both productive and receptive activity and that it is in this fact that the distinctive opportunity for aesthetic experience lies.[24] But this would mean that the paradigm of the hero would then extend over the entire span from dream to art, from a solipsistic to an intersubjective, self-transcending experience: "because of their emphasis on disguise, dreams look more to the past, to childhood. But in works of art the emphasis is on disclosure; thus works of art tend to be prospective symbols of one's personal synthesis and of man's future and not merely a regressive symptom of the artist's unresolved conflicts. The same emphasis upon disclosure is the reason our pleasure as viewers of art is not the simple revival, even accompanied by an incentive bonus, of our own conflicts, but the pleasure of sharing in the work of truth that comes about through the hero."[25]

Ricoeur's elaboration of Freud's theory of the aesthetic experience gives me the opportunity to call attention to an as yet unresolved problem in my undertaking. The boundary between everyday and aesthetic experience does not distinguish definitively between the hero of the daydream and the hero in the work of art. The process of identification with an ideal model which one wishes to become does not always attain a personal synthesis. It can also slip back into the fantasy the daydreamer always entertained about himself. The switch of aesthetic experience from the appropriation of what is other to the confirmation of one's own desires and expectations is something we encountered time and again in the demarcation of interaction patterns. Can the shifts from upward-looking admiration to mere marveling at the extraordinary, from free emulation to unfree imitation, from a compassion that will act to the sentimental enjoyment of pain, from sympathetic to aggressive mocking laughter and other forms of regression—can all these be explained by psychoanalytic theories of ambivalence? Do the progressive interaction patterns as forms of subject formation according to the model another offers correspond to Freud's concept of identification with the father ("to become and to be like him"), and do the regressive interaction patterns as substitutes for an annulled object choice correspond to his concept of the choice of the father as an object ("what one wants to have") such that the ambivalence of identification, which can be the expression of tenderness and simultaneously the desire for removal, becomes manifest when the free state of suspension of the aesthetic attitude is lost?[26]

I prefer leaving the answer to these questions to more competent disciplines and simply point out that the third possibility which Freud discusses in chap. VII of "Group Psychology and the Analysis of the Ego"—namely, identification based upon the possibility or desire of putting oneself in the same situation"—might well be the most likely explanation for a primary level of the lyrical experience. Freud's example is the desire of the girls in a boarding school to also have a secret love affair like one of their fellow students who is happy but plagued by jealousy. "One ego has perceived a significant analogy with another upon one point" and accepts, "under the influence of a sense of guilt . . . the suffering involved in it."[27] Identification here is not with a person (who may even be unloved) but comes from the readiness to put oneself in the same situation and has its analogue in the reception of lyric poetry; here also, what is being looked for is not the identity of the person but a significant analogy through a lyrical persona that stakes its identity in boundary experiences of daily life.[28] Aesthetic sublimation would then lie in the movement by which the receiving subject rises beyond its emotional identification with the concrete, often incidental situation to the pleasurable recognition of that "universal analogy" which the lyric self causes to shine forth as the meaning of its experience.[29] Aesthetic regression would then occur when the state of suspension of the lyric experience becomes one-sided; it can turn into an insufficient distance in which the receiving self takes its satisfaction in a sentimental self-enjoyment for which the experience of the other merely serves as a triggering mechanism.

In what follows, explanations of the table of interaction patterns will be primarily historical. I felt it necessary to work out the five levels of aesthetic identification separately and diachronically, by using examples from the literary tradition with which I am familiar, and only then to describe their functional connection synchronically or in reception processes with changing identification levels. For application in empirical reception protocols, the matrix of five levels may well be too narrow. It could perhaps be coordinated with Holland's model of the interaction of "fantasy content and the defensive or other management of the fantasy," which he himself considers too broad and which, in view of the shaping and reshaping of "literary affects," he feels to be in need of further differentiation.[30] But my model did prove useful in tracing the historical change in the figure of the comic hero to changing attitudes of aesthetic identification and to thereby bring out the reason for our pleasure in an aesthetic experience which even today has not been lost. The essay that has been incorporated in this volume as section C1 is based on the fundamental distinction between laughing *at* and laughing *with* the literary hero. Laughing at is derived from the comic of the counterimage, laughing with from the affirmation of the pleasure principle, and takes the analysis of the affective functions of the comic (relief, protest, solidarization) as far as the humoristic catharsis: here, in the switch from laughter *at* to laughter *with* a humoristic figure who rises above the destruction of its purposes, we reach the highest level of self-affirmation in a world that is not ideal.

By taking the perfect hero out of his ideality and placing him into awkward situations and by making his unheroic straits the object of enjoyment for the uninvolved spectator, the comic of the counterimage breaks the spell of admiring identification. As the interpretations of travesties of Vergil by Scarron, Blumauer, and Marivaux demonstrate, this pleasure can even lie in relief from the heroic seriousness of the literary legacy. But the affective potential of comic catharsis can also be articulated as a protest against the prevailing social authority and finally be transformed into solidarization with the unheroic hero so that society may be made to acknowledge hitherto suppressed aspects of human nature. The Rabelaisian comic of the grotesque, on the other hand, which comes from the affirmation and the consummation of the pleasure principle, eliminates the cognitive distance between reader and hero in a laughing sympathy; and the community of laughers that comes into existence in this fashion experiences this sympathy as the liberation of the body and the triumph over fear and all the powers of an established order. Here, we are dealing with an outstanding interaction pattern of associative identification: the collective subject of the laughter, the group of revelers Rabelais constantly addresses and portrays, coopts the outsider and constitutes in the pleasurable inversion of all the agencies of social reason the insularity of the exceptional state that defines the festive occasion. The response to the humors, finally, where human nature presents itself in quirkish one-sidedness and harmless weakness, is a sympathetically attenuated variation of the laughter *at*: Mr. Pickwick, as a likeable "average man," is first placed on the path of a heroic supergreatness and then laughed at; on his picaresque road in his struggle against the disfavor and injustice of reality, he achieves the curious dignity of humor Freud described, so that the comic of innocence at which he smiles exacts a growing admiration from the reader. The humoristic hero reconquers for admiring identification that terrain from which the laughter at the downgraded hero had banished it.

2. Historical explanation of the interaction patterns

a) Associative identification

By associative identification, we mean an aesthetic behavior that realizes itself most clearly in assuming a role in the closed, imaginary world of a play action. It should be noted that play action here is not a representation for spectators, since the associative identification of the players does away with the dichotomy of players and viewers, actors and spectators. This determination can be described as the constitutive negativity of play: As antithesis to the praxis of life, it interrupts the homogeneous experience of time and space where it sets against the world of daily purposes and needs a heterogeneous world of play in which the participants observe freely acknowledged rules and thereby realize a more perfect order.[31] The negation of the praxis of life by the imaginary world of play, the festive occasion, and, finally, the spectacle itself does not, however, preclude a turning back from aesthetic to practical experience. The insular disconnectedness of the spectacle resembles the play action of the festival which, according to Helmut Kuhn, potentially contains art within itself in that it is marked by a "twofold extension into life, and this by a tendency toward periodic repetition and through ceremonial which is an emanation that pervades daily life and shapes mores."[32]

What is being called "emanation" here can be even more plausibly explained by the training and socializing function of play. If the aesthetic attitude required in play can open up to communicative experience, this is not due to any "aura of festiveness" but a result of the fact that, like any playing child, the player must learn to accept rules, to observe them, and thereby to understand them. But that also requires a readiness on his part to put himself into another's role, indeed even "to take the attitude of everyone else involved in that game."[33] And since the player can be both judge and one side when the roles are assigned, participation in the play action brings the recognition of the other's role and the other's side and thus leads to the acknowledgment and comprehension of the inherent justice of play.[34]

What was described here as associative identification in aesthetic behavior is a central element in George H. Mead's social psychology. The individual cannot become a subject for himself except "to the extent he first becomes an object for himself," to the extent he experiences himself in the assumption and acknowledgment of roles from the perspective of a social group of this world, sees himself in the relativity of his role (persona), and develops his identity.[35] The society-creating function of the associative identification of play thus lies in the circumstance that the player can develop his identity to the degree that in play he adopts attitudes and learns modes of communication which, as expectations of others' actions, orient social life.

This theory can be illustrated by a famous historical example of the transposition of literature into social praxis. In the European tradition, the emancipation and sublimation of sexual love can hardly be envisaged without the literary ceremonial of medieval courtly service. With it began the playful training in the social norms of the love ethic which was then passed on by those classes that set the tone at a given moment and which is still recognizable today in "language games" such as flirting, love declarations, rejection, reward, termination. In the originally norm-setting troubadour poetry, lyric forms such as the canzona or alba, which confined themselves to the intimate tie between individual lover and his mistress, were framed by genres of a more public character such as tenson and partimen (poems of dilemmatic dispute) and the ceremonial of the *courts d'amour*. From the situations and forms of communication of courtly love, the latter genre developed playful legal proceedings and trials which incorporated the role of the lonely, suffering, and loving singer vis-à-vis his uniquely admired mistress associatively in a social scene.[36]

What makes play attractive, namely, the chance it offers to engage in a form of action according to established roles, seems to remain potent even when the aesthetic object does not call for associative identification but only for the role of observer. This is testified to by examples in which the reader himself takes the step from individual to associative identification, exchanges his passive reader's role for active participation in a social ceremonial, and thus returns to the work of art the status of a game. This is instructively shown in the history of the reception of what was probably the most influential seventeenth-century novel, *Astrée* by Honoré d'Urfé.[37] This enormous pastoral novel first produced an entire register of social forms of reception among what was initially an aristocratic audience. The response extended from modish insignia and the writing of love letters, question and answer games, masquerades of shepherds and sheperdesses, and casuistic discussion to the founding of an "Académie des parfaits amants." Such an academy was established by twenty-nine persons of the "plus illustres maisons de la Germanie" from which a letter to the author, Honoré d'Urfé, has survived. It testifies to the liberating function of the play action and its effect on the praxis of social life when the participants express the hope that the literary roles from the *Astrée* had been assumed "pour pouvoir ci-apres tant plus doucement, et avec cette mesme liberté, que nous voyons comme au vieux siècle d'or, reluire en la vie" (in order to shine in life more gently and with the same freedom which was enjoyed in the Golden Age).[38] The purpose of this letter is to involve the author of the *Astrée* himself in the play action. The twenty-nine signers (who have interpreted the novel as a code of rules for their game and exchanged their names, titles, and clothes for those of the "gentils Bergers, brave Cavaliers, excellentes Nymphes et gratieuses Bergères") not only ask d'Urfé to continue his inimitable work in the interest of their game. They go further and request that he adopt the name of Celadon in their circle since no one among them is worthy of playing that role.

The span of the associative identification of aesthetic behavior extends from the shepherds' masquerades of the *Astrée* readers to the "Wirtschaften, Mummereyen und Balletten" of the bourgeois public to which Gottsched devoted a separate chapter in his *Critische Dichtkunst* ([1730], II, 5). Historically, it extends back to the Christian beginnings of the religious play and is present in current tendencies of the Living Theater or "happenings" which aim at "bridging the stage."[39] The purpose in both cases is to bring the viewer out of his contemplative distance. But whereas in the religious play, the faithful is associated with a community whose identity is guaranteed by the already known course of the history of salvation, the individual in the happening (which can occur anywhere) is drawn into an unforeseeable action and associated with a community that is born of chance. Being called on to participate in a common action without guaranteed meaning, he runs the risk of failure. Procedures of such "staged authenticity" furthermore harbor the danger that they will make him so uncertain that the aimed-for activation of the viewer easily degenerates into adaptive behavior.[40]

The strong inducement to cross the barrier of solitary reception and to actively participate in the social realization of a world of play can be traced back to both the desire for the festive enjoyment of a free existence and that for a festive infraction of what is permitted. One can subscribe to Kurt Badt's view and derive the understanding of art as the "celebration through praise" from the former, the association for purposes of play and conviviality which is experienced as liberation from work and purposive behavior.[41] To have fallen under the ideology-critical suspicion of accommodation does not mean that this social function of the aesthetic has become passé. For although such celebration through praise has ever been harnessed to idealize relations of domination and to transfigure their order, art always overcame its subservience, and this because it could produce solidarity with moments of a shared past which testify to the greatness and suffering in human history and which could certainly fall victim to a more evil accommodation, that of forgetting, if the communicative and simultaneously conservative power of the aesthetic experience did not counteract this.

Because of the transition to collective aesthetic behavior, the associative identification with play and conviviality is especially exposed to the fundamental ambiguity of the imaginary. The regressive movement of associative identification has been grasped in Freud's well-known definition of the festival (which makes no mention of the sublimating movement toward the enjoyment of a free existence): "A festival is a permitted, or rather an obligatory, excess, a solemn breach of a prohibition. It is not that men commit the excesses because they are feeling happy as a result of some injunction they have received. It is rather that excess is the essence of a festival; the festival feeling is produced by the liberty to do what is as a rule prohibited."[42] Augustine's warning against the collective fascination of gladiatorial games is a classic instance of this. We have already seen that even the religious play of the Middle Ages was not immune to such regressions. Through aesthetic pleasure, the enjoyment of play can liberate the public from the constraints and habits of its everyday, and it is precisely for this reason that it can be tempted unwittingly to let itself be drawn through associative identification into ritual acts which cause its initially free aesthetic attitude to turn into the servitude of collective identities.

b) Admiring identification

Admiring identification refers to the aesthetic attitude that defines itself in terms of the perfection of a model and still remains on the far side of the separation into tragic or comic effect, for the norm-setting admiration of a hero, saint, or sage does not commonly derive from either tragic emotion or comic relief. Rather, admiration demands that through its perfection, the aesthetic object transcend expectation in the direction of the ideal and therefore prompt an astonishment which "does not cease when the novelty wears off."[43] It follows that it is not the mere marveling at the extraordinary or the perfect but only the distancing act in which consciousness measures itself against the object of its astonishment that makes admiration an aesthetic affect that disposes the individual toward acknowledging and adopting models and patterns. This is also the reason the rhetorical tradition could distinguish unfree imitation (mimesis-*imitatio*) from free emulation (zelos-*aemulatio*) by using the concept of admiration: "imitation (mimesis) is an activity which copies the pattern through precise observation; emulation (zelos), however, is a striving of the soul which is moved to admiration by what appears beautiful to it."[44]

Max Scheler's well-known theory of models and leaders makes no allowance for the role aesthetic experience plays. Both historically and in social praxis, it is not just heredity (sexual choice), tradition, and faith in individuals that are constitutive for the creation and transmission of exemplary figures. Regarding faith in individuals, Scheler wrote: "We first love and hate entire, whole persons because of the total value impression they make (Gestalt). Where we love and hate, we also tend to assent or reject, follow or resist."[45] The concept of Gestalt, which is defined here as "impression of total value," obscures the fact that the "undivided whole" which inspires the affective relation to the model is not so much the indefinable individual totality of a person as it is its perfection in one dimension for which we admire it as heroic, beautiful, holy, sage, etc.[46] or reject it where we see the corresponding counternorms. That affective relation which, according to Scheler, explains why "everyone views . . . the model he adopts and follows as also being the good, the perfect, as what ought to be"[47] can be defined more precisely: it is admiration that Descartes already saw as the first of all the *passions de l'âme* because it disposes us in favor of a thing before we can tell whether it is beneficial for us ("avant que nous connaissions aucunement si cet objet nous est convenable ou s'il ne l'est pas").[48] Whether to esteem or despise ("estime et mépris, vénération et dédain")—a decision from which, according to Descartes, self-esteem and self-contempt follow— is determined by something secondary, a later understanding about the good or harmful effect the occasioning object has on us. This classical definition of admiration clearly shows that it is the aesthetic evidence of the perfect and its power to exceed all expectation that touches off the aesthetic affect of admiration for a model, heightens its distinctive quality, and makes tempting its adoption as a pattern of behavior. Historically, the eminently social function of aesthetically mediated identification always emerges where a taste and trend assert themselves, where more profound changes in private or social behavior are initiated by recognizable literary interaction patterns, and where personal models symbolize and further the formation and consolidation of group identities. In Rousseau's *Nouvelle Héloïse*, for example, there is testimony that those among the young who had earlier looked for prestige as drinkers and toughs now wanted to be seen as lovers.[49] The famous "Werther fever" in Germany was later matched in France by the effect of Chateaubriand's *René*, which Sainte-Beuve described as a "kind of moral disease of the imagination" afflicting entire generations of the young in the early nineteenth century. "Such was the magical effect of those small masterpieces which came at just the right moment: they are like a mirror in which everyone recognizes himself and learns what to call himself, as it were. Without that, people would have vaguely and for long attempted to discover who they were and not have understood themselves. But suddenly one sees oneself in another, in the great artist of the generation one belongs to, and exclaims, 'that's me, that's certainly me!'"[50]

Aesthetically mediated identification can do more than give a "name" to a latent need such as *Weltschmerz* (ennui) in this case, and it can do more than give it an admirable form as a complex behavioral pattern. Admiring identification is also superior to reflective action that is governed by the maxims of everyday social praxis in the sense that it condenses historical experience in the growing sequence of personal models and transmits them from one generation to the next.[51] In the constitution of the collective memory of religious groups or social classes, the series of models has an often underestimated import.[52] In genealogies, it serves the glorification, preservation, and transmittal of the ancestors' illustrious deeds. In religious communities, it inspires the emulation of the heroes of the faith and martyrs. In galleries of resplendent figures, from popular heroes such as the Nine Worthies[53] to the large numbers of famous sinners, penitents, and blessed (by which Dante in the gigantic creation of a canon represented classical, Christian, and contemporary history through figures and elevated them to a permanent memorial), it brings to mind the past of all mankind. And it legitimates even the largest-scale revolutionary actions if the zero hour of the new beginning of history is followed by a phase of consolidation of the revolutionary movement which, by way of its own martyrs, early pioneers, and distant models, now proceeds to a step-by-step appropriation of the previously negated past as an "inheritance" which rightfully belongs to it. The ideological advocacy of socialist society's claim to the German cultural legacy has renewed this paradigm in our time. The recourse of the revolutionaries of 1789 to models of the Roman republic is probably the most famous historical example. In his *Sentimental Education*, Flaubert cast an ironic light on the repetition of this paradigm by the 1848 revolutionaries: "And as each person took his cue from a model, one copying Saint-Just, another Danton, a third Marat, he [Sénécal] tried to resemble Blanqui who was imitating Robespierre" (III, i). It is in this very phenomenon that Marx saw the cause of their failure and therefore demanded that the social revolution of the nineteenth century take "its poetry not from the past but only from the future." From the point of view of ethical rigorism, the revolution of the future cannot be at one with any model and requires no legitimation through a heroic past. Its "poetry" is the poetry of the zero hour of the new society as it creates itself *ex nihilo*: "Earlier revolutions have needed world-historical reminiscences to deaden their awareness of their own content. In order to arrive at its own content, the revolution of the 19th century must let the dead bury their dead."[54]

As an example of the historical change of one figuration of heroic models, we may mention the rise of the courtly novel around 1150. The presence of two archtypical forms of admiring identification can be demonstrated in this event in the history of literature. The new heroes of King Arthur's Round Table (Erec, Yvain, Gawain, Lancelot, and Perceval) are entering into competition with the old paladins of the Charlemagne legend (Roland, Olivier, Guillaume). The new heroic type is the courtly knight-adventurer who sets out alone, overcomes the dangers of a magic world, thereby brings "joy" to the courtly society around King Arthur, and wins the beloved lady for himself. Around the middle of the twelfth century, this new hero began to become more popular with the crusader knight. The crusader is the outstanding fighter of his army who dies heroically as he achieves victory over the heathens, is therefore admitted to the Christian paradise, and leaves behind an example to be emulated.[55] Admiration for the older type which bears Roland's stamp is inspired by a bravery and utter readiness for sacrifice which transcends all expectation.[56] Here, admiring identification unites author, singer (*jongleur*), and the public in the collective remembrance of a norm-setting earlier time of national history, the heroic age of Charlemagne. At the correlative levels of the accidents of adventure and the testing of love, admiration for the later heroic type as defined by Chretien's Arthurian romances is nourished by the extraordinary with a fairy-tale flavor. In its identification with the admired hero, the (reading) public here turns its back on the realities of the everyday and of history because it wants to satisfy a need for escape in the perfection of the imaginary. At the same time, the reader is initiated into the norms of perfect love through which the man with a courtly education is to set himself apart from the ordinary mortal.[57] The two heroic types that survived the Middle Ages thus satisfied a twofold need of admiring identification: the epic or legendary hero the need for collective remembrance of the glorification of the historical deed that heightens everyday reality, and the fairy-tale or novelistic hero the characteristic interest in unheard-of events which fulfills the reader's wish for rare adventure and perfect love in a wish-fulfillment world beyond everyday reality.

The fascination of the second pattern grew more intense in the twelfth century because with the material of celtic provenance, literary fiction was distinguished for the first time in medieval epic poetry from historical and legendary reality and experienced as a pleasure sui generis. John of Salisbury testifies to this in a philippic that addresses itself to the victorious procession of Arthurian romance. His critique of the pleasure the monks take in their reading traces the fascination of the stories around Arthur, Gawain, and Tristan (which were clearly popular in monasteries as well) to the affect of admiration for the perfect hero ("aliquis vir prudens, decorus, fortis, amabilis et per omnia gratiosus," some man, prudent, proper, brave, lovable, and gracious in all things) which the trials and tribulations of the adventure (pressurae vel injuriae eidem crudeliter irrogatae, oppressions, injuries, or cruel afflictions to the same) usually transform into mawkishness and even tearfulness. But such emotions are neither meritorious nor conducive to salvation.[58] In this early account of the pleasures that may be found in the imaginary events of an adventure story, the degenerate form of admiring identification already becomes palpable. It sets in with regularity when the originally norm-setting meaning of the experience of the hero (in the Middle Ages: adventure as the path of courtly education) pales, and the reader finds his satisfaction in the mere marveling at the adventure and the pleasure he takes in the erotic wish fulfillment of *his* hero. The history of the novel shows this debasement in the continual degeneration of admiring identification into that self-affirmation which popular fiction with its well-known mechanisms foments.

Admiration as aesthetic affect thus requires an attitude that must occupy a middle ground between inadequate and excessive distance, an attitude that has clearly become quite precarious in the age of the mass media. The "dream factory" which satisfies the demand for a "better world" sublates the cognitive distance of admiration, and the flooding of the viewer with stimuli can set off defensive strategies of unimpressionableness which cut off all aesthetic communication.[59] The inviolability of the spectator which has thus been provoked has its objective correlate in the phenomenon of the modern superhero who, in his perfect apathy, has already left the tradition of the heroic far behind and can therefore no longer be admired but at most merely marveled at.

c) Sympathetic identification

By sympathetic identification, we refer to the aesthetic affect of projecting oneself into the alien self, a process which eliminates the admiring distance and can inspire feelings in the spectator or reader that will lead him to a solidarization with the suffering hero. Aesthetic experience shows time and again how admiration and compassion follow each other. The admired model of a hero may appear as unattainably perfect or sink so low that it becomes nothing more than the object or spur of daydreams. The new norm of an imperfect, more "daily" hero in whom the spectator or reader can recognize the scope of his own possibilities and with whom he can solidarize as a being of the same "stuff and substance"[60] as himself can be set against the hero who has moved out of reach or degenerated to a frozen cliché.

In all periods of the history of literature, there are examples of this sequential relationship of admiring and sympathetic identification. With the blossoming in the twelfth century of the genre of the miracle in the romance literatures, the unknown sinner on whom the miracle is performed supplants the legendary hero who was a well-known saint.[61] The perfection of the saint in whose vita virtue is incarnate and where the confirming miracle demonstrates God's power also confronts the Christian viewer with the problem that although he is being called on to emulate this figure, he may hardly dare hope that he will ever attain to the perfect norm of the saint.[62] It is understandable, therefore, that over against a perfection that is out of reach, that is unchangeable, and that stands above fear and pity, there should be set up an attainable *imitabile* at this time. It was the imperfect, ordinary object of the miracle through whose exemplary conversion God's saving power—often mediated through Mary's compassion—could manifest itself. During the same period, we find an early model of the "average hero" in a moral satire on estates and occupations, Etienne de Fougère's *Livre des manières* (around 1170); with the comment that "many another woman of low birth still among us" lives like her, the simple model of a "Marguerite" is held up against the reprehensible idealized images of high courtly love.[63] The repudiation of the much and unquestioningly admired ideal images of feudal knighthood and its heroic period is nowhere testified to more impressively than in the rhymed chronicle of the third crusade by Ambroise. As he recounts the siege of Acre, the author presents an extended comparison which measures the suffering of the crusaders against the exploits of the heroes of the entire epic tradition. Compared with the woes of the anonymous fighters at the gates of Acre, what do the great names of the famous line from Alexander through Pippin and Charlemagne down to Arthur and their much-sung individual exploits amount to, considering that there is no telling what things about them are true, what invention. That is the tacit question his heroes' gallery suggests:

> Mais de ço que tantes genz virent
> E qu'il meismes le soffrirent,
> Cil de l'ost d'Acre, les meschiefs
> Qu'il orent es cuers e es chiefs
> Des granz chalors, des granz freidures,
> Des enfermetez, des enjures,
> Ço vo puis jo por veir conter.[64]

(But of what so many saw and what they had to suffer, the men of the army outside Acre, of the misery in their hearts and on their faces, of great heat and great cold, of diseases and injustices, I can tell you the unvarnished truth.)

But let us look at some more recent examples. During the century of the Enlightenment, admiration and compassion as the principal affects of the aesthetic effect are at the center of the new dramaturgy with which Diderot and Lessing initiated the turn of the bourgeois stage as a "moral institution" away from the prevailing aesthetic doctrine of French classicism. "The compassionate human being is the best human being, the most disposed to all social virtures, to all forms of magnanimity. So the author who makes us compassionate also makes us better and more virtuous."[65] Lessing's famous thesis also lies behind Diderot's demand that the world of the stage be returned from its unreal sublimity to the solid basis of daily reality and that equality be established between the bourgeois spectator and a hero of his kind. "The admired hero is the subject of the epic; the pitied one the subject of the Trauerspiel."[66] To this allocation, there already corresponded at this time the beginning decline of the epic which still occupied the highest rank in the classical hierarchy of genres.

Admiration can be an intermittent "point of rest" in bourgeois drama where "the spectator can recover sufficiently to sustain his compassion."[67] According to Lessing, admiration by itself is less likely to change the spectator's feelings because it can only take him to an emulating identification with the hero if he is capable of "understanding a good quality when it is presented to him." Pity, on the other hand, achieves identification more directly: it "improves without our having to contribute anything; it improves both the man of sense and the dunce."[68]

According to Diderot, the new stage, which is to make the spectator feel sympathetic identification with persons of his life world, does not simply call for the elimination of admiring distance from the perfect hero and more highly placed persons. A precondition of admiring identification is that a new, middle genre, the drama or *genre serieux*, overcome the classical opposition of tragedy and comedy and that the classical world of timeless characters be replaced by "circumstances," i.e., persons in the circumstances of their life and occupations.[69] But how can an average hero like Diderot's *père de famille* who must no longer be a model of heroic perfection and be neither tragic nor comic arouse the interest of the spectator in a dramatic action from which Diderot would exclude all contrasting characters such as Lillo's and Moore's villains and angels of innocence? This is the point at which we notice a birfucation in the development of bourgeois drama.

Diderot hoped that the pathetic quality of the situation would inspire both an aesthetic and a moral interest and raise the bourgeois "hero" from the private and merely personal to the level of exemplary generality. Lessing, on the other hand, already spoke of the "development of his character" in his critique of the *Fils naturel* and thus announced a principle of the coming period of German classicism, the subjective hero who attempts to maintain his individuality amid all that befalls him.[70] A threshold of individuation in the history of aesthetic experience defines itself here and along with it, the problem of aesthetic identification poses itself in a new form. The hero of the older tradition had always become the object of admiring or sympathetic identification because there was something general which transcended his individual biography: the perfection of a quality or the exemplary nature of his suffering. But how could the modern "hero" be simultaneously the subject of an individual story and exemplary, unique personality, ideal image of human perfection, singular individual, and generalizable model? It may well be that this dilemma was nowhere grasped with more intelligence and resolved with greater rigor than in *Emile*'s educational program. *Robinson Crusoe* is the only novel Rousseau permits him to read, for all the effort of an enlightened education would go to waste, were Emile to wish just once "to be someone other than he is" ("qu'il aime mieux être un autre que lui").[71]

Since Diderot, Lessing, and Rousseau, the problem of the normativeness and individuality of the bourgeois hero has given rise to a variety of solutions with reference to which narrative prose in the period after the end of classical individualism could be interpreted and put into perspective. In Balzac's *Comédie humaine*, the modern French novel realized Diderot's program of "circumstances" by a comprehensive *histoire des moeurs*, critically elaborated the tension between individual and society in the ironically seen, imperfect "heroes" of Stendhal and Flaubert, and turned sympathetic identification into highly effective models and patterns of legitimation in the popular novel of Eugene Sue, the two Dumas, Ernest Feydeau, and others.[72]

In the much maligned Entwichlungsroman, the German novel during this period not only realized the program of aesthetic education as the society-negating experience of the self-sufficient individuality. It also found in Hegel's prognoses of an "objective humor" the principle of poetic realism which made possible a reconciliation of subjective reflection and individual surrender to a changed social reality, as Wolfgang Preisendanz has shown.[73] Whereas the novel of "objective humor" took seriously the critical demand to confront the classical individuality with the "prosaic conditions of the world," the degenerate forms of the *Bildungsroman* turned into a cult of "great individuals." Sympathetic identification with the bourgeois hero thus became reverence for a "historical greatness" which was out of reach of all imitation or emulation.

The mythicizing of the hero into the "great individual" in the imaginary museum of historicism on the one hand, and his impressment in the services of the ideological interests of established bourgeois society on the other are two, typically nineteenth-century instances of regressive sympathetic identification. It is instructive in this context to compare Flaubert's *Madame Bovary* and its criticism of the system with Dumas's system-conforming *Dame aux Camelias*. Hans-Jörg Neuschäfer has pointed to a set of rules of enormous influence which informs Dumas's novel and continued to have its effects down to Eric Segal's *Love Story*. Through it, the sympathetic identification of the reader is first elicited and then made to serve the hypocritical rule of bourgeois morality.[74] The need for entertainment and escape is met by a subject that has the lure of the forbidden and illegitimate, the erotic passion of the wealthy young bourgeois Armand for the courtesan Marguerite. Because the prostitute is noble and consumptive and therefore stirs compassion, social conscience is soothed to such a degree that the fate of "ces pauvres créatures" can become a source of edification for the bourgeois reader who need not feel responsible for it. And at the end, the bourgeois will to order can feel fully vindicated. For the threatening conflict with the son who might violate the bourgeois taboo by an engagement rather than enter a permissible liaison is avoided because the father secretly engineers the renunciation of the "dame aux camelias." Both material interests and moral sympathies are now satisfied: the "honorable prostitute with bourgeois leanings" is metamorphosed into "the saintly prostitute who sacrifices herself for the bourgeoisie." The upshot is that "the interests of the bourgeoisie now sanctify what before had to be avoided at all cost, promiscuity."[75]

Escape, confirmation, and tranquilization are also norms that Flaubert's *Madame Bovary* brings into play, but at the highest level of literary achievement. In contrast to Dumas's novel, the escapist theme of forbidden love is here problematized as the pathology of an everyday "heroine" who becomes a victim of her reading even more than of her milieu. Emma Bovary's decline is a "pharamakos" story, not a confirmation but—as the proceedings instituted against Flaubert make clear—a provocation of official morality and in particular of the narrowmindedly bourgeois educational system. The conscience of the reader is all the less assuaged since it is not only Flaubert's impersonal style that makes his judgment uncertain. There is also no "positive character" (*personnage sage*) in the entire book who might condemn Flaubert's scandalous heroine, and this is what the prosecutor objected to most vehemently. The reproach of "immorality" is a novum for it is no longer based on the violation of a norm of the prevailing morality but rests wholly on the circumstances that the reader cannot identify with any character in the novel.[76] It is not only the possibility of sympathetic identification that is made more difficult for the reader because Emma Bovary's fate is ironized (he can hardly feel that the provocatively trivial "heroine" is someone like him); there is the further fact that the customary ideal measure of contrastive norms is withheld. Without suspecting it, Napoleon III's prosecutor was the first to officially register and criticize an aesthetic procedure —the ironic form of refused identification—that had not yet been canonized.

Ironically, the accusation of Flaubert anticipates an aesthetic norm which was to become eminently successful in a social order of anti-bourgeois provenance, and that is the "positive hero" of socialist realism. The aesthetic norm, which is raised to the level of dogma there, illustrates most impressively the decadent form of sympathetic identification. The "positive hero" of socialist realism should not be altogether perfect and call forth admiration; nor must he be pitiable, let alone comic. But neither must he negate the prevailing morality and thus prompt critical reflection, and even less satisfy the need for escape. Fundamentally, he is thus a modern version of the dilemma of Diderot's *père de famille* who could no longer be a perfect hero in the traditional sense nor yet a subjective one in the modern. Because of his blank positivity, he falls into that *genre ennuyeux* which, even before Voltaire's ridicule, frustrated sympathetic identification whenever the reader was not considered mature and therefore given no alternative but to affirm existing norms.

d) Cathartic identification

By cathartic identification we refer to the aesthetic attitude, already described by Aristotle, that frees the spectator from the real interests and affective entanglements of his world, and puts him into the position of the suffering and beset hero so that his mind and heart may find liberation through tragic emotion or comic relief. This definition already extended to both the tragic and the comic effect of art in classical theory[77] and could be documented by the poetics of various periods of "classicism" in the European literatures. Schiller's formulation reads as follows: "To produce and nourish in us the freedom of the mind and soul is the admirable task of comedy, just as it is tragedy's task to help recover aesthetically the freedom of mind and soul when some affect has violently destroyed it."[78]

This is the place to recall Kommerell's interpretation of Aristotelian catharsis according to which it is the goal of catharsis to liberate the mind and soul from affects because they jeopardize "a desirable composure as the condition for higher intellectual pursuits."[79] Correspondingly, German classicism also understood the hiatus between the aesthetic and the practical attitude as the condition for giving man his moral freedom through the experience of art. Aesthetic education in the sense of Schiller's idealism cannot lay down patterns of action. Rather, it must restore the capacity for freely chosen action and therefore treat its object in such a way "that it is not our reason that is referred to the rule of the will but rather our imagination that is referred to the capacity of the will."[80] Historically, it is with the cathartic identification in the emancipatory process of the aesthetic experience that the threshold of autonomy has been reached; the spectator is allowed the tragic emotion or sympathetic laughter only to the extent that he is capable of detaching himself from the immediacy of his identification and rises to judgment and reflection about what is represented.

This understanding of cathartic identification seems to preclude a search for phenomena of cathartic poetry in the Middle Ages, considering that they are a paradigmatic period of preautonomous art. And where indeed would it be found in a literary canon that knew neither the classical principle of distinct stylistic levels nor the pure forms of classical tragedy and comedy and their mutually exclusive effects? As historical poetry, the epic of the Christian Middle Ages is situated within the providential frame of the history of salvation. The death of a hero such as Roland, Olivier, or Vivien may inspire tragic emotion. But such emotion must remain episodic because on the soil of Christian faith, it cannot be an ultimate. The audience that is moved by the suffering of the hero is to admire him as a fighter for the faith and to recognize in his fate the workings of providence. Hagiography also does not aim at a cathartic identification with the suffering martyr or saint but negates all compassion in the higher interest of the *gloria passionis*.[81] André Gide's dictum that genuine tragedy is unthinkable on Christian soil is confirmed during this period at least and also seems to hold good for comic catharsis. Only the low genre of the farce which we find in all literature serves laughter exclusively. But the comic function of these farces, which Robert Guiette taught us to see anew as an antithesis to the symbolism of all higher genres,[82] is exhausted by its quality as pure *divertissement*. It lays no more claim to any truth of laughing insight than do the comic interludes in the mystery plays whose ambivalent effect can no longer be looked for in any "liberation of the heart and mind" but rather in rituals of mocking laughter, as R. Warning has shown.[83] On all higher levels of the literary canon, one finds episodic comedy, more frequently satire, occasionally irony and parody, perhaps the smile (as in the case of Lancelot, the courtly lover in extremis), but not, as far as I can see, the ultimately liberating laughter of comic catharsis.

There are nonetheless literary phenomena in the high Middle Ages which subliminally presuppose a cathartic effect among the public. In Troubadour poetry, the joy of singing can be thematized in such a way that the poet's poietic activity produces his catharsis. We have already mentioned the cathartic effect of the chanson de geste;[84] if, according to Jean de Grouchy's testimony, it could serve to give the working population a welcome relief from the sufferings of everyday life and send it back to work in a more cheerful frame of mind, this "liberation of the heart and mind" is an effect of aesthetic pleasure which here also can ignore all indoctrination. During the same period, the blossoming lyric poetry of the troubadours takes on, as *poésie formelle*, the quality of what is already almost autonomous poetry.[85] Increasingly detached from social functions, it gives the listener the pleasure of formal variation while the poet finds a cathartic satisfaction in the poietic activity itself. The basic scene of the canzone in which the perfect but unapproachable beloved becomes the inexhaustible source of the poet's emotions draws the lyric persona into an erotic dialectic between desire for love and resistance, fear and hope, overpowering affects and imaginary fulfillment. This "sweet sorrow" for which the lover is rewarded in the fulfilling joy of being granted his wish may, for the poet, already find its resolution in the successful form and harmony of his canzone.[86] Corresponding to the liberation of the heart and mind, to which the lyric subject attains through the poetic sublimation of his affects, is the aesthesis of the listener who can enjoy the linguistic game of variation and innovation from poem to poem and thus avoid the monotony the modern reader feels vis-à-vis the wholly conventionalized language of this lyric.

Its history of reception shows us another interesting historic change in the aesthetic attitude. The obligatory impersonality of this poetry (which demanded of the poet that the personal aspects of his experience be wholly absorbed in the inner movement of an abstract lyric self) apparently no longer satisfied later listeners. Biographies of troubadours from the thirteenth century show how the imagination of the recipients availed itself of the figures of the old poets and imbued the empty shell of their idealized persona with significance. Cases where a personal drama is ascribed to the admired poet or a love adventure seen behind a favorite poem are difficult to explain by an interest in literary history which did not develop until later. Rather, there must have existed a need for individuation on the part of the recipients which can only be called "romantic" and which corresponded to the literary form of the "Vies des Troubadours." In the desire to see the abstract perfection of the lyric self embodied in a personal fate, the aesthetic activity of the later reader goes beyond the cathartic interaction pattern and confers on the poets of the past the aura of admiring identification.

In modern literature, the developing autonomy of art brings it about that cathartic identification is understood as the condition that will aesthetically liberate and thus facilitate reflection, and is expressly demanded of the enlightened reader and spectator. In the judgment of new classes of readers, Condorcet saw a "nouvelle espèce de tribune" which would do more to further the spread of enlightened thought than the tyrannic force of seductive persuasiveness. Blankenburg's *Versuch über den Roman* addresses itself to the "thinking reader" who is called on to learn through the hero of the novel how to correctly judge his own feelings.[87] But it was Schiller who showed the highest regard for the aesthetic judgment of the enlightened public when he gave it the status of a jurisdiction which he denied to historians and insisted on its autonomy vis-à-vis secular law: "I know that some of the best historians of our time and classical antiquity have captivated the hearts of their readers by their electrifying delivery. But this is a usurpation of the writer's office and offends the republican freedom of the reading public whose right it is to pass its own judgment. It is also a violation of boundaries for this method is wholly and distinctively that of orators and poets."[88]

In French classicism, the freeing of moral reflection through cathartic identification was already the highest justification for both tragedy and comedy. One need only recall Racine who maintained in his preface to *Phèdre* that the power of the passions portrayed was no less capable of sharpening the moral judgment on virtue, vice, and the measure of retribution than were the prevailing schools of moral philosophy. In his preface to *Tartuffe*, Molière similarly claims that the most effective means of moral instruction for the improvement of manners and morals were less suitable than the *ridiculum* of his comedy: "On souffre aisément des répréhensions, mais on ne souffre la raillerie. On veut bien être méchant, mais on ne veut point être ridicule" (people have no trouble putting up with recriminations but they will not be mocked. People do not mind being wicked but do mind being ridiculous). The claim that tragic or comic catharsis would raise the public of the classical stage to free reflection and thus make it an autonomous and public authority of moral judgment was the strongest provocation to ecclesiastical orthodoxy. The primary motive behind this ecclesiastical criticism is the rejection of this claim as illegitimate, even though less weighty objections to the morally destructive effects of the theater disguise it. In his "Sermon sur l'hypocrisie," for example, Bourdalou attacks Molière's presumption to judge hypocrisy, considering that it does not come within his purview to correct this evil. It is suggested that only the authority of the church can distinguish true from false piety, that Molière therefore merely creates confusion, and ultimately ridicules the most sacred things.[89]

The ingenuity of some of the critics of threatened orthodoxy, however, was already bringing to light some of the negative aspects of cathartic identification and anticipated arguments that arose later in the criticism of the Enlightenment philosophers. Wasn't it a fact that the seductive power of illusion counteracted the alleged moral effect of catharsis? Wasn't the emotional involvement in the imaginary fate of a hero always about to degenerate into pleasurable identification with the passion portrayed? Rousseau's previously quoted argument that the growing bewitchment of the spectator gradually causes his initial horror of evil to turn into sympathy for Phèdre already finds an explanation in Bossuet's "Traité de la concupiscence" which today would be called psychoanalytical.[90] Emotional identification with the tragic heroine can mobilize older or repressed needs and make the spectator secretly enter into the theatrical role because his own passion responds to the situation that is being represented: "On voit soi-même dans ceux qui nous paraissent comme transportés par de semblables objects: on devient bientôt un acteur secret de la tragédie; on y joue sa propre passion; et la fiction au dehors est froide et sans agrément, si elle ne trouve au dedans un vérité qui lui réponde" (one sees oneself in those who seem to us as though transported by similar things: soon, one becomes a secret actor in the tragedy. One acts out one's own passion there, and the fiction one sees before one's eyes is cold and unpleasurable if it does not encounter within oneself a truth which answers it).[91]

The spectator's emotional involvement in comedy can turn into another extreme which frustrates the return to free moral reflection. Sympathetic laughter at the *déraison* of the miser, the imaginary invalid, or the misanthrope does not necessarily lead to what Joachim Ritter called the "positivizing of the negative," i.e., to the reconciling insight that in the comic conduct of the character types, the prevailing norm of social reason comes to be revealed as arrogant, substanceless, and ridiculous.[92] Sympathetic laughter can also degenerate into mocking laughter which makes the comic figure the "butt of the laughter of others, often mixed as it is with malice,"[93] and lets the spectator find pleasure in the mistaken belief in his superiority. Finally, sympathetic laughter can turn into an archaic ritual of laughter which drives Molière's great monomaniacs from the stage or, expressed differently, excommunicates them from the society of "rational people," as Rainer Warning has shown.[94]

e) Ironic identification

Ironic identification refers to a level of aesthetic reception where an expectable identification is held out to the spectator or reader only to be subsequently refused or ironized. Such procedures of ironizing identification and the destruction of illusion serve to pull the recipient out of his unreflected advertence to the aesthetic object and thus prompt his aesthetic and moral reflection. They may aim at quickening his aesthetic activity and making him aware of the preconditions of fiction, unnamed rules of reception, or alternative possibilities of interpretation. But by its negation or by moral provocation, they can also bring about the questioning of the aesthetic attitude as such.

With such peak achievements as Sterne's *Tristram Shandy* or Diderot's *Jacques le Fataliste*, interaction patterns of aesthetic experience that propose to free the receiving or enjoying subject by such procedures so that he may engage in activity of his own have moved into the foreground of the literary scene since the Enlightenment. In the nineteenth century, these patterns constituted a counterauthority to the belief in progress and the need for entertainment which an increasingly commercialized bourgeois literature sought to satisfy. As forms of protest by avant-gardist art against manipulated consumption and ideological cooption, they have been dominant since the Second World War and can be exemplarily elucidated in the work of Max Frisch whose novels and plays have thematized the problematics of received and contested, imposed and refused identity in a great variety of ways. Here, however, we will begin by looking for them in earlier periods when they were not yet in the foreground. For the normativeness of the hero was not first problematized in literature when the autonomous individual arrived on the scene or when the hero, according to a never decreed but generally observed convention, could only appear in quotation marks, as if to thus symbolize his decline. What form does ironic identification take when its normative opposite pole is the exemplary hero (without quotation marks) and individuality as a subjective counterauthority is not yet available?[95]

Ironic identification (which in later periods constitutes the opposite pole to the norms of a periodically returning, affirmative classicism) appears in the Middle Ages as the counterauthority to the heroic idealism of knightly epic and novel. Usually, it takes the tone of cheerful satire and sounds the full seriousness of negation only in exceptional cases. The most common pattern is the ironization of the hero who is to be demoted from his unquestioningly accepted epic ideality and placed among the realities of everyday life. The recognition of ideal norms of heroism against a comic background is the pleasure such texts afford. It results not so much from a questioning of their validity as it is due to temporary relief from their authority. The reader whom the ironic presentation frees from an admiring identification can laugh at the behavior of the hero in an exceptional state, though when that behavior appears as epic seriousness, he feels obliged to respect it. When the famous knight William in the *Moniage Guillaume* must continue his earlier hero's career in the monastery and constantly makes a nuisance of himself because the monkish *vita contemplative* is so small-scale, one always laughs at the expense of the monks. The unheroic exceptional state thus ultimately confirms the knightly ethos as the highest, unquestionably prevailing ideal.[96] To expose the knightly norms themselves to laughter, the literature of the twelfth century characteristically resorted to the protective guise of travesty. When, in the *Roman de Renart*, Chantecler confronts his fearful "ladies" in the vainglory of a blasé pride, stays at his post—a fearless knight—at that exposed point that is the manure pile, falls asleep from boredom and is then seized with horror by a mere dream, and quickly flees into the chicken coop, the episode not only parodies the prophetic dream of the serious epic but attacks the epic hero himself. In Chantecler's disintegrating heroism, animal poetry unveils what the perfect knight, unlike the rest of creation, never seems to experience: fear for his life.[97]

Like the ideality of the knightly ethos which rises above all the weaknesses of human creatureliness, the ideality of courtly love with its code of perfect conduct was already ironized and parodied during its flowering and taken to a state of balance which allowed the reader to freely enjoy the distance to the absolute heights of the *fin'amor*. Genres that belong here include the *sotte chanson* or the obscene farce in which the perfect sublimation of the courtly epic turns into its literal opposite which then reveals itself no less absolutely in sexual or scatological clarity. The middle level between the extremes of the admiration for perfect love and the uninhibited laughter at the irresistibility of the sexual drive is seldom observed in literature. We find it in the figure of the hero whose very imperfection makes him lovable, whom no one really laughs at for his foolishness, and who appeals to the sympathetic smile of a public that is familiar with the convention. His burlesque variation is Aucassin, the clumsy but imperturbable lover who is forever surpassed by his beloved Nicolette and her heroic virtues, always roused when it is almost too late to act, and, having been tested, finds the expected fairy-tale happiness of eternal love in Torelore. His sublime variation is Lancelot, the ecstatic lover who, even in the least appropriate situations, cannot free himself of his spell, always skirts the ridiculous, yet finds the reader increasingly sympathetic.

In what was for the contemporary public an unheard-of violation of a taboo, the break with the expectable identification is brought about here at the very beginning of the adventure, as Lancelot mounts the ignominious cart. The scandal that the "chevalier de la charette" is none other than the chosen one and thus the redeemer figure of the threatened Arthurian society then finds its emotional counterweight in no less extreme tests which demand of the altogether too perfect lover that he expose himself to ridicule for the sake of his beloved queen. For the ecstatic lover who almost falls from his horse when he sees the lost comb in Guenièvre's golden hair or who in the tournament blindly lashes out behind him because he cannot avert his gaze from his beloved is a target of mockery and laughter only for the foolish but brings a smile of sympathetic identification to the lips of those who make up the growing circle of solidarity.[98] In a carefully measured alternation of astonishment and tender feeling, admiration and sympathy, the originally withheld identification is restored step by step, and what can happen when the ideality of the norm of the *fin'armor* is realized *in extremis* is made clear to the reader with a courtly education. Finally, in the sentimental climax, when Guenièvre grants Lancelot her favors on the condition that this be a unique occasion, the absolute claim love enjoys in this exclusive society is renewed and confirmed.

There is a work from the High Middle Ages which not only temporarily suspends heroic and courtly ideality but irrevocably transcends its sphere, and that is the *Roman de Renart* (around 1176). The adventure of Renart, the most important precursor of all modern antiheroes, makes impossible any identification with the perfect hero and lover. By describing the ethical characters of the animal figures and their realm under the rule of King Nobles, the licence of travesty is employed to shed light on the unideal aspects of human nature and feudal society which the idealism of knightly and courtly poetry had suppressed. The medieval antihero accomplishes this ironic reduction by unmasking the knightly behavior of his antagonists as mere pretense and exploiting their creaturely weaknesses and hidden qualities to outwit them. In this process, the very legitimation of feudal rule is called into question. The proceedings instituted against Renart for adultery with his godmother and for many instances of impiety can never come to an end because his case brings out into the open the contradictions between the worldly norms of *amour courtois* and canonic law, and the highest feudal court splits into parties. A judgment thus cannot be made which means a succession of ever new trials from which, in the face of all knightly and courtly ideas of justice, the wily fox emerges unscathed. But the reader who merely finds the ruses of this unheroic "hero" amusing and is not offended by the violation of a poetic justice which is ordinarily observed acknowledges implicitly that the ideality of the old epic and heroic world has lost its validity and henceforth remains in the distant horizon of a defunct past, a no longer actualizable literary fiction.[99]

If one were to set about writing a history of the antihero, this triumph of the rascal over the heroic ethos of the knightly world would define a turning point. From now on, the novel as a genre whose peak achievements are predominantly ironic found its point of departure in the negation of an anterior ideality—the "transcendental home" of the hero (Lukács). Cervantes turned the ironic relation of epic ideality and present novelistic actuality into the sharper antinomy of a prosaic present and a chimerical past which survives only in the hero's consciousness, and thematized this antinomy in the fable of the setting out of the last knight. If Ortega y Gasset and Lukács are right, and the modern novel subsequently acquired its poetic substance from criticizing and demythicizing an anterior ideality which had become an unquestioned order, this process in the history of the genre also brings about a change in the aesthetic experience of the reader who, as Don Quixote, emerges in a new form. For as a belated hero who seeks to realize the chimera of knighthood in opposition to an alien world, he is originally a reader par excellence, a reader who is no longer content with his receptive role and therefore sets out to make what he has read the code of his conduct, who imperturbably displays to nonreaders the ecstasies of the pleasure of reading, and who—as an interpreter of genius—knows how to remedy the poverty of reality by his inventive imagination whenever it refuses to conform to his expectations and desires.

In the footsteps of Sterne, Diderot developed an even more effective procedure to serve the didactic intent of curing the reader no longer able to identify with Don Quixote's foolishness of his addiction to old knighthood novels. Whereas Cervantes had transposed the outdated hero into the modern role of acting and interpreting reader, Diderot makes the enjoying reader the "hero" of his novel and now demands a considerable measure of reflection from him. In *Jacques le Fataliste*, the novel reader finds himself alongside the two protagonists in a role specifically programmed for him, participates by addressing questions to the narrator, is constantly confronted with his expectations, and has his naiveté demonstrated to him: "In Diderot, the true fool is not Jacques but the reader who thinks that the traditional novelistic artificiality makes him safe. Not the interpreting imagination of the hero but the interpreting imagination of the reader is taken ad absurdum."[100] The fictive role of the traditional reader is built into Diderot's novel so that the real reader may be refused identification with his representative, the intent being to enlighten him about his prejudices, to set his self-critical reflection in motion, and call on his judgment regarding the large questions raised by the novel all of which the narrator presents as open: fiction and reality, master and servant, freedom and necessity, and even the digressions which all end in the open-ended casuistry of daily life.

By a turn in the development of narrative technique which Flaubert's novelistic oeuvre and his reflections in the correspondence had paradigmatically elaborated, aesthetic experience at the level of ironically withheld identification acquired new possibilities in the nineteenth century. Doing away with the omniscient narrator not only forces the reader to work out the nexus of meaning in the fable and not infrequently to decide among several possible interpretations. Without prior orientation and the meaning-creating mediation of the narrator, he can now be placed directly into the alien horizon of expectations of the portrayed characters, is obliged to deduce what they are without being told their qualities, must distinguish their self-deception from their hidden motives, and may gradually become aware that the alien consciousness into whose world he is being drawn *nolens volens* makes excessive demands on his readiness to identify and may even shock his sensibility. At the very outset, in "Au lecteur,"[101] Baudelaire had already ironically invited the reader of romantic lyric poetry (who opened the *Fleurs du Mal* with the expectation that he would share the exquisite moments and sublime sentiments of the poet) to become "mon semblable—mon frère" which necessarily made him a hypocrite since he was also expected to identify with the spleen of his "brother" and a catalog of vices that could hardly be considered edifying.

It is not only at the highest levels of avant-gardist experiment that twentieth-century literature has utilized the procedures of ironic identification, as when Jean Genet's work, for example, obliges the reader to adopt the role of voyeur because the author wants to provoke his reflection as he is shocked into withholding identification, or when, as in a work such as Robbe-Grillet's *La Jalousie*, he is locked into the total immanence of a consciousness through which he can experience the classic affect of jealousy with unanticipated intensity, thanks merely to a "special way of seeing." Such procedures have meanwhile been adopted even in minor genres like the detective story. The reader of such stories is accustomed to abandoning himself to imaginary dangers and anxieties under the reliable guidance of a modern hero, the detective; he may now realize with horror that he must see the murder story from the perspective of the criminal.[102] And in the novels of Boileau and Narcejac, he may even have to live the fate that he had always seen from the other side and with equanimity. Using the perspective of the victim is the most extreme way of depriving the reader of his ultimate certainties and exposing him without any support to a growing fear which can nonetheless transform itself into an odd aesthetic pleasure: "In the context of the story, one is defenseless (like the victim) and must experience with him the terrors of a progressive dematerialization of the world which is also a poeticization, however. For poetry is that sublime, delicate coloration the world takes on when guarantees of security disappear and one can no longer reliably judge what are supposedly well-known things."[103]

There is still the question how, at the level of ironic identification, the norm-breaking experience which sets reflection free can miss the goal and fall back into deficient aesthetic behavior. Through its commercialization, the constantly accelerating process of avant-gardist art seems to have maneuvered itself into a closed circle of production, aroused need, and consumption in our century: in the case of the provoked reader or observer, innovation with shock effect, unpalatable estrangement and irritating ambiguity pass over into new habits of reception which soon make him look on the initially refused identification as an enjoyable scandal.[104] At the other extreme are demands made by experimental art, which include historical knowledge, an expertise in interpretative techniques, and patience in deciphering which can only be satisfied by an esoteric group of recipients. The dismantling of the narrative function can go too far and become a contentless language experiment; dematerialization can turn into a monotonous ascesis of perception, and ambiguity can be exaggerated and decline into the directionlessness of arbitrary solutions.[105] All this not infrequently squashes a residual interest on the part of the reader, though even when the reader himself is expected to become the principal character, i.e., to take the place of the empty identity of the vanished hero or to act as if he were the author, such interest is required. The line that separates all this from aesthetic indifference cannot be crossed with impunity. It is found where it is wholly incumbent on the reader or observer to generate the equivalent of the aesthetic pleasure being denied him, where, in other words, there is no aesthetic inducement that would make him prefer the reflection or activity demanded of him to some other way of spending his time.

After the "death of the hero" and the "withdrawal of the author," the extreme attempt has been made to confer identity on the reader alone, but here the irony of refused identification leads to a communicative vacuum. A radio play by Claude Ollier about the *Death of the Hero*[106] drew a radical consequence from this fact, though that consequence is rather calamitous for the literary and revolutionary program of the Tel Quel group. The reader who first wishes to interrogate the author about the disappearance of the "hero" declares his readiness to let himself be tutored in productive reading. What he learns in the author's school he must then apply to the reality of the street outside his window. As he begins to "read reality" in this fashion, he unwittingly describes the arrival of the murderers in front of the house, i.e., he describes the story of his own murder as if it were a literary fiction. The receptive student identifies himself in the most perfect manner conceivable with the literary event, and this up to his own, albeit literary, murder. The death of the ideal reader as an imaginary reenactment of the earlier death of the literary hero is immediately followed by the death of the author: at the end, the mentor is liquidated by the murderers who did in his all-too-docile pupil. All that now remains is the listening witness of the play who may learn from this case that the avant-gardist principle "the main character is the reader" is passé, as is the author and, last but not least, the listener. For as the final element in this rat's tail of negativities, he can escape the fear of his own demise only if he is of an allegorical turn of mind and believes with the medieval reader that the meaning of death is a future resurrection, a resurrection in which hero, reader, and author will share along with the rest of mankind. *Summa summarum*: should a *tabula rasa* be the best nursery of a new productivity, this autodafé of the aesthetics of negativity would entitle one to the most handsome hopes for a revolutionary art, an art of the future and one that would create a new solidarity.

C. On Why the Comic Hero Amuses

1. The comic hero seen negatively and positively (laughing about and laughing with)

Sigmund Freud discovered a source of the pleasure in the comic in a curious contrast which can serve very well to introduce our topic: "Thus a uniform explanation is provided of the fact that a person appears comic to us if, in comparison with ourselves, he makes too great an expenditure on his bodily functions and too little on his mental ones; and it cannot be denied that in both these cases our laughter expresses a pleasurable sense of the superiority which we feel in relation to him. If the relation in the two cases is reversed—if the other person's physical expenditure is found to be less than ours or his mental expenditure greater—then we no longer laugh, we are filled with astonishment and admiration."[1] As an example of the comic in the excessive expenditure of physical effort, he gives the movements of a clown or those of a child who is learning to write and "follows the movements of his pen with his tongue stuck out."[2] A (less convincing) example of the comic in inadequate mental expenditure is the kind of nonsense an ignorant candidate produces during an examination. Freud quickly abandons the explanation of comic pleasure as due to a feeling of superiority and adopts instead the principle of "difference of discharge" which we observe when others make too much or too little effort: "In the former case I laugh because he has taken too much trouble, in the latter because he has taken too little."³

The reversal of this relationship (where we no longer laugh but "are filled with astonishment and admiration") describes an aspect of the experience of the hero who is taken seriously. The person who can make light of physical exertions that are difficult for the ordinary mortal and who can go to greater psychological expense where we would make things too easy for ourselves is customarily admired as a hero. At first glance, this account seems to contradict the epic convention which, since Homer, defines the hero by labors, i.e., by greater physical and psychological effort, and places him above the ordinary mortal for that reason. But it is precisely for this judgment that Freud advances a reception-aesthetic cause in his (later) explanation of Aristotelian catharsis. The spectator or listener who has experienced too little and sees himself as a poor wretch to whom nothing of consequence happens would like to be a hero, and the poet makes this possible and enjoyable for him by having him identify with an imaginary one. For a presupposition of the cathartic "liberation of mind and feelings" is not only the discharge of one's own affects but also the "certainty that it is someone other than himself who is acting and suffering on the stage, and, secondly, that after all it is only a game which can threaten no damage to his personal security."⁴ It is thus the saving of greater expenditure which makes the spectator enjoy the suffering and even the heroic death of the admired hero. Marveling, he can take pleasure in the hero's effortless overcoming of the greatest physical exertions and admiringly identify with the larger than life-size heroic passion he could muse about in daydreams and childhood games but which was denied the poor fellow in everyday reality.

The aesthetic pleasure of identification with a hero as here explained is perfectly compatible with a cognitive function. For precisely in the case of the hero, the aesthetic pleasure of identification as "incentive bonus" or "forepleasure" may have a regressive effect and lead to the "release of greater pleasure from deeper psychic sources."⁵ But I should add that it can also act progressively and call for the adoption of social norms of action which the hero, the saint, or the sage conveys through the perfection of a point of view or attitude and authenticates as a model.⁶ This collaboration of the affective and the cognitive function may also be presumed where admiring identification encounters the comic, i.e., where the hero no longer transcends what is expected and achieves the ideal, but where he must assert himself in comic situations.

Turning the "serious" hero into a "comic" one has at least two fundamentally different aspects, depending on whether the comic derives from the degradation of a heroic ideal to its opposite, or the elevation of the material and physical in human nature. If one understands the comic hero as the degradation from an expected perfection and ideality, this corresponds to determinations familiar from the tradition of parody, travesty, pastiche, or even satire. A parody or travesty can exploit the discrepancy of "high" and "low" on both the formal and the substantive plane in order to attack its object, in most cases a text of authoritative rank, by critical imitation[7] or the artistic heightening given the imitation in one's own "excellent invention."[8] It can thus take aim at the individual norm of an author, the authoritative one of a classical model, the formal one of a genre, the typical one of a hero, and, along with all this—as T. Verweyen has shown—the more or less explicitly defined norms of reception.[9] The target of a parody that uses a comic hero can thus be the authority of a norm handed down from the past. But when this classical object of the parody is itself taken as medium or pretext, the target can also be the validity of norms that have currency in the social life and conduct of the contemporary public.

All these cases involve a comparison between parody and what is parodied. The comic hero is not comic in himself but against the horizon of certain expectations; he is comic because he negates these expectations or norms. In this variety of the comic which we call the "comic of the counterimage," comparing is itself clearly part of the process of reception: the person who does not know or fails to recognize[10] what a given comic hero negates need not find him comic. This already makes clear the cognitive function of this kind of comedy. Through the comic hero, aesthetic or moral norms can be thematized; their apparent "naturalness" or never explicitly formulated currency can be brought to consciousness; they can be ridiculed with the intent to amuse or problematized by critical seriousness. But in this sphere of aesthetic experience also, we find an intermediate possibility between affirmative and destructive tendencies: norms need not simply be affirmed or attacked through the comic hero; a release or justification of what is repressed under the rule of idealized norms and excluded from literary representation can also be initiated.

From the point of view of reception aesthetics, these three functions can be summarized as follows: what the hero reveals through the comic of the counterimage may be received either as amusing and therefore ultimately affirmative relief from a sanctified tradition or as a protest that is seriously meant but safe because presented in comic guise. It may also be taken as the beginning of a solidarization, however, if prevailing norms are not merely attacked through the comic hero but the incorporation of what was previously suppressed or excluded leads to the creation of new norms.

Under the heading "methods of degrading," Freud also gave a psychogenetic explanation for the pleasure that is the motor of the cognitive functions of the hero. What all comic methods, caricature, parody, and travesty (also unmasking as a nonliterary device) have in common is that they "degrade the dignity of individuals by directing attention to the frailties which they share with all humanity, in particular the dependence of their mental functions on bodily needs. The unmasking is equivalent here to an admonition: such and such a person, who is admired as a demigod is after all only human like you and me. Here, too, are to be placed the efforts at laying bare the monotonus psychic automatism that lies behind the wealth and apparent freedom of psychical functions."[11] For Freud, this description primarily confirms his theory on differences of expenditure; he took no further interest in the aesthetic function of relief and protest which could be derived from it, and certainly did not look into the function of solidarization. What is also interesting in his "mechanism for the production of comic pleasure" is the observation that this pleasure derives solely from the difference in expenditure in procedures of degradation and is therefore "independent of the reality of the comic situation so that everyone is in fact exposed, without any defense, to being made comic."[12] The comic effect of degradation is indifferent to the dignity and worth of a person; its mechanism cuts through both the conventions of morality and poetic justice: we laugh at the hero who falls down before we can ask whether he deserved to be tripped. In this flagrant immorality of situational comedy, the pleasure in the inversion of hierarchical positions and the symbols of power reveals itself; placing the hero into a comic situation destroys the spell of admiring identification and allows the laughing spectator to enjoy a moment of superiority and unconcern vis-à-vis the hero who is ordinarily his superior.

It is this laughter from a feeling of superiority which Baudelaire wanted to trace back to a satanic root because it is directed at "a sign of weakness or disaster among his fellows."[13] As is well known, Baudelaire contrasted this imitative "significative comic" with a creative "absolute comic" which is no longer based on the arrogation of superiority over one's fellows but no less satanic for that reason: "in this case, laughter is still the expression of an idea of superiority—no longer now of man over man, but of man over nature."[14] This distinction, whose prototypes for Baudelaire were Molière's comedy on the one hand and Rabelais's comic on the other, presupposes a concept of the comic hero which can no longer be understood by the categories of degradation and the counterimage. The Rabelaisian hero is indeed eminently suited to illuminate the origin and function of the grotesque as a kind of comic effect that does not derive from the counterimage of a heroic ideality but which manifests itself, in figures like Gargantua and Pantagruel, as the release and affirmation of repressed creatureliness. So far, the grotesque hero who sparks collective laughter which triumphs over fear, compulsion, and repression has not been of interest to the Freudian theory of the hero. It is therefore appropriate here to recall Mikhail Bakhtin, whose *Rabelias and His World* —a book that did not become known until late—gave us the essential insight into the Rabelaisian heroes as figures of grotesque laughter.[15] If one compares Bakhtin's definition of grotesque comedy with the descriptive model of the comedy of the counterimage as developed according to Freud, the result is this:

The comedy of the counterimage comes from a degrading of the ideal to a level that permits the reader or spectator an identification with the hero which he can experience as relief from or protest against the pressure of authority, or as solidarization. Grotesque comedy derives from the elevation of the creaturely and the bodily to a level where the distance between reader or spectator and hero disappears in a sympathetic laughter which the community of laughing onlookers can experience as a liberation of the sensual and a victory over fear and all the power of the world and its norms, and thus as a triumph of the pleasure principle. In the former case, the comic catharsis can be explained as an economy of emotional effort, in the latter as a gain in intensity due to the liberation of repressed nature. In the former case, it is conveyed through the distance-creating imagination, in the latter through a sympathy that eliminates distance. The pleasure in the comic here presupposes unconcern and thus the capacity to recognize and enjoy the humorous coming to nought of heroic expectations. It is a laughing *about* (Baudelaire's "significative comic") and contrasts with grotesque laughter which, as a laughter *with* (Baudelaire's "absolute comic"), is sparked by a laughable figure. It is a laughter that eliminates the opposition of spectator and hero and conveys even to the solitary later reader a sense of the "insularity of the exceptional state" in which the original community of laughers experienced the liberation of laughter and the body.

Such manifestations of grotesque laughter clearly constitute the opposite pole to Freud's theory of pleasure as arising from an "economy of expenditure upon feeling." Figures of laughter such as the grotesque mime, the naive fools of Aristophanes' comedy, and the unabashed fools of medieval soties, but also the Rabelaisian heroes with the exuberance of their physical functions, certainly do not save their public any expenditure upon affects. On the contrary: both in themselves and in the laughing public, they liberate and mobilize the affects that were repressed by a strict external or inner censor. The comic heroes in this "festive drama of bodily life (copulation, birth, growth, eating, drinking, defecation)"[16] still have their being beyond the well-known distinction Hegel wanted to draw between classical and modern comedy: "whether the folly and one-sidedness of the dramatis personae appears laughable to the audience only or to themselves as well, whether therefore the characters in the comedy can be mocked solely by the audience or by themselves also."[17] Grotesque laughter does not make the comic hero "the butt of the laughter of others, often mixed as it is with malice."[18] but creates, by way of the liberated affects, understanding between the hero and those who laugh at him. The fundamentally unconscious nature of this "belief in the truth of laughter" also excludes the possibility that laughable figures like the heroes of Aristophanes can be "laughable to themselves," as Hegel puts it. The grotesque laughter at such figures makes clear that Hegel read an idealist concept of the "truly comic" into Aristophanes' comedies. For in that poet's characters, he thought he could discover "higher natures," fully conscious of their indestructible subjectivity, who were raised so far above their own contradictions that they could bear the frustration of their aims and achievements.[19]

There is, however, another variant of the comic hero which is based on such a degree of consciousness of self. Freud defined it as "humor" and saw it as possessed of a special dignity by which it differed from the joke and the comic: "Like jokes and the comic, humor has something liberating about it; but it also has something of grandeur and elevation, which is lacking in the other two ways of obtaining pleasure from intellectual activity. The grandeur in it clearly lies in the triumph of narcissism, the victorious assertion of the ego's invulnerability."[20] The agreement with the Hegelian account is obvious: in contrast to the tradition of the humors which appear comic because they cannot free themselves of the *one* quality of their nature (like Molière's characters which Hegel belittled), the humoristic hero's relationship to himself permits him "to protect himself from suffering" and to assert the pleasure principle against the demands and the unpropitiousness of reality. Freud explained this attitude by a shift of cathexis: the superego, heir to the parental agency, tries to console the ego by humor.[21]

We have now arrived at certain determinations which allow us to delimit some variants of the comic hero, or attitudes toward him. Invested with the negative quality of the counterimage, the *unheroic hero* of parody and travesty or an antihero and rogue like wily Renart may also become a comic figure that moves between jest and seriousness and can attack the validity of ideal literary or social norms in that sphere. The *comic hero* in the English tradition of humors or the French hero of the *caractères* can also be subsumed under the principle of the counterimage if such figures represent the variety of human nature but contradict its ideality through their constrained or quirkish one-sidedness. Invested with the positive quality of the affirmation of the pleasure principle, the *grotesque hero* who triumphs over his fear can do his part to make the unofficial truth of laughter prevail, and thus create a laughing rapport with his public. The *humoristic hero*, finally, who is able to laugh at himself, can, through the triumph of consciousness over the demands and the harshness of reality, release in the spectator or reader a humoristic response to the world. He can thus reestablish admiring identification on that level of gaiety which the laughter about the degraded ideal hero broke through.

If the first two variants in this account, the unheroic and the comic hero, fall into the category of *laughter at*, and the latter two, the grotesque and the humoristic hero, into the category of *laughing with*, it must not be overlooked that this contrast is not wholly one of an objective typification but is constituted in part by the aesthetic attitude of the spectator. Laughter at a variant of the comic hero often turns into laughing with him. Initially, we may have laughed at Renard, Lazarillo, Falstaff, Mister Pickwick, and then have realized that we suddenly join in their laughter. This applies even more to the three functions of relief, protest, and solidarization which may be produced by either of the two kinds of laughter. Since the relieving, protesting, and solidarizing functions of laughter at a hero depend on both the horizon of expectations of the work and the attitude of the viewer, he can choose to content himself with the comic catharsis even though the text was intended as a protest or as an offer of solidarization. Protest and solidarization are more dependent on the social horizon of expectations at a given moment and therefore especially subject to a horizon of understanding that does not remain unchanged in the process of historical reception. The following interpretations cannot make allowances for aspects that relate to the history of reception. They are merely intended to serve as an explanation of the reasons the comic hero amuses us, and were taken from the history of literature as representative examples and without any other claim.

2. The deflation of the classical ideal of the hero in the Vergil travesty of the seventeenth and eighteenth centuries

The literary "rebirth of antiquity" was accompanied by an abundant flowering of parodistic and travestying literature. It has remained the stepchild of a literary history which—more than the humanists of the Renaissance themselves—was deeply concerned with the classical legacy. Quite recently, Jürgen von Stackelberg could still justifiably feel that to rise to the defense of this "reversal of humanist imitatio" or "reverse of the medal on whose obverse is stamped the worship of antiquity" was very much called for indeed.[22] This is especially true of the poetry in burlesque verse which had a faddish vogue during the age of Louis XIV alongside classical literature. One of its peak achievements was the *Virgile travesti* Scarron wrote between 1648 and 1653, during which period he advanced to the middle of Book VIII. After him, and up to 1740, the work was taken to Book XII and went through forty editions. Like all works of this genre, its language lives off the contrast with the genres of serious literature. More specifically, it uses the vocabulary that the canon of serious poetry excluded. On this level, Michel Gillot's apt formulation also applies to Scarron: "life's revenge on literature."[23] With an eye toward the exemplariness of the classical epic which stood at the apex of the hierarchy of genres during the classical period, this Vergil travesty casts the cheerful light of burlesque comedy on the entire repertory of acknowledged and implicit epic and heroic norms. Whether Scarron intended more than relief from the seriousness of the hallowed model so that "life's revenge," in 1648, in the midst of the confusions of the Fronde, took aim at more than literary norms, can hardly be decided in retrospect. From the most frequently edited continuation, I have selected a passage from the twelfth canto, with the decisive duel between Turnus and Aeneas, because the author, a certain Jacques Moreau de Brasei, was a master at giving an edge to the tendencies of Scarron's travesty.[24]

Turnus becomes a comic hero through a comic of the counterimage which constantly brings in what the ideality of the Vergilian epic excluded. Where Vergil immediately begins with an account of Turnus' heroic fury as the Latins are being defeated and describes it as "pure affect" by utilizing the Homeric simile of the wounded lion (XII, ll. 1-9), the travesty makes the natural image with its emphasis on the purity and greatness of the passion almost entirely disappear in a sequence of nonideal, daily occurrences: the great hero has slept poorly, pondered inconsequential matters in a tragic situation, and vented his bad humor at the domestics. Later, as he is about to give a dressing down to his prospective father-in-law, a big fly gets caught in his hero's throat:

> Comme il voulut ouvrir la bouche
> Un bourdon, une grosse mouche,
> Entra dans son vaste gosier,
> et détourna ce vieux routier,
> Un moment, d'étaler sa rage
>
> (XII, p. 201)

(The war horse, about to open his jaw, / got a buzzing fly stuck in his maw / which mishap kept him for a while, / from venting his bile.) None of these situations fits in with what is expected of the heroic. Bringing the hero down into the reality familiar to the reader is amusing not simply because the circumstances with which even—and indeed precisely—a Turnus in his epic outsize cannot deal are so utterly commonplace. It also shows that a Vergilian hero is too sublime to ever do, or be: sleep ("doucement sans faire de bruit / ou s'il eut la puce à l'oreille," softly without making any noise or as if he were on guard, XII, p. 199), be perplexed ("que faire en cette extrémité? / Se pendre, c'est déloyauté; / Se noyer, ce seroit folie; s'enfuir, c'est quitter Lavinie"; What should I do in this extremity? / To hang myself would be disloyalty; / to drown myself, stupidity; / and fleeing would mean leaving Lavinie; XII, p. 200), be clumsy or act improperly ("rompt la dentelle d'un colet, / Donne un soufflet à son valet, / Renverse sa chocolatière, / Nomme putain sa chambrière, / Fait un soleil à son miroir, / Sans s'étonner, sans èmouvoir"; tears the lacework of a collar, slaps his valet, overturns his chocolate pot, calls his chambermaid a whore, moons the mirror, and all without surprise or emotion; ibid.), or have doubts about his role:

> Pardi! la chose est peu commune;
> Etre brave, et de plus heureux,
> Est moins des hommes que des dieux
>
> (ibid.)

(Forsooth! The gods perhaps, but certainly few men are valorous and happy too.)

The continuator of 1706 already saturated the comic contrast between the expected heroic ideality and a situation made trivial with details from the everyday world of civil life, whereas Scarron was mostly intent on commenting on the high epic style with vulgar turns of speech. As when, the storm breaking, he has "pious Eneas" begin his plaint to heaven in these words:

Alors Aenéas le pieux,
Regardant tristement les Cieux,
Lâcha ces pieuses paroles:
Je serai donc mangé des soles,
Cria-t-il, pleurant comme un veau,
Et je finirai dedans l'eau?

(I, p. 8)

And gazing heavenward, pious
Aenéas sighed: / 'it's not
my wish / to perish and to
nourish fish!' / And bleating
like a sheep, he
asked, / 'Must I then go to my death
in the deep?'

or when he calls the tears his hero weeps as he separates from Dido "crocodile tears" ("Mais il ne s'y faut pas fier, / Ce sont larmes de crocodile, / Quoi qu'en dise Messer Virgile"; But do not give them credence. They are crocodile tears whatever Master Virgil may say; IV, pp. 234–44) and corrects Vergil's sublime authority by pointing out that he overlooked the unavoidable surfeit of his hero:

En cet endroit, maître Maron
N'a point approfondi l'affaire
Tellement qu'il se peut bien faire,
Que maître Aenéas étoit sou,
D'avoir toujours femme à son cou

(IV, p. 277)

But here, maître Maron /
did not really probe the matter. /
For master Aenéas, we know
better / was truly loth of a
female that / clung to him
like a piece of cloth.

or when he describes the appearance of the amazonlike virgin Camilla and reflects on the varying effect she had on the ladies who envied her, and on men:

Mais les hommes la convoitèrent,
Faisant, à son intention,
Mentale fornication,
Ou fornication mentale,
En tous sens la chose est égale

(VIII, p. 473)

> But men desired her, / and
> dreamt of fornication /
> or fornicated having her in
> mind. / It's really two of
> a kind.

In the Vergil travesty, the rebellion against the authority symbolized in the ancient gods usually does not go beyond providing relief, as is appropriate for the burlesque genre. When, in the twelfth canto, Turnus complains pathetically before the duel and bemoans his role after his defeat by Aeneas, the ideality of the hero's fate is ironically downgraded: it becomes the right of the stronger ("Eh bien, j'ai mérité la mort, / Parce que je suis le moins fort"; Well then, I do deserve to die, since I am the weaker. XII, p. 259). But coming from the mouth of this comic hero, this really sounds melancholy. The heights of disrespect toward the ancient gods point in the same direction. By reducing the authority of the divine ruling couple to the level of a banal matrimonial dispute between dame Junon, "véritable attrape-minon" and "son vieux lance-tonnere" (XII, p. 211), the continuator pokes fun toward the end at the epic structure of a second, higher plane of divine action and intervention. The greatness of those who rule, seen through the linguistic magnifying glass of a conversational tone, as it were, seems both comic and humanized ("Votre conduit me chiffone, / Entendez-vous bien, ma mignonne? / C'est votre mignon qui le veut, / Qui l'ordonne . . ."; Your conduct irks me, do you hear, my beloved? It is your beloved who wants it, who orders it; XII, p. 251). Such play with the suspended seriousness of the governing authority can also at times be directed at prevailing conditions, as when Juturna's seduction by Jupiter is first wittily commented on and then related to the (royal?) custom of bestowing sinecures:

> Il le poussa si loin, je pense,
> Qu'il en vint à la complaisance
> De lui donner dans son cabat
> Deux lecons du noviciat
> De ce qu'on appelle hyménée,
> Dont la belle, d'une fournée
> Fit à la fois deux embrions
> Qui sont de vaillant champions.
> Le bon Jupin, pour récompense,
> Lui fit don d'une présidence

(XIII, p. 212)

(He pushed and pled, and finally had the pleasure of acquainting her with the marriage bed. / The twins she produced are champions now. / And Jupiter, to show his gratitude, / gave her a post of some magnitude.) But neither Scarron nor his continuators modified the latent because no longer relevant ideology of their classical model although its stoic fatalism probably shocked the Christian public of the seventeenth century and its norms of "bienséance" in at least two places in the twelfth canto: when Jupiter must finish off the heroically fighting Turnus with an apparition (ll. 843ff.), and when "pious Aeneas" remorselessly puts his helpless enemy to death. The Vergil travesty of the eighteenth century did in fact object to this.

Whereas the French travesty contents itself with a dig at Aeneas ("Lui fit avec irrévérance / Un grand trou dans sa vaste pance," Proceeded to make, without any respect, a big fat hole in his big fat belly, XII, p. 260), the German version calls Jupiter's chitchat with the fury "a trick which cannot be forgiven" (p. 305) and criticizes the god's authority as bellicose: "There's nothing quite like the delight, it seems, Jupiter feels when people fight" (p. 298). During the course of the Enlightenment, the tone and tendency of the travesty became sharper. In *Vergils Aeneis travestirt* (Vienna, 1782–94)[25] the procedures of disparagement used by Scarron no longer merely serve as comic relief from the hitherto unshakable authority of classical education. Blumauer put them in the service of the attack by Josephine enlightenment on superannuated authorities, especially the pope and the clergy, satirized heroic valor and the relentless course of destiny, and thus undermined the legitimations of the ruling powers. The comic disintegration of Jupiter's and the intervening Olympians' mythic power aims at the transfigured historical image of the church and the absolute monarchy. Blumauer's travesty shows the decisions and counsels of the masters of world history to be acts of utter arbitrariness and despicable ingratitude or revolting horse trades.[26] And in this process, the Vergilian myth of Aeneas' world-historical mission and the origin of Rome is turned into a philosophical satire on the founding of the Papal states and the Rome of the popes. Blumauer's Mercury is given an order from the emperor which he is to pass on to Aeneas who is sipping cocoa on Dido's couch:

> Frag' ihn, ob er denn glaubt, dass man
> im Bette Reiche finde?
> Und ob er seinen Vatican
> Auf einem Sopha gründe?

(ll. 1849–52)

(Ask him whether he believes that one finds empires in bed? And whether he establishes his Vatican on a sofa?) What principally contributes to stripping heroic events and all mythical and historical greatness of any ideality is that Blumauer not only occasionally substitutes all too human behavior for the expected pathos of epic gestures but transposes the entire action without any qualms whatever into the totally unheroic world of everyday Vienna. Instead of visiting Juno's temple after his arrival in Carthage, Aeneas decides on a rather more profane spot:

> Doch ein Kaffeehaus in der Näh'
> Liess unsern Mann nicht weiter:
> Er ging hinein, trank Milchkaffee
> Und las den Reichspostreiter.
> Aneens Flucht aus Trojens Glut,
> Sein Sturm, sein Schiffbruch und sein Mut
> Stand alles schon darinnen
>
> (ll. 358–64)

(A coffeehouse proved too much to resist. Inside, he sipped a café au lait, and read the *Reichspostreiter*. His flight from burning Troy, the storm, his shipwreck and his valor, had made the headlines already.) Aeneas reading Aeneas' story in the newspaper is an example of Blumauer's skillful raising of things to a higher power: such a "travesty within the travesty" reaches its hardly surpassable climax in the feast in Dido's palace, as the last course is being served:

> Auch Kirschen, Ananas sogar
> Und Erdbeer' im Burgunder,
> Und dann die Torte—ja die war
> Der kochkunst grösstes Wunder:
> Sie präsentierte Trojens Brand,
> Und oben auf den Flammen stand
> Aeneas—ganz von Butter
>
> (I, ll. 447–83)

> And cherries, even pineapple
> and strawberries in wine /
> and then the cake—it truly
> was a culinary feat / with
> Aeneas above a Troy incarnadine /
> made wholly of butter and
> ready to eat.

With Blumauer, what is comic in thus turning the Vergilian hero into a very ordinary mortal slips easily into satire. Where this happens, the heroes seem not so much comic heroic models as ridiculed and degraded ones, as when Aeneas, in burning Troy, is barely restrained from laying hands on Helena ("Und als ich schon vom Leder zog, / Die Hexe zu tranchieren, / Da zupfte Venus mich am Rock," as I was drawing my sword to cut up the witch, Venus tugged at my coat, ll. 862–64) and is then escorted through the flames by Venus ("Ich ging nach Haus, da hatte mich / Mama in Schutz genommen, / Sonst wär' ich diesmal sicherlich / Gebraten angekommen," My mother shielded me on my homeward track / for otherwise I would have been ashes / by the time I got back, ll. 883–86) or when he notices that he has lost Creusa ("Patsch!—schmiss ich meinen Vater weg. / Und lief im allergrössten Dreck / Zurück, um sie zu suchen," I threw my father to the ground / and ran back through the deepest mire / to search for Creusa in the fire, ll. 950–53).

In 1794, Blumauer's continuator, Schaber, tried to give the travesty renewed relevance but also deprived it of its prerevolutionary pathos of progress. Now, Turnus' heroic furor is trivialized, his speech sounds like that of dwelling students, the fight for Lavendel (i.e., Lavinia) is fought as a duel, and ultimately made to refer to the war of the Coalition against the Jacobins ("Und schwuren, dass das deutsche Blut / Nie sollt'zu Wasser werden," and swore that German blood would never turn to water, p. 292). In this process, Schaber sets the absurdity of the spilling of blood against the martial glory of all rulers who lust for conquest ("Dafür sind ja Soldaten da, / Dass sie der Grossen Händel / Mit ihrem Blut ausmachen," that has always been soldiers' fate / to shed their blood, to suffer pain / for others' gain). In Blumauer's work, the Enlightenment criticism of the inhumane norms of power politics and their legitimation by heroic literary models also includes the poets who, like "Mr. Maro" at poor Dido's undeserved death (to console her, she is allowed to first read parts of *Werthers Leiden*) play a cat-and-mouse game with their hero:

> Ihr Herr'n aus deren Federn Tod
> Und Leben willig fliessen,
> Sagt, macht Ihr euch denn nicht vor Gott
> Und Menschen ein Gewissen
> Ob eurer Feder Mordbegier?
> Bedenkt doch, dass die Welt—und ihr—
> Viel lieber lacht als weinet

(ll. 2010–16)

> Ye poets from whose pens
> Life and death so readily flow
> Should you not perhaps forego

your murderous vehemence?
I say you should try
considering that all of us
would rather laugh than cry.

The solidarizing function of the comic is more apparent in Marivaux. In his criticism of militarism and hero worship, the affirmation of a eudaemonistic morality is plain. Not only do the classical heroes in *L'Homère travesti, ou L'Iliade en vers burlesques* (1716) ridicule traditional norms of heroic greatness. They also derive comic effects from openly avowing their creaturely feelings, fears, and desires. In the famous scene describing Hector's leave-taking, Andromache expresses what heroic widows normally keep to themselves:

Ah! grands dieux! Lorsque j'envisage
L'affligeant état de veuvage,
Je sens qu'un lit est bien affreux,
Quand, dans ce lit, on n'est plus deux
                            (V, ll. 849–53)

How grievous, o ye gods /
to be without a man, and solitary /
to have no one to share one's bed /
because all men are temporary.

Although Hector is ready to bow to the fate the gods have decreed — albeit with the disrespectful comment "Vous verrez Hector généreux, / Dire à cela: tant pis pour eux" (you will see generous Hector say to that: so much the worse for them) — he finds it insupportable that he should be cuckolded after his death: "Mais je me sens presque la fièvre, / Quand je pense qu'un vilain Grec / Viendra pour vous baiser le bec" (but I almost feel feverish when I think that some villainous Greek / will shortly come along, and kiss you on the beak, V, ll. 917ff). J. v. Stackelberg has shown that Marivaux's opposition to the heroic becomes most impressive when he treats death without pathos or solemnity, refuses to idealize it, and not infrequently uses understatement ("Vivre est un bien, la sepulture / Est deplaisante à la nature," life is a good and burial displeases nature, I. p. 74). His comic heroes claim the right to openly admit their cowardice as they face death. In their "murderous combat," Hector and Ajax inflict only two scratches on each others nose and chin. When the spectators from the two hostile armies demand more, the two adversaries agree not to go all out: "c'est une manière / De se battre trop meutrière, / On veut bien être un peu blessé, / Mais non pas rester trépassé" (This is altogether too lethal a fight / A wound or two may be all right / But to die? / fie, I say, fie!; VI, ll. 49–52). The solidarizing function of the comic becomes apparent in the circumstance that those aspects of human and creaturely existence that were previously suppressed in the classical epic are being raised to a new norm through the unheroic hero:

> Crains-tu la mort? Je ne t'en blâme;
> Rien n'est tel qu'un corps avec âme,
> Rien n'est plus doux que de pouvoir,
> Boire et manger, et se mouvoir
>
> (II, p. 99)

(Are you afraid of death? / I understand that well, and must admit / there's nothing sweeter than to draw your breath / to have a body for your soul / to eat, to drink, and to be fit.) The solidarization is most impressive in Hector's death scene where J. von Stackelberg has justifiably praised the "simultaneity of the sublime and the ridiculous."[27] Toward the end, Marivaux has the mortally wounded Hector ask Achilles to blow his nose for him and then describes this humane gesture in the following verse:

> Là dessus, Achille se panche,
> Dit, le torchant avec sa manche:
> Je perds si souvent mon mouchoir,
> Que je ne veux plus en avoir.
> L'autre reprit, je te rends grâce,
> Ta manche est cependant bien grasse:
> Mais, quand on meurt il est égal,
> De se moucher ou bien ou mal.

(Achilles thereupon bends down / and wipes his nose with his sleeve / 'I've lost so many a handkerchief, / I no longer carry them.' / 'I thank you,' Hector says, 'but I am queasy / and find your sleeve really awfully greasy. / And yet, when I come to think of it, / so close to death, what matter / if one's nose is blown worse, or better?') In such passages, one cannot fail to note that with the comic heroes of his Homer travesty, Marivaux is no longer taking aim at the distant authority of the classic epic but at the still valid norms of its reception and their powerful preceptive influence, and thus at an instrument of legitimation of the prevailing morality. The final verses of his work express this openly: only "thanks to our stupidity" was the classical hero considered great, for what are they but "des malheureux tueurs de gens" (wretched killers of people), no better than a modern surgeon: "Moi, je dirai qu'un Chirurgien / A ce Héros ne cède en rien." The parody

of epics is certainly not the most effective way to introduce new norms
into social life and action, and the bourgeoisie of the eighteenth century
disseminated its ideals and models in other literary forms, principally the
novel and the theater. Yet the comic hero of an epic which died in this
period and lived only in parody prepared the ground for the new everyday hero of this rising class. The dissolution of heroic ideality in everyday reality and the connected justification of the repressed, "unheroic"
desire for happiness gave rise to an insight that is far ahead of all later
critique of ideology and which was expressed by Marivaux in a memorable formulation: "tout ce qu'on rapporte de grand en parlant des
hommes, doit nous être bien plus suspect que ce qu'on en rapporte de
grotesque et d'extravagant" (all the great things we are told about men
should be viewed with much greater suspicion by us than the grotesque
and extravagant things we hear [in his *Télémaque travesti*, 1715]).[28]

3. The Rabelaisian hero as a figure of grotesque life

What Baudelaire saw as absolute or grotesque laughter and wished to
set against the classicist tradition of distancing "laughter about,"
Mikhail Bakhtin later uncovered in the more universal context of the
phenomenon he called the "culture of folk humor." Depending on
the normative power of prevailing moralities, its manifestations are
more or less subliminal, are forced into subcultures or remain "insular," limited to the license of certain festive occasions such as the classical or medieval saturnalia or the carnivals of our period. Rabelais's
work brought an enormous breakthrough: in this inexhaustible summa of grotesque laughter, the *poeta doctus* of the Renaissance breaks
free of the secular burden of Christian dogmatics and classical learning,
of the compulsion of an ascetic morality and the veiled dogmatism of
a language that distinguished between high and low, forbidden and
permitted, sacred and profane.[29] Although it may not do full justice
to Rabelais's creative individuality,[30] his humanist or Erasmian credo,
and the questions about a new practice of life, Bakhtin's interpretation nonetheless provides us with the indispensable key that will help
avoid the familiar aporias of philological and positivist research.
Gargantua, Pantagruel, and the other books of the Rabelaisian cycle
do not fit neatly into a history of the novel; Rabelais's grotesque language and his handling of the sacrosanct sources cannot be understood
by classicist concepts of parody and travesty or the comedy of the
counterimage; and his figures in their fantastic dimensions as giants,
fools, or rogues cannot be classed as individual heroes. The laughter
at Gargantua or Pantagruel, Frère Jean or Panurge is never confined

to the figure that prompts it. It is the liberating and desecrating laughter of a group of eaters and drinkers who are always also portrayed and addressed, and it is infectious. It is, above all, grotesque laughter because it continually testifies to the triumph over every kind of fear.

That it is inappropriate here to expect anything like a novel or norms of probability immediately becomes apparent when one looks back at the relationships between the Rabelaisian cycle and the medieval *roman* and the chronicles about giants, the already distant model and the immediately preceding tradition. The entire repertory of heroes as found in the most successful medieval novels is once again evoked for the reader of Rabelais but now in the form of a burlesque heroes catalog which includes all those whom Epistemon encountered in the nether word: Alexander, who must repair old shoes, and Lancelot who must work as a flayer, are first among classical heroes and the "chevaliers de la table ronde." They find themselves in a merry round with historical figures such as Pope Julius II (street-vendor of pastries), Cleopatra (reseller of onions), Trajan as a frog catcher, and Dido as a seller of mushrooms. In the lower world, all the celebrities from the epic and legendary tradition are condemned to atone through lowly labor for their prerogatives as "gros seigneurs" whose role Rabelais allots to the philosophers, so severly disadvantaged in this world.[31] This carnivalesque inversion of the hierarchy is matched by a promotion of previously secondary figures to principal ones: the giants, members of the servant personnel of the power of evil in the Arthurian novel and finally dissolved into nothingness along with all other magical beings, are now beyond all servitude and alone determine the epic action. It is certainly true that Rabelais found his principal figures with their giant dimensions in the popular chronicles and skillfully exploited their success. These giant heroes, which had already appeared on the side of the beneficent powers in those accounts, here occasionally come close to the paragons among human rulers, but this is not the full extent of Rabelais's decisive innovation.[32]

Pantagruel, for example, who was known from folklore as nothing more than a little devil who scatters salt into the mouths of drinkers attains, as son of the giant Gargantua, not only the epic dignity of a ruler but also mythical greatness: born in an hour when the world almost perished of thirst, he will, as Roy des Dispodes, one day become the ruler of all thristy persons. From the tiny demon who served as a witty explanation of thirst, Rabelais develops an outsize comic power which can decree both the torments and the stilling of physical and spiritual thirst and thus has control over an inexhaustible source of human happiness.[33] Pantagruel and Gargantua being autocratic rulers, the grotesquely exaggerated powers, deeds, and pronouncements of the Rabelaisian "heroes" are raised to a higher level and become expressions of the irrepressibility of the body: the laughter at their giant hunger, the insatiable sexuality, or the monstrous scatology of their "Faits et dits heroiques" restores the corporality of human existence, which had been suppressed by epic ideality, to its rightful place and puts in the wrong those who take moral offense at this emancipation of creatureliness. To the degree Gargantua and Pantagruel, Frère Jean and Panurge and their trabants inspire grotesque laughter, they stop being comic as individual heroes and become subordinate actors in the eternally recurring, festive "drama of bodily life."[34] Laughter here is no longer about conduct that evokes ideal norms of heroic greatness in the very act of falling short of them: the reason for the grotesque laughter lies in the ephemeral relief from moral taboos whose burden and pressure were probably first consciously felt in this act of the festive liberation of laughter and the body.

Thus the stations of a hero's life (which Rabelais copied from the medieval chivalric romance "from the ancestor catalogue, the miraculous birth of the hero and his childhood up to his being tested in combat against the evil heathens")[35] also become a new occasion for laughter which has little in common with the traditional pleasure in parody. Gargantua's birth may serve as example (chapters iii to vii): it is not miraculous in the sense of a one-time occurrence with epic prefiguration but enormous through the dimensions of a cosmic event whose episodes burst all epic conventions. One need only call to mind the extravagant descriptions of the pregnancy, the onset of the birth as a result of an extremely unappetizing meal of tripe, the disreputable speeches of the drunk, the consoling words Grandgousier finds for the woman in labor, "hurry up with this one and soon we'll make another," the first cry of the newborn, "à boire, à boire," his gigantic thirst which can be stilled only with the milk from seventeen thousand three hundred and nineteen cows, and so on. In his dramatic revival of 1968 (surely the highest level of current Rabelais reception!), Louis Barrault not only blended the shocking climax of the "propos des bien yvres"—Christ's desecreated "I am thirsty" ("sitio")—into the birth but has the cross collapse in the joyous frenzy of a kermis à la Breughel after giving the crucified a "gentil vin blanc."[36] Rabelais probably would not have minded this daring interpretation. However, the achievements of the adult giant hero in the pursuit of the ideal of "arma et litterae" are not really comic because they parodistically refer to a heroic model but as "deeds and pronouncements" that shift or altogether eliminate the traditional border line between body and world, as Bakhtin observes.[37]

Faits et dits heroiques: this title of Books III, IV, and V also comes closest to doing justice to the intent of the earlier books. For the announced "faits et prouesses espouventables" of Pantagruel not infrequently make it seem as if the grotesque action were being told only for the sake of a witty saying. They so far exceed all epic expectation and are so enormous that an action mocking all probability also mocks all heroic ideality and may perhaps be said to ignore rather than to imitate and parody it. In the war against Picrochole, Gargantua insults the opposing forces for lacking all military art and discipline, though this certainly does not prevent him from achieving his victories through pranks and ruses the laughter at which stifles all thought of knightly rules and epic justice. Gargantua, for example, uproots a large tree in spite of its sacred origin (it had grown from the staff belonging to Saint Martin) and uses it to kill his enemies in the castle of the Vède ford, enemies who had already been decimated by a flood of urine because Gargantua's mare had had to "relieve her belly" (chap. XXXVI). And later, Gargantua does not really have to undergo what might be called heroic efforts: the large canon ball with which a "ruffian gunner" hits him on the temple he takes for a berry, the nine thousand and five smaller bullets and rocks which fly at and about his head for a swarm of flies. And as he combs his hair before the victory celebration, his father, Grandgousier, laughs derisively at the "lice" falling from his head which he must have picked up at some "lousy college" (chap. XXXVII). Such points which the contemporary reader probably no longer appreciates were presumably even at that time no longer aimed at the heroism of a faded knighthood; they simply abolish it and derive most of their comic effects from the lack of proportion between real (often overly precise) dimensions and irreal excessive ones which exposes to laughter what is fear-inspiring in war, be it passed down in the epic tradition, or historical.

The collective subject of this laughter, the eating and drinking guests, reappear here. The enormous victory banquet is introduced by the charming episode in which Gargantua prepares a salad from huge lettuce leaves as an hors d'oeuvre and devours six fearful pilgrims who had hidden there (chap. XXXVIII). It is to Herman Meyer that we are obliged for having shown that all the elements of this grotesque story are a reworking of the text of the 123rd psalm and that it "ridicules the deplorable medieval custom of interpreting passages from the Bible as prophecies of events in daily life."[38] But Rabelais here pretends not merely to the "freedom of humoristic inversion" the humanist *poeta doctus* had, he also lays claim to the newly won freedom of his grotesque style to do away with the limits of the individual body. The direct occasion for the grotesque laughter is the disproportions: great fear of the small pilgrims—tiny objects for the giant appetite, their point of convergence in the image-field "snail in the salad" merely a guess at this moment. When Gargantua has already put five of the pilgrims into his mouth without realizing it, a table companion notices what he takes to be a snail's horn under a lettuce leaf though it is actually the staff of the sixth, "seeing which, Grandgousier said to Gargantua: 'look, Gargantua, that's a snail's horn. Don't eat it!'—'Why not? They are good this month.'" The punch line is due to the ambiguity but ultimately also to the Rabelaisian idea of the *one* grotesque body which is cosmic and universal, i.e., which "transgress[es] the limits of [its] isolation."[39] The famous counterpart is the episode analyzed by Erich Auerbach in which Alcofribas discovers a "new world" in Pantagruel's mouth where things are no different from what they are at home, in France (chap. XXXII).[40] It need only be added to this already classical interpretation that the point of the newly discovered yet familiar everyday world refers to the real 1598 event but also discovers in the grotesque laughter Pantagruel's mouth as horizon and thus the body as encompassing world. The grotesque detail that Maître Alcofribas must answer various questions about what he ate and drank as he reports to Pantagruel about his sojourn in his throat (questions which include the unavoidable one, "'But where did you cack?'—'Down your throat, My Lord'") fits in with this view. The discovery of the world in Pantagruel's mouth, which began with the description of cabbage-planting peasants, ends with the natural consequence of consumption and digestion. The reader who laughs about Pantagruel's more than generous reaction (the good-natured giant gives Alcofribas the "domain of Salmagundi") thus has his attention directed to the fact that the well-ordered world with its beautiful arrangement of forests and fields, villages and towns, was created and is being maintained by the endless cycle of physical life.

It must finally be mentioned that the epic occasion for the voyage of discovery into Pantagruel's mouth was a gathering thunderstorm from which the giant sought to protect his frightened companions "as a hen covers her chicks," by sticking out his tongue and making it serve as an umbrella. It is no accident that here also, we encounter a deeper motivation which showed up principally in the antiheroism of the quoted examples but which subliminally conditions the entire thematics of grotesque laughter to a greater or lesser degree. It is the element of vanquished fear in which Bakhtin saw something like the primordial process that gives rise to the manifold manifestations of the grotesque. According to him, "festive folk laughter presents an element of victory not only over supernatural awe, over the sacred, over death; it also means the defeat of power, of earthly kings, of the earthly upper classes, of all that oppresses and restricts."[41] Because the forms of the grotesque, unlike the ugly, are comic not simply as counterimages of the beautiful but as symbols of vanquished fear (simply as counterimage, the ugly does not touch off laughter in any event), they were probably more acceptable in the Middle Ages in that coexistence with the official Christian cult and faith which appears so odd and incredible to the later observer. If parodies on sacred texts or acts of worship (as, for example, the drinkers' mass in Paul Lehman, *Die Parodie im Mittelalter*, 1922) were not felt to be the same thing as the Vergil travesty of the Enlightenment, i.e., were not experienced as a disparaging attack on a no longer accepted authority and therefore tolerated by those in power, this may have been due to an attitude that grants to laughter a truth of its own—a province of the trivial, of a world turned upside down, in the midst of powers that were sure of themselves and could thus establish the curious institution of carnival license. The "insularity of the exceptional state," not the conscious, critical antagonism to the sobriety and coerciveness of institutions, made possible the "festive liberation of laughter and body."[42] Rabelais so enormously extended the insular limits of this exceptional state, his figures of grotesque laughter have triumphed so hugely over the great inner censor, the "fear of the sacred, of prohibitions, of the past, of power"[43] inculcated in man over thousands of years, that in his novels an inversion seems to have occurred in which it is the sacrosanct gravity of the official that is accorded mere insular validity. That this epochal turn in the history of how poetry functions is not directly owed to Renaissance man's legendary self-liberation but that, in Rabelais's case, it was fought for and wrested from a powerful external censor that never let up and that this turn had to be purchased at the price of a lifelong fear of persecution, expresses a fundamental biographical and genetic ambivalence on which, after Jean Louis Barrault, especially Michel Butor has justifiably based his interpretation of Rabelaisian laughter.[44] This laughter cannot really be measured by the yardstick of the modern aesthetics of negativity because it cares nothing about negating or affirming social conditions but brings to light an anthropological truth which time and again has been suppressed, a truth which even the institution of carnival license tended to turn into something innocuous, namely, that "le rire est le propre de l'homme."

4. The comic of a one-sided portrayal of human nature (humor)

The type of comic hero who does not affirm the pleasure principal but presents a one-sided nature and causes a laughter that is equally distant from grotesque laughter and the pleasure of parody is only a marginal phenomenon in the tradition of French literature.[45] But English literature exemplarily represented it at a time when both comedy and the novel were at their height. That it created a tradition makes one wonder whether national psychology is really as inconsequential as is often alleged. Charles Dickens's successful first novel, *The Posthumous Papers of the Pickwick Club* (1836–37) lives off this tradition of humors.[46] The members of this highly respectable "scientific" club set out to extend their research into nature to the observation of characters and manners (p. 2). Mr. Pickwick, the founder of the club, faintly resembles Plato, Zeno, Epicure, and Pythagoras (chap. 15), and is the brilliant author of "Speculations on the Source of the Hampstead Ponds, with Some Observations on the Theory of Tittlebats" (p. 1); he is accompanied by three companions who portray three aspects or sides of human nature.

Mr. Tupman, an enthusiast of female beauty, Mr. Snodgrass, a poetry enthusiast, and Mr. Winkle, a sports enthusiast, make up a trio which becomes comic because it contradicts expected roles. For the ladies' man who becomes ever rounder is successful only once, with an old maid, and that success hardly goes beyond the delightful confession scene ("Miss Wardle! said he. The spinster aunt trembled till some pebbles which had accidentally found their way into the large watering-pot shook like an infant's rattle," p. 97). Because he entrusts himself to Mr. Jingle, a fraud who makes false promises of marriage, the latter promptly supplants him in the affections of his beloved. The second member of the trio whom Mr. Pickwick praises for a "strong poetic turn" (p. 11) has nothing of the poet except the romantic manner ("poetically enveloped in a mysterious blue coat with a canine-skin collar," p. 3), does not produce a single verse, and ends his poet's career with a respectable betrothal. And finally, the dandy in the new green hunting coat turns out to be no more than a would-be hunter and sportsman who is as inept with the rifle as on skates and avoids a duel only at the price of considerable absurdity, his adversary being no less of a coward than he (chap. 38). The comic of these humors does not derive from a caricature of the heroic in the form of conqueror, poet, and "Nimrod." Rather, it lies in a portrayal of charming weaknesses that is not intended to be critical, in the emphasis on the pardonable inclination of the average man to play the role of human greatness. But since this is a daydream, every attempted realization brings its unavoidable disintegration.[47]

The comic of the other groups of individuals who come into contact with the traveling Pickwickians has a simpler structure. What is involved here are characters and social roles that are restricted to a dominant quality or quirk and which have a comic effect because their behavior unwaveringly maintains that dominant quality no matter what the situation. Mr. Jingle's speech, for example, draws on an inexhaustible supply of stories which he tells in a witty imitation of the staccato style of stenography as a sometimes appropriate, sometimes inappropriate comment; the identical speech pattern is repeated in any number of situations until at the end, unmasked as a swindler, he describes his fall into misery with the same trick but with a grotesque gallows humor: "all shirts gone—never mind—saves washing. Nothing soon-lie in bed-starve-die-Inquest-little bone-house-poor prisoner-common necessaries-hush it up-gentlemen of the jury-warden's tradesmen-keep it snug-natural death-coroner's order-workhouse funeral-serve him right--all over-drop the curtain" (pp. 597–98). There is also the idiosyncrasy of the "fat boy," Mr. Wardle's servant, who falls asleep no matter what the occasion so that the coach must have a special seat to keep him from tumbling down. But when this exceptional young man acts unexpectedly and does not fall asleep for once—and the reader has been waiting for this, of course—it is unfailingly at the wrong moment so that he becomes dangerous to lovers, for example, because he overhears their secrets and can produce considerable if ultimately amusing confusion in the family circle (chaps. 8, 54).

This family circle describes the most conventional series of humors, all of which are comic through their banality. Jovial toward the rest of the world, Mr. Wardle is the principled family head within his domain, strict, yet willing to yield when the happiness of his daughters demands it. Of the latter, hardly more can be said than that their colorless role as charming, romantic (but also proper), and sensitive young girls wholly defines them. Other family members such as the elderly, always hysterically laughing spinster or the old lady who seems to be in the novel only because she is hard of hearing are monochrome. There are also humors that become comic only because there is a pair.[48] Bob Sawyer and Benjamin Allen, for example, are two medical students, witty tipplers, whom Dickens uses to satirize the medical profession through the tall stories its practitioners tell (chap. 32) and by the tricks employed when a new practice is opened (chap. 38). More than in the case of this couple, which puts familial dignity to a severe test yet allows one to hope that it will someday be a credit to that family, Dickens uses the comic of the pair in the case of Mr. Pott and Mr. Slurk, the rival editors of the two local papers, the Eatonsville Gazette and Independent. They hate each other like poison, champion the interests of their respective parties to the point of physical combat (chap. 51) as if unbridgeable gulfs lay between "blue" and "buff" principles, attack each other's journalism with a withering sarcasm, and are comic because in their hyperbolic style, they resemble each other as two peas in a pod.

A classical pair in the tradition of humors, father and son, is embodied in this novel by Mr. Weller and Sam, the old coachman and Mr. Pickwick's pert and clever "valet." What Dickens has stressed here is the difference in the comic resemblance ("like father like son"), especially in the attitude toward popular wisdom. Whereas Weller senior philosophizes with usually mild resignation about marriage, the advantages of being a coachman, and the dangers widows anxious to marry pose for him, and awaits with ironic patience the hour he can square accounts with the perpetually drunk Methodist minister, Weller junior is always ready with a witty reply, a better advocate for his master than learned counsel (chap. 34), and eminently successful with the opposite sex (thanks in part to a love letter of his own devising "that verges on the poetical," p. 454). Sam is perfectly capable of commenting on anything that may develop, and of doing so with a pessimism that differs from his father's coachman's philosophy, a point to which I will return. An exhaustive analysis of the humors in the *Pickwick Papers* should study in some detail how Dickens transforms social roles into humors: the many-faceted portrayal of the law with all its quirky, mulish, innocuously ignorant but also unscrupulous and corrupt types and authorities would be an excellent field for such an undertaking. This cannot be done here. Instead, we will turn to the principal figure, Mr. Pickwick, who, though himself part of the tradition of humors, transcends it in a distinctive way.

5. The comic of innocence — the innocence of the comic (Dickens's comic hero)

As he gets into the *Pickwick Papers* and begins to reflect about his experience with the characters, the reader will probably realize that though they offer an always identical occasion for laughter or reason for our pleasure which is determined by their respective humor, there is at least one, Mr. Pickwick himself, who breaks through this convention and who surprises us by gradually forcing us to realize that our estimate of the hero changes in the course of the picaresque action. If we initially find him amusing or laughable as just one among other traveling Pickwickians, our attitude can rise to admiring identification to the degree that Mr. Pickwick abandons his pretentions to the role of philosopher (chap. 2), involves himself from innate kindness in the affairs of others, and finally, as a true humoristic hero, "victoriously asserts," in the debtor's prison, "the ego's invulnerability" against all cowardly adaptation to reality and the glaring injustice of the world.

The manner of Mr. Pickwick's introduction does not at first appear to really set him apart from his traveling companions. For just as it is only in their daydreams that they achieve an extraordinary destiny, so Mr. Pickwick initially seems comic only because the records of the Pickwick Club and the narrator identify him as a famous, a "colossal-minded man," (p. 165), the bearer of an "immortal name" (chap. 12). Yet he certainly does not exceed the common measure. Through the contrast between the heroic greatness expected of him as head of the club, and his perfectly unheroic qualities of patience, good humor, sensitivity, cheerfulness, and kindness — all of which go perfectly with the appearance of an elderly gentleman with a "bald head and circular spectacles" (p. 2) — Mr. Pickwick is comic as an involuntary hero. But the enumeration of these qualities already shows that Mr. Pickwick is a rounder figure than the one-sided humors that keep him company. The preeminent attribute of his nature is neither a particular weakness nor an aberrant pretension but a disarming innocence which allows him to emerge unscathed from even the most delicate situations and often makes one smile rather than laugh. For this reason, Mr. Pickwick has been incorrectly called the "Don Quixote of the Biedermeier." For the "hero" of the Pickwickians does not pursue a fixed idea of heroic supergreatness but contents himself with the role of an "observer of human nature" (p. 11). He does not interpret events to then attempt to impose a universal principle on a hostilely neutral reality but responds to the expectations and demands on his "fame" by the innocence of a conduct that ostensibly makes him a comic hero. But since the innocence of this comic not infrequently shames his friends and his adversaries, he actually turns increasingly into a humoristic figure.

The comic of innocence into which Dickens transforms this charming average man's ironic elevation to the level of heroic supergreatness is pervasive in the action of the novel. Where the situation calls for heroic transport, as after the "defiance" delivered by Doctor Payne (chap. 3) or the impertinences of Mr. Jingle (chap. 10), Mr. Pickwick's wrath erupts too late and nothing more than a glass of brandy or a prosaic admonition of his servant is needed to promptly dissipate the heroic affect: "Mr. Pickwick's mind, like those of all truly great men, was open to conviction. He was a quick and powerful reasoner; and a moment's reflection sufficed to remind him of the impotency of his rage. It subsided as quickly as it had been roused. He panted for breath, and looked benignantly upon his friends" (p. 131). Where the situation brings with it all the torments of absurdity, as in the chase after a hat that is rolling before the wind ("smiling pleasantly all the time, as if you thought it as good a joke as anybody else," p. 50), or when he is caught behind the gate of a "young ladies' seminary" which is in an uproar because of him (chap. 16), when he falls asleep in a barrow after too much punch and wakes up in the Pound (chap. 20), or slides on the ice and crashes through it and into the cold water, Mr. Pickwick always knows how to preserve some of the curious dignity of his innocence in these comic entanglements: "And when he was knocked down (which happened upon the average every third round), it was the most invigorating sight that can possibly be imagined, to behold him gather up his hat, gloves, and handkerchief, with a glowing countenance and resume his station in the rank, with an ardour and enthusiasm that nothing could abate" (p. 414). A climax of this comic of innocence is the marvellous scene where, in the labyrinthine inn, Mr. Pickwick mistakenly wanders into the room of an unknown "middle-aged lady" and, already half-undressed, is surprised by her arrival, hides behind the bed curtains, and must embark on a complicated retreat. And this happens to "one of the most modest and delicate-minded of mortals (p. 309), whom the mere thought of having to show his nightcap to a lady fills with apprehension" (chap. 22). This most harmless of mortals, the very antithesis of a ladies' man, is also unlucky enough to be suspected of having broken a promise of marriage and to almost fall victim to the machinations of a widow scheming to marry, and to the unscrupulousness of her two lawyers. The climax of the plot is reached when the comic of innocence which up to this point had been acted out at the level of unproblematical cheerfulness, turns into an innocence of the comic which touches the sublime and comes to embody the Freudian concept of the humoristic hero.

"Like jokes and the comic, humor has something liberating about it; but it also has something of grandeur and elevation," Freud wrote.

"The ego refuses to be distressed by the provocations of reality, to let itself be compelled to suffer. It insists that it cannot be affected by the traumas of the external world; it shows, in fact, that such traumas are no more than occasions for it to gain pleasure."[49] The humoristic attitude as described here also characterizes in Mr. Pickwick what I referred to as the preservation of the curious dignity of his innocence in the episodes mentioned.[50] This innocence is subjected to an *experimentum crucis* when he refuses to accept the unjust judgment in the trial of Bardell against Pickwick and prefers being taken to Fleet prison than pay what is for him an insignificant compensation. The explanation Mr. Pickwick gives the "supercilious serjeant,"—"that unless you sincerely believe this, I would rather be deprived of the aid of your talents than have the advantage of them" (p. 431)— already gives his rejection of the claim of reality an ethical motive which, though fed by the assertion of the pleasure principle, yet points beyond it. This does not mean that the humoristic hero of the *Pickwick Papers* acts in the name of a universal principle; instead, he simply rebels because "I am innocent of the falsehood laid to my charge" (p. 430). Mr. Pickwick does not evoke principles of justice that have been violated, nor does he criticize the evil reality of this society, though this might be warranted by his reputation as a "philosopher." Rather, the humoristic attitude which asserts itself in his person in the face of the contrariety of real conditions turns against all philosophical theories and carries on what had hitherto been a subliminal polemic against philosophers. Mr. Pickwick had previously expressed this in these terms: "it has somehow or other happened, from time immemorial, that many of the best and ablest philosophers, who have been perfect lights of science in matters of theory, have been wholly unable to reduce them to practice" (p. 253). As a theoretician, Mr. Pickwick can only claim to be a very modest luminary (one need only recall his "theory concerning the sticklebacks"), but he turns out to be "a most extraordinary man" in practice (p. 570) and this not because he knows how to "reduce knowledge to practice" but because he can victoriously assert the innocence of human nature against the encroachments of an evil reality.

However seriously this decision must be taken, however great Dickens's skill in exploiting this situation in order to cry out against conditions and abuses in the English judicature of his time, it is also true that the story intermittently preserves the humoristic attitude. It is in the medium of comic innocence that the victoriously asserted innocence of the comic manifests itself time and again in the behavior of the humoristic hero. We need only recall the stage requisite already familiar to us from a number of comic situations which now takes on the quality of a symbol of the "inviolability of the self" for the Biedermeier hero: Mr. Pickwick's nightcap. After his first walk through the prison he is close to despair: "he was alone in the coarse vulgar crowd, and felt the depression of spirit and sinking of heart, naturally consequent on the reflection that he was caged and cooped up, without a prospect of liberation" (p. 579). Sitting down on his small iron bed, he pulls his nightcap from the pocket into which he had providentially put it during the morning, and his equanimity returns. The rowdiness of his drunk cell mates, whose rough jokes and provocations he suffers until the nightcap is violently pulled from his head, rouses him from the sleep of the just. As though stung by a tarantula, he jumps from his bed, develops a "very unexpected gallantry" (p. 582), and retrieves not only the attribute of a "worthy gentleman" but also wins the admiring recognition of his dubious new companions.

The reader may be surprised that so much fortitude is no better rewarded at the end of his stay in the debtors' prison, that the sly lawyers get away unscathed, and that it takes the strenuous and tearful intervention of the charming Arabella who must appeal to his magnanimity to lure Mr. Pickwick from the prison. But the humoristic hero stands above a simple satisfaction of poetic justice.[51] His material defeat is made up for by the "victoriously asserted inviolability of the ego," though not without a final word which the gentle Mr. Pickwick feels free to address to Dodson and Fogg: "'you are,'" continued Mr. Pickwick, resuming the thread of his discourse, 'you are a well-matched pair of mean, rascally, pettifoggin robbers.' 'Robbers'! shouted Mr. Pickwick, breaking from Lowton and Perker, and thrusting his head out of the staircase window. When Mr. Pickwick drew in his head again, his countenance was smiling and placid, and, walking quietly back into the office, he declared that he had now removed a great weight from his mind, and that he felt perfectly comfortable and happy" (p. 751). We have here the finest example of what I should like to call "humoristic catharsis."

It is more than merely a stereotype of the classic bourgeois novel when the author bids his hero a somewhat melancholy farewell at the end: "Let us leave our old friend in one of those moments of unmixed happiness, of which, if we seek them, there are ever some, to cheer our transitory existence here" (p. 799). As a humoristic hero, Mr. Pickwick is viewed with growing sympathy, a sympathy which Molière's characters (enslaved by their affects) or the comic epic hero (who, as a counterimage of the ruling tradition, produces laughter by disparaging the ideal) elicit less often. This growing sympathy presupposes an understanding between author and reader which—as John Bayley recently explained—is rooted in a kind of social compact, a common "patronage" toward a society that we need and hate but which for that very reason we can also love.[52] A humoristic hero who is comic because of his innocence and appealing at the same time thrives only in a world in which we can share his hatreds and loves, his contempt and his admiration.

In Don Quixote, the prototypical counterimage comedy, this level of identification is missing. For although it is true that he comes close to the humoristic hero because, an unpropitious reality notwithstanding, he clings to his stubborn interpretation of a last knight, his rejection of the claim of reality is unfree: "this only is his lunacy that he is and remains so sure of himself and his business."[53] Unlike the humoristic hero therefore, he cannot laugh at himself and the disintegration of his purposes so that the reader also can only laugh at, not with him. Nor did Dickens take more from Cervantes than the master-servant relationship which he modified. The friendly solidarity that develops gradually and almost imperceptibly between Don Quixote and Sancho Pancha exists between Mr. Pickwick and Sam Weller from the very beginning. Dickens does not problematize it; it is touching rather than funny. In response to the Cervantine tradition, it becomes comic only where master's and servant's relationship to reality diverge. It is a difference that can be expressed in terms of the contradiction between theory and practice.

In Cervantes, master and servant become a comic pair in part because they use contrasting keys to interpret reality: the master the key of the "theory" of the novel of chivalry, the servant that of the practical wisdom of the proverb. Neither succeeds. The master fails because he anticipates a later, famous philosopher and subscribes to a dictum attributed to him: "if reality does not accommodate itself to my theory, so much the worse for reality." The servant, because in his difficulties he draws on a special "dowry for use against a hostile world. With Sancho Pancha, the wisdom of the proverb answers Don Quixote's utopian rationalism and unrestrained consciousness of freedom."[54] Werner Krauss, whose unsurpassed appreciation of the Spanish proverb I should like to recall here, already noted that Sancho's key—the proverb as practical insight into, and derived from, any and every situation and congealed in a catchword—fails before the test of this journey. His "theory" fails not merely because the aristocrat Don Quixote has uprooted the peasant Sancho Panza who, when afraid, always recites a whole string of proverbs when the occasion seems to warrant it. The deeper reason is that for the first time,

Cervantes here makes us ironically aware of the immanent contradiction between an experience that is interpreted by rules, and the praxis
of life whose reality one can never wholly catch up with. Even in
their grotesque sequentiality, the proverbs with which Sancho comments on the journey and the interpretations of his master are not all
that nonsensical, let alone a piece of pure nonsense poetry. In their
very contradictions, they continue to relate to an initial situation, illuminate its ambiguity, become entangled in the casuistry of life, and
thus make the reader feel the fundamental contradiction of the
proverb as a category of practical experience. For as retrospective insight, it cannot also be a guide to action nor, as a truth tied to a
specific situation, a timeless rule.

In the case of another comic couple in the Cervantic tradition of
master and servant, Diderot's *Jacques le Fataliste et son maître*, the
servant is also promoted in the sense that he espouses a philosophical
theory that his master does not care for. Here, the entwinement of
theory and practice and their contradiction become a source of the
comic in a different way. The master who argues for the philosophical
theory of the freedom of the will before a skeptical Jacques is in practice incapable of taking even the simplest decision without the aid of
his servant. He is ironized as his "automaton" for which everything
revolves around his tobacco box, his pocket watch, and his curiosity
about Jacques's tales. When he tells his own life story, everything is
so totally predictable that Jacques, a smart listener, can anticipate
all points and becomes so bored that he falls asleep before the story
reaches its climax. The servant to whom Diderot has here allotted the
role of reason and thus the traditional legitimation of the master[55]
constantly quotes the fatalistic phrase of his captain, and resembles
Sancho in this respect, "que tout ce qui nous arrive de bien et de mal
ici-bas était écrit là-haut" (that all the good and bad that happens to
us here on earth was written in heaven). But in practice, his actions
contradict this, show him capable of dealing with any difficulty and
the master of any situation, so that the praxis disavows his fatalistic
theory which only governs his ex-post-facto interpretations. If one
wishes to see a barometer of the prerevolutionary bourgeoisie in the
mirror of Diderot's *Jacques le Fataliste et son maître*, the frequently
evoked dialectics of master and slave must be qualified by the per-
ceptibly growing friendly solidarity of this comic couple, and it must
also finally be taken into account that neither of them is right in the
end; not a particular philosophical theory but the metaphysical claim
that ultimate questions can be answered and the world therefore interpreted is refuted in Diderot's novel by practical reason.

In Dickens, the process of mutual recognition between master and servant is already presupposed. From beginning to end, their relationship is friendly: Mr. Pickwick is proud of his valet and accepts him as "an original" who may take certain liberties (chap. 22), and Sam praises his master,[56] voluntarily follows him into prison, and would rather not marry his beloved Mary than leave Mr. Pickwick even though the latter now retires. In Dickens, master and servant are therefore not really comic as a pair but only through their different interpretations of reality. Mr. Pickwick refuses to see only "the worst side of human nature" (p. 430) and survives in the world through the innocence of his humoristic attitude. His servant Sam beautifully complements him by his presence of mind and the sharpness of his mother wit. Not infrequently, the success his practical wisdom brings makes for a witty contrast with the pessimistic tenor of his "philosophy." It is really this contrast which casts in a comic light the otherwise round character who is not comic through any inherent inadequacy. As when Sam is pursued by Mr. Jingle, introduces himself, and simultaneously gets himself out of a tight spot: "'Here you are, Sir,' said Mr. Weller, emerging from a sequestered spot where he had been engaged in discussing a bottle of Madeira, which he had abstracted from the breakfast table an hour or two before. 'Here's your servant, Sir. Proud o' the title as the Living Skellinton said, ven they show'd him'" (p. 206). The pointed form and the often almost macabre substance of his comments ("now we look compact and comfortable, as the father said ven he cut his little boy's head off, tu cure him o' squintin," p. 384) characterizes his speech as the expression of an original, and it is not by chance that these sayings, a subspecies of the proverb, have entered the vocabulary as "Wellerisms." They constitute the pessimistic counterpart of the humoristic attitude. Yet here too, it is only a single facet of the comic inexhaustibility of the inherently so serious contradiction between theory and practice that is brought to light in the *concordia discors* of master and servant.

D. On the Question of the "Structural Unity" of Older and Modern Lyric Poetry (Théophile de Viau: *Ode III;* Baudelaire: *Le Cygne*)

> For art to be born, it is necessary that the relation between represented objects and man be of a different nature than that imposed by the world.[1]

1. On the debate over Hugo Friedrich's theory of modern lyric poetry

The still continuing discussion that Hugo Friedrich set off with his *Die Struktur der modernen Lyrik*[2] (1956) has recently been enriched by a contribution of H. O. Burger's which deserves special interest because he raises a fundamental objection and supports it by skillfully chosen texts.[3] His criticism does not concern itself with the secondary problem involved in the unavoidable choice that H. Friedrich first had to make among numerous authors belonging to various national literatures and then from their lyric production, but questions the underlying historical determination: whether the structure of modern lyric poetry can justifiably be derived from an opposition to the norms of the traditional, classical, and humanist poetics with which the "literary revolution of the 20th century," especially Baudelaire, Rimbaud, and Mallarmé—H. Friedrich's "classics" of modern lyric poetry—broke. In Burger's words, "didn't Friedrich make it a little too easy for himself when he described this premodern lyric poetry? This may be the reason that in his book, modern lyric poetry appears so markedly as the reversal of everything that went before and seems best understood in negative categories. In spite of the enormous differences, isn't there also a certain structural unity between 'modern' and 'classical' lyric poetry?"[4]

Burger believes he can uncover such a structural unity by way of a novel definition of the lyric experience which also includes a rehabilitation of the concept of experience which H. Friedrich "loathed in poetics." That novel definition is the "experience of exorbitance," one of life which is not wholly contained in the world. Expressed differently: "where our attitude toward existence and the idea we have of it are called *world*, there *life* is our experience of existence as world bursts open. It is my view that to present or evoke experiences of this kind is the innermost essence of poetry."[5] Reading this, the Romance scholar will first be pleased to note that with this definition Burger has moved away from the customary aesthetics of the experience of individuality even though he does not specifically say so. His "experience of exorbitance" no longer sublates the tension between "experience" and "poetry" in the immediacy of lyric self-expression but in the presentation of another world, a world which is new because "created in language."[6] But half of this additional step is retracted on the very same page. This "bursting open" of an existing world in the verbal creation of lyric poetry does not "first and foremost involve a new world but something that is other than world: the 'marvellous' in the widest sense of that term."[7] And for Burger, that "widest sense" turns out to be surprisingly encompassing, for in it, poetic practice from the seventeenth century to the present, from Marino to Mallarmé, is to find a common denominator. "If the mannerists of the Baroque started off from Marino's ''E del poeta il fin la meraviglia, Chi non sa far stupir, vada alla striglia,' the later poets from post-Baroque classicism to early Romanticism wrote variations on Boileau's thesis concerning 'cet extraordinaire et ce merveilleux qui fait qu'un ouvrage enlève, ravit transporte.' And the same thread is spun further in Mallarmé's 'ontological scheme,' as Friedrich called it, and in Gottfried Benn's lecture on 'Probleme der Lyrik' (1951) which became the 'Ars poetica' for Germany's younger generation."[8]

To probe this apparent agreement by investigating the concept of the "marvellous" in the history of poetic theories and the application of the "far stupir" in poetic practice would certainly be an engaging undertaking. Since we cannot come anywhere near that distant goal at this time, we follow the route also chosen by Burger who seeks to support his thesis by a comparative structural analysis of classical and modern poems. We will consider two, fairly long ones with a similar motif from older and from modern French poetry where the postulated structural unity behind all stylistically conditioned differences would have to manifest itself. Since what ultimately counts in this comparison is that the "marvellous" or the "bursting open" of an existing world and the appearance of something that is "other than world" show itself as a structural correspondence in the two poems, it is methodologically indicated that we approach the texts by asking how the authors realized Marino's "far stupir" or—in modern terms— how they "alienated" familiar reality and made the "other world" of poetry appear in this estrangement.

In the case of this poetic procedure, in which G. R. Hocke sees a characteristic of mannerism as opposed to the classical style[9] (in Burger, this distinction is relativized),[10] a further conceptual analogy to Burger's "merveilleux" might be mentioned which at first glance seems to confirm the structural unity of "baroque" and modern lyric poetry which Hocke emphasizes. For the modern concept of "alienation" did not just become fashionable in our time, especially through Brecht's epic dramaturgy. In its application to poetics, we probably find it first[11] in the very poet Hocke wanted to place "at the beginning of the Neo-mannerism of our time," in Baudelaire's essay *Notes nouvelles sur Edgar Poe* (1857).[12] The passage refers to the special care Poe had bestowed on the treatment of rhyme: "Just as he has shown that the refrain is capable of infinitely varied applications, so also he has sought to renew, to redouble the pleasure derived from rhyme by adding to it an expected element, the strange,[13] which is the indispensable condiment, as it were, of all beauty."[14] Along with other definitions of the *beauté moderne* (such as surprise, the bizarre, melancholy), this Baudelairean concept, especially significant here because of the explanatory elaboration, seems to correspond perfectly to the atemporal typicality of that literary mannerism which Hocke, in a development of chapter 15 of Curtius's *European Literature and the Latin Middle Ages*, tried to identify as a "European constant" from Marino and Gongora to Mallarmé and T. S. Eliot.[15] Whether with complete justification or, expressed differently, whether Baudelaire with his new definition of the beautiful merely renewed a thousands-of-years old "expressive gesture" going back to the Asianic style of antiquity or created a new one which ran counter to all previous tradition (a style which corresponded to his sense of the onset of the wholly different historical world of the modern period) is the wider problem which I wish to pursue here by a comparative structural analysis.

2. The modernity of the classical in Gide's selection from the *Maison de Silvie*

Decisive in the choice of an example from the older tradition was not only the thematic analogy (swan motif) but also the fact that André

Gide incorporated a portion from the third ode of Théophile de Viau's *Maison de Silvie* (1624) in his *Anthologie de la poésie française*. The criteria for his choice lead us directly into the problematics of "classical" and "modern form". And the rationale Gide advances for these criteria in his preface also presents to us the special situation of lyric poetry during the century of French classicism and thereby the reason it seemed appropriate to represent this epoch by a poet who ignored Malherbes's classical rules, yet enjoyed a special and sustained esteem among the public of French classical literature.[16] Gide's remarks go back to a dispute with A. E. Housman who provoked him into a very appealing apology of French poetry by this question: "How do you explain the fact that there is no such thing as French poetry, Mr. Gide? . . . I know, of course, you have had Villon, Baudelaire . . . But between Villon and Baudelaire, what long and constant misapprehension has brought it about that rhymed discourses were considered poems, discourses which certainly contain wit, eloquence, virulence, pathos, but never any poetry!"[17] The widespread prejudice —deliberately overstated here—that French lyric poetry suffers from a chronic lack of feeling clearly shows that Gide's interlocutor himself subscribed to a historically determined and therefore episodic canon of the beautiful: the concept of poetry romanticism cherished, a movement which had its roots in Germany and England. By contrast, it is the "classical" principle of *contrainte* (restraint) which anti-romanticism had revaluated that Gide placed at the head of his canon as he made the selections for his new anthology which was to rebut this prejudice: "Might one not say that however troublesome to the ill-considered flight of fancy, however vexing to the spontaneity of the poet these rules may occasionally be, they make up for this by leading him to produce more art, a more perfect art, and often an art which no other country can equal?"[18] This principle results in the modern esteem for the artificial, rhetorical style, for the formal beauty of an art whose language and style are pure, an esteem which was reflected in the rediscovery of the lyric poetry of the Baroque: it is Gide's intent to present "the most perfect examples of verbal mastery and oratorical persuasion." But neither is his anthology meant to conceal "what French poetry atypically offers in the way of the musical."[19] This second criterion relates to the "revolution without predecessors" with which Baudelaire opened a new path for poetry.[20] Gide says nothing about the alleged difference between this specifically modern musicality of the lyric and similar determinations of the older, rhetorical and verbal tradition. In the case of the section from Théophile's third ode, it is a question that first arises in the following form: did Gide here wish to provide an example of classical *maîtrise verbale* and *persuasion oratoire* or did he want to show a specifically modern side in the poet of French *préclassicisme*? It is obvious that Gide's procedure made it necessary to detach the concepts "classical" and "modern" from their tie to a historically circumscribed period. The extent to which the typological and atemporal contrast posited in this fashion is itself the result of the temporally conditioned aesthetic judgment of a twentieth-century critic will become clear to us from Gide's abridgement, from what he included and from what he omitted.[21]

(i) *Dans ce Parc un valon secret*
tout voilé de ramages sombres,
Où le Soleil est si discret
Qu'il n'y force jamais les ombres,
Presse d'un cours si diligent
Les flot de deux ruisseaux d'argent
Et donne une fraischeur si vive
A tous les objets d'alentour,
Que mesme les martyrs d'Amour
Y trouvent leur douleur captive.

(ii) *Un estanc dort là tout auprès,*
Où ces fontaines violentes
Courent, et font du bruit exprès
Pour esveiller ses vagues lentes.
Luy d'un maintien majestueux
Reçoit l'abord impetueux
De ces Naiades vagabondes,
Qui dedans ce large vaisseau
Confondent leur petit ruysseau
E ne discernent plus ses ondes.

(iii) Là Melicerte, en un gazon
Frais de l'estanc qui l'environne,
Fait aux Cygnes une maison
Qui luy sert aussi de couronne.
Si la vague qui bat ses bors
Jamais avecques des thresors
N'arrive à son petit Empire,
Au moins les vents et les rochers
N'y font point crier les rochers
Dont ils ont brisé les navires.

(iv) Là les oyseaux font leurs petits
Et n'ont jamais veu leurs couvees

Souler les sanglants appetits
Du serpent qui les a trouvees.
Là n'estend point ses plis mortels
Ce monstre de qui tant d'autels
Ont jadis adoré les charmes,
Et qui d'un gosier gemissant
Fait tomber l'ame du passant
Dedans l'embusche de ses larmes.

(v) *Zephyre en chasse les chaleurs,*
Rien que les Cygnes n'y repaissent,
On n'y trouve rien sous les fleurs
Que la fraischeur dont elles naissent.
Le gazon garde quelques fois
Le bandeau, l'arc et le carquois
De mill'armours qui se despouillent
A l'ombrage de ses roseaux
Et dans l'humidité des eaux
Trempent leurs jeunes corps qui boüillent.

(vi) *L'estanc leur preste sa fraischeur,*
La Naiade leur verse à boire,
Toute l'eau prend de leur blancheur
L'esclat d'une couleur d'yvoire.
On void là ces nageurs ardents
Dans les ondes qui'ils vont fendants
Faire la guerre aux Nereides,
Qui devant leur teint mieux uny
Cachent leur visage terny
Et leur front tout coupé de rides.

(vii) *Or ensemble, ores dispersez,*
Ills brillent dans ce crespe sombre
Et sous les flots qu'ils ont persez
Laissent esvanoüir leur ombre.
Parfois dans une claire nuict
Qui du feu de leurs yeux reluit,
Sans aucun ombrage de nuës,
Diane quitte son Berger
Et s'en va là dedans nager
Avecques ses estoilles nuës.

(viii) *Les ondes qui leur font l'amour*
Se refrisent sur leurs espaules
Et font danser tout a l'entour

L'ombre des roseaux et des saules.
Le Dieu de l'eau tout furieux,
Hausse pour regarder leurs yeux
Et leur poil qui flotte sur l'onde,
Du premier qu'il void approcher,
Pense voir ce jeune cocher
Qui fit jadis brusler le monde.

(ix) Et ce pauvre amant langoureux
Dont le feu tousjours se r'allume
Et de qui les soins amoureux
Ont fait ainsi blanchir la plume,
Ce beau Cigne à qui Phaëton
Laissa ce lamentable ton,
Tesmoin d'une amitié si saincte,
Sur les dos son aisle eslevant,
Met ses voilles blanches au vent
Pour chercher l'object de sa plaincte.

(x) Ainsi pour flatter son ennuy
Il demande au Dieu Melicerte
Si chacun Dieu n'est pas celuy
Dont il souspire tant la perte,
Et contemplant de tous costez
Le semblance de leurs beautez
Il sent renouveller sa flame,
Errant avec des faux plaisirs
Sur les traces des vieux desirs
Que conserve encore son ame.

(xi) Tousjours ce furieux dessein
Entretient ses blessures fraisches,
Et fait venir contre son sein
L'air, bruslant et les ondes, seches,
Ces attraits empreints là dedans,
Comme avec des flambeux ardens
Luy rendent la peau toute noire:
Ainsi dedans comme dehors
Il luy tient l'esprit et le corps,
La voix, les yeux et la memoire.

(i) In this park a small, secret valley, fully hidden by dark branches, above which the sun shines so discreetly that it never penetrates its shadows, presses two silver streams onward so diligently and gives such a freshness to everything in it, that even love's martyrs find their suffering captivated by it.

(ii) A pond, toward which the impetuous brooks flow, making noise intentionally to wake its sleepy waves, dozes close by and receives with majestic calm the violent arrival of these vagabond Naiads, who then—ceasing to set apart its waves—merge their little stream into the pond's larger waters.

(iii) Here, Melicertes, on a cool lawn within the pond, provides a home for the swans, who in turn provide him with a crown. Though the waves breaking upon his shores never bear treasurers to his little kingdom, at least no winds or rocks cause pilots to lament the destruction of their ships.

(iv) Here, birds who hatch their young have never seen their nestlings satiate the bloody appetite of the snake. Here, too, the monster [Scylla] whose charms were once adored at so many alters and whose plaintive voice now lures the soul of the passerby into a tearful ambush, has never extended her mortal folds.

(v) Here, Zephyr drives out the heat of the day. Here, only swans feed, and nothing lies beneath the flowers but the coolness from which they grow. Occasionally, on the lawn one comes upon the blindfolds, the bows, and the quivers of a thousand Cupids who undress in the shadows of the reeds and dip their burning bodies in the waters of the pond.

(vi) The pond offers them its coolness. The Naiad pours them drink. All around them the water takes on, from the whiteness of their skins, the luster of ivory. These ardent swimmers can be seen lunging through the water, waging attacks against the Nereids, who hide their tarnished faces and their wrinkled foreheads before the Cupids' smoother complexions.

(vii) Now together, now dispersed, the swimmers shine in the darkness and then allow their shapes to disappear beneath the water. Sometimes, on a clear, cloudless night glistening from the brilliance of their eyes, Diana, having left her shepherd, comes here to swim in the company of her naked stars.

(viii) The waves make love to them, curling around their shoulders and making the reflected reeds and willows dance around them. Melicertes, furious, standing on tiptoe to see their eyes and their hair outspread upon the water, thinks he sees in the first to approach the young charioteer [Phaethon] who once set fire to the world.

(ix) And this poor languishing lover [Cycnus], whose passion continually rekindles and whose loving cares have turned his feathers white, this beautiful swan to whom Phaethon gave his sad song—token of so pure a friendship—raises his wings over his back and sets his white sails to the wind in search of the object of his sorrow.

(x) He asks Melicertes whether every god is not the one whose loss he so greatly mourns, and so he feeds his torment. And seeing on all sides the reflection of their beauty, he feels his love renewing and retraces with illusory pleasure the path of the old desires his heart still preserves.

(xi) This mad enterprise endlessly re-opens his wounds and sets against his breast the air—burning—and the waves—dry. Those charms, stamped into his heart as if with burning torches, blacken him all over: thus, inside as well as out, his search for the one he loved holds his spirit and his body, his voice, his eyes, and his memory.

Théophile's third ode comprises eleven stanzas of ten lines and eight syllables each. From the 110 lines, Gide chose stanzas, i, v, vi, vii, and viii (through the fourth line) and created a skillful transition between i and v by using the first line of ii. If this transition could have been fitted into the form of the stanza, his version would not have revealed that it was due to a cut: by his selection, Gide produced a new, autonomous whole. His forty-five lines are not merely connected formally; they also provide a pervasively motivated sequence of images, i.e., the unity of a perspective which extends from the beginning toward the end. Its center is the pond. With the park, the hidden valley, and the two brooks, the first stanza gives a sort of frame within which the pond appears as scenery which is subsequently brought to life by swans, amourettes, water nymphs, and nereids, which is visited by the moon goddess and her stars, and which, at the end, when everything dissolves in the reflection of the water's surface, still remains visible in its own contours ("l'ombre des roseaux et des saules," l. 74). The visual unity of this perspective is matched by a movement of images which gradually becomes denser and more intense, and is then contained. The description of the park in the first stanza remains static. As the scene gradually fills with figures, the segment of what is shown becomes ever narrower, the rising moon forms a calm contrast with the spirited climax of the playful combat between amourettes and nereids until at the end, we see nothing more than the play of the waves, the medium of all that moves, and, as reflecting surface, its point of rest.

The unity of the perspective Gide created is generally characterized by the fact that it restricts itself to what a painter could also have shown on canvas. In spite of all movement, his version contains neither a temporal-epic process which extends beyond the unity of the scene, nor elements of a suprasensible world or some anterior myth which might break through the sensory appearance of the figures. In his version, the adopted mythological personnel (zephyr, amourettes, naiads, nereids, Diana and her shepherds) no longer point to a higher, mythical world of which the portrayed, natural landscape would be only a copy. His selection makes the heightening of the representation by mythological personifications appear as no more than an ornament of the description, artificial metaphors, which become pure visual phenomena in the landscape of the park. "Diane quitte son berger / Et s'en va là dedans nager" (ll. 68–69) is, in Gide's sequence of images merely a periphrasis for the reflection of the moon in the water where the mythological reference (son berger = Endymion) no longer matters. In the "tableau" that Gide cut out of Théophile's ode, everything mythological remains subordinate to the poetic description and points that description to nothing other than what manifests itself in the representation.

But in the same version also, what is portrayed cannot be understood as the copy of a real landscape, the park of Chantilly, to which Théophile's ode actually refers. What is preserved of that landscape — park, valley, brooks, pond, swans, grass, reeds, and willows — are only the most general features and typical of almost any park of the period. If the poem nonetheless produces the impression of an autonomous unique creation, that is not due to the object itself or some biographical relationship of the poet to what is portrayed, but solely and exclusively to his artful description (*maîtrise verbale*). This disappearance of what is portrayed behind the manner of its presentation is made a shade clearer by Gide than by Théophile because in his abridgement, the description no longer seems to have a purpose other than itself. This gives us an explanation for his criterion of the "musical" which, in the case at hand, can hardly refer to special acoustic effects of euphonious verses. Rather, the analogy to music must be seen in the missing or vanished relationship of a visual phenomenon to something that also exists independently of it; in Gide's version, the precious and mannerist style has the effect of a free-floating play of words and constantly detaches the description from its object. Bodies and things dissolve in an animated restlessness which, in the play of water, light, and shadow, takes on a life of its own, becomes pure phenomenon, a phenomenon which means only itself and no longer points to any transcendent meaning (cf. ll. 45–50, 53–54, 61–64, 71–74).[22] The principle of the "musical" being applied here presupposes, for Gide, the specifically modern development of lyric poetry which Baudelaire's poetics initiated. It is a poetry whose tendency toward abstraction or "de-realization" has its complement in the concurrent development of painting, i.e., in its progressive detachment from the object.[23] For G. R. Hocke, on the other hand, there is nothing specifically modern about this phenomenon. Rather, it is a structural element of mannerism which has been present since the sixteenth century (Marino).[24] But if a structural unity between "baroque" and modern lyric poetry did in fact exist, it would have to be possible to demonstrate it here as well, and would mean that the identical principle would apply to both "versions" of the ode to whose original we now turn.

If one fits Gide's selection back into Théophile's ode, one soon discovers that the twentieth-century critic did not really proceed so differently from a photographer who manages to discover an unexpectedly modern aspect in an old picture by skillfully reproducing part of it.[25] In both instances, the viewer fails to see his expectation fulfilled as he turns back from the segment to the whole, recognizes the illusion of the "imaginary museum" to which he succumbed, and now faces the task of finding another form of access to the work of art which, in its strangeness, also makes him conscious of its historical distance. It could be shown that G. R. Hocke's results have largely come about by such a modernizing selection procedure in the first place, as in the case of the ode *Ce ruisseau romonte à sa source / Un boeuf gravit sur un rocher* (*This rivulet wends up to its spring / A steer climbs upon a rock*), for example, which he sees as a showpiece of "alogical montage."[26] But here, the omitted context gives the allegedly completely abstruse verse Hocke selected a wholly different, perfectly consistent meaning: by the use of dire omens and the appearance of Charon, the preceding stanza announces an imminent vision of the beyond ("Je voy le centre de la terre," I see the center of the earth) so that the "upside-down world" of the alogical verse takes on the encompassing aspect of an apocalyptic landscape. (Many of the grotesque images following the "un boeuf gravit sur un rocher" do in fact come from the biblical apocalypse.)

3. Théophile's ode in the horizon of experience of Baroque lyric poetry

That Théophile's ode was wholly transformed in Gide's abridgement, and that such transformation is only minimally related to the cut in its length, becomes apparent primarily in the fact that the ode in its entirety lacks that perspectivist unity which Gide—more "classical" than the poet of "préclassicisme" in this respect—brought out or, more precisely, brought *to* the ode by his cut.[27] If, for the moment, we disregard the historical conditions of its form and attempt to grasp the peculiarity of its composition from the effect it produces on the reader as he goes through the entire poem, it would seem as if the poet had specifically intended to constantly interrupt, indeed to make impossible a continuity of perception by the ever recurrent and ever surprising change in the subject of the stanzas and by the arbitrary sequence of images, metaphors, and mythological elements. Between the description of the park (i) and the bathing scene of the amourettes (v) which Gide had placed organically into the natural framework of the park, as it were, we find three stanzas that take us farther and farther from the pond, the setting which provides the unity. It is true that the second stanza continues the theme of the "deux ruisseauz" which now mingle their waters with that of the pond. But already in the following stanza, the frame of this tableau is broken (iii): with "Là, Melicerte, en un gazon," a sudden shift occurs from the natural landscape of the park and pond to the atemporal present of an idyllic and mythological world. Sudden, because in contrast to Diana, whom Gide retains, there is no natural complement for Melicertes; the god of the sea here does not represent something else but is himself present among the swans, as stanza x shows. While this presence is related to the frame by "son petit Empire" (l. 27), his atemporal being is simultaneously presented by the perspective on the mythological history of the sea which now follows. With two negated hypotheses ("si la vague . . . jamais . . . n'arrive," ll. 25–27, and "Là les oiseaux n'ont jamais vu, ll. 31–32), the poet manages the transition into what has become doubly unreal by such negation. By an implicit and also quite implausible syllogism (pond and sea are waters, which means that even this small realm of Melicertes may be threatened by the sea), the Scylla myth is contrasted with the evoked idyll. With this, we have already come so far away from the first idea which touched off all this that it requires some reflection to see that line 41: "Zephyre en chasse les chaleurs" (l. 31) must be referred back to "un gazon" (l. 21) through "en" and via "Là" (l. 31).

After eliminating the mythological "digression," Gide started again with line 41. The result is that in his version, the swans appear only incidentally, as purely decorative elements in the scene, and instead, the amourettes move into the very center of events. For Théophile, however, the swans are incomparably more important: that they determine the image of the peaceful idyll in stanzas iii and iv has a connection with the later appearance of the one mythological swan (l. 85) by which the destruction of the idyll is intimated. This significant nexus also is not explicit but obscured by the incoherence of the sequence of images. Where a new subject appears, such as the amourettes in v after the swans in iii and iv, it takes its place directly next to the old one.[28] Similarly, it is without recognizable motivation that the peaceful idyll of the bathing amourettes turns into the combat with the nereids. "On void là . . ." (l. 55). This transition makes evident that the unity does not lie in the continuity of a temporal process but solely in the principle of a continuing metamorphosis which the poet's eye discovers in his unchanging poetic subject and which it has transposed into a continuing change of its manifestations.

This "baroque" procedure attains its climax in the other stanzas Gide omitted. The impressionistic final image with which Gide's "tableau" comes to an end does not stand by itself in Théophile. He has the god of the sea emerge from it and introduces again quite abruptly and initially as a mere fear the figure of Phaeton into his pond idyll (viii). In the following stanza (ix), the unreality of this idea has suddenly become a visible reality and the incoherence of the presentation is even intensified by an unannounced change of subject. For "et ce pauvre amant langoureux" (And this poor languid lover, l. 81) does not refer back to "ce jeune cocher" (this young coachman, l. 79), as one might expect, but forward to "ce beau Cigne à qui Phaeton / Laissa ce lamentable ton" (this pretty Swan to whom Phaeton left his sorry tune, ll. 85–86). The following motivational chain would be conceivable here: *Dieu de l'eau* (*God of the Water*)—threat to the idyll—Phaeton's fall into the sea—plaint of his friend Cygnus—his metamorphosis into a swan. That such a motivation is not explicit in the text shows how little is gained by calling Théophile's method a mere set of associations. The characteristic quality of his procedure is precisely that he omits necessary or natural connecting links.

There is something else involved here: in contrast to the deliberate arbitrariness in the sequence of images, the unity of the image within the stanzas is strictly preserved. Most of the stanzas have a center and a climax of their own,[29] are often only paratactically connected,[30] and only rarely show an element that ties in with what follows. Although there is a more direct nexus between the plaintive gesture of the swan and the final two stanzas, a surprising turn is provided. Only after some reflection does one see that the question addressed to Dieu Melicerte (x) must refer to the amourettes. And with the verse about the futile "faux plaisirs" (l. 98), the question takes an unexpected direction which is not dictated by the Phaeton-Cygnus myth. The final stanza returns to this myth, but this time also with a surprising deviation from the preceding situation which now appears in a twofold metaphoric inversion. In contrast to Ovid's Cygnus (*Metamorphoses* II, ll. 379–80):

> stagna petit patulosque lucus ignemque perosus
> quae colat, elegit contraria flumina flammis

> Whom Lakes and Ponds (destesting fire) delight;
> And Floods, to Flames in nature opposite[31]

the abandoned friend who has been metamorphosed into a swan here vainly seeks to cool himself in the waves. Théophile presents the opposition between fire and water in an image and, in a precious inversion, turns it against the swan:

> Et fait venir contre son sein
> l'air, bruslant et les ondes, seches
>
> (ll. 103–4)

(And has, thrust against his breast, the air, burning and the waters, dry). Then the swan suffers a further metamorphosis not present in the tradition: his "furieux dessein" (frightful plan) now dyes his plumage black which his "soins amoureux" (loving needs) had earlier caused to become white (ll. 83–84). Stanza xi in Théophile thus provides a no less effective ending than the one found by Gide, but it is an ending that now sublates the sequence of images in precisely the opposite sense. Whereas Gide allows everything figurative to ultimately dissolve in the sensory and natural appearance of the animated surface of the water, Théophile transposes the natural appearance of the objective world into the unreality of a metaphoric plane by two precious pointes. With its oxymoron "les ondes seches" (dry waters, l. 104), the first almost makes one forget that here, in an abstracting metamorphosis, the pond is being evoked a final time. The second pointe – "Luy rendent la peau toute noire" (Makes the skin all black, l. 107) – carries the theme of the disturbed idyll with the paradoxical emblem for the swans to its grotesque climax, yet the poet does not as yet reveal to us the external reason for the intimated catastrophe and the plaint of the swan.

The procedure just analyzed, which conforms to the general aesthetic canon of his epoch and especially its idea of the genre of the "ode descriptive,"[32] was characterized most aptly elsewhere in his *Maison de Silvie* by Théophile himself. There, he has the nightingale say of its song in praise of Silvie:

> Si mes airs cent fois recitez
> Comme l'ambition me presse,
> Meslent tant de diversitez
> Aux chansons que je vous adresse,
> C'est que ma voix cherche des traits
> Pour un chacun de vos attraits.
>
> (IX, ll. 41–46)

(If my songs sung over a hundred times as ambition presses me, mix so much diversity in the song I sing you, it is because my voice seeks airs for every one of your charms.) The poetic principle of *diversité*,[33] which governs the form of Théophile's presentation, wholly corresponds with the object of his poem whose substance is also seen in a multiplicity of features or dissolved into such a multiplicity of aspects. Every feature of the object ("un chacun de vos attraits") demands the manner of description appropriate to it ("traits"):[34] the technique of the poet consists in embellishing and metaphorically or mythologically heightening every component of his object that is to be praised (in our case, the park with the pond, grass, and swans). This produces a discontinuous movement: the object itself becomes a mere occasion, dissolves in the *diversité* of its aspects, and creates the impression of a restlessly moving surface whose *beau desordre* has its new, no longer substantial unity in the continuing metamorphosis of the field of vision.[35] To simply deny that the mannerist principle of *diversité* has any unity whatever is therefore a mistake. It is simply not one that should be looked for in a "composition logique" or a perspectivistically rigorous "unité de mouvement" which would be "classical definitions."[36] Rather, it lies in the movement itself which dissolves all objects aperspectivistically into a "beautiful" (and therefore not purely arbitrary) disorder. Through this "estrangement," it can strike us as "modern," though in a sense that differs from the use of that term as applied to Gide's abridgement.

To agree with Hocke and to see in this seemingly modern "estrangement" of the objective world a constant stylistic element of mannerism would presuppose that Théophile did in fact mean his readers to be taken aback by a deliberate obfuscation, and that his poetry "no longer has much in common with classical communicating."[37] This raises the question whether the effect produced by the precious style of our ode was a pure "art du langage"[38] or whether it was to serve a higher purpose which would confer what the poet considered its ultimate meaning on the ode. For the reader of our time, for whom the original horizon of expectations of the poem has receded into the distant past, and to whom *La Maison de Silvie* as a whole is no longer immediately accessible for that very reason, the *description poétique* as used by Théophile in his third ode[39] seemingly turns the underlying Horacian precept *ut pictura poesis* into its opposite. The ornament of metaphors and personifications which has become its own end here eliminates the object in its sensory manifestation as it abolishes the coherence of the images, and it was precisely that sensory appearance which Gide's abridgement had emphasized. There arises the impression of a "certain indifference to what today we call the content of a poem,"[40] although in contrast to Gide's version, it is not a description for its own sake that is involved here. How then are we to understand the concept of a *description poétique*, considering that this impression makes it seem a *contradictio in adjecto*?

The contradiction can be more easily resolved if one goes back to the various passages in which Théophile refers to this poetic principle. The traditional image-field, the "poet as painter," is amply represented in the *Maison de Silvie*.[41] At the very beginning of his poem, Théophile calls it a "peinture" (i, l. 2). Later, he speaks of his "enterprise du tableau" (vi, l. 85) and of the "pinceau d'un faiseur de rimes" (the brush of the rhymester, viii, l. 47), and characteristically employs the concept even when he remembers Chantilly in prison, "mes sens en ont tout le tableau" (my feelings have the whole picture of it, viii, l. 105). That *peindre* means no simple portrayal but a glorification and praise of the subject ("et si j'ay bien loue les eaux, les ombres, les fleurs, les oyseaux . . . ," and if I have praised well the waters, the shadows, the flowers, the birds . . .) is implicit at the very start, in the image of the "golden stylus":

> Pour laisser avant que mourir
> Les traits vivans d'une peinture
> Qui ne puisse jamais perir
> Qu'en la perte de la Nature,
> Je passe les crayons dorez
> Sur les lieux les plus reverez.
>
> (I, ll. 1-6)

(Before dying, to leave the living strokes of a painting that will never die, unless Nature herself be lost, I sketch the golden pastels over the most revered places.) The connection established here between poet and "la Nature" takes us into wider contexts. In the *Maison de Silvie*, the "poet as painter" motif is paralleled by another: "nature also can paint." Just as the rays of the sun "portray" themselves in the midst of uncertain shadows in the waters of the spring and the branch "impresses" its *peinture* in their mirror to then efface it again ("efface et marque," vi, l. 110), so the poet's image of Silvie can also be received and eternally preserved there:

> Je scay que ces miroirs flotants
> Où l'objet change tant de place,
> Pour elle devenus constans
> Auront une fidele glace,
> Et sous un ornement si beau

> La surface mesme de l'eau,
> Nonobstant sa delicatesse,
> Gardera seurement encrez
> Et mes characteres sacrez
> Et les attraits de la Princesse.
>
> (I, ll. 101-10)

(I know that this floating glass where the object forever changes place will, having become changeless for her, turn into a faithful mirror; and under such a handsome ornament the very surface of water, despite its delicacy, will surely keep indelible both my sacred characters and the charms of the Princess.) This especially deft, precious, and gallant figure contains a twofold *concordia discors*: the fluid, ever mobile element appears as a preserving, stable mirror in which the "sacred letters" of the poet can be engraved in the same way as the living features of the Silvie he celebrates.[42] The two themes, poet's image and nature's copy, move together, combine metaphorically, and thus cause a secret analogy to manifest itself. We now have the explanation of the poet's initially expressed conviction that his *peinture* can only fade when all nature passes away (see I, ll. 1–6).

This equivalence is relativized elsewhere. Its higher rank is returned to nature;[43] actually, Silvie's glory has no need of his poetry, heaven itself has taken care "de la peindre par tout le monde" (to paint her everywhere, I, l. 114). Her eyes are "painted" in the sun, her charms in Aurora (I, ll. 115ff.); the winter snow competes with the whiteness of her complexion (II, ll. 97–100), and before her, the elements cease their eternal strife (II, ll. 25–30). That this is not merely a word play of precious gallantry becomes clear in another passage where the latent Platonism which underlies the analogy of poetry and painting in Théophile is made explicit:

> Le Ciel nous donne la beauté
> Pour une marque de sa grace,
> C'est par où sa divinité
> Marque tousjours un peu sa trace.
>
> (IV, ll. 41-44)

(Heaven gives us beauty as a token of its grace. It is the way in which divinity always marks its little track.) At the end of the ever more manifest step-by-step progression, Théophile gives a Christian turn to this Platonism. Whereas in the description of the "cabinet de verdure" in the seventh ode nature still appears as the ultimate, divinely authorized agency "pour nourrir le monde,"[44] a tradition which points back to Alanus, the tenth ode climaxes in a final and highest image of *peinture* which assigns absolute rank, the power over the beginning and end of all things, to Christ:[45]

> Il fait au corps de l'Univers
> Et le sexe et l'age divers;
> Devant luy c'est une peinture
> Que le Ciel et chaque Element,
> Il peut d'un trait d'oeil seulement
> Effacer toute la Nature.

(X, ll. 85-90)

(To the body of the Universe he gives a variety of sexes and ages. Before Christ, heaven and every element are but a painting, and by nothing more than the blinking of an eye He can efface all of Nature.)

For the question that concerns us, it is decisive that this Platonism with its Christian heightening not only determines Théophile's concept of the beautiful ("Tous les objects les mieux formez / Doivent étre les mieux aymez," All the best modeled objects must be the best loved, IV, ll. 45-46) but also gives its deeper meaning to his *description poétique*. The modern reader will not do justice to the intention of the text until he realizes that the estrangement of the object by the precious style is not Théophile's ultimate object. The precious manner of his *peinture*, which at first glance seems to make poetic description and its objects diverge so that, for the modern reader, the natural landscape begins to dissolve in the disconcerting aspect of *diversité*, simultaneously transforms for Théophile and his contemporary public the singular, merely factually real into the general truth of a timeless, spiritual reality. The park of Chantilly in its unique, historical form and the unique situation of the *poète maudit* is translated back into the imaginary space of an idyllic and mythological landscape by the *crayons dorés* of the poet. Only behind the contingent world which encloses his life, the poet's *peinture* raises a curtain before the always already familiar because always identical horizon of another, higher world. The mannerist elements of his style are merely the words through which the translation is accomplished. Théophile's "estrangement" of the objective world differs from the apparently identical procedure of modern poets (which Hocke calls "neo-mannerist") in that it can be dissolved again as this higher, spiritual reality is beheld — that it is merely the medium of a translation, merely a transitional step, and not as yet a sustained, bizarre, and beautiful reflection of a subjective poetic experience which refers only to its own world.

This means that J. Tortel's judgment in the *Cahiers du Sud* volume, which pioneered the reassessment of Théophile's epoch, must be revised: "The fundamental realism of preclassical poetry must be underlined. The movement of the language is from reality to the dream, it does not take the opposite direction."[46] That the movement of the poetry starts off from sensory reality does not preclude its leading back to an antecedently existing, suprasensible world and thus finally conforming once more to the medieval meaning of "realism." The existence of G. Macon's detailed monograph on the history of Chantilly[47] makes it possible to confirm in a great many particulars in the case of the *Maison de Silvie* that while Théophile's representation as a whole is based on nonfictitious scenery, he reshaped it to so large an extent into the timeless landscape of an idyll that hardly a single specific feature of Chantilly's historic form remained. The stags and swans are an especially instructive example. In an account dating from 1602, they are mentioned as the special glory of the park Henry IV loved above all others: "Everything is enchanting at Chantilly, the large carps, the swans in their pools, the tame stags and does that roam the park and lead their young to the castle, even the peacocks and turkeys which scatter during the day and return at night to Bucamp."[48] There was something special about the stags at Chantilly. Ever since the beginning of the fifteenth century, there had existed a "gallery of antlers where Martin de Meilles had painted stags from nature (and which) was decorated with the most handsome heads of stags that could be found."[49] It must have still existed in Théophile's day, for it is mentioned in 1603 that the trophies had to be refurbished.[50] In March 1607, the king spent ten days at Chantilly and bagged no less than nine stags.[51] Soon thereafter, a chronicler reports that he had seen a completely white stag in the park which the Marechal de Montgomery had preserved after its death and kept in his collection as a curiosity.[52] Accordingly, it seems most likely that even the theme of the "white stags" in Théophile's second ode is no invention. There is, nonetheless, a distance of the imaginary between the stags in Théophile's ode and those in the park which makes unrecognizable for the later reader all correspondence between poetry and reality. For the poet copies Ovid and introduces the white stags in the *Maison de Silvie* as tritons who, like Actaeon surprising the bathing Diana, undergo a metamorphosis when they behold Silvie and are consoled by the privilege of wearing her color:

> La Princesse qui les charma
> Alors qu'elle les transforma
> Les fit estre blancs comme neige,
> Et pour consoler leur douleur
> Ills receurent le privilege
> De porter tousjours sa couleur

(II, ll. 75–80)

(The princess, who cast her spell over them, made them white as snow when she changed their shape. And to console them in their grief, conferred upon them the privilege of always wearing her color.) The mythological description so completely overlays the particular event (odd appearance of a white stag) which it (presumably) interprets poetically that the real occasion for the inspiration could at best be divined by initiates but was inaccessible to Théophile's wider audience. The anterior mythological world into which Théophile transposes the actual event has a higher poetic validity for him and his contemporary readers than the actual reality on which his *description poétique* was based.[53] This description can also refer to something that has already been portrayed, i.e., as *poésie-peinture*, it can compete directly with the fine arts. For the Ovidian motifs present throughout the entire cycle presumably do not go back directly to the text of the *Metamorphoses* but rather to their representation in the tapestries that made Chantilly famous.[54] For Théophile, the mythological personnel of the third ode (Melicertes, Scylla, Diana, Phaeton, Cygnus) were thus not merely a recollection from his humanist education but something he had before his very eyes. As such, they were no less real than the landscape surrounding him. This also defines more closely the horizon of expectations into which Théophile placed his *Maison de Silvie*. His poetic procedure ("I do not wish to gather up the thread of my subject. In a variety of ways, I abandon and take up again my object"),[55] which strikes the twentieth-century reader as a modern alienation effect, takes the seventeenth-century reader, whose familiarity with his mythological and allegorical world of images Théophile takes for granted, through the dissolution of the object back to the familiar horizon of another, higher reality which first gives meaning to the everyday world. This applies equally to the personal situation of the poet who was the object of a criminal prosecution; for with the *Maison de Silvie*, he celebrated a place of refuge which his patron Montmorency had granted him. It is true that there are stanzas that directly express the personal distress of the incarcerated poet,[56] and this probably most strongly in the eighth ode where Théophile evokes the image of Chantilly in his "noire tour" (l. 101).[57] But the very stanzas that contain this evocation are framed at both the beginning and the end of the ode by verses in which Théophile sees his fate already traced in the traditional figure of the nightingale. The Philomela myth is justification for his now also beginning to sing "sur les caprices du destin" (l. 19): the poet's subjective experience appears before the same background as the poetically transformed objective world. This transposition of the lyric subject to a mythical plane, a subject which seeks and finds the meaning of his poetic experience by reference to a still unquestioningly presupposed spiritual reality, manifests itself both in the *diversité* of his changing and interchangeable identifications (Phaeton, Damon, Philomela),[58] and in the fact that the self of the poet in such transformed identity is itself one element among others in the idyllic and mythological landscape. This takes us back to the theme of the swan in the third ode.

Like the stags, Théophile also placed the swans in the park of Chantilly into a mythological nexus which is no longer apparent in Gide's version. One might have expected Théophile to take up a tradition of the Pleiade where—as R. J. Clemens shows—the classical motif of the *cygnus musicus* was one of the most common images for the poet or the *douceur* of his poetry. What is more, the new school had referred to themselves as "les nouveoux cygnes, qui ores par la France vont chantant" (the new swans, that now sing throughout France) in order to suggest that they viewed themselves as the direct successors of the classical and early Italian authors.[59] But in Théophile, there is hardly a trace of the famous passage in Plato's *Phaidon*[60] nor of the other ideas that the Pleiade had taken from classical tradition and developed[61] (that the swan is sacred to Apollo, that, together with the nightingale, he has the sweetest voice and a prophetic gift). Instead, our poet went back to the Ovidian swan,[62] thereby created a monument to his friendship with Thyrsis (Des Barreux), and, in his role as poet, equated himself with Phaeton. But it is only the following ode (IV) which provides the key for this interpretation, and even there the biographical connection must be guessed at. In the present context, it is important that the mythological element (Phaeton's fall into the sea and the swan's dirge) anticipates the real event (the sentencing of Théophile[63] presented in the fifth ode in the form of a prophetic dream): the poet's subjective experience is seen in terms of the objective meaning of the mythologically heightened fate. Théophile's poetic achievement here lies primarily in juxtaposing two conventional image-fields, the *locus amoenus* with the swan idyll and the Phaeton myth with the swan's dirge, in a novel and bold fashion which also defines his distance as *poète moderne* from the poets of the Pleiade and their platonic-Christian conception of poetry.[64]

A stanza from sonnet CXV from *L'Olive*, in which Du Bellay celebrates Ronsard's poetry, may serve as a parallel and typical contrast to Théophile's treatment of the swan motif:

> Quel cigne encor' des cignes le plus beau
> Te prêta l'aele? et quel vent jusque'aux cieulx

Te balança le vol audacieux,
Sans que la mer te fust large tombeau?[65]

(What swan still the most ravishing of swans lent you its wing? And what wind to the very heavens propels your daring flight, without the sea ever becoming your wide tomb?). For this stanza also, a central motif of Renaissance lyric poetry which Leo Spitzer examined in a comparative interpretation of sonnet CXIII from L'Olive must be premised, and that is the platonic-Christian idea of the "yearning of the soul, exiled on this opaque earth from the splendor of Heaven, from the source of light whence it came—this subject matter, highly poetic in itself because of its suggestion of a different world, different from and more beautiful than our own."[66] Like Théophile later, Du Bellay links the swan motif and the image of the sea as grave (alluding to Phaeton or Icarus)[67] in this stanza, but in the opposite sense: the poet-swan whose wings (i.e., the wings of poetry) carry him above the profane world and closer to his true home remains untouched by the danger that is evoked only by negation. The idea of death to which the poet had reconciled himself in the preceding sonnet CXIII[68] passes over into that of immortality which can become his if he sings of his love in which the idea of the beloved and the idea of perfection coincide.[69] In line with this and like most poets of the Pleiade, Du Bellay follows Plato's interpretation of the swan song: "when these birds feel that the time has come for them to die, they sing more loudly and sweetly than they have sung in all their lives before, for joy that they are going away into the presence of the god whose servants they are."[70] Théophile's third ode, on the other hand, corresponds with the interpretation rejected by Plato but still to be found in Polybius where the swan's dirge is "the plaintive plea of someone whose life or purpose is frustrated."[71] In Théophile, the upward movement (equally suggested by Phaeton) is missing; his portrayal begins directly with the abrupt fall which destroys the swan-and-amourette idyll and gives rise to the futile plaint of the lonely swan, a plaint which is not attenuated by any conciliatory thought and which, in a melancholy that rises to the pitch of fury, the ode maintains up to the end.[72] To the extent that in his *description poétique*, he places the park of Chantilly back into the anterior, Platonic world of the beautiful, Théophile proceeds no less "classically" than a Renaissance poet. But in the destruction of the timeless idyll to which he elevates and into which he transforms the catastrophe of his personal destiny, the expectation of an always possible end of nature also announces itself ("la perte de la Nature," I, 4). It is an expectation that finds voice elsewhere in his work as well[73] and gives expression to a consciousness of the uniqueness and nonrepeatability of existence which was foreign to classical beliefs and which cannot but cast doubt on the Platonism of another imperishable world of the beautiful that is directly accessible to the poet and therefore ultimately on the classical principle of the *imitatio naturae*.

4. Baudelaire's renunciation of Platonism and the poetics of remembrance

Significantly, Baudelaire's modern version, like Mallarmé's later swan sonnet, continues the interpretation of Théophile's swan myth as a motif of melancholy and in so doing also makes thematically visible the move away from the Platonic concept of the beautiful, a turn which was so decisive for the development of a modern poetics. As we begin, there is probably no better way to document this turn than by a remark in the article "Le Beau" in the Encyclopedia of 1752 which Diderot makes in the course of his criticism of Hutcheson's doctrine of a "sens interne du beau." "Notice, by the way, that a truly unhappy being would be one that had the inner sense of beauty but only recognized the beautiful in things that were harmful to it. As far as we are concerned, Providence has arranged matters in such a way that a truly beautiful thing is also normally a good one."[74] This sentence still expresses the unquestioned conviction of a preordained Platonic unity of the beautiful and the good or of a congruence of aesthetic experience and moral effect. In imagining a possibility it does not consider realizable, Diderot's remark anticipates a hundred years before Baudelaire the counterposition of that modern poet, "who hardly conceives of a type of beauty which does not harbor misfortune" and thus places the (anti-Platonic) meaning of the title of his *Fleurs du Mal* and his new definition of the beautiful "that brings a notion of melancholy with it"[75] into the light of its genuine historical significance.

But Baudelaire's turn from the "famous doctrine of the indissolubility of the Beautiful, the True, and the Good" is not to be traced here primarily as a phenomenon in the history of ideas (as, for example, in the discussion of the "heresies" of traditional poetics which he initiated).[76] Instead, it is to be documented through the structural change that becomes palpable in his modern treatment of the swan motif. A comparative analysis of Baudelaire's *Le Cygne* (1859) is instructive for the additional reason that it is part of the *Tableaux parisiens* which — as this subtitle makes clear — seemingly continue the tradition of the *poésie-peinture* which we brought out in the discussion of Théophile's ode. Seemingly, for beginning already with the *Salon de 1846*, Baudelaire progressively freed himself from the painterly realism of the Parnassian style, as G. Hess has shown, and went beyond the limits that were peculiar to a descriptive poetry that competed with painting.[77] In the *Salon de 1846*, which contains his program for nonrealistic art, the new concept for his modern procedure first occurs where "the sterile function of imitating nature" is replaced by the re-creation of the essence of the world, of "nature's intentions, 'le surnaturalisme.'"[78]

I

    (i) Andromaque, je pense à vous! Ce petit fleuve,
        Pauvre et triste miroir où jadis resplendit
        L'immense majesté des vos douleurs de veuve,
        Ce Simoïs menteur qui par vos pleurs grandit,

    (ii) A fécondé soudain ma mémoire fertile,
        Comme je traversais le nouveau Carrousel.
        Le vieux Paris n'est plus (la forme d'une ville
        Change plus vite, hélas! que le coeur d'un mortel);

    (iii) Le ne vois qu'en esprit tout ce camp de baraques,
        Ces tas de chapiteaux ébauchés et de fûts,
        Les herbes, les gros blocs verdis par l'eau des flaques,
        Et, brillant aux carreaux, le bric-à-brac confus.

    (iv) Là s'étalait jadis une ménagerie;
        Là je vis, un matin, à l'heure où sous les cieux
        Froids et clairs le Travail s'éveille, où la voirie
        Pousse un sombre ouragan dans l'air silencieux,

    (v) Un cygne qui s'était évadé de sa cage,
        Et, de ses pieds palmés frottant le pavé sec,
        Sur le sol raboteux traînait son grand plumage.
        Près d'un ruisseau sans eau la bête ouvrant le bec

    (vi) Baignait nerveusement ses ailes dans la poudre,
        Et disait, le coeur plein de son beau lac natal:
        'Eau, quand donc pleuvras-tu? Quand tonneras-tu, foudre?'
        Je vois ce malheureux, mythe étrange et fatal,

    (vii) Vers le ciel quelquefois, comme l'homme d'Ovide
        Vers le ciel ironique et cruellement bleu,
        Sur son cou convulsif tendant sa tête avide,
        Comme s'il adressait des reproches à Dieu!

II

(viii) Paris change, mais rien dans ma mélancolie
N'a bougé! Palais neufs, échafaudages, blocs,
Vieux faubourgs, tout pour moi devient allégorie,
Et mes chers souvenirs sont plus lourds que des rocs.

(ix) Aussi devant ce Louvre une image m'opprime:
Je pense à mon grand cygne avec ses gestes fous,
Comme les exilés, ridicule et sublime,
Et rongé d'un desir sans trêve! Et puis à vous,

(x) Andromaque, des bras d'un grand époux tombée,
Vil betail, sous la main due superbe Pyrrhus,
Auprès d'un tombeau vide en extase courbée;
Veuve d'Hector, hélas! et femme d'Helenus!

(xi) Je pense à la négresse, amaigrie et phtisique,
Piétinant dans la boue, et cherchant, l'oeil hagard,
Les cocotiers absents de la superbe Afrique
Derrière la muraille immense du brouillard;

(xii) A quiconque a perdu ce qui ne se retrouve
Jamais! jamais! à ceux qui s'abreuvent de pleurs
Et tettent la Douleur comme une bonne louve!
Aux maigres orphelins séchant comme des fleurs!

(xiii) Ainsi dans la forêt où mon esprit s'exile
Un vieux Souvenir sonne à plein souffle du cor!
Je pense aux matelots oubliés dans une île,
Aux captifs, aux vaincus! . . . à bien d'autres encor!

The Swan

I

Andromache, I think of you! The stream
The poor, sad mirror where in bygone days
Shone all the majesty of your widowed grief,
The lying Simois flooded by your tears,

Made all my fertile memory blossom forth
As I passed by the new-built Carrousel.
Old Paris is no more (a town, alas,
Changes more quickly than man's heart may change);

Yet in my mind I still can see the booths;
The heaps of brick and rough-hewn capitals;

The grass; the stones all over-green with moss;
The debris, and the square-set heaps of tiles.

There a menagerie was once outspread;
And there I saw, one morning at the hour
When Toil awakes beneath the cold, clear sky
And the road roars upon the silent air,

A swan who had escaped his cage, and walked
On the dry pavement with his webby feet,
And trailed his spotless plumage on the ground.
And near a waterless stream the piteous swan
Opened his beak, and bathing in the dust
His nervous wings, he cried (his heart the while
Filled with a vision of his own fair lake):
'O water, when then wilt thou come in rain?
Lightning, when wilt thou glitter?'

                      Sometimes yet
I see the hapless bird—strange, fatal myth—
Like him that Ovid writes of, lifting up
Unto the cruelly blue, ironic heavens,
With stretched, convulsive neck a thirsty face,
As though he sent reproaches up to God!

II

Paris may change; my melancholy is fixed.
New palaces, and scaffoldings, and blocks,
And suburbs old, are symbols all to me
Whose memories are as heavy as a stone.
And so, before the Louvre, to vex my soul
The image came of my majestic swan
With his mad gestures, foolish and sublime,
As of an exile whom one great desire
Gnaws with no truce. And then I thought of you,
Andromache! torn from your hero's arms;
Beaneath the hand of Pyrrhus in his pride;
Bent o'er an empty tomb in ecstasy;
Widow of Hector—wife of Helenus!
And of the Negress, wan and phthisical,
Tramping the mud, and with her haggard eyes
Seeking beyond the mighty walls of fog
The absent palm-trees of proud Africa;
Of all who lose that which they never find;

> Of all who drink of tears; all whom grey Grief
> Gives suck to as the kindly wolf gave suck;
> Of meagre orphans who like blossoms fade.
>
> And one old Memory like a crying horn
> Sounds through the forest where my soul is lost . . .
> I think of sailors on some isle, forgotten
> Of captives, vanquished . . . and of many more.

If we begin by asking how the outer structure achieves that unity of perspective which Gide had introduced into Théophile's ode by his modernizing abridgement, it becomes apparent that the modern poet has at his command a number of expressive means from which a new form of vision must derive. The verse- and rhyme scheme (Alexandrines in stanzas of four lines each with crossed rhymes) is extremely simple and of "classical" rigor. But Baudelaire constantly breaks up the symmetry of the four-line stanza by the syntactic overlapping of the periods. Through this irregular interlinking, the appeal of the asymmetrical (varying length of the images which match the syntactic units) and a consequent, ever new effect of surprise and tension is achieved which intensifies and "explosively" resolves itself toward the end in an abruptly sped-up sequence of nine exclamations in seven lines. Yet the run-on lines must continue to be perceptible for the reader because only then can Baudelaire's intended effect, the perpetual contrast of rhythm and image,[79] "de monotonie, de symetrie et de surprise,"[80] come into full play. This specifically "musical" principle is counteracted by the overall architectonic bipartition in which the seventh stanza emerges as a first climax between the six preceding and the six following ones. It is precisely the stanza that dwells on the accusing gesture of the swan and which, because of its position, corresponds to the final stanza—the second climax—of the poem. Regarding their images, the two principal sections thus set off from each other are also distinguished by a glance which travels first in one, then in the opposite direction and are thus made to contrastively refer to each other. Whereas in the first section, the field of vision becomes progressively more constricted as we move from the landscape of the Trojan war to the panorama of the "Nouveau Carrousel," the old menagerie, the "waterless stream" with the swan and the single gesture of his neck (detail in close-up!), in the second section, the perspective expands from the smallest image, the swan ("une image m'opprime," l. 33, "to vex my soul"), the evoked figure of Andromache, the negress, and the collectively named further groups of exiles ("A quiconque . . . à ceux . . . Aux maigres orphelins . . .

aux matelots . . . Aux captifs, aux vaincus! . . . à bien d'autres en-core!" "of all . . . of all . . . of meager orphans, sailors, capitves, vanquished . . . and of many more,") to the entire temporal and spatial, mythical and exotic expanse that is the world. Because in both sections, the end refers back to the beginning, the movement of images becomes circular and it is this which gives its final perfection to Baudelaire's conscious composition. The reason for the introductory invocation, "Andromaque, je pense à vous" (l. 1, "Andromache, I think of you"), is given only at the end, in the still implicit comparison which becomes palpable only in the image of the swan. And with the return of the key word *souvenir*, we note that between "Et mes chers souvenirs sont plus lourds que des rocs" ("to me whose memories are as heavy as a stone") in the first, and "Un vieux Souvenir sonne à plein souffle du cor" ("And one old Memory like a crying horn") in the last stanza of part II, there has occurred a metamorphosis whose meaning must still be explored.

In his *Notes nouvelles sur Edgar Poe*, Baudelaire had called for and justified this poetic procedure as a specifically modern structure and in explicit opposition to the poetics of inspiration and experience of the Romantic school. It differs from Théophile's form of *description poétique* not merely because it excludes the arbitrary. The strict modern structure which obeys the *dessein prémédité* also lacks the linear order of the lyric event which still underlay the "classical" unity of perspective which Gide's version had achieved. The modernity of perspective realized in Baudelaire's poem manifests itself in the fact that it is no longer tied to the sensory appearance of a continuous event which extends from a beginning through a middle toward an end. It thus corresponds to an important observation of his poetics as developed after Poe, "[that] all epic intent obviously results from an imperfect sense of art."[81] The perspectival unity of modern lyric poetry no longer lies in the achieved likeness of a lyric event or subjective experience but comes from the artificial creation of a "new world," a creation which obeys only the rules of the imagination. It is a world that presupposes a destruction and estrangement of the familiar objective world at the beginning of the creative act.[82] Baudelaire's *Le Cygne* is exemplary because it presents to us both the process of alienating the familiar and the *sensation du neuf*[83] which the imagination creates.[84]

As in Théophile before but with the opposite intent this alienation also shows itself in the use of mythology. Whereas in the earlier poem, the kind of transposition occurred which allows the purer image of an already familiar, atemporally true, and different world to shine through, Baudelaire takes the opposite route. After the abrupt call to Andromache with its evocation of Racine's tragedy, he introduces the mythical into the existing world and thus strips the real urban panorama of its familiar aspect. In the reader's horizon of expectation, this strangeness sets in because the poet, "by adding that unexpected element, strangeness," inverts the natural sequence of real occasion and mythical evocation. Why his *mémoire fertile* brings the figure of Andromache before his eyes becomes apparent only when one recognizes in the fifth stanza that "ce petit fleuve" (l. 1) is to be referred both to the mythological river ("ce Semois menteur," l. 4, "The lying Simois") and to the actually remembered waterless stream ("près d'un ruisseau sans eau," l. 20). The myth thus appears as an element of personal recollection whose particular meaning the reader cannot yet guess, even if he is perfectly familiar with the underlying verse from the *Aeneid*: "falsi Simoentis ad undam," and the general meaning of the Andromache fable.[85] But even when the imaginary analogy between Andromache and the swan dying of thirst, an analogy that comes from the poet's recollection, can be intuited by the reader, the myth still remains alien in another sense, for it is precisely now that the poet sees the swan as a "mythe étrange et fatal" (l. 24). The swan which is dying of thirst and in which Andromache's fate becomes incarnate for the poet remains a stranger in a world which, because of his accusing gesture, itself seems strange. This disconcerting aspect of the surrounding world also precedes the contrast that gave rise to it ("un cygne . . . le coeur plein de son beau lac natal," l. 22, "his heart the while filled with a vision of his own fair lake"). The poetic inversion of cause and effect thus deprives the anecdotal event of any remainder of an *intention épique*: to completely understand it, a second reading must from the very beginning view the poem with a glance that looks back on it from the end. The estrangement of the urban panorama, which ultimately derives from the contrast to the exile of the beautiful, expresses itself in the accumulation of prosaic detail in the third and fourth stanzas. After a paradoxical and abrupt change in the expectation aroused by the sentimentally evoked "vieux Paris" (ll. 7–8), that world appears as a chaotic, smashed "forme d'une ville," as the disorderly, desolate burial ground of a vanished past into whose dead silence the banal noise of the beginning working day all of a sudden blares.

The peculiarity of this contrasting thematics of part I has not been adequately understood when one reduces it to a simple denominator, as J. D. Hubert has done: "this chaos of the real is opposed to the poetic order which is symbolized by the swan as it opens its beak before the waterless stream."[86] For even the *ordre poétique* does not remain self-contained and in symbolic perfection, untouched by the *étrangeté* of the external, surrounding world. Image and meaning have entered a relation of inappropriateness: in the mythical gesture of his plaint, the swan can no longer give a higher meaning to the situation in which he appears. His image refers only to itself, to its lost origin in a mythic ideality which is no longer timelessly present but seems removed to an unbridgeable distance. There is more: in the bizarre gesticulation of his neck ("sur son cou convulsif tendant sa tête avide," l. 27, "with stretched, convulsive neck a thirsty face"), its plaint also rebels against the meaning of his traditional fate. Here also, the rebellion against that "mythe étrange et fatal" does not await the poet's explicit interpretation ("comme s'il adressait des reproches à Dieu," l. 28, "As though he sent reproaches up to God") but already manifests itself in the gesture of the swan which, according to the Ovidian tradition to which line 25 alludes, is reserved to man alone.[87] Before our eyes, the meaning of the Platonic interpretation of the swan song turns into its opposite: Baudelaire's swan remains before the "empty ideality" of a "ciel ironique et cruellement bleu" (l. 26, "cruelly blue, ironic heaven"), just like the estranged cityscape which remained immobilized in its reified chaos. The progressive transformation of things into the familiar no longer respects the traditional *ordre poétique*; its retransformation into a new world of the beautiful which occurs in part II can therefore no longer start from an already existing mythic objectivity but must find its own origin.

In this retransformation, we see the decisive innovation of the *Fleurs du Mal* which seals the break with traditional poetics or—if one wishes—one of the "positive categories" of modern lyric poetry which Burger misses. For Baudelaire is not only the poet of "contentless ideality," the modernity of his poetry is more than a merely thematic negation of Platonism. He goes beyond the alienation of the familiar horizon of lyric experience which, in *Le Cygne*, leads to the dissonance between a destroyed outer reality and a worldless mythic symbol: the tension of "Spleen et Ideal" has its opposite pole in a new *ordre poétique* which no longer derives from a picturesque copy of nature or the transparency of a more beautiful Platonic ideality but which presupposes the creation of a different, purely imaginary, and therefore world-immanent sphere of the beautiful by language, "that suggestive magic that contains both object and subject, the world external to the artist, and the artist himself."[88]

This inverse poetic process which in *Le Cygne* sets in at the beginning of part II evolves here step by step in the medium of remembrance.

In this process, it is essential that remembrance as subjective interiorization not simply set itself against an external reality that has congealed into allegory. During the transition into the inner world, external reality is not extinguished all at once; rather, it moves into the inner world with the entire weight of its objects, indeed, it is precisely and only there that its images attain to the extreme degree of their strangeness:

> . . . Palais neufs, échafaudages, blocs,
> Vieux faubourgs, tout pour moi devient allégorie,
> Et mes chers souvenirs sont plus lourds que des rocs.
>
> (ll. 30–32)

> New palaces, and scaffoldings, and blocks,
> And suburbs old, are symbols all to me
> Whose memories are as heavy as a stone.

One of the functions Baudelaire gave the allegorical form becomes visible here. Whereas in the older poetry, allegory served to distinguish the sensory appearance from the suprasensible meaning of things and its personifications and emblems pointed to the timeless truth of a higher world of *universalia ante rem.* the opposite occurs in Baudelaire: here, allegory does away with the gulf between outward appearance and spiritual significance, object and subject. In this modern use, it loses its referential character and its emblems congeal into the indecipherable signum of the world. It is precisely through this process, however, that they can become the pivotal points where the sudden switch from outside to inside, the equation of alien reality and the "morne incuriosité" of the "Spleen" can take place.[89] Remembrance from which the counterimage of the new and the beautiful ("un monde nouveau, la sensation du neuf") will gradually emerge is thus enclosed by the alien world of objects at the beginning. "Et mes chers souvenirs sont plus lourds que des rocs." ("To me whose memories are as heavy as a stone.") Here, it still appears in an image of melancholy on which things weigh immovably and therefore more heavily than would be appropriate to their nature ("mais rien dans ma mélancolie n'a bougé," ll. 29–30, "my melancholy is fixed"). And the first of the following evocations also is not yet wholly free from this compulsion of heaviness: "Aussi devant ce Louvre une image m'opprime" (l. 33, "And so, before the Louvre, to vex my soul). But in the same stanza, there is the contrasting gesture of the swan which is being given a different interpretation as the image recurs: "avec ses gestes fous" (l. 34, "with his mad gestures") is raised to a higher level in the next line by "ridicule et sublime" ("foolish and sublime"). The following evocation incorporates this tension in the analogy of Andromache and swan which has become explicit only now, and simultaneously increases it, from "vil betail" (l. 38) to "en extase courbée" (l. 39, "Bent o'er an empty tomb in ecstasy"). The counter-world of the beautiful which is being summoned in ever fresh images ("les cocotiers absent de la superbe Afrique," l. 43, "the absent palm-trees of proud Africa") makes the banal reality (la négresse, amaigrie et phtisique, pietinant dans la boue," ll. 41–42, "the negress, wan and phthisical, tramping the mud") recede more and more until finally, along with the objective world, the inner world, the subject of the poetic experience, appears transformed:

> Ainsi dans la forêt où mon esprit s'exile
> Un vieux Souvenir sonne à plein souffle du cor!
>
> (ll. 49–50)

> And one old Memory like a crying horn
> Sounds through the forest where my soul is lost . . .

The liberating blow of the horn of remembrance can break the spell of melancholy. From the frozen chaos of the alien reality, the immanent poetry of remembrance can give birth to another, unreal, and yet autonomous world of the beautiful which sets itself against the "empty ideality" of the old swan myth as a new, "supernatural" creation of the imagination.

That it should be precisely the short paragraph entitled "empty ideality" in H. Friedrich's Baudelaire chapter[90] that is so readily misunderstood, as if it maintained that the decisive "lyric statement" of the poet had here been given its "definitive formulation," merely shows how strongly some of H. Friedrich's readers still subscribe to what Baudelaire called "didactic heresy." What is overlooked is that H. Friedrich himself contrasted the section "language magic" and this central theme and that the former can also comprehend what we identified here as a structure with an inverse direction. It should be added that in Baudelaire, the retransformation of the estranged reality into a new world of the beautiful frequently occurs in the medium of remembrance, as in Le Cygne, but that it is not invariably tied to that medium. In the second "Spleen" poem, for example, it is remembrance which, in a gradual intensification of the images of petrified recollection, remains the medium of estrangement until the very end, and the final image ("un vieux sphinx ignoré du monde insoucieux, / Oublié sur la carte," An old sphinx ignored by a careless world, / Forgotten on the maps) seems to put its seal on this calamitous process (as the allegory of a being no one remembers and that therefore must remain eternally unredeemed). And yet it is precisely in the ambivalence of this final image that the switch takes place from which the unreal counterworld of the beautiful emerges and transfigures from the end what had first been evoked only under the aspect of the "Spleen": "et dont l'humeur farouche / Ne chante qu'aux rayons du soleil qui se couche" (and whose ill humor / Sings only to the rays of a sun that sets). In a mythological inversion of what tradition reports about Memnon's statue in Thebes, perhaps also in allusion to the owl of Minerva, the forgotten sphinx sings as the sun sets and thus transforms the melancholy landscape of the "Spleen" at the end into the bizarre beauty of a pure sound that detaches itself from its source and is meant for no one.

This process which his poem *Le Cygne* thematizes by its reshaping of the Platonic myth about the poet-swan, and its transformation into a modern concept of the beautiful, Baudelaire once referred to in *Le Peintre de la vie moderne* as a "forced idealization": "All the material that burdens memory is sorted, ordered and harmonized, and undergoes that forced idealization that is the result of a childlike perception, i.e. a keen perception which is magic because of its artlessness."[91] Not only does his swan poem carry out the process of this idealization thematically; in the previously mentioned irregular interlinking of its syntactic units, it also sets it before us in images. Whereas their movement leads to a confused piling up and chaotic congealing of the materials of recollection in part I, where the destruction of the "formes d'une ville" becomes visible all the way to the asymmetrical contrasting image of the thirsting swan; in part II, the imaginary counterworld of the beautiful emerges from a linear sequence of evocations which connect in an articulated order like a festive procession. With the inverse movement of this form of composition, Baudelaire has moved farthest from the tradition of *poésie-peinture*. Here, the object, the urban landscape which includes the swan motif, is no longer described statically and objectively. Baudelaire's poem, which leads us away from the object by the estrangement of the familiar and then allows it to arise again in unexpected beauty after the imagination has transformed it into a *sensation du neuf*, includes the path of evocation in its representation and thus announces the specific form of Mallarmé's lyric,[92] the poem which in its portrayal causes the object itself to disappear in order to find its real theme in the composition of a poem.

5. Lyric poetry as "dream of a world in which things would be different" (postscript 1977)

The history of lyric aesthesis into which I placed the above investigation now makes it possible to raise anew the question about the "structural unity" of older and modern lyric poetry and to answer it in a way that differs from my attempt in the polemics against H. O. Burger and G. R. Hocke.[93] The working out of the hermeneutic difference between Théophile's baroque poem and Baudelaire's modern "poetry of remembrance" elucidated the dissimilarities of their understanding of the world. What remained unmentioned was the common horizon of lyric experience which overarches even the epochal differences, Théophile's Platonism and Baudelaire's anti-Platonism. What separates older from modern lyric poetry emerged in the swan poems because the lyric aesthesis directs the glance in opposite directions: through the continuing metamorphosis, the incoherent transformation of views, and the *beau désordre* of the landscape of the park, Théophile's ode takes us into the antecendently familiar horizon of a mythical world of the true, the beautiful, and the good. Baudelaire's poem estranges the familiar cityscape, allows it to sink into the livid indifference of "Ennui," and then brings forth from remembrance a counterworld of the beautiful which has its truth already in its for-itself and no longer points to any origin other than the composition of the poem. The choice of my examples does not imply that a changed principle of production and reception is the only element by which older and modern lyric poetry differ. If they allow an epochal boundary to become tangible, that is not meant to imply that lyric poetry after the *Fleurs du Mal* can be called "modern" only if it follows Baudelaire's pattern. But it can show what justification Hugo Friedrich had for seeing a certain tradition of the modern lyric which Baudelaire initiated as the inversion of all that preceded.[94]

This inversion of lyric aesthesis still follows the scheme of Platonic anamnesis in Théophile, whereas Baudelaire merely quotes the ideality of a "ciel anterieur oú fleurit la beauté" (an anterior heaven where beauty flowers)[95] to set against it a different, immanent world of the beautiful that memory creates; the inversion becomes paradigmatic by virtue of the fact that in this poem, Baudelaire specifically thematized the modern rejection of the Platonism of the older tradition. Yet today, I would certainly agree with Burger and say that the older and modern lyric, which here, on this threshold of our modernity, form a fundamental contrast which becomes apparent in the process of lyric aesthesis, still have a common element: in both cases, expectation does not direct itself toward the recognition of a portrayed, already familiar or experienced reality but the appearance of what is other than the world of daily familiarity. Whether lyric aesthesis on the far side of the threshold of autonomous art transposes its object back into the horizon of a mythic ideality or thereafter discovers a new aspect of the world in a reality that is empty of meaning because always already known—the experience of lyric poetry always leads beyond the sphere of the realities of daily and historical life. H. O. Burger was clearly thinking of this fundamental experience of lyric aesthesis when he used the concept "exorbitance." But he stopped halfway when he attempted to prove the "structural unity" of older and modern lyric poetry by employing categories that derive from classical representational aesthetics.

If we look back once again at Burger's interpretation, it becomes clear that by the relativization of classicism and mannerism, his approach almost imperceptibly led him to a modernization of the "classical" which alone enabled him to discover an apparent structural unity between the older and the more modern form of lyric poetry. This modernization first shows up in the formulation by which he draws the line between classicism and mannerism: "starting out with the concluding lines of Goethe's *Auf dem See* and Hölderlin's *Abschied*, I contrast the adequate symbol and the evocative equivalent."[96] There is the tacit assumption here that Hölderlin's evocative figure already has the function of T. S. Eliot's "objective correlative." Then Burger attempts to show the structural unity of classical and modern poetry by comparing Hölderlin and Mörike with Marie Luise Kaschnitz, Karl Krolow, and Paul Celan. But this involves a *petitio principii*, for Hölderlin's obscure style and Mörike's poetry with its surprising (precious-mannerist) final points represent, after all, the "most modern" aspects of classical German poetry. The circle of the argument closes with the claim: "The evocative equivalent in the modern poem is a logical development of the adequate symbol of the classical one."[97] But his conclusion applies only to the step from Goethe to Hölderlin and Mörike, not to the further step toward the dominant development of modern lyric poetry and Baudelaire. For there, it necessarily obscures the decisive break between the older and the more modern "dark style" which Burger's examples themselves also make palpable.

In the final lines in Hölderlin's ode *Der Abschied*, for example, which Burger quotes as an instance of an "evocative equivalent,"[98] what seems unmotivated and obscure at first glance defines itself for every Hölderlin reader when he translates back into its preexistent horizon the mythicizing image which surprisingly leaps out of its context, and recognizes in the "golden aufduftenden Lilie" a cipher of the poet's belief in a recoverable "whole world." As such, this figure is a dark image, i.e., a no longer representational "evocative equivalent" only from the perspective of the existing, secular world but an "adequate symbol" in the context of the other, Platonic world of the beautiful and the true. However, those images from modern German poems which Burger wants to bring into parallelism with Hölderlin's "Lilie" are "equivalent" neither under a Platonic nor a secular aspect but remain dissonant. As "exorbitant images," "Die Wolke, die über ihre Köpfe dahinfuhr, schwarz und herrlich" (the cloud which sailed above their heads, black and magnificent), in the poem of M. L. Kaschnitz, and Hölderlin's "Lilie," fail to come together at precisely the point "they leave the world behind,"[99] Where Hölderlin "exorbitates harmoniously into a world that is whole" with his evocative figure, M. L. Kaschnitz proceeds inversely and ironically undoes the equivalence of the cloud which had seemed to point to a higher, more essential world above the banal burial scene, and takes us "dissonantly back into a pathetic reality" as Burger himself had to note in his study of Krolow's love poem.[100] If the exorbitant image, which—in a precise inversion of Hölderlin's procedure—is introduced in a perfectly matter-of-fact and banal manner and then surprisingly annuls the expected equivalence between image and transcendent meaning, still serves a definite if ironic statement, Kaschnitz's second poem (*Genazzano*) destroys all equivalence by the alogical connection of speaker's statement and past tense (the persona's death appears as having already occurred). Verses such as:

> Hier stand ich am Brunnen
> Hier wusch ich mein Brauthemd
> Hier wusch ich mein Totenhemd
> Mein Gesicht lag weiss
> Unterm schwarzen Wasser
> Im wehenden Laub der Platanen

(Here I stood by the well / Here I washed my bride's shift / Here I washed my shroud / My face lay white / under black water / in the flowing leaves of plane trees) are equivalents neither of a portrayable reality nor of an antecedent meaning of the experience of death; in their bizarre irreality, they correspond to nothing but Baudelaire's "perception du neuf"—the perception of that "new world" which the modern poet knows how to produce himself, according to the underivable rules of the imagination. What Burger shows in his conclusion, that adequate symbol and evocative equivalent come together where they leave visible reality behind and cause another, more essential world to appear, is only seemingly the structural unity of classical and modern lyric poetry but in fact the structural unity of classical and (older) mannerist form. For this, one must be grateful to him, for in Hocke's book, this structural unity is prematurely interpreted in terms of philosophical views cast in the dark Heideggerian style which can hardly be shown to be present in the perceivable structure of the text and presumably cannot make wholly supererogatory a structural analysis of complete texts.[101]

If a common horizon of lyric experience is to lie in the expectation that another world opens up to us in and through the lyric experience, one should first recall a sentence from Malraux's *Voices of Silence* which I used as an epigraph at the beginning of this essay: "For art to be born, it is necessary that the relation between represented objects and man be of a different nature than that imposed by the world." But with this definition, the question concerning an overarching experience common to both the older and modern European lyric poetry is only reduced to a fundamental aesthetic attitude which, according to Malraux, did not apply to poetry and all the arts until they had achieved autonomy in the Renaissance: "The Middle Ages were as unaware of what we mean by the word 'art' as were Greece and Egypt, who had no word for it. For this concept to come into being, works of art needed to be isolated from their functions. What common link existed between a 'Venus' which *was* Venus, a crucifix which *was* Christ crucified, and a bust? But three 'statues' can be linked together."[102] With the idea of an autonomous art which became dissociated from all functions of everyday life, there also set in, since the Renaissance, a change in the hitherto purely normatively determined relationship to past art as a binding canon of masterpieces, a canon which had also created a barrier to the reception of the historical diversity of art. To the degree that the "fine arts" detached themselves from the life-world functions of preautonomous art, an ever expanding historical understanding also gave rise to that attitude of "aesthetic differentiation" (Gadamer) which finally, in the *musée imaginaire* of the nineteenth century, made available to itself the art of the past of all cultures, epochs, and styles. The common denominator that allows one to place side by side in the imaginary museum the classical goddess, the crucified Christ, and a Michelangelo statue is their reduction to "aesthetic objects." Ignoring their functions in the everyday world annuls temporal distance to such a degree that the otherness of preautonomous art becomes aesthetically experienceable and enjoyable as a "different world of the past." Malraux's thesis needs to be supplemented in two ways. It does not adequately explain how this capacity for otherness of the world which the experience of autonomous art opens up for us is to be conceived in relation to a given life reality which it negates. And it leaves open the question: in what sense did aesthetic experience on the far side of the threshold of autonomous art involve that expectation of another, more beautiful world which often gives us the easiest hermeneutic access to the alien reality of past ideals, desires, and dreams?

How must the relationship of man and world be conceived in the experience of art if it can "differ in kind" from the pragmatic one which the reality of daily life imposes on us, and if it is yet to give us experience of this, our common world? In his *Rede über Lyrik und Gesellschaft* (1975), T. W. Adorno raised this question with a dialectical rigor which Malraux lacks. Here, lyric poetry is understood as "something opposed to society" and eminently "social" for that very reason. According to Adorno, it is distinguished from other forms of aesthetic experience by the demand that it "conjure up the image of a life which is free of the compulsion of prevailing praxis, usefulness, and the pressure of mulish self-preservation,"[103] But Adorno believed that this demand of lyric poetry was of recent date, a "form of reaction to the reification of the world" and therefore "modern through and through." That may hold for the ideological-critical implication of his thesis but certainly does not exclude the historical possibility that older lyric poetry could also express "the dream of a world in which things would be different,"[104] and did in fact express it in a multiplicity of ways. The expectation that the lyrical experience would open up for us this capacity for otherness of the world on solemn as on daily occasions—the occasional lyric situation—has been met in the tradition of the West by the classical song of praise in Pindar's manner, the Anacreontic occasional poem, Christian-medieval poetry as the spiritual or secular "poetry of the invisible," the already self-conscious *Canzoniere* of Petrarch with its "poetry of absence," the Platonizing and the sensuous lyric poetry of the Renaissance, and certainly young Goethe's so-called poetry of experience.[105] The question that must still be answered is this: what is the specific achievement of the lyric experience in the fulfillment of this expectation, and how is the boundary between older and modern lyric poetry to be drawn?

The pure capacity of the world to be other, the "exorbitance" into the imaginary or marvelous, defines lyric experience as little as does the simple expression of something experienced or the praising of a thing. As the experience of something that seems unlike the daily reality imposed on us, lyric poetry preserves something of the horizon of the real world it transcends. It can attain to this otherness by merely allowing the world to arise anew—and this wholly through poetic language—from the occasioning motive of a familiar situation, and through the transforming power of verse. In the reception of lyric poetry, reality and fiction, daily and aesthetic experience do not confront each other as two utterly opposed worlds. Rather, lyric experience creates that kind of relationship between daily reality and the "other world" of poetry where, through the transformations of linguistic form, the occasion is raised to new meaning and the lyrically seized situation can make the whole of a universal analogy appear in the horizon of fiction.[106]

In spite of all the metamorphoses of the *description poétique*, the park he celebrates does not wholly disappear from the reader's imagination in Théophile's ode. To the extent that he retranslates the concrete, complex order of the idyllic place through the *beau désordre* of poetry into the timeless truth and perfection of the idea, the historic park of Chantilly also derives an unsuspected plenitude of meaning from the mythological horizon of the beautiful. And in the analogy of the "end of Nature," the poet can discover the hidden significance of the threat to his personal fate. In Baudelaire's swan poem similarly, the concrete occasion, the destruction of old Paris through Haussmann's brutal renovation, remains present to the end. The counterworld of the beautiful, which the "peintre de la vie moderne" evokes with the solemn triumphal procession of his recollections, acquires its luminosity in no small part before the background of an estranged ambiance, in a protest against the loss of the "forme d'une ville" which the gesture of the thirsting swan in its "beauté inutile" condenses in a symbol. And even where modern lyric poetry seems to take an almost indifferent object as pretext—as Mallarmé does his fans and tombstones—in order to draw the reader into a referenceless *jeu de la parole* and to make him experience what the possibilities of language are, the disappearing objective equivalent preserves an ultimate poetic function: it opens up the complex game of word and verse which the reader can concretize only when the testing and rejecting of new meanings is tied to the horizon of a thematic vanishing point which reduces the arbitrariness of interpretation to the "complex, succinct perception" (D. Henrich) of lyric experience when, in the concrete instance of the *Tombeau de Verlaine*, the opening line, "le noir roc courroucé que la bise roule," limits the polysemy of possible interpretations to the range between tombstone in an occasional or literal sense, and the emblematic rock on Christ's grave.

The last example is taken from *Blindness and Insight* (1971) in which Paul de Man continues the discussion on "lyric poetry as paradigm of the modern period" with a detailed critique of my earlier study and of Karlheinz Stierle's investigations into the dark style as the beginning of modern lyric poetry.[107] I hope that my present argument has reached—and advanced grounds for—a position from which the hitherto unresolved differences can be mediated. De Man's critique can be summarized in four arguments: (1) Modernity is neither an autonomous aesthetic value nor a unique historical-period concept which would suffice to grasp lyric poetry since Baudelaire as a paradigm of *modernitas*. (2) The development of lyric poetry since the turn that de Man also understands as a "crisis of representation and the autonomous self" is not a straight line, let alone a genetic process in which, from Baudelaire through Verlaine to Mallarmé and Valéry, every "son" takes up the position of his "father" to then carry a progressive irrealization and depersonalization of the lyric to the next higher level. (3) Even if the "disappearance of the object" in the literary sequence of these "fathers" of our modernity is acknowledged as a dominant and overarching tendency, an objective equivalent or "natural image" remains—in the poetry where this has occurred—the indispensable prerequisite for the obscurity of the modern lyric. (4) Especially Baudelaire's position is only one-sidedly understood by the poetics of a "perception du neuf." The characteristic signature of his ambivalent "modernity" must be looked for in a development that runs "from the sensory richness of the earlier poems to their gradual allegorization in the prose versions of the "Spleen de Paris."[108]

There is no need for me to specifically address myself to the first point because my history of the concept of *modernitas*, which de Man did not yet have available to him at the time,[109] explains modernity as a poetological category and also as a historical phenomenon par excellence, i.e., as the ever renewed attempt at self-definition by rejection of a past, and traces it from the classical "Querelle des Anciens et des Modernes" to the threshold of our present understanding of modernity. De Man's pair of categories, "blindness" and "insight" on the other hand, emphasizes the hermeneutic principle that one cannot get behind the self-understanding of any given period, a principle I also subscribe to. Regarding the second point, I have already conceded that although the literary sequence of the French "fathers of our modernity" exemplarily represents the crisis of representation and the autonomous self, that cannot be considered the only true motto of the modern lyric in toto. I corrected the "blindness" of a modernist theory that sees Baudelaire's poetics of *nouveauté* as a total break with the entire tradition by calling attention to the "dream of a world in which things would be different" as the overarching horizon of lyric aesthesis. On the third point, I hope that agreement can come from my proposal to define the specific achievement of lyric aesthesis through the dialectics of prompting occasion and universal analogy. What de Man sees as the ambivalence of lyric language, which is "representational and non-representational at the same time,"[110] is in harmony with this dialectic. But both his and my definition will only become methodologically concretizable for purposes of interpretation if it is premised that the objective and the irreal in lyric aesthesis enter into a relation where their horizons become reciprocally substitutable, i.e., where the objective world becomes the horizon of the fiction, the fiction the horizon of the objective world—a clarification of the constitution of lyric experience which we owe to Karlheinz Stierle, who not only theoretically but recently also practically corrected the "blindness" of his earlier Mallarmé interpretation with this insight.[111]

Regarding the fourth point, I agree with de Man that Baudelaire's poetics remains contradictory when one looks at the implicit theory of his lyric practice. This is already brought out in my aesthesis chapter in the unmediated juxtaposition of "Spleen" and "Ideal," shock, *beauté fugitive*, and the correspondence of the data of remembrance.[112] From my point of view, however, the allegorization of poetry which de Man stresses actualizes the use of allegory precisely in the service of depersonalization. For in Baudelaire's modern use, personifying allegory can no longer point to an antecedently known spiritual significance of things. As an "allegory without a key," it turns the traditional emblems into the undecipherable signum of things that have lost their aura in the spleen and that dominate the psychological inner landscape as alien realities to such an extent that the self can no longer integrate them in any personal experience.[113] This is the reason the interpretation of Baudelaire requires no allegoresis, no retranslation into an antecedently known significance, or clarification of what is opaque. In contrast to such reductions, the demand I once formulated with a view to Mallarmé and which I still insist on today (with the addition that the "presque" in the Mallarmé quote be underlined) applies to Baudelaire as well; what counts is not simply to elucidate what is opaque but to move inversely, to follow the transposition of the theme from clarity into mysteriousness, and to grasp in the disappearance of the object a complementary process, the writing of the poem in its *beauté inutile*, as the aphorism in which Mallarmé defined the nature of poetry would have it: "à quoi bon la merveille de transposer un fait de nature en sa presque disparition vibratoire selon le jeu de la parole, cependent; si ce n'est pour qu'en émane sans le gêne d'un proche rappel, la notion pure" (why should we perform the miracle by which a natural object is almost made to disappear beneath the magic waving wand of the written word, if not to divorce that object from the direct and the palpable, and so conjure up its essence in all its purity.[114]

E. *La douceur du foyer:* Lyric Poetry of the Year 1857 as a Model for the Communication of Social Norms[1]

1. From the image-fields of the poem to the communicative function of the lyric

The lyric has always been a stepchild of the sociology of literature, and, Walter Benjamin's fragmentary Baudelaire studies notwithstanding, that is what it has continued to be for the new materialist theory of literature. Whether it be the mimetic relationship of representation or form and reality, the cognitive relation of literature to a state of society, or the communicative function of poetry, up to now it has usually been the novel that was preferred as the paradigm for such questions. As a purely linguistic act, lyric poetry seems to inherently elude all mimesis or "referential illusion." This is reason enough to devote particular attention to Michael Riffaterre's attempt to grasp the representational or descriptive achievement of lyric poetry through the use of structural linguistics.[2] Because a number of years have passed since Riffaterre's method began to apply structural linguistics to the relationship of text and reader, this attempt is also guided by the principle "Le poème n'est pas un aboutissement mais un point de départ" (the poem is not an end but a point of departure).[3] This principle and its application in interpretation coincide with the aims of the theory of reception aesthetics that I espouse. But it is not our purpose here to measure the two methods against each other but to take both to a point where they can answer the question whether and how communicative functions can be uncovered in the representational achievement of the lyric. This question touches on a problem which sociology is also interested in and where that discipline would welcome an offer from the field of aesthetic praxis, and that is the passing on, elaboration, and legitimation of social norms through literature.

Riffaterre's point of departure is the observation that neither the ordinary reader nor even traditional criticism takes autonomous art as its yardstick: below the highest level of aesthetic reflection, the poem is measured against experienced reality, its authenticity admired or a mimetic faithfulness missed. Yet this customary reception of the average reader does not mean that he naively equates the verbal signs of the poem with real objects in the world; the average experience of lyric poetry also does not start off from an external reality but "from words" which allow one to see something in "just such a way" and therefore make that thing appear poetic.[4] The faithfulness of the poem is measured against the cliché or "mythology" or, more simply, the idea the reader has about the represented world, not any actual knowledge of what it is like. The poetic representation is more convincing than simple verbalization because it is "overdetermined," not because it is similar or probable. "Overdetermination" as a category through which structural analysis tries to get at the effect of poetic representation comes from the combination of three elements, according to Riffaterre: the linguistic code, the thematic structure, and overlapping descriptive patterns. The first requires explaining only when the author's linguistic code has become so remote historically that the later reader needs a translation into the code of his language. The thematic structure is the syntagmatic level; it becomes effective and perceptible to the degree that the reader becomes a *decodeur* and successively registers those deviations from expected conventions by which the author as *encodeur* elicits the attention of a future audience.[5] The descriptive system constitutes the paradigmatic level; it is interacting "image-fields" (as Harald Weinrich baptized them),[6] i.e., the associations called forth by certain words which have an adequate connotative potential. They evoke in the reader a self-contained sphere of ideas which are often recognized when just one *single* element of such a system is presented (for example, *carillon* for the entire image-field *horloge*).

In his analysis of Victor Hugo's "Ecrit sur la vitre d'une fenêtre flamande," Riffaterre demonstrated in exemplary fashion what structural stylistics can accomplish when it uncovers how these three structures interact. The analysis does not proceed from a represented reality to its representation or description in the poem but shows inversely "comment la représentation crée la chose représentée, comme elle la rend vraisemblable, c'est-à-dire reconnaissable et satisfaisante à la lecture."[7] (how the representation creates the thing represented, how it makes it probable, i.e., recognizable and satisfactory when read.) In the horizon of the unfolding of the syntagmatic system and its correction,[8] the interpretation can trace from word to word, more precisely from image-field to image-field, how, between "surprise" and *rétroaction*, the meaning of the thematic structure is decoded for the reader.[9] And because the context permits one to infer the implicit norm from its changes or its fulfillment, overdetermination can be observed without recourse to historical knowledge or aesthetic values. This means that the analysis of the reception process acquires objectifiable data ("le contraste résultant de cette interférence est le stimulus stylistique," the contrast that results from this interaction is the stylistic stimulus).[10]

If we now turn back and try to answer the question how the representational achievement of a poem can acquire a communicative function, and how the receptive experience can convey an interaction pattern of social life to the solitary reader, we find that Riffaterre's procedure must be taken beyond the individual poem and the aesthetic norm as inferred from the context. The poetic text that spellbinds the reader by its overdetermined elements or interplays and that ensures its controlled decoding must also prove to be the carrier of a meaning or "message." And if it is not just through its poetic form but also through its context that the poem is to impose attention, the poetic message must differ from mere information. It might, for example, disclose in the open horizon of its possibilities and uncertainties a situation whose significance has paled to matter-of-factness in the routine of everyday life. By way of a situation whose meaning the lyric "I" discloses by engaging itself in it or dealing with its risks, the poetic message can unfold an interaction pattern which enters the reader's horizon as expectation of meaning. It is certainly true that not every lyric text contains a message which the reader can interpret as the answer to an implicit question or the solution of a real-life situation. But even in the extreme case of that modern lyric poetry which refuses any and every "message" by negating evoked situations and annulling any possible significance, and which lays claim to being enjoyed and thought about in its self-referentiality alone, a situational referentiality and the meaning-disclosing achievement of the lyric message are implicit.

But when it becomes a question of demonstrating the explicit or implicit, hidden or refused poetic message being conveyed to the reader in the aesthetic enjoyment of a poem, structural analysis cannot remain within the context-immanent circle of inferred norm and deviation, descriptive system and interaction. It then becomes necessary to inquire about the norm which, as *expectation*, conditions the thematic structure and, as *idea*, can enter into the experience of a reader who came to know it through the reception of the poem. For though it is true that the literary description of reality does not directly refer to *things*, it certainly relates to our *idea* of them. It does so either by affording us the evidence of recognition or by conveying this idea to a young and still inexperienced reader for the first time and thus preforming his future expectation. To that extent, it is not entirely correct to say, "Qui n'a jamais veillé au chevet d'un mourant n'en est pas moins sensible à la force évocatrice du mot 'rale.'"[11] (Though someone may never have sat by a dying person's bedside, he will still be sensitive to the evocative power of the word *death rattle*.) For someone who has sat by a dying person's bedside, the evocatory power of that word may bring an additional resonance that comes from memory. But the person to whom this poem conveys the first idea of a death scene will already have his expectation oriented by the aesthetic norm when he encounters such a situation in real life. Aesthetic experience appears as a world unto itself and may yet refer to the same thing as practical commerce. With a view toward the representational function of lyric poetry, it must therefore be asked what the aesthetic attitude adds when it conveys, inaugurates, or allows one to recognize the idea of an object, an action, or a situation.

It is only with regard to the image-fields that are relevant to the discovery of the norms of everyday reality that this question is of interest here. So far, Riffaterre has not ordered his descriptive systems in accord with such relevancies. His starting point is the semantic potential (the *semes* and their respective codes) of concepts that are capable of generating one or more descriptive systems. He shows how the unfolding of descriptive sequences in poetry follows certain rules (of tautological or oxymoronic generation, for example), and includes rhetorical patterns, allegorical keys, mythological elements, and symbols. Such descriptive systems or image-fields can range from the smallest compass of a classical epithet to the meaning potential of symbolic words with a rich tradition which can function in more than one context. The step from image-field in a representative function to descriptive pattern in a communicative one is taken where the system of lexical associations fits into a model that evokes a situation. To test whether an image-field contains an interaction pattern, one must determine if the descriptive pattern can be formulated as a "language game." As an example, we take Riffaterre's analysis of the use of *carillon* in different contexts and according to a variety of semantic codes. As the reader takes in certain adjectives that pertain to the "ringing of a bell," the direction of meaning of the descriptive pattern has already been decided for him: "Si la sonnerie était un tocsin appelant aux armes, les sons de la cloche seraient de 'bronze' ou 'd'airain,' metaux des armes poétiques. Si la cloche tintait dans un clocher de village, elle serait 'enrouée' comme le gosier d'un rustre. Si la cloche n'est que la clochette tout prosaique d'un portail de jardin bourgeois, le 'fer' vulgaire suffirait."[12] (If the ringing were an alarm calling to arms, the sounds of the bell would be bronze or brassy, for these are martial metals. If the bell tolled in a village steeple, it would be hoarse, like a peasant's throat. But if that bell were simply that perfectly prosaic little bell at the garden gate of a burgher's house, common iron would do.) As tocsin, stroke of the clock, or tinkling, the image-field of *carillon* can metonymically evoke a warning, the round of village life, or the signal of an arrival. The description of the situation becomes an interaction pattern when, as language game, it refers to rules and defines or legitimates such rules which tell the reader what is involved and what must be done when, for example, there is a call to arms, the church bell regulates daily activities, or the bell at the garden gate announces a visitor (famous as the scene of Swann's arrival in Marcel Proust's "Combray").

Compared with the lexical code of conversational language, the descriptive system of structural stylistics represents a first reduction to those words that can function in the poetic code of lyric poetry as the germ of normlike ideas. They are not directly derivable from the lexical order of a language but presuppose extralinguistic, historically determined choices and thus a mutual consensus of those of its users who are familiar with the poetic code.[13] This initial reduction must be supplemented by a second one when in and behind the descriptive subsystems of a poem, those interaction patterns or language games are to be discovered by which lyric poetry, inherently designed to make known rather than to communicate or represent, can also take on a communicative function. Such interaction patterns which develop in social existence when actions become habitual express themselves in expectations which solidify into social norms. These patterns can be passed on from one generation to the next although they need never have been expressly formulated or codified as is true of prescriptions with the force of law, religious commandments, or ethical maxims. What is involved here is habitual knowledge or role behavior that can be learned through action or from models and of which the outsider

or the distanced historian is a better observer than the participant.
For to the latter, the ambient institutional world of intersubjective
behavior is generally so self-evident or so opaque that he does not become conscious of its norms and rules until a malfunctioning occurs.
Unless, that is, art or literature make him aware of them. For it is
one of the most important if least explored achievements of the aesthetic experience in social praxis that it gives voice to the mute institutions of the social world, thematizes norms that prove themselves,
and conveys and justifies those that have been passed down. But it
also problematizes the constraints of the institutional world, makes
the roles of others understandable, creates consensus about newly developing norms, and thus counteracts the dangers of reification and
ideologizing.

The sociology of knowledge, whose conceptual apparatus I used in
the above,[14] seems to have barely paid attention to the function of
aesthetic experience in the constitution of social reality.[15] In the investigation being started here, I intend to describe this function by
means of a historical example and thus to build a bridge between the
reception-aesthetic theory of literature and the sociological theory of
the world of everyday reality.[16] It is true that the sociology of knowledge cannot furnish a perfect systematics of all the interaction patterns that underlie the everyday world of what is already a historically
remote bourgeois life world which is yet part of the prehistory of our
present, the year of publication of the *Fleurs du Mal* (1857). But our
investigation can benefit by adopting its theory of the structure of
the social world. This structure can be demonstrated both as process,
in the phases of habitualization, institutionalization, legitimation,
and internalization (by primary and secondary socialization), and can
also be understood as result, in the gradated relevance of social roles,
institutions, and subuniverses. What we have called interaction pattern
or language game up to now does not occur in isolation in social praxis
but appears in a closed horizon of expectations. Individual *norms of
behavior* are subordinated to pervasive role demands, standardized
roles fit into *institutions* through a process of mutual typification,
and their order is secured by forms of *legitimation* which "give a normative dignity to its [i.e. the order's] practical imperatives."[17] Such
legitimation, finally, can confer the character of, or, if one prefers,
the ideological appearance of, an autonomous subuniverse on such an
order. Because the reality of everyday life is normally assimilated
through such firmly circumscribed forms of meaning and modes of
experience, the present analysis must aim at grasping the individual
interaction pattern in the context of the subuniverse that encloses

and legitimates it as the horizon of the life world. Since it is only in rare cases that the documents of social history indicate how such sub-universes are set off from each other in collective thought, it should be all the more rewarding to examine what information about sub-universes and their boundaries in the bourgeois life world of the nine-teenth century can be derived from the lyrical representatives of com-municative patterns.

2. Synchronic analysis of a lyrically represented subuniverse: *La douceur du foyer*

> Encore la plupart n'ont-ils jamais connu
> La douceur du foyer et n'ont jamais vécu!

(Indeed, many a one has never even known / The hearth's warm charm. Pity such a one.) It was surely Baudelaire who, at the lyric's highest level in 1857, most powerfully evoked what the end of work's daily round—that time when the sky encloses the city "like a large alcove"— brings for the bourgeois family. In "Le crépuscule du soir," the al-ready trite theme of happiness at the hearth once more acquires a painfully insistent, poetic power because the poet evokes it from the perspective of the excluded, the prostitutes, the criminals, the gam-blers, the hospitalized, for there is the pathos here of that *douceur* being denied them. In the untranslatable verbal amalgam which fuses social ideal, sacral origin, and the poetry of the everyday, the *douceur du foyer* returns at all stylistics levels of lyric poetry during this year as an autonomous, quoted or implicit theme. The underlying social norms which this communicative pattern conjoins in a subuniverse and conveys into the praxis of life are to be discovered through a synchronic analysis of the following 1857 texts:
from Victor Hugo's *Les Contemplations*:
  1. "La vie aux champs" (I, vi)
  2. "Le rouet d'Omphale" (II, iii)
  3. "Paroles dans l'ombre" (II, xv)
  4. "Il lui disait" (II, xxi)
  5. "Aimons toujours" (II, xxii)
  6. "Intérieur" (III, xviii)
  7. "Elle avait pris ce pli" (IV, v)
  8. "O souvenirs! printemps! aurore!" (IV, ix)
  9. "A Mademoiselle Louise B." (V, v)
from Charles Baudelaire's *Les Fleurs du Mal*:
  10. "Les bijoux"

11. "Le balcon"
12. "Je n'ai pas oublié, voisine de la ville"
13. "Le crépuscule du soir"
by other authors of poems written during the same year:
14. Louis Bouilhet, "Démolitions"
15. Blaze de Bury, "Chaperon-Rouge" (Intermède romantique)
16. L. Damey, "Le Grillon"
17. Alfred Lemoine, "La veuve"
18. Andre Lenoyne, "Où sont-ils?"
19. Andre Lemoyne, "Stella maris"
20. Leon Magnier, "Rêve agreste."

This selection was made from a corpus of about 700 lyric pieces which a seminar at the University of Constance[18] collected, classified, and interpreted as representatives of communicative patterns for a cross-sectional analysis of the literary horizon of expectation in 1857. Not all the texts in this corpus originated in 1856/57. Many of the poems that Victor Hugo collected and published in his *Les Contemplations* in 1856 go back to a much earlier period. Since my reception-aesthetic inquiry is not based on a magic symbolism of contemporaneity but on a theory of the absence of contemporaneity in phenomena of an identical period, the representation of various levels of sources in this analysis was vital: the canon of the preceding lyric tradition by the successful work of Victor Hugo; the avant-gardist provocation by Baudelaire's *Fleurs du Mal*, and the daily production of lyric pieces in the journals of 1857, poetry that was intended for instant consumption. I reprint a sample of the latter type, I. Damey's "Le Grillon," in the appendix.

a) The basic situational pattern (roles, place, time)

> La mére, dans son fils, croit trouver ton image.
> La moitié de son coeur est là, dans un berceau.
> *Le Marin*
> Et son autre moitié? . . .
> *L'Etoile*
> L'autre moitié voyage,
> Essayant sur les mers de suivre ton vaisseau.
> *Le Marin*
> Quand Dieu laissera-t-il les heureux vivre ensemble? . . .

> The mother thinks she finds your image in her son
> There lies half of her heart, nestled in a cradle.
> *The Sailor*
> And the other half . . . ?

> *The Star*
> The other half travels,
> Trying, on the high sea, to follow your vessel.
> *The Sailor*
> When will God ever let the happy live together?

In this dialogue between the far away sailor and the "stella maris," the sentimental tone of an already dated romanticism conjures up the "primal situation" which underlies the lyrical pattern. The object of such longing is the smallest circle that ensures the permanence of bourgeois happiness: father, mother, and child or, mythologically, the "holy family." Lemoyne's poem (#19) also makes clear that in the view of these sources, it is the mother who has the strongest because mediating role in the trinity of the bourgeois family. "One half of her heart" belongs to the child in the cradle, the other to the distant husband whose fate it is to die heroically "with his captain" at sea, for fatherland and family. The situational pattern shows a symmetric apportioning of roles and obligations: the mother represents the authority of the family within, the father vis-à-vis the outside. "Inside" and "outside" relate to each other as safety and danger, realm of happiness and proving ground.

The realm of happiness of the hearth is the gentle sphere of the woman. Her dominant role reveals itself most beautifully in the mythological garment of Hugo's "Rouet d'Omphale" (#2). In the luxurious atrium, the spinning wheel stands still. As the archaic attribute of the bourgeois hearth, it does not merely keep at bay the monsters punished by Hercules' club. For the deeper meaning of this ecphrasis is as follows: "the monsters were tamed by the virile, strong hero, but that hero was tamed by woman's gentleness."[19] The woman retains this dominant role even when the bourgeois trinity is reduced to the couple or expanded to include several children. Our synchronic analysis shows unmistakably that Baudelaire sets a self-sufficient duality against the happiness of the family, the artist's *intérieur* against the homey hearth, the ecstasies of sensory communication or sublimated remembrance against the hearth's quiet joys. But even in the *intérieur* of "Les bijoux" (#10), the elevated position of the mistress ("du haut du divan," from the head of the divan) intimates the same seductive power by which Omphale subdued the hero. And if, in "Le balcon" (#11), the *douceur du foyer* (home sweet home) is provocatively claimed for the solitary couple, the mistress assumes the dominant role as "mère des souvenirs" (mother of souvenirs), which means here that it is only the harmonizing power of remembrance that can create the perfect concord of a self-sufficient happiness.

This aura which first and only derives from recollection is absent from those pieces in which Hugo evokes situations of past familial happiness. The source of melancholy is the misfortune connected with the recently married daughter Leopoldine. Around her on whom Hugo often confers a mother's obligations, the scene is animated by the "quatre douces têtes" (the four sweet faces) of the children, a grieving mother, the reading grandfather who may be joined by a friend of the family. Hugo thematizes the latter as poet in "La vie aux champs," romantically unhoused but a person who knows things ("le poète en tout lieu / se sent chez lui," Everywhere the poet feels at home, #1, l. 3). But Hugo also confers on him the function of introducing the children to the experience of life. Because of this, the poet as someone from outside becomes the counterpart of the woman's gentle law and the mother's educational principle and takes over the role of paternal authority. If one considers that the latter normally goes unmentioned in the basic lyric pattern of the *douceur du foyer*, it seems as if Hugo had wanted to strengthen the weakened position of the father by having him trade roles with the poet.

The basic situational pattern of the *douceur du foyer* is both temporally and spatially removed from the praxis of the everyday reality of work:

> O soir, aimable soir, desiré par celui
> dont les bras, sans mentir, peuvent dire: aujourd'hui
> nous avons travaillé! . . .

(O evening, lovely evening, desired by those whose arms can say in truth: Today we have labored!) The temporal frame is "le soir charmant, le soir qui soulage" (The charming evening that solaces, #13), the time after the daily work is done, when the family has often gathered in the light of the lamp for supper, talk, or singing, in short for all those things suggested by the untranslatable German *Feierabend*. The lamp is the true center of the hearth. The hour it is lit signals the beginning of the narrative (#1, l. 30). Its circle of light symbolizes the intimacy of a private familiar world (#19). In Baudelaire's *intérieur*, on the other hand, it goes out and the body of the mistress acquires the fantastic attraction of the uncanny in the flickering light from the fireplace ("Il inondait de sang cette peau couleur d'ambre," It drowned in blood this amber-colored skin, #10).

The other attributes of the hearth as center of the bourgeois world can be gleaned from the poem "Où sont-ils" by Lemoyne (#18). The elegiac contemplation of a deserted house brings together and poeticizes traces of absent life: the open window, the rising smoke, the sound of a harp or a piano from the salon, the mute ancestor portraits, the empty armchair, and the chirping of the cricket which will have to find another hearth when, with the dying fire, the life of a family comes to an end. The windowpane also is a symbol of the self-contained world of the bourgeois hearth. It checks curiosity from both beyond and within (#16, l. 24) and, while protecting and revealing the happiness of those living behind it, may also merely stimulate it. Baudelaire uses this motif in the only poem of the *Fleurs du Mal* in which the mother is present, although even here, he does not name her; the evening sun must transform its natural light on tablecloth and curtain into candlelike reflections, for it refracts behind the pane, appears as "grand oeil ouvert dans le ciel curieux" (a great open eye in the curious sky, #12), and thus becomes the excluded eyewitness to the calm happiness of the diners. The inversion of this symbolism can be found in Hugo's "Intérieur" (#6); here, the evening sun makes the window of a worker's flat light up and hides from the passer-by that inside, a terrible quarrel is taking place between the three persons of a family that is anything but holy. I will return to the ideological function of this poem.

b) The basic normative pattern (maxims, values, sanctions)

> Je leur parle de tout. Mes discours en eux sèment
> Ou l'idée ou le fait. Comme il m'aiment, ils aiment
> Tout ce qu je leur dis. Je leur montre du doigt
> Le ciel, Dieu qui s'y cache, et l'astre qu'on y voit.
> Tout, jusqu'à leur regard, m'écoute. Je dis comme
> Il faut penser, rêver, chercher.

(I speak to them of everything. In them, my words sow either idea or truth. As they love me, they love all I tell them. I point out the heaven, God hidden within, and the star seen there. Everything down to their eyes listens to me. I say how one must think, dream, and seek.) In its life-world function, lyric poetry does not evoke the basic situational pattern and poetically heightened ideal of the *douceur du foyer* for its own sake. As social paradigm, the lyric theme and its variations always also convey experiences, modes of conduct, and norms of everyday knowledge. The mostly unexpressed or hidden function of poetic patterns for the process of so-called primary socialization is overtly thematized in Hugo's "La vie aux champs." There, the poet tells the children in the narrative situation of the hearth not only "comme il faut penser, rêver, chercher" (how one must think, dream, and seek, #1). He also gives more or less concrete advice about the giving of alms ("donnez l'aumone au pauvre humble et penché," give alms to the poor, humbled and gnarled, l. 60) and how to react to instruction or reproach. He anchors all moral teaching in the promise: "Qu'être bon, c'est bien vivre" (Being good means living well, l. 67) and tops it off with a short theodicy: God has no need of evil, which means that even in pain and tears, man can find "la bonté." In the variations on the basic pattern, the scope of clearly expressed or implicit behavioral norms extends from the skill of the female hand which can spread "contentment, lumière, propreté" even in the poorest hut ("Au dedans, ah, c'est là qu'une main économe / Arrange toute chose avec activité," Within, yes, there a thrifty hand takes care of everything busily, #15) to the touching admonition to the man working at his books that he bestow an occasional glance on the person he loves (#2). Otherwise, the thematized activities at the hearth are appropriate to the situation of the *Feierabend*. Work is excluded from the hearth's realm of happiness; only the spinning wheel points to an archaic phase of domestic production (#2, #15, #19). Where work at the spinning wheel is expressly described, as in Lemoine's "La veuve" (#17), it is an element in the sad sight of a destroyed harmony, one of the attributes of a widow's desolation for whom the brief happiness of married life has turned into a long torment:

> Dans son grand fauteuil assise,
> Tandis que ses doigts courants
> Tirent l'aiguille, indécise,
> Sa voix s'éteint dans son chant.

(In her great armchair, seated while her running fingers draw the needle, adrift, her voice is drowned by its song.) As the most familiar witness to the joys and misfortunes of the hearth, the armchair is also encountered elsewhere (#15). In Lemoine's poem, the rarer counter-image of "vicissitudes" is held up against the ideal image of the *plaisirs du foyer*, the sad fate of a bereaved woman whose husband and children have died one after the other so that she is now in permanent mourning (#17). This counterimage variation is neither a genuine boundary crossing nor in any way closer to reality than the positive variations. Rather, it is an instance of what might be called a procedure of *counteridealization*. It is directed at the negative side of a phenomenon. But because it merely describes the "reverse of the same coin," the implicit positive norms are neither subjected to doubt nor broken through by negative ones. On the contrary, as predicates of abundance, the positive norms emerge more insistently and are covertly substained by predicates of deficiency. These positive norms and their counterimages or negative correspondences can be listed as follows (principally derived from #16 and #17):

gaîté (gaiety)	− tristesse (sadness)
compagnie (company)	− solitude (solitude)
rêverie (revery)	− souci (concern or worry)
douceurs (pleasant things)	− tourment (torments)
plaisirs (pleasures)	− travail (work)
bonheur (happiness)	− malheur (unhappiness)

In its function of making communicable social norms, lyric poetry does not restrict itself to the idealizing means of poetic suggestion and imagery. Covertly or openly, it can also threaten social sanctions. An outstanding example from our collection, "Le Grillon" by Damey, documents this (#16; see appendix). It is a successful pastiche of the La Fontaine fable, a genre which clearly survived in the popular literature of the nineteenth century, the tendency of literary historians to fix its death around the end of the Ancien Regime notwithstanding. In Damey's piece, the youngest madcap is told every day by his "Mère Grillon": "Enfant, sachez-le bien, le bonheur est dans l'âtre" (Mother Cricket: My child, mind you, happiness is in the hearth). But he cannot resist his curiosity, takes a short excursion to the window, unexpectedly finds this threshold to the world of the others open, lands in the sunlit field, and frolics with the crickets there until he suddenly becomes terribly afraid. The reckless excursion into the world on the far side of the window ends in homesickness: "Oh! qui me donnera d'en retrouver la route!" (Please! Who can tell me how to get home!). And the moral of the story is as follows: "there are those who only learn to appreciate the "douceurs du foyer" when they no longer have the chance to enjoy them" ("Heureux qui les comprend, plus heureux qui les goute!" Happy he who knows them, happier still he who enjoys them!).

c) The subuniverse and its closed boundaries

> Voyant rouler ainsi qu'une onde
> Nos longs jours aux flots bleus,
> Nous formerons un petit monde
> De sages et d'heureux. (#20)

(Seeing our long days of blue breakers roll like the wave, we will fashion our little world of the happy and wise.) The sociology of knowledge takes as its staring point that we experience the reality of the everyday world in "finite provinces of meaning," as "enclaves within the paramount reality which are marked by circumscribed meanings and modes of experience."[20] To bring before our eyes the comprehending horizon of the everyday world which is shared by all its inhabitants, an effort of consciousness, a "shift of attention" away from the direct orientation toward a world of professional activity, play, religious cult, science, or the arts is therefore required. This may occur in the "commutation" from one "enclave" to another, the intrusion of a political interest (as when one listens to radio news, for example) or, more fundamentally, in the questioning of the autonomous validity of such enclaves. How the subuniverses of our everyday world are set off from each other has already emerged in our review of the *douceur du foyer* paradigm. Aesthetic experience has this advantage over other social-historical sources: it thematizes the knowledge of the everyday world which has become matter-of-fact through routine. The analysis of the paradigm can show in the medium of lyric poetry how the boundaries of a subuniverse (*petit monde*) are anchored, idealized, and sanctioned in collective thought. But as a pattern of communicative interaction, lyric poetry can also counteract the force of established institutions when it becomes hortatory or uses ironic means to recall to consciousness what may have been excluded or suppressed. In Damey's fable, the boundary between the familiar and the alien world is first rendered innocuous by the circumstance that the boundary-crossing "fugitive" encounters his like in the "outside" world. But then the small difference between the subuniverse of the domestic and the field cricket suffices to bring to consciousness the high risk of a life beyond one's own four walls, a life which only curiosity could delude one into seeing in the alluring colors of a freer existence. The imprudent crossing of the boundary is unavoidably followed by sanctions. For it is not simply that everything is different "outside"; the "escapee" becomes the stranger for whom the hoped-for pleasure turns into remorse and the tardy perception that the "plaisirs sans regrets et sans indiscrets" (pleasures without regret or indiscretion, l. 13) can only be had on the "inside."

Jurij Lotman's literary semiotics[21] confirms that the insight to be gained from the structure and explicit doctrine of this poetic fable is no accidental result. One of his most important pairs of concepts for the organization of a spatial structure is the opposition "open": "closed": "close space is interpreted in texts in terms of various common spatial images—a house, a city, one's motherland—and is endowed with certain features: 'kinship,' 'warmth,' 'security,' and so on. It stands in opposition to open-ended, 'outer' space and its features: 'strangeness,' 'enmity,' 'cold,' and so on. Opposite interpretations of 'open' and 'closed' are also possible. In this case, the boundary becomes the most important topological feature of space. The boundary divides the entire space of the text into two mutually non-intersecting subspaces. Its basic property is impenetrability. The way in which the boundary divides the text is one of its essential characteristics. This division can be between insiders and outsiders, between the living and the dead, between rich and poor. What is more important is that the boundary which divides space into two parts must be impenetrable, and the internal structure of each of the subspaces must be different." From this typology of what he calls "artistic space," Lotman derives a coordination of certain types of space with certain types of hero, his concept of event ("an event in a text is the shifting of a persona across the borders of a semantic field," p. 233), and his categorical pair, texts with and texts without plots. After what has been said, it should be apparent that one of the reasons Lotman's typology is so fertile is that the artistic space articulated around a boundary represents, or better, renders imaginable, the structure of delimited subuniverses. The element which the aesthetic attitude adds to the situations of practical life is that it makes explicit the latent boundaries of meaning of semantic fields, that it thematizes them as self-sufficient boundaries, and that it gives them the form of a modellike perfection.

The interaction model *la douceur du foyer* knows only figures of the closed, inner space, to use Lotman's terminology, not heroes of the outer, open world. The sole exception is the arrival in the secure circle, the hearth, of a guest from far away. The person who wishes to satisfy his longing for the far away and yet not surrender the security of his familiar world can listen to such a stranger who has experience of the world or has traveled far and wide and who will talk about "foreign lands and seas." This phrase is the title of a piano piece that is one of the famous *kinderszenen* by R. Schumann (died 1856) and which I mention here because it belongs to the same subuniverse. From the perspective of inner space, it thematizes the desire for what is distant not as the experience of the world "outside" but as a longing for "foreign lands and seas" such as can express itself this side of the threshold, within the realm of the *douceur du foyer*, without risk. Part of the ideal self-subsistence of this subuniverse is also the curious aura of distance peculiar to it—an idea of the foreign which has always already cushioned the shock of the alien, the unexpected, the fearful. In his "La vie aux champs" (#1), Victor Hugo assigns this theme to the role of the unhoused poet. The guest who arrives in the evening presents himself as the understanding friend of the children, bewitches them with "contes charmantes qui vous font peur la nuit" (charming tales that make you afraid of the night, l. 31), and by a mixture of story telling and instruction introduces them to the experience of what is both spatially and temporally remote. Names are mentioned which symbolize the fate of important peoples, of Jews, Greeks, and Romans, on the world historical stage. Then the temporally most remote nation, "l'antique Egypte et ses plaines sans ombre" (Egypt of old and its shadowless steppes, l. 7) is evoked on its still existing site, and this scene is painted as a disquieting landscape of death. It sends a shudder down the spine of the "voyageur de nuit" as which the poet places himself into his own enormous canvas at the end. What began in the homey light of the lamp (l. 30) ends in a nocturnal vision of the sphinx, a masterpiece of the mixture of the "grotesque and the sublime." Yet for the listener, the effect of the uncanny is cushioned by the pleasant sensation of a thrill which can even find the macabre metaphors of shroud and death masque aesthetically enjoyable, provided the idea of death, normally excluded from the realm of happiness of the *foyer*, remains consigned to the farthest reaches of spatial distance.

It is clearly part of the means of idealizing a subuniverse that the relationship between nearness and distance be brought into a state of balance which is used here to covertly make the opening up of the view beyond the boundary subserve the idealization of that familiar realm of happiness that is home. From a distance, the familiar world of nearness can itself take on an aura, i.e., "the unique appearance of a distance, however close it may be," in Benjamin's formulation.[22] This happens in "Stella maris," where the sailor, the image of longing, the "cher pays que tojours voit mon âme" before his eyes, heroically dies on the distant sea (#19). If the poetic form affirmatively idealizes the province of meaning of the "foyer paternal, abri de la sagesse" (the paternal hearth, shelter of wisdom, #16) in such variations, it can open up the perspective on a familiar distance and thereby make the reader forget the nearness of other subuniverses that are excluded from the realm of happiness of bourgeois existence. In the synchrony of the texts assembled here, the provocative lines of an evening poem therefore strike one not merely as a bold metaphor or poetic license but as a transgression of tabooed boundaries:

> Voici le soir charmant, ami du criminel;
> Il vient comme un complice, à pas de loup . . .

(The charming evening, friend of crime, comes in stealthily like an accomplice . . .) It is Baudelaire who foils the expectation of his reader in "Le crépuscule du soir" (#13) because as evening falls and the bourgeois family happily and "without hatred shuts out the world," he evokes the luckless urban life of all those for whom this hour is the start of their "daily" round on streets and in places of amusement, or when the tortures of the night set in in hospitals. The common denominator of the existence of prostitutes, criminals, gamblers, and invalids in their excluded subuniverses is that they cannot say about themselves, "aujourd'hui nous avons travaillé." And this means that they have forfeited the right to the happiness of the *douceur du foyer*. Here Baudelaire touches on the question of the legitimation and the ideological function of this communicative pattern.

d) Legitimation and ideological function

> Oh! de la mère-grand vénérable demeure,
> Cher cadre où, dans le buis et l'ébène enchassé,
> Nous sourit gravement le tableau du passé;
> Eden où notre enfance a célebré son heure,
> Théâtre fortuné de nos plus doux émois,
> Où, dans la profoundeur des sentiers et des bois,
> Au murmure de l'herbe, au chant des sources vives,
> S'éveille dans nos coeurs pour la première fois
> Le sentiment sacré des croyances naives;
> Oh! je te reconnais, séjour calme et bénie,
> De la paix domestique humble et dernier asile,
> Que la main du Seigneur protège comme un nid,
> Des orages lointains qui grondent sur la ville!

(Oh, grandmother's venerable dwelling, cherished home where, set in wood and ebony, the picture of yesteryear gravely smiles at us. Eden, where our childhood celebrated its hour, happy stage of our tenderest feelings where, in the depths of paths and woods, to the murmur of grass, to the song of springs, first awakens in our hearts the sacred feeling of childish beliefs. Oh, I recognize you, calm and blessed abode, the humble and last refuge of domestic tranquillity which God's hand protects like a nest from the distant storms that rumble over the city.) This bucolic variation on our theme from Balze de Bury's "Chaperon-Rouge" (#15) contains a good deal of the subject matter a communicative pattern can use to explain and to openly or covertly justify the traditional validity of social norms. Even if the pattern of *la douceur du foyer* has the special, biographically occasioned advantage that it sets the norms for a subuniverse which is the world itself for children during the phase of their primary socialization, it is also true that it must be transmitted from one generation to the next, explained to descendents, and defended against the claims of other groups or disadvantaged classes and their competing subuniverses. This can be done openly, through proofs, symbols, or the invocation of agencies of legitimation. But either intentionally or unintentionally, the poetic rationale can also serve to cloak an unavowed interest. In such a case, poetic legitimation takes on an ideological function.

In the text at hand, a first legitimation derives from the invocation of an old and tested tradition: the *foyer* has the aura of venerability of a "cher cadre" (dear frame) from which the picture of the past smiles at us, of a "saint heritage" which is there and need merely be appropriated by the next generation. A second legitimation lies in the allusion to Eden as the paradise of childhood, an appropriation of the long-since "secularized" central element of the popular Christian image of history which all political doctrines lay claim to. With the sentimental turning back to the time of first youth everyone remembers, it acquires an emotionally inexhaustible potential for authentication. Thus Hugo also praises the family vacation in "O Souvenirs! printemps! aurore!" as a piece of paradise brought down to earth ("j'entrevoyais un coin des cieux," I envisioned a little spot in the skies, l. 52). A third agency of legitimation is nature itself. The clichés of *locus amoenus* in our text suggest that the blessings of nature have been vouchsafed the hearth, that nature protects it from the hostile world and turns it into the final refuge of a simple, peaceful life. But Victor Hugo also makes nature a competing agency when he shifts the *douceur du foyer* to a country seat and crowns a rustic family idyll with the words that such a life is man's creation of which he may well be proud for it rivals nature's.

> Et, dans l'hymen obscur qui sans fin se consomme,
> La nature sentait que ce qui sort de l'homme
> Est divin et charmant
>
> (#9, l. 76)

(And, in the dark marriage endlessly consummated, nature felt that what issues from man is divine and charming.) In Hugo, the beauty of nature can also serve as that forum before which man feels ashamed of his *laideur sociale* (collective ugliness). In "Intérieur" (#6), the previously mentioned negative variation on our basic pattern, Hugo went counter to the connotations of harmony and intimacy which the title of the poem causes one to expect and produced what was an uncustomary degree of unpoetic reality, considering the time of its composition (1841): a proletarian milieu, a "mauvais ouvrier" (bad worker) who comes back from the tavern drunk and calls his scolding wife a prostitute, the exchange between the two in disjointed exclamations and sentence fragments, a hungry child who cries from fear. Although meant as a denunciation of social conditions, the poem stays within the bounds that are characteristic of Hugo. The frame of the provocative scene has the effect of a counteridealization and covertly confirms the ideality of the bourgeois *foyer* which the *intérieur* of the *pauvre demeure* matches element by element, just as the "unholy trinity" of father, mother, and child is the counterimage of the "holy" one and all that is ugly here is beautiful there. The simile at the end, which defuses the social dynamite of the central scene as the Vergilian allegory of the *discordia demens* does at the beginning, is ambiguous. It seems at first as though nature were specifically called on to conceal a human turpitude from the eyes of outsiders and to create the impression that the world as a whole continues to shine in its God-created beauty:

> Et leur vitre, où pendait un vieux haillon de toile,
>
> était, grâce au soleil, une éclatante étoile
>
> Qui, dans ce même instant, vive et pure lueur,
>
> Eblouissait au loin quelque passant rêveur!

(Their window, where pieces of old canvas hung, became, thanks to the sun, a bursting star that at that very moment—a pure and living light—dazzled some passing dreamer from afar.) If understood in this way, the poem would reveal the romantic theodicy à la Chateaubriand as an illusion, and the windowpane could be judged a metaphoric concretization of ideological make-believe. But such ideology-critical intent is far from Hugo's mind. The preceding lines lend a moral and edifying meaning to the contrast between the beautiful glow of the setting sun and the ugly sight of the "couple hideux, que rend deux fois infâme la misère du coeur et la laideur de l'âme" (hideous couple whom poverty of heart and ugliness of soul make doubly loathesome, l. 19);[23] it is precisely in its beauty that nature is the measure by which man is to recognize how far he has fallen in the "poverty of his heart" and the "ugliness of his soul" from an order God intended, which manifests itself in the beauty of external nature and which should also prevail in the inner harmony of the hearth.

A fourth legitimation which has become even more of a cliché is presented in this text from the "Chaperon-Rouge" in the picture of the nest over which God holds his shielding hand. The author of the piece called "Intermède romantique" clearly took this metaphor literally. He has the hunter who appears at the end of the story

act as "justicier" of the divine protector and punish the unheard-of
outrage ("Ce que les temps avaient de respect entouré, l'aieule
centenaire au coeur évangélique et la vierge innocente, il a tout
devoré," What time had once surrounded with respect, the centenary
ancestor with the evangelical heart and the innocent virgin, now he
devoured all). Oddly enough, however, this is no longer of any use to
Red Riding Hood or her grandmother for their obligatory resurrection does not take place. Why can it no longer take place in 1857? It
is perhaps at this trivial level that in the unorthodox, definitive end
of "chaperon rouge" there is suggested something of the growing
sense of the public consciousness that as a realm and ultimate asylum
of the bourgeoisie ("de la paix domestique humble et dernier asile,"
the humble and final refuge of domestic tranquillity), the *foyer* is as
threatened by historical reality as the houses of old Paris are by
the remorseless progress of urban civilization. What may be intimated
here and possibly in the lines "des orages lointains qui grondent
sur la ville" (faraway storms scolding over the city) is perhaps openly expressed by Louis Bouilhet and made the object of a denunciation:

> Ah! pauvres maisons éventrées
> par le marteau du niveleur!
> Pauvres masures délabrées,
> Pauvres nids qu'a pris l'oiseleur!

(Ah! the poor houses gutted by the leveler's hammer, poor dilapidat-
ed huts, poor nests the fowler has taken.) The destroyed nest here
stands at the beginning of the description of the view the city offers
after batallions of Viollet-le-Duc's workers began tearing up the wide
boulevards of Napolean III's metropolis. Not only have pick and axe
cut a nexus of past and future life that has grown over the centuries
and found its embodiment in monuments. They have also laid bare
the inside of this existence, the "secrètes anatomies" (l. 11) of the
bourgeois *foyer*, and shamelessly profaned its well-guarded life, from
the "chambre aux agonies" (room of agonies) to the "alcoves de
l'amour" (alcoves of bliss), before the eyes of the multitude. The
macabre sequence of anatomical, slaughterhouse, and burial ground
images, which Bouilhet finds for the "carcasses nues" of the old
bourgeois houses along the periphery of the new boulevards, ends
elegiacally, with a gesture of helplessness:

> Pour les couvrir, montez, o lierres!
> Brisez l'asphalte des trottoires!

Jetez sur la pudeur des pierres
Le linceul de vos rameaux noirs!

(O ivy, please climb to cover them! Break the asphalt of the sidewalks! Throw over the ever-shy stones the shroud of your black branches!) Here, romantic nature is once more pathetically invoked against a superior civilization, but in the process, the subuniverse of the *douceur du foyer* is sentimentally removed to the "never more"; it takes on the beauty of ruins.

It should not come as a surprise that it is only in the last example that a contemporary reference becomes tangible. In the area of aesthetically mediated experience, interaction patterns are subject to a process of detemporalization and idealization which increases their suggestiveness and also poetically legitmates their norm-setting or norm-sustaining function. But the semblance of timeless validity also fits such communicative patterns to serve as means of ideological obfuscation. In our context, ideology means that lyric speech veils an interest of the powers that be, that communication is distorted by an asserting which simultaneously suppresses what it does not care to be known, that a group interest claims universal truth for its particular interpretation of the world. Our paradigm shows the turn from poetic legitimation to an ideological support function at more than one level.

In an ideology-critical perspective, the function of the soothing maxim "Eh! palais ou chaumine, / Qu'importe à qui se trouve bien?" (Oh! Palaces or thatched huts, for those living in them does it ever matter? #16) is most easily seen through: it is the preservation of the property-owning class. Less transparent is the sentence that Hugo puts into the mouths of the children because he wishes to praise the poet as a friend of the family who introduces them to bourgeois morality: "Il est du même avis que Monsieru le curé" (He is of the same mind as our Priest, #1). This phrase which seems so revelatory in its ideology can be prematurely set down on the wrong side of the ledger if one overlooks that in all pieces with religious themes Hugo's *Contemplations* develop a lay catechism to which an orthodox "Monsieur le curé" would hardly assent. But if ideological, this sentence does not reveal an alliance of "throne and altar" when it is seen in context, but rather a laical position. Most interesting for the ideological function of the interaction pattern *la douceur du foyer* is what it excludes, suppresses, or fails to mention, and that because it gives itself the appearance of a self-justifying ideality and the implicit dignity of the normative which it can confer on the knowledge it conveys.

Baudelaire's evening poem, which evokes the luckless existence of groups that remain excluded from the *douceur du foyer*, made conscious the insulation and perhaps even the tacit tabooing of the boundary to other subuniverses which the poetic form renders even more intense. There is also ideological insulation in Hugo's "Intérieur" where the norm of harmony of the bourgeois hearth is confirmed by its counterimage, as if it were only the *laideur de l'âme* and not conditions of social misery which deny such harmony to a worker's household. But the ideological function of poetic interaction patterns need not be confined to the exclusion, nonrecognition, or the passing over in silence of other subuniverses. It may also serve to cloak the interests of a power actually at work within the tabooed boundaries of a subuniverse. One of the results of this investigation was that the lyric production of 1857 represents the *foyer* as the realm of happiness of the bourgeois world as if it were the gentle sphere of the woman where a merely subordinate role accrues to husband and father whose mythological archtype is being called to mind in the Red Riding Hood intermezzo by a picture that hangs on the wall over grandmother's bed: "une image grossière / représentant Joseph et la Nativité" (a roughly drawn picture showing Joseph and the Nativity, #15). Does the *douceur du foyer* pattern have an ideological intent in failing to mention the authority that was the father's and the family head's in the bourgeois classes of the Second Empire? To answer this, one must look at the social history of the family and at contiguous interaction patterns and subuniverses where their synchronic distribution could already be determined in a preliminary manner during the original investigation of the entire lyric communications system.[24]

3. The social function of the lyric experience and its communications system in the life world of 1857

It is well known that in nineteenth-century France, the family as social institution was shaped by the reform decrees of the early years of the Revolution and the regulations of the *Code civil* which annulled in part the emancipatory elan. The revolutionary step that was in line with the principles of freedom and equality was the secularization of marriage; understood as a civil contract between free partners, it implied both its dissolvability (right to divorce) and equality within the family (equality of man and wife, dismantling of the primacy of paternal authority, equal rights of inheritance for the children). The *Code civil* retained secularization and dissolvability, limited the grounds for divorce, and reinstituted the principle of paternal authority to a considerable extent: "L'idée de protection est marquée par le fait que l'autorité paternelle s'exerce jusqu'a la majorité et cesse par l'émancipation et le mariage mais elle s'exerce sans limites, avec un droit de correction, survivance des lettres de cachet, et une administration des biens sans contrôle. Bref la famille apparaît tout entière dans la main du père de famille qui jouit d'une autorité quasi-romaine sur la personne de son épouse et de ses enfants ainsi que sur leurs biens." (The idea of protection is characterized by the fact that paternal authority is exercised until the children come of age and that then, and by marriage, it comes to an end. But it is exercised without limits, includes the right of punishment, the survival of *lettres de cachet*, and total freedom in the administration of property. In short, the entire family is in the hands of the family head who enjoys a quasi-Roman authority over his wife, his children, and their possessions.)[25]

This great power of the paternal authority is nowhere mentioned in the family portrait that the interaction patterns of the subuniverse *la douceur du foyer* convey. Yet this does not permit the inference that our corpus of lyric texts already reflects an advanced phase of emanicipation. In the synchrony of the lyric interaction patterns of 1857, there is no trace of the ideas of individual or social emancipation such as George Sand or the early socialists advocated. The paternal authority which the bourgeois husband and family head still enjoyed in the nineteenth century is tacitly passed over in the thematized realm of bourgeois happiness. Yet it is implicitly presupposed, as if the institution of bourgeois marriage and family had not in fact lost more and more of its normative validity during this period, a consequence of the industrial revolution and the proletarianization of the masses which also becomes apparent in the changed work- and living habits of a daily round which is no longer shared by the entire family.[26] Whereas the lyric interaction pattern creates the impression that the *foyer* is the gentle sphere of the woman, examples from another literary genre, the novel in both its peak achievements and all the way to its "trivial" levels, make clear that paternal authority still enjoyed an undisputed power more in line with the social reality of the Ancien Regime than with mid-century conditions. Whether this distribution of the functions of communicative patterns between the lyric and the novel has more than purely formal grounds cannot as yet be decided (the pater familias does not differ from any other *agent fondateur* in that the preservation of his role — and the challenge to it — clearly require stories). The richness of interaction patterns of paternal authority in the French nineteenth-century novel is most impressively shown in a documentation "Le père dans le texte" which was undertaken with ideology-critical intent by the journal *Manteia*.[27] The father-son relation occupies the foreground. The classic situation shows the son who rebels against the father, thereby provokes the exercise of paternal authority, is then "put on the right path," and becomes a father himself in the end. The modern inversion of this situation would be the suffering of the son without father, according to the psychoanalytic scheme "Que la souffrance du fils 'sans père' le libère de cette mort, la lui fait expier . . . et tres fortement l'y rattache (à ce qui en Lui ne saurait perir)" (That the suffering of the son "without a father" liberates him of this death, makes him atone for it . . . and strongly ties him to the death [to that which in Him could not perish]).[28] The analysis shows very clearly how the power and the halo of authority are enhanced in the interaction pattern by a balancing of what is said and what is left unsaid (economic interests, for example).[29] But it makes no mention of the interaction pattern of paternal love and especially Père Goriot's role as martyr (*ce Christ de la paternité*) so that that figure is suffering a second parricide here.

If the *douceur du foyer* interaction pattern is ideologically regressive when one considers that the father's role goes unmentioned, it seems on the other hand to justify the assumption of a progressive tendency in the bourgeois upper class when one looks at the role of the child. Our pattern restricts the family to the trinity of mother, father, child. Where more than one child is mentioned, the number remains quite small ("ces quatre douces têtes" #8, l. 41). This limited number of persons implies a norm which only emerged in a diachronic examination. During the nineteenth century, a change in the social structure of France took place which was no less revolutionary for the social comportment of the family than the principle of *Egalité*. I am referring to the turn from the patriarchal family with an uncontrolled number of children who were accepted as a natural event to the small bourgeois family which, toward the end of the eighteenth century, began to deliberately restrict itself to two children.[30] In the former, family life was determined by the uninterrupted biological cycle of birth and death (high infant mortality), the woman's usually lifelong role as mother, and the unequal treatment of the children (only the heir spent more time at home whereas the other children had to be provided for as expeditiously as possible, by marriage, an army career, holy orders, and so on).[31] The new idea of a household with two children which the spread of contraception made possible was tantamount to a denaturalization of the family; the familial community was no longer put up with but chosen. This also meant that it could now be dissolved again by the legal institution of divorce or supplemented by its counterpart, adoption, that it could be changed, in other words, without regard to any sacramental barriers or blood ties.[32] The sociological investigation of P. Aries has shown how this change in family structure which first developed in the bourgeois class also began to spread to the milieu of farmers and workers after about 1880, and how both wife and child attained to an unprecedented social standing. Along with this, a hitherto unknown affective potential was released. The children who had been seen sui generis since Rousseau grew up in a sphere of new intimacy and stayed at home longer. And what they were taught no longer aimed at establishing them professionally but at giving them an intellectual and moral education. The woman, freed from the slavery of continual pregnancies and encouraged by the expansion of schools, now took a more active part in education and domestic life but principally in domestic affairs whose supervision was increasingly entrusted to her. Given this social process, a social reality does in fact seem to correspond to the "gentle sphere of the woman" in the lyric pattern of the *douceur du foyer*. Yet this does not preclude the possibility that the literary idealization of this reality in turn ignores all factual and economic dependence on the authority of the father. For in the ideal image, "Le bonheur est dans l'âtre," the woman's and mother's belief in her preeminence could thus be confirmed, and the latent interest of the husband and father in this projection of harmonious happiness inside the *foyer* could be kept secret.

We cannot here go into the literary prehistory of the *douceur du foyer* motif, though it would be tempting to compare its manifestations as interaction pattern in successful bourgeois society with a literary testimonial to the rising eighteenth-century bourgeois class. One need only call to mind the striking analogies in a poem that was so thoroughly trivialized in the nineteenth century, Schiller's "Glocke." Instead, we will conclude with a view at the overarching communication system of French lyric poetry in 1857 within which our paradigm has its place. In establishing this synchronous system, the following were used: Victor Hugo's *Les Contemplations*, Baudelaire's *Fleurs du Mal*, Pierre Dupont's *Chants et chansons*, and some 200 individual lyrics, all of them taken from journals that appeared in 1857. This gives a total of approximately 700 poems. The sociological theory of A. Schütz and T. Luckmann provided the interpretive frame for the determination of the factual articulation of the putative communications system into its subsystems and "axes of relevance."

In constituting the life world in human action, there is the inital premise that its dimensions "are organized around the 'here' of my body and the 'now' of my present" and that I experience the reality of the everyday world as an intersubjective world which I share with others (*Mitwelt*).[33] The "here-there" situation organizes the life world as surrounding world, the "face-to-face" situation organizes it as a world in which I engage with others. The temporal boundary of the "now" can open either of these situations toward the dimensions of the "no longer" and the "not yet," include both the past and the future. Within these dimensions, the fundamental experiences of social praxis and the interaction patterns they present and convey can be grasped and set forth along three axes of relevance: the here-there situation grounds the relationship of self and surrounding world and is staggered, extending from the nearby to the far away, from the milieu to nature to cosmos. The face-to-face situation grounds the relationship of self and my world (*Mitwelt*). As the prototype of all social interaction, it extends from the face-to-face experience of the other through the "you" and the "we" to the collective subject of human history. Between these two axes of relevance, the biography of the individual can be understood as an integrative process which makes subjectively plausible and meaningful the whole of a given milieu and *Mitwelt*, and achieves this through the succession of institutionally set phases.[34] The three axes of relevance are overarched by a symbolic world of meaning as an objective agency of legitimation which can manifest itself in cult (religion), aesthetically (in art), and theoretically (in science). As one examines the function that a specific medium of the aesthetic experience such as the lyric may have for the communications system of a historical life world, the selection or the horizon characteristic of such a medium must be noted. In our case, the axis of relevance of the surrounding world carries a greater number of elements than that of the *Mitwelt* and the biographical relevancies show surprising gaps. The legitimating symbolic world of meaning takes on the form of a lay catechism.

In 1857, the "here-there" situation beginning with which the reality of the everyday or life world organizes itself as surrounding world still appears primarily in interaction patterns of romantic derivation. It constitutes itself from the basic relationship of "I": loneliness and "harmony with nature" (*Correspondences*) through the proximity of experienced space (*Promenade/Paysage*) and experienced time (*Les heures du jour, les saisons*) to spatial distance (Baudelaire's "Invitation au voyage"; "Any where out of the world") and the cosmological horizon (Hugo's "A la fenêtre pendant la nuit"). But nature as experienced surrounding world is now confronted by the new reality of metropolitan and industrial civilization which lyric poetry either adopts in patterns of urban poetry (Baudelaire's *Tableaux parisiens*) or deplores elegiacally as the end of "vieux Paris." The world of work as such is usually still viewed in poems that describe venerable occupational roles, although a hint of the milieu and the standardized life of factory work is given in Pierre Dupont's praise of the silk industry in Lyon ("La Soie").[35] The *douceur du foyer* subuniverse ignores, as we noted, the reality of working for a livelihood. The bourgeois "foyer" still belongs to the romantic substrate of a surrounding world that is experienced as naturally given. As the closest and most familiar "world within my reach," it fits into lyric poetry on this axis of relevance.

In the lyric production of the year 1857, the face-to-face situation beginning with which reality organizes itself as *Mitwelt* is usually confined to that "I:you" relationship which the sociology of knowledge calls "the privileged other." Our corpus extends the fundamental romantic relationship of poet and lover, *amant* and *amante* to the familial relations between father, mother, and child and allows existences that are marginal to the social hierarchy such as the beggar, the blind man, the chiffonier, or the prostitute to occasionally emerge within its circle of vision. The "I:we" relationship is present primarily in patterns of festive life (Hugo's "La fête chez Thérèse," Dupont's festivals, P. Veron's "Un mardi gras a Saint Cloud") or in politically engaged lyric poetry (Dupont's "Le chant des ouvriers"). Collective remembrance articulates itself in excerpts from history which may be standardized as major events, models (Dupont's "Le cuirassier de Waterloo"), positive or negative exemplars, or sequences of martyrs (Hugo's "Les Malheureux"). This horizon, still wholly limited to the ideal of order and the interests of the ruling bourgeois class, is transcended in at least one instance, Baudelaire's discovery of the theme of "La Foule" for lyric poetry. Or, more precisely, where, from the perspective of the flaneur ("l'homme de la foule"), he discovers and poetically justifies a new interaction pattern of modernity, the urban masses, which Hugo had still described in moralistic terms and even resisted as threatening.

If one inquires about the symbolic world of meaning which, as horizon and agency of legitimation, heightens the interaction patterns within the horizon of *Umwelt* and *Mitwelt*, one encounters a change of function of the literary medium which was already registered by contemporary criticism. What had in earlier times been one of the eminent tasks of the epic, to "parler de Dieu," it was noted, had now been assumed by the lyric.[36] And it is true that Victor Hugo's "A Villequier" is not the only poem that answers all the questions a father struck by undeserved misfortune may put to the "père auquel il faut croire" (father in whom we must believe, l. 21). There are a good many edifying poems in the *Contemplations* and pieces with an inverse tendency in the *Fleurs du Mal* which could be used to put together a kind of laical catechism that would answer practically any question that had already been settled in Christian instruction.

With the evoked subuniverse, the *douceur du foyer* interaction pattern idealizes norms and values of bourgeois life and creates from them an innerwordly conception of happiness. The institutionally determined phases and initiation thresholds of the biographical axis of relevance can be represented by the lyric interaction patterns below, which are often expressed in paired opposites (missing items in italics):

Phase	Threshold	Norm
birth		
	infant	mother love, *paternal love/authority*
childhood		
	amant, amante	couple of lovers
youth		
	wedding	
middle of life		marriage/"douceur du foyer"
old age		
death		

The various key words merely name areas of experience for which, using the procedures being tested here, explicit or implicit norms would still have to be discovered in lyric documents. Regarding the place value of our paradigm, a shift of the biographic phases that occurred in the nineteenth century must be noted. The entire span from birth to death ("C'est l'existence humaine sortant de l'enigme du berceau et aboutissant à l'enigme du cercueil," It is human existence arising from the enigma of the cradle and ending in the enigma of the shroud)[37] is not subdivided by chronological breaks but is still articulated by the symbolic contrast between "youth" and "age," though *jeunesse* is set off from *enfance*. In line with this, we have interaction patterns which standardize the two thresholds between child and youth, *fille* and *amante* on the one hand, and the "âge riant des amours" and marriage, *amante* and *mère* on the other.[38] The biographical axis of relevance thus shows not only the standardization of a world that is unique to the child, a world whose discovery for pedagogy goes back to Rousseau, for the lyric to Hugo. It also indicates that puberty which Rousseau had still brought to public consciousness as a "second birth" has in the meantime come to be seen and standardized as an extended, autonomous stage.[39] The prolongation of this adolescence lacks uniformity in the lyric patterns; it extends from the poetry of "first love" to the threshold of the wedding[40] and on to the prose of marriage. But it can also comprise the inverse register of a "vert paradis des amours enfantines" (green paradise of vernal loves) and a "jeunesse (qui) ne fut qu'un tenebreux orage" (youth which was all a tenebrous storm) and end as a thirty-year-old takes leave of "the dream of youth."[41] The last-mentioned testimonial, Henri Cantal's "Après trente ans," describes the threshold as if it were also the transition to old age. Neither here nor elsewhere is the middle of life seen as a phase of fulfillment, of the seriousness of life, of victories and defeats. Its conspicuous absence on the axis of biographical relevance is obscured by the now familiar *douceur du foyer* pattern. That the mother-child relation should be standardized on the biographical axis as "mother love" but that the conflictive one between father and son should be absent in the medium of the lyric is in keeping with this.[42] Such omissions confirm the same poetic function as the failure to mention paternal authority did before: poetically mediated as the subuniverse of the *douceur du foyer*, this interaction pattern of bourgeois society in the Second Empire can make up for such gaps because the concept *foyer* and its connotations of warmth and security, satisfied needs (including economic ones), and self-sufficient community, of a ritual evoked by the fire on the hearth, is characterized by an ideality which can be more obscurely potent than a mere fiction or utopia of a harmonious life together. For in the present, it seems to fulfill older desires which are legitimated by an immemorial, sacral origin.[43]

Appendix

Le Grillon

[From "Fables et Contes par M. Louis Damey" in the *Revue contemporaine*, 1857, pp. 578 ff.]

C'était un grillon familier
Eclos aux rayons du foyer;
Pour monde il avait la cuisine,
Pour gîte un terrier spacieux,
Héritage des bons aïeux.
Quel palais! direz vous. Eh! palais ou chaumine,
Qu'importe à qui se trouve bien?
De la gaieté toujours, pas la moindre castille,

Chants du soir, souper de famille
Où chacun babille
A propos de rien,
Douce rêverie,
Plaisirs sans regrets
Et sans indiscrets;
Où mieux, je vous prie,
Dans l'incognito
Passer la journée
Que sous le manteau
De la cheminée?
Mère grillon disait, redisait chaque jour:
"Enfants, sachez-le bien, le bonheur est dans l'âtre".
Mais le plus jeune, hélas! capricieux, folâtre,
Leur faussa compagnie; il voulait fair un tour,
    Un petit tour à la fenêtre,
Rien qu'un tour. Le destin voulut qu'en ce moment
Elle fût grande ouverte. Or quand il vit paraître
Aux splendeurs du soleil tout un monde charmant,
Fleurs, herbes, fruits enfin un pays de cocagne,
La tête lui tourna, si bien qu'en clin d'oeil
    Il sautillait dans la campagne.
Là les grillons forains lui firent bon accueil
    Tout en se gaussant de sa mine
    Et de ses parfums de cuisine;
On alla grillonant et par monts et par vaux;
Le fuyard admira ces spectacles nouveaux,
    Rit beaucoup, jasa davantage
    Quand il eut bien ri, bien jasé,
    Il se prit à penser; le sage,
    A ce qu'on dit, fait l'opposé.
    Ce regard jeté sur lui-meme,
    Hélas! dans une angoisse extrême
    Plongea le grillon familier.
Plus de chants, plus de ris, plus de jeux dans la plaine;
Sous les feux du soleil il se trainait à peine.
Ses joyeux compagnons regagnant leur terrier
Lui dirent: qu'as tu donc? — J'ai le mal du foyer.
Au foyer paternel, abri de la sagesse
D'où le vent du caprice exila ma jeunesse,
Ainsi le souvenir me ramène, mes soeurs.
Oh! qui me donnera d'en retrouver la route!

Douceurs de la famille, eneffables douceurs,
Heureux qui les comprend, plus heureux qui les goûte!

The Cricket

He was a household cricket, born among the shelves of the fireplace. For a world he had a kitchen, for a bed he had a spacious hole inherited from good ancestors. "Some palace!" you say. Well, palace or shack, what does it matter to one who finds it good? Good cheer always, not the least little quarrel.

Singing after supper, the family meals where everyone chatters about nothing in particular, sweet reveries, pleasures without regrets—and without the presence of the indiscreet. Where better, I ask of you, to spend the day incognito than under the mantle of the chimney?

Mama cricket said and said again each day: "Children remember this, happiness is within the hearth. But the youngest—Alas! capricious and playful—sneaked away. He wanted to take a walk, a little walk to the window, just a little walk. Destiny had it that at this moment it was wide open. And when he saw appear in the splendors of the sun an altogether charming world—flowers, herbs, fruits,—a fabulous world. He fell in love in the blink of an eye, and jumped into the countryside.

There the outdoor crickets gave him a good reception, at the same time teasing him about his appearance and his kitchen odor. They all went cricketing over hills and valleys. The runaway admired these new sights, laughed a lot, and chirped even more. After he had laughed a lot and chirped a lot, he began to think. The wise, it is said, do the opposite. He took a good look inside himself; and this look, alas, threw the cricket into extreme anguish.

No more singing, no more laughing, no more games in the field; under the hot sun, he could scarcely drag himself along. His cheerful playmates went back to their lairs and said to him, "What's bothering you?" "I am homesick. My memories carry me back to the paternal hearth, the home of wisdom, whence I've been banished by the capricious whims of youth, my sisters. Oh! Who will show me the way! The pleasure of the family home, its indescribable delights—happy are those who understand them, happier still those who enjoy them."

Notes

Notes

Introduction

1. Jauss, *Literaturgeschichte als Provokation* (Frankfurt: Suhrkamp Verlag, 1970), English translation by Timothy Bahti: *Towards an Aesthetics of Reception*, Introduction by Paul de Man (Minneapolis: University of Minnesota Press, 1982); p. 7.

2. Under the title "What Is Meant by Literary History and to What End Is It Studied?" it was delivered on April 13, 1967. This is obviously an ironic allusion to Schiller's "Was heisst und zu welchem Ende studiert man Universalgeschichte." Feeling perhaps that too few in his audience had noticed the nature of the provocation intended, Jauss altered the title by labeling his project a provocation. The inaugural lecture was therefore published under "Literaturgeschichte als Provocation der Literaturwissenschaft" (1967) and was eventually foreshortened to *Literaturgeschichte als Provokation*.

3. Harald Weinrich, "Thirty years after Ernst Robert Curtius' Book *Europäische Literatur und lateinisches Mittelalter* (1948)," *Romanic Review* 69, 4 (1978), p. 262.

4. Ibid.

5. Jauss, *Zeit und Erinnerung in Marcel Proust's 'A la Recherche du Temps Perdu'* (Heidelberg, 1955).

6. Jurii Tynjanov/Roman Jakobson, "Problemi izučenija literaturi i jazika," in *Texte der Russischen Formalisten*, ed. Wolf-Dieter Stempel, vol. II (Munich: Fink Verlag, 1972).

7. Gadamer, *Wahrheit und Methode* (Munich, 1960), English translation as *Truth and Method* (New York: Seabury Press, 1974).

8. Adorno's seminar had been disrupted throughout the academic year 1968–69 with the distribution of leaflets, name calling ("Teddy," to remind him of his American sojourn), and so on. Students finally occupied Jürgen Habermas's office. Adorno opposed their forceful removal. Yet when it took place on January 31, 1969, at the instigation of the rector of the university, Adorno was photographed shaking hands with the police officer leading the raiding party. The gesture of courteous leave-taking was represented as evidence of Adorno's "treachery."

9. Theodor W. Adorno, *Kierkegaard: Konstruktion des Ästhetischen*, G. S. vol. 2 (Frankfurt: Suhrkamp, 1979), pp. 60-69.

10. Geoffrey Hartman, *Criticism in the Wilderness* (New Haven and London: Yale University Press, 1980).

11. F. R. Leavis, *The Living Principle. 'English' as a Discipline of Thought* (New York: Oxford University Press, 1974).

12. Collected in *Beyond Culture*, Uniform Edition (New York: Harcourt Brace Jovanovich, 1965), pp. 50-76.

Preface

1. Jauss, *Negativität und Identifikation — Versuch zur Theorie der ästhetischen Erfahrung* (1972), published in 1975.

2. On this matter, I refer to: *Gebremste Reform — ein Kapitel deutscher Hochschulgeschichte. Universität Konstanz 1966 to 1976*, ed. H. R. Jauss and H. Nesselhauf (Constance, 1977).

3. "Zur Frage der 'Struktureinheit' älterer und moderner Lyrik" (already published in 1960) supplements chap. A6 (Aesthesis), "Interaktionsmuster der Identifikation mit dem Helden" (1975) and "Über den Grund des Vergnügens am komischen Helden" (1976) chap. A7 (Catharsis), "La douceur du foyer" (1975) chap. A8 (Aesthetic experience among the problems of everyday life: problems of delimitation).

4. On this, see M. Fuhrmann, *Alte Sprachen in der Krise?* (Stuttgart, 1976), who here and elsewhere advances reasons for the revision of the classical canon and has worked out proposals for transforming or reshaping reception theory into new paradigms of literary education from the perspective of the Latin scholar.

5. On this, see Striedter (1976) and the anthologies of texts (and their introductions) in *Texte der russischen Formalisten*, vol. I: *Texte zur allgemeinen Literaturtheorie und zur Theorie der Prosa*, ed. J. Striedter (1969), vol. II: *Texte zur Theorie des Verses und der poetischen Sprache*, ed. W.-D. Stempel (1972); see also F. Vodička, *Die Struktur der literarischen Entwicklung*, ed. J. Striedter (1976) and M. Cervenka, *Der Bedeutungsaufbau des literarischen Werkes*, ed. W.-D. Stempel (Munich, 1977).

6. By K. Mandelkow (1974), P. U. Hohendahl (1974), G. Labroisse (1974), M. Naumann (1973), and R. Warning (1975).

7. See Schlaffer (1974), with the representative title *Erweiterung der materialistischen Literaturtheorie durch Bestimmung ihrer Grenzen*, and the two "Repliken" by W. Iser and H. R. Jauss in Warning (1975) which address themselves to Naumann (1973).

8. This is Naumann's position (1973), pp. 18ff. Recently, M. Naumann also made the sphere of distribution part of the dialectic of production and reception ("Das Dilemma der 'Rezeptionsästhetik,'" in *Poetica* 8 [1976], pp. 451ff.) But he reduces it to the element of circulation and limits it historically to the socialization process of bourgeois literature, which means that the revalidation of interaction ("exchange" as communicative action) for a new Marxist literary theory remains to be accomplished.

9. "In production, the person objectifies itself, in consumption the thing subjectivies itself, in distribution, society takes over the mediation between production and consumption in the form of general, prevailing conditions. In exchange, they are mediated by the accidental determinacy of the individual" (*MEW*, vol. 13, p. 621).

10. "Arbeit und Interaktion," in Habermas (1968), p. 45. These approaches have been taken up again and developed further in *Zur Rekonstruktion des historischen Materialismus* (Frankfurt, 1976), esp. pp. 160ff.

11. Borinski (1914) still has the richest sources although they are wholly oriented to the continuing influence of classical antiquity and must therefore be constantly reinterpreted.

12. In a public discussion with J.-P. Faye, J. Ricardou, and others, on December 9, 1964, which was published as "Que peut la litterérature?" in the collection *L'inédit* (Paris, 1965), pp. 107-27. In chap. 3, I will return to Roland Barthes who, in his *Pleasure of the Text* (1975), rediscovers the reader in his solitary, philological pleasure.

13. In *Les voix du silence* (Paris, 1951) there is no acknowledgment whatever of the debt to Benjamin.

14. In *Counterrevolution and Revolt* (Boston: Beacon Press, 1972).

15. "Nachwort," in *Wahrheit und Methode*, 3rd ed. (Tübingen, 1973), pp. 539-540.

16. Ibid.

17. Gadamer (1960), p. 84; in English translation (New York: Seabury Press, 1975), pp. 73ff.

18. Ibid., pp. 81ff. and 76ff. respectively.

19. I refer the reader to the detailed analyses by Hannelore Schlaffer in her "Kritik eines Klischées: 'Das Kunstwerk als Ware," in Schlaffer (1974), pp. 265-87.

20. On the ambiguity of the concept "manipulation" and the justification of rhetoric against the suspicion of an unavoidably compulsory creation of opinion, see H.-G. Gadamer in Apel (1971), pp. 304ff.

21. In Schlaffer (1974), pp. 282ff., with reference to H. H. Holz, *Vom Kunstwerk zur Ware*, 2nd ed. (Neuwied, 1972).

22. "Resüme über Kulturindustrie," in Adorno (1967), pp. 60-70.

23. *Gesammelte Werke*, vol. 18 (Frankfurt, 1967), p. 167.

24. Adorno (1970), p. 339.

25. In France, Louis Althusser's panideological theory had a paradigmatic effect. According to it, all social activity unavoidably comes under the sway of the ideological apparatus of the state and the imaginary functions as ideology's principal instrument for turning concrete individuals into dependent subjects (play on the two meanings of *sujet*) without their being aware of it. Since the "production of aesthetic interest" can then only serve the reproduction of the ideological code, the best advice would be to suspend aesthetic experience until the conditions for free art have been reestablished by the class struggle. This is Charles Grivel's conclusion in a monumental cross-sectional analysis of novels written during the 1870-80 decade. It is based on Althusser's "Idéologie et appareils idéologique d'état," (in *La Pensée* [June 1970], pp. 1-36). See *Production de l'intérêt romanesque. Un état du texte* (The Hauge/Paris, 1973).

26. Against Adorno who, in his "Resüme über Kulturindustrie" seems to have overlooked the fact that the spheres of high and low art were emphatically not distinct for thousands of years but were one in their practical function until the time of the emancipation of the fine arts.

27. See my article in *Poetik und Hermeneutik VIII*, to be published in vol. II of the German edition of *Ästhetische Erfahrung und literarische Hermeneutik*.

28. *Critique of Judgment*, trans. James Creed Meredith (Oxford: Clarendon Press, 1952), § 8.

29. Ibid., § 32; here, I follow the interpretation of Günter Buck (1967), p. 181.

A. Sketch of a theory and history of aesthetic experience

1) What does aesthetic experience mean?

1. Tam multa, tamque mira diversarum formarum uibque varietas apparet, ut magis legere libeat in marmoribus, quam in codicis, totumque occupare singular ista mirando, quam in lege Dei meditando (Epist. ad Guillelm. Abbat., cap. xii). (So numerous and so wondrous appears the variety of diverse figures that one is disposed to read marble rather than books, and to take possession of the whole by staring at these single things rather than by meditating on the law of God).

2. M. D. Chenu, *La théologie au 12e siècle* (Paris, 1957); and Hans Robert Jauss, *Alterität und Modernität der mittelalterlichen Literatur—Gesammelte Aufsätze 1956-1976* (Munich, 1977), pp. 170ff.

3. Cantus autem iste debet antiquis et civibus laborantibus et mediocribus ministrari, donec requiescunt ab opere consulto, ut auditis miseriis et calamitatibus aliorum suas facilius sustineant et quilibet opus suum alacribus aggrediatur." Quoted from J. Wolf, "Die Musiklehre des Johannes de Grocheo," in *Sammelbände der internationalen Musikgesellschaft*, I, p. 90. (This music, moreover, should be dispensed to the old, the workers, and the feeble, while they rest from their allotted tasks, so that they may more easily sustain themselves having heard of the misery and misfortunes of others, and apply themselves to whatever their task is with alacrity.)

4. Daniel Poirion, "Chanson de geste ou épopée?" in *Travaux de linguistique et de littérature* X, no. 2 (Strassbourg, 1972), pp. 7-20.

5. Quoted from Nisin (1959), p. 19.

6. A. Adler (1975) uses this formulation as the rationale for his new approach which no longer interprets the old French epic as historical mimesis. Instead, he adopts the view that the epic can intensify a situation to an extreme degree and thus make recognizable a problem and its possible solutions. The original of Busch's line is: "Was im Leben uns verdriesst, man im Bilde gern geniesst."

7. According to T. Luckmann, "Persönliche Identität, soziale Rolle und Rollendistanz," in *Poetik und Hermeneutik VIII*.

8. "So dass wir eine Weile hingerissen / das Leben spielen, nicht an Beifall denkend," from "Todeserfahrung," in *New Poems*. Translation in text is J. B. Leishman's.

9. According to W. Preisendanz, *Poetik und Hermeneutik III*, p. 604.

10. "Les tambours battaient la charge. Des cris aigus, des hourras de triomphe s'élevaient Frédéric, pris entre deux masses profondes, ne bougeait pas, fasciné d'ailleurs et s'amusant extrêmement. Les blessés qui tombaient, les morts étendus n'avaient pas l'air de vrais blessés, de vrais morts. Il lui semblait assister à un spectacle." English version in text is from Gustave Flaubert, *Sentimental Education*, trans. Anthony Goldsmith (New York: Dutton, Everyman's Series), p. 268.

11. "Ces passion que j'aurais voulu avoir, je les étudiai dans les livres." Gustave Flaubert, *Novembre*, ed. R. Dumesnil (Monaco, 1946), pp. 70-71.

12. "Je n'avais aucune idée des choses, que tous les sentiments m'étaient déjà connus." English version in text is from Jean Jacques Rousseau, *The Confessions* (London: Dent, 1960). This translation is used throughout.

13. According to D. Harth (1970), pp. 85-93.

14.   Cil livres les fist moult haster;

    Dona lor sens d'aus entramer.

    Ensamble lisent et aprendent;

    A la joie d'amor entendent;

    Quant il repairent de l'escole,

    Li uns baise l'autre et acole

              (ll. 229-34)

(This book hurries them on; I gave them the idea of loving each other. Together they read and learn, and begin to understand the joy of love. When they get back from school, one kisses the other and falls into embraces.)

15. End of the preface. The Klopstock passage is in the letter of June 16: "sie sah gen Himmel und auf mich, ich sah ihr Auge tränenvoll, sie legte ihre Hand auf die meinige und sagte-Klopstock!" "Und du, gute Seele, die du eben den Drang fühlst wie er, schöpfe Trost aus seinem Leiden, und lass das Büchlein deinen Freund sein, wenn du aus Geschick oder eigener Schuld keinen näheren finden kannst."

16. "Trieb und Leidenschaft," in *Merkur* 25 (1971), pp. 307-15.

17. Jolles (1923/33), p. 293.

18. Ibid. p. 287.

19. "Jolles illustrates this by persons who dress up as Edam cheese or the ten of hearts. These are roles which could not be enacted throughout the night of the masked ball and are absurd because they refer to no desirable world."

20. "Ernst eines Vor-Scheins von möglich Wirklichem" Bloch (1959), vol. 1, pp. 108-9, and chap. 21: "Tagtraum in entzückender Gestalt: Pamina oder das Bild als erotisches Versprechen" (daydream in charming shape: Pamina or the picture as erotic promise).

21. See L. Spitzer (1959), who showed that the meaning of Troubadour poetry was the poetic inversion of the Augustinian "noli foras ire: in interiore animae habitat veritas" (do not leave home, truth dwells within your soul, ibid., pp. 363-417).

22. Kant, *Critique of Judgment*, trans. James Creed Meredith (Oxford: Clarendon Press, 1952), §43.

23. As did Jacob Burckhardt: "To give tangible form to that which is inward, to represent it in such a way that we see it as the outward image of inward things, as a revelation—that is a most rare power. To re-create the external in external form—that is within the power of many. But the other awakens in the beholder or listener the conviction that only the creator of this work could do this, and so is indispensable." Jacob Burckhardt, *Force and Freedom. Reflections on History* (New York: Pantheon, 1943), p. 313.

24. *Dialogo sopra i due massimi sistemi del mondo* (1632), quoted by Löwith (1971), p. 252, note 8.

25. See Löwith, ibid., pp. 69ff; and Blumenberg (1964).

26. "le genie n'est que l'enfance retrouvée à volonte, l'enfance douée maintenant, pour s'exprimer, d'organes virils et de l'esprit analytique qui lui permet d'ordonner la somme de matériaux involontairement amassée." English version in text is from *Baudelaire as a Literary Critic*. Selected essays introduced and translated by L. B. Hyslop and F. E. Hyslop (University Park, Pa.: Pennsylvania State University Press, 1964), p. 295.

27. The by no means adventitious similarity between Marx's famous statement about the "eternal charm" Greek art exerts on us "as the never returning stage . . . of man's historic childhood where it unfolded most beautifully" and Schiller's theory of the naive has most recently been called attention to by G. Ter-Nedden when he wished to defend the realm of aesthetic creation against the reductionism of materialist ideology critique. See "Gibt es eine Ideologiekritik ästhetischer Sinngebilde?" in Schlaffer (1974), pp. 251-64.

28. "L'enfant voit tout en nouveauté, il est toujours ivre." English version in text is from Hyslop and Hyslop, *Baudelaire*, p. 294.

29. In Freud, however, the return of the repressed in aesthetic experience also includes the temporary admission of what is forbidden (during festive occasions, for example).

30. "Je n'ay pas plus faict mon livre que mon livre m'a faict, livre consubstantiel à son autheur, d'une occupation propre, membre de ma vie." (*Essais*, II, 18). (All Montaigne translations in this book are taken from the Donald M. Frame translation.)

31. See Ter-Nedden, "Gibt es eine Ideologiekritik ästhetischer Sinngebilde?" p. 257, and also Jacob Burckhardt in his theory of the three powers state, religion, culture in WW VII, 20.

32. Lotman (1977), p. 1.

2. Critique of Adorno's aesthetics of negativity

1. Sartre (1940), p. 234.

2. See Jauss (1970), pp. 177ff.

3. Giesz (1971), p. 30.

4. Adorno (1970), p. 15. In all further quotations, page number is given in the text.

5. P. Bourdieu, *Zur Soziologie der symbolischen Formen* (Frankfurt, 1970), pp. 103ff.

6. Starobinski (1970), pp. 9-33.

7. Since Adorno does not distinguish sharply enough between original classicism and a classic exemplariness that is the result of historical development (in my terminology, between the first and second change of horizon during the process of reception), his polemics against what is exemplary in classical Greek art are as unjust as his critique of classicism is contradictory (see pp. 240-44 as against p. 339): the "neutralization" noted there already occurs along the "path of the classical," before it becomes "the social price of aesthetic autonomy."

8. See Adorno (1970), pp. 12, 347, 358, 386. The exaggerated polemics against directly social functions of preautonomous art such as entertainment ("as testimony to the failure of culture, it always juts into it," p. 32), consolation, or encouragement (pp. 56, 66) — indeed, amusing art altogether — is to be seen in this context: "The wrong which amusing art and certainly all art that entertains commits is one against the dead, against accumulated and speechless grief" (p. 67).

9. Diderot, *Entretien sur le Fils Naturel*, ed. Vernier, *Oeuvres esthetiques* (Paris, 1959), p. 153; Lessing, *Hamburgische Dramaturgie*, 75. Stück, and elsewhere.

3. Aesthetic pleasure and the fundamental experiences of poiesis, aesthesis, and catharsis

1. "und was der ganzen Menschheit zugeteilt / will ich in meinem innern Selbst geniessen." English version from *Faust*, trans. Walter Arndt (New York: Norton, 1976). Note that *savor = geniessen!*

2. See H. Paul, *Deutsches Wörterbuch*, 5th ed., ed. W. Betz.

3. The article "Genuss" in J. Ritter's *Historisches Wörterbuch der Philosophie* (Basel/Stuttgart, 1974) discusses only the development since the seventeenth century and announces an article with updated information on the use of *uti* and *frui* in the tradition.

4. See Fuhrmann (1973), pp. 10-11; and Kommerell (1957), p. 256.

5. Fuhrmann (1973), p. 85: "But Aristotle saw that there were states of excitement that have a place in man's psychic economy and which therefore must not be repressed but released in the proper way. And according to him, poetry did not have direct but inverse effects, as it were: poetry, his doctrine states, is not contagious, it inoculates."

6. Kommerell (1957), p. 103.

7. Blumenberg (1973), p. 107.

8. All quotations from Augustine's writings in the text of this book are from *Great Books of the Western World* (Chicago: Encyclopedia Britannica, 1952), vol. 18.

9. Blumenberg (1973), p. 106.

10. According to Blumenberg (1973), p. 108.

11. On this, see H. Friedrich, "Uber den Briefwechsel Abelard-Heloise," in *Romanische Literaturen* (Frankfurt, 1972), p. 67; and Helga Meyer, "Das französische Drama des 20. Jahrhunderts als Drama der Wiederholung," unpublished dissertation (Heidelberg, 1952), chap. IIb.

12. According to Blumenberg (1973), pp. 108-9.

13. Fuhrmann (1973), pp. 92-94.

14. According to K. Dockhorn (1966), p. 181.

15. Dockhorn (1966), pp. 184-205.

16. Ibid., p. 178.

17. Ibid., p. 173, and already in Dockhorn, *Die Rhetorik als Quelle des vorromantischen Idealismus* (1954).

18. Dockhorn (1966), p. 176.

19. Ibid., p. 186.

20. The parallel key passage: "because with the division of labor there arises the possibility, indeed the reality, that mental and material activity – that enjoyment and labor, production and consumption, will fall to different individuals" (etc.) in *MEW*, vol. 3, p. 32.

21. See Conze (1972), p. 202.

22. Brecht, *Gesammelte Werke* (Frankfurt, 1967), vol. 12, p. 406.

23. "Writers and day-dreaming," in *The Standard Edition of the Complete Psychological Works*, general editor James Strachey (London: Hogarth Press, 1962), vol. IX, p. 151. All further quotations from Freud are from this edition and are referred to as *Works*.

24. See Imdahl, *Who's Afraid of Red, Yellow and Blue III* (Stuttgart, 1971), #147 in *Werkmonographien zur bildenden Kunst*.

25. To name just two antipodes. See Badt (1968), p. 103 and Werckmeister (1971), p. 83.

26. Geiger (1913).

27. Gadamer (1960), p. XV; p. XIII in the English translation.

28. Roland Barthes, *The Pleasure of the Text*, trans. Richard Miller (New York: Hill and Wang, 1975), p. 23.

29. Giesz (1971), p. 30.

30. Sartre (1940), pp. 239ff.

31. Ibid., p. 245.

32. Giesz (1971), p. 33.

33. Ibid., p. 32. Geiger (1913) also had already reached the point where he improved Kant's formulation of "disinterested pleasure" to "uninterested interest" (p. 660). But even here, he still disputed that the self was in any way involved in the constitution of the aesthetic object; this was in line with his adherence to the classicist ideal of pure contemplation which also made him bracket all cathartic pleasure as mere "effect" of the aesthetic experience from the latter's phenomenological description (p. 593).

34. Iser (1976) writes: "to be in the presence of a mental representation or image therefore always means experiencing a certain irrealization. For such a representation means a positing of something irreal in the sense that through it I am engaged with something which lifts me out of the reality in which I find myself." pp. 226–27.

35. What is, according to Geiger (1913), the "absorption of the observing self in the enjoying one, the 'self-forgetfulness' of esthetic enjoyment" also comes under this heading.

36. Giesz (1971), p. 33; actually, my interpretation of the 'state of suspension' as the enjoyment of self in the enjoyment of what is other merely develops an implication Giesz had left unexplored when he equated self-enjoyment and "sensuousness."

37. *Poetik and Hermeneutik III*, pp. 646–47.

38. *Psychopathic Characters on the Stage*, in *Works*, vol. VII, pp. 306ff; *Writers and Day-dreaming*, vol. IX, pp. 145ff.; in the section on "phantasy" in the twenty-third of the *Introductory Lectures*, vol. XVI, pp. 371ff.

39. Freud, *Works*, vol. VII, p. 306.

40. Freud, *Writers and Day-dreaming*, vol. IX, p. 153.

41. On Proust's conception of the *poésie de la mémoire* and its inversion of Platonic anamnesis, see Jauss (1955a), especially p. 272ff.

42. "Man does this in order, as a free subject, to strip the external world of its inflexible foreignness and to enjoy in the shape of things only an external realization of himself." Hegel's *Aesthetics*, trans. T. M. Knox (Oxford: Clarendon Press, 1975), p. 31. (All further Hegel quotations are from this translation.)

43. Petrarch, *Canzoniere*, #23, l. 4.

44. Zimmermann (1977), p. 172.

45. Letter to J. F. Rochlitz, dated June 13, 1819, in *WA* IV, vol. 31, p. 178.

4. The ambiguity and refractoriness of the beautiful

1. H. Blumenberg, *Poetik und Hermeneutik I*, p. 20.

2. On the ontological presuppositions of the ambivalence of Platonism in the history of the theory of art ("It was always both justification and debasement of artistic activity"), see H. Blumenberg, *Poetik und Hermeneutik I*, p. 15.

3. Plato, *Phaedrus*, 265b.

4. Fuhrmann (1973), pp. 80ff.

5. Borinski (1914), vol. I, pp. 2ff. In what follows, I was unable to make use of M. Warnke, *Bildersturm — Die Zerstörung des Kunstwerks* (Munich, 1973) which reached me only after this book had gone to press.

6. According to Borinski (1914), vol. I, pp. 70ff.

7. Panofsky (1960), p. 6.

8. According to Blumenberg (1957), p. 281.

9. See Borinski (1914), vol. I, p. 4.

10. Bossuet, *Maximes et réflexions sur la comedie* (1694): "Le premier principe sur lequel agissent les poètes tragiques et comiques, c'est qu'il faut intéresser le spectateur; et si l'auteur d'une tragédie ne sait pas émouvoir, et le transporter de la passion qu'il veut exprimer, ou tombe-t-il, si ce n'est dans le froid, dans l'ennuyeux, dans le ridicule, selon les règles des maîtres de l'art? . . . Ansi tout le dessein d'un poète, toute la fin de son travail, c'est qu'on soit comme son héros, épris de belles personnes, qu'on les serve comme des divinités, en un mot, qu'on leur sacrifie tout, si ce n'est peut-être la gloire, dont l'amour est plus dangereux que celui de la beauté même" (The first principle of tragic and comic poets is that it is essential to interest the spectator. The masters of the art already formulated the rule that if the author of a tragedy cannot move the audience and transport it by the passion he wishes to express, he becomes cold, boring, and ridiculous. . . . It is thus the aim of the poet and the object of his work that one be like his hero, in love with beautiful women on whom one attends as though they were goddesses, in short, that one sacrifice everything to them except perhaps glory, the love of which is more dangerous even than the love of beauty; p. 282).

11. Bourdalou, *Sermon sur l'hypocrisie*, see below.

12. Bessuet, *Maximes sur la comédie,* quoted in Hervieux (1911), p. 334.

13. "It follows from these first observations that the general effect of the theatre is to strengthen the national character, to augment the natural inclinations, and to give a new energy to all the passions. In this sense it would seem that, its effect being limited to intensifying and not changing the established morals (manners), the drama would be good for the good and bad for the vicious" (p. 20). Translation from *Politics and the Arts: The Letter to M. D'Alembert on the Theatre*, ed. and trans. Allan Bloom (New York: Free Press, 1960). The translations in notes 14–17 are also from this edition.

14. " . . . every useless amusement is an evil for a being whose life is so short and whose times is so precious. The state of man has its pleasures which are derived from his nature and are born of his labors, his relations, and his needs. And these pleasures, sweeter to the one who tastes them in the measure that his soul is healthier, make whoever is capable of participating in them indifferent to all others" (p. 16).

15. "People think they come together in the theatre, and it is there that they are isolated. It is there that they go to forget their friends, neighbors, and relations in order to concern themselves with fables, in order to cry for the misfortunes of the dead, or to laugh at the expense of the living" (pp. 16–17).

16. "I suspect that any man, to whom the crimes of Phaedra or Medea were told beforehand, would hate them more at the beginning of the play than at the end. And if this suspicion is well founded, then what are we to think of this much-vaunted effect of the theatre?" (p. 23).

17. "And since the very pleasure of the comic is founded on a vice of the human heart, it is a consequence of this principle that the more the comedy is amusing and perfect, the more its effect is disastrous for morals (manners)" (p. 34). On the critique of the *Misanthrope* which has become famous, see p. 36 of this work.

18. On this, see Ritter (1971), especially p. 558.

19. H.-J. Neuschäfer's argument "Für eine Geschichte der nichtkanonisierten Literatur" (reference here is to the middle level of nineteenth-century popular novels) in Neuschäfer (1976), pp. 7–31 criticizes this position.

20. Otto K. Werckmeister's *Ende der Ästhetik* (1971) with its demand that all aesthetics be turned over to the guillotine of ideology critique to free the memory of the dead of the transfiguring deception of art (p. 79) is symptomatic.

21. According to K. Schefold, *Griechische Kunst als religiöses Phänomen* (Hamburg, 1959), p. 114, with the significant qualification: "one is surely justified in saying that Leochares, Praxiteles and Skorpas were more in line with Plato's demands on art than hieratic art such as the Egyptian which was ultimately the only one he allowed" (p. 115). According to T. Hölscher (*Jb. d. dt. Archäolog. Instituts* 89 [1974], p. 107), a number of fifth-century artists viewed "the new, the 'modern' as decisive progress, an optimism that prevailed in widely differing spheres of life at the time and which was based on pride in human 'techne,' the capacity to make things through one's own resources."

22. Jauss (1977), especially the introductory essay, "Alterität und Modernität der mittelalterlichen Literatur."

23. Borinski (1914), vol. I, p. 3.

24. Borinski (1914), vol. I, pp. 84–85.

25. Borinski (1914), vol. II, pp. 5ff, 13ff.

26. Baudelaire (1951), p. 1021.

27. Diderot, *Oeuvres esthétique*, ed. P. Vernière (Paris, 1959), p. 402.

28. Ritter (1971), p. 559, with reference to Alexander Gottlieb Baumgarten, *Metaphysica* (Halle, 1739), § 521: "Perfectio phaenomenon s. gustui latius dicto observabilis est pulcritudo."

29. *Critique of Judgment*, § 17.

30. "The affirmative character of culture," in Herbert Marcuse, *Negations, Essays in critical theory*, trans. Jeremy J. Shapiro (Boston: Beacon Press, 1968).

31. Ibid., p. 131.

5. *Poiesis: the productive side of aesthetic experience*

1. On this, Blumenberg (1957) is still unexcelled. I also base my discussion on Mittelstrass (1970) and on the results of two seminars at Constance which we held jointly, and to which I owe essential insights.

2. On this, see Conze (1972) and W. Bienert, *Die Arbeit nach der Lehre der Bibel* (Stuttgart, 1954); an abbreviated version of the latter is in Bienert's article "Arbeit," in *Die Religion in Geschichte und Gegenwart* (Tübingen, 1957).

3. Gadamer (1960), pp. 286–87.

4. Blumenberg (1957), pp. 273ff.

5. "Man is 'homo sapien' but collectively at least, he is that perhaps only through the accomplishment of 'homo artifex' which is his first definition." It is on this interpretation of Gen. 1, 26 that M. D. Chenu has based his *Theologie du travail* (Paris, 1955). The renewed biblical mandate to transform nature into a human world through work is intended to annul the classical (and cartesian) opposition of theory and practice and the Lutheran separation of nature and grace, to lessen the theological misunderstanding of the industrial world, and to again reconcile technique and nature.

6. According to A. Borst, *Lebensformen im Mittelalter* (1973), pp. 203–14, especially p. 213: "medieval forms of life had to make much greater allowance for the natural milieu than do modern ones because control over nature had not yet been perfected. All the more unanimous was the belief that human historicity and sociability had to realize themselves in the struggle against, and the victory over, nature. Which means that the difference between the ascetic who rises above natural conditions, and the technician who changes them, is not so very great."

7. Guillaume de Conches, *Glossen zum Timaeus*, quoted by Rüfner (1955), p. 261.

8. Meyer Schapiro (1948).

9. Ibid., p. 148.

10. Guiette (1972), pp. 50–51.

11. On this, see the commentary of N. Pasero who correctly emphasizes the deliberate paradox of high rank and technical know-how and the counterfactual sequences of "conosc" and "non sai" in poems IV and VI (*Guglielmo IX d'Aquitania: Poesie*, ed. N. Pasero [Modena, 1973], pp. 159ff).

12.   Farai un vers de dreit nien:
            non er de mi no d'autra gen,
            non er d'amor ni de joven,
            ni di ren au,
            qu'enans fo trobatz en durmen
            sus un chivau

                                    (IV, ll. 1–6)

13. Lewis (1964), p. 85.

14. Documentation in Jauss (1964), esp. pp. 9, 25ff., 47ff., 64.

15. As a result of philosophical-historical and conceptual-historical works by Blumenberg (1957) and (1973), Mittelstrass (1970) or Conze (1972), A. Tilgher's older book, *Homo Faber* (Rome, 1920), is now outdated.

16. Mittelstrass (1970), p. 349.

17. Blumenberg (1957), p. 268.

18. According to R. Warning, article "Genie" in *Historisches Wörterbuch der Philosophie* ed. J. Ritter, vol. 3, p. 297. Literary theoreticians of the eighteenth century, such as Alexander Gerard, Edward Young, and William Duff, frequently chose seventeenth-century natural scientists to exemplify the concept of natural genius, as was shown by F. Fabian (in *Europäische Aufklärung, Herbert Dieckmann zum 60. Geburtstag*, ed. H. Friedrich and F. Schalk [Munich, 1967], pp. 47–68).

19. Mittelstrass (1970), pp. 175, 178.

20. Valéry (1960), vol. I, pp. 1192ff., 1201, 1252ff. *Collected Works*, vol. 8, pp. 54ff., 66, 134ff.

21. Nicolas of Cusa, *De beryllo*; Hieronymus Cardanus, *De arcanis aeternitatis*; see Rüfner (1955), pp. 269ff., 273.

22. "Oratio de hominis dignitate," quoted by Rüfner (1955), p. 272.

23. On this, see Blumenberg (1957), p. 281, which states that Leibniz's doctrine of the infinity of possible worlds was first used as an argument by Breitinger in his *Critische Dichtkunst* (1740) where it justifies the poet's autonomous creation.

24. Vico, *The New Science*, trans. Thomas Goddard Bergin and Max Harold Fisch (Ithaca: Cornell University Press, 1968), p. 104.

25. Fellmann (1976), p. 72.

26. Ibid., p. 17.

27. Ibid., p. 71, also with reference to Vico's statement: "invenire enim fortunae est, facere autem industriae" (invention is a matter of luck, making one of diligence).

28. Ibid., p. 73: "It is true that Prometheus' theft of fire is mentioned . . . but the emphasis shifts from the discovery of fire to its preservation and use. According to Vico, this consists in the burning down of the primeval forest which is the interpretation given Hercules' first labor, the slaying of the Nemean lion."

29. Karl Marx, *Ökonomisch-philosophische Manuscripte* (1944), *MEW* Erg.-Bd.1 (1968), p. 574.

30. *Critique of Judgment*, § 43.

31. According to J. Mittelstrass, in a draft for the seminar mentioned in note 1.

32. Karl Marx, *Selected Writings*, ed. David McLellan (New York: Oxford University Press, 1977), p. 82.

33. In his dialectic of the appropriation of nature, Marx used definitions which can already be found in Hegel's *Ästhetics* under the heading "The work of art as the product of human activity." (This includes the notion of doubling: "by doubling himself not only in consciousness, intellectually, but through his work, in reality, and therefore seeing himself in a world created by himself.")

34. Marx, *Die Frühschriften*, ed. S. Landshut (Stuttgart, 1971), p. 237.

35. Ibid., p. 241.

36. Valéry, *Collected Works*, vol. 8, pp. 118–19.

37. Blumenberg (1964), p. 307, with reference to Valéry (1960), vol. II, p. 681 (éd. de la Pléiade).

38. On this, see Friedrich (1956), p. 51: "Poe's idea is the inversion of the sequence of poetic acts which the older poetics had postulated. What seems to be the result, the 'form,' is the origin of the poem; what seems to be origin is 'meaning,' result."

39. Valéry, *Collected Works*, vol. 8, p. 124.

40. Blumenberg, (1964).

41. Valéry, *Dialogues, Collected Works*, p. 144.

42. Blumenberg (1964), p. 301.

43. Ibid., p. 318.

44. Ibid., p. 304, with p. 308: "As aesthetic, technical being, man needs integral nature. The finality of nature ruthlessly cuts across the finality of homo faber, 'construire' and 'connaître' are antinomic, and as compared with nature, man's artificial and artistic work is based on an act of renunciation: he can only act and create because he can 'disregard.'"

45. O. Marquard, *Poetik und Hermeneutik III*, p. 379. In what follows, I refer to the tenth discussion, "'Op,' 'Pop,' and the Forever Ending History of Art" (pp. 691–705).

46. Imdahl (1969) explains this turn in the history of art which radically changed the relationship of the arts that have traditionally been strictly separated to the extra-artistic as a result of Kandinsky's 1912 theory. He shows how the "Great Abstraction" provokes the "Great Realism" as a presence of the real and the concrete which itself falls under the criterion of the Great Abstraction and thus makes possible the *objet trouvé*. Imdahl's conclusion: "Though this is necessary under the conditions of the traditional concept of art, art need not be made, it can also be discovered in the unmodified real object. The Great Abstraction makes possible within the Great Realism the art-relevant 'object trouvé'" (p. 224).

47. From Duchamp, *Conversations avec Marcel Duchamp*, quoted by Imdahl (1969), p. 225.

48. Imdahl (1969), p. 226.

49. On this, see J. Wissmann, "Pop Art oder die Realität als Kunstwerk" in *Poetik und Hermeneutik III*, pp. 507–30; and Imdahl (1969), pp. 214ff.

50. Wissmann, *Poetik und Hermeneutik III*, pp. 517ff.

51. According to Imdahl (1969) who interprets Jasper Johns's painting of the flag as "a case where reality and art in the sense of concrete art overlap" according to the definition by Theo van Doesburg (p. 218).

52. On this, see Jauss (1961) where the revelant texts, especially Goethe's *On truth and probability in works of art* (1797) and Diderot's *Entretiens sur le 'Fils Naturel'* and *Salon de 1763* are quoted and interpreted.

53. Imdahl (1969), p. 218.

54. In *Poetik und Hermeneutik III*, p. 700.

55. Tom Wolfe, "The Painted Word—What you see is what they say," in Harper's Magazine (1975), pp. 66–92 (later published as *The Right Stuff* [New York: Farrar, Strauss, and Giroux, 1979]).

56. Valéry, *Collected Works*, vol. 13: *Aesthetics*, p. 46.

6. Aesthesis: the receptive side of aesthetic experience

1. Geoffrey H. Hartman, *The Fate of Reading* (Chicago: University of Chicago Press, 1975).

2. Walter Benjamin, "The Work of Art in the Age of Mechanical Reproduction," in *Illuminations* (Schocken Books, 1969), pp. 217–51. Quotation from "Der Surrealismus" (1929), in *Angelus Novus*, vol. 2 (Frankfurt, 1966), p. 202.

3. Benjamin, *Illuminations*, p. 223.

4. Hartman (1975), p. 253.

5. As Kracauer (1960) showed in his film aesthetics and interpreted as a "redemption of physical reality."

6. Benjamin, *Illuminations*, p. 236.

7. The essay "La littérature industrielle" (1839) makes the lapidary statements that romanticism is over and done with, that *art pur* had its moment, and that literature now has not merely become a business but, having become commercialized, has also eliminated literary criticism, i.e., degraded it to the level of advertising: "As it penetrates the dream and makes it over in its own image, industry also makes itself dreamlike and fantastic. The demon of Literary propriety goes to people's heads." (*Choisir les meilleurs textes*; Saint-Beuve, introduction by A. Therive [Bruges, 1936], p. 183.) W. Benjamin explained *l'art pour l'art* as a rebellion of nonconformism which had made the attempt "to insulate art from technical development" (1955), vol. I, p. 419.

8. Henrich (1966), p. 12.

9. Here I am using the definitions of aesthesis which resulted from the phenomenological inventory (chap. 1).

10. Starobinski (1961), pp. 9–27.

11. Starobinski (1961), p. 17: "The look constitutes the living tie between the person and the world, between the self and the others: "The writer's every glance again brings into question the status of reality (and of literary realism), as it does that of communication (and of the human community)."

12. K. Reinhardt devoted an unforgettable interpretation to it. See "Der Schild des Achilleus," in *Freundesgabe für E. R. Curtius* (Bern, 1965), pp. 67–78. *Iliad* quotation from Richmond Lattimore's translation (Chicago: University of Chicago Press, 1961).

13. Reinhardt, "Der Schild des Achilleus," p. 67.

14. On the history of the concept *kalos*, see M. Fuhrmann, *Poetik und Hermeneutik III*, pp. 585ff.

15. K. Reinhardt, op. cit., p. 71.

16. Erich Auerbach, *Mimesis*, trans. Willard R. Trask (Princeton, N.J.: Princeton University Press, 1953), chap. 1.

17. Ibid., pp. 4–5.

18. Reinhardt, "Der Schild des Achilleus," p. 72.

19. H. Blumenberg, *Poetik und Hermeneutik I*, p. 11: "The classical conception of reality which makes possible Plato's doctrine of ideas without being identical with it presupposes that

the real presents itself as such, through and by itself, and that, when this occurs, its persuasive power is irrefutable."

20. Ibid.

21. Homer, *Odyssey: A New Translation*, ed. Albert Cook (New York: Norton, 1967).

22. K. Rahner, "Odysseus am Mastbaum," in *Griechische Mythen in christlicher Deutung* (Zurich, 1966), p. 301.

23. "denn das Schöne ist nichts/ als des Schrecklichen Anfang." *Duino Elegies*, I, ll. 4–5. Translation in text is Leishman's.

24. According to K. Rahner, "Odysseus am Mastbaum," especially pp. 282, 288.

25. According to J. Starobinski, "Montaigne et les masques," in *Poetik und Hermeneutik VIII*, especially p. 51: "Let the sirens sing, imaginary temptations lure him. He delights in feeling his separation and his indigence but without wanting to end his lack by possession. Space opens and deepens because in it, desire deploys its impulse. . . . The hiatus which the call of absent pleasure creates thus becomes the space where the powers of the intelligence and of judgment can have free play." Montaigne quotes the sirens in *Essays* II, xii and xvi. Pages 360 and 469 in the Donald M. Frame translation (Stanford, Calif.: Stanford University Press, 1948).

26. § 23: "Quelle der romantische Poesie."

27. This is still the basic definition of Christian allegory in Winkelmann, "Gedanken über die Nachahmung," . . . in *Kunsttheoretische Schriften* (Baden-Baden, 1962), p. 43.

28. Jauss (1977), pp. 28–34, from where this summary is taken.

29. Grimm (1977), pp. 138ff.

30. Jauss (1977).

31. PL 189, 1537c; commented on in Grimm (1977), p. 141.

32. On this, see Grimm (1977), pp. 67ff.

33. Ibid., p. 141; the following quotation is in R. Grimm's translation.

34. Grimm (1977), p. 172: "An allegorization of allegory advances as the original 'paradisiacal' accessiblility of meaning in the work of creation the reason for the allegorical significance of things (in holy scripture and in nature). This new treatment of allegorical motifs in the interpretation of paradise discovered sensuousness in allegorical and etymological correspondences which it was believed had already petrified." Following the Augustinian argument that "allegorical meaning, far from disavowing literal and historical meaning rather presupposes and confirms it," poetic allegory tries to rescind that original spirituality of creation which became material and temporal after the fall . . ." (ibid., p. 139).

35. "Intueri possumus in homine velut quemdam alterum mundum, totum in exiguo, e coelo terraque commistum, habentem sub se visibilem creaturam, supra se invisibilem, in unius mentis angustia, universitatis semina complectem" (We are able to see in man a sort of second world, the whole in small compass, a mixture of heaven and earth, having under him the visible creature, above him the invisible, in the confines of one mind, woven together the seeds of the universe; PL 189, 1528bc).

36. Grimm (1977), p. 142.

37. PL 189, 1534c.

38. As after the warning by the very old shepherd: "crescebat ex prohibitione cupiditas," in *Le Familiari*, ed. V. Rossi, vol. I, p. 155; on the entire matter, see Ritter (1963), pp. 140ff., and Blumenberg (1973), pp. 142ff.

39. The choice of these examples is not random. Not only did Rousseau choose a motto from the *Canzoniere* for his *Nouvelle Heloise*, but he quotes verses by Petrarch on eight different occasions (Petrarch is the most frequently quoted author in that work).

40. Friedrich, *Epochen der italienischen Lyrik* (Frankfurt, 1964), esp. p. 204: "He presents even the most radiant moments of her physical and spiritual beauty as a recollection of

the lover who brings back to mind how he once saw her and how many mountains and how much water now lie between her and him. In this poetry, recollection and spatial distance take on more painful qualities than in earlier poets."

41. Ibid., p. 206.

42. Ibid., p. 216.

43. Ibid., p. 210-214.

44. Canzone #310:

Ze forio torna, e'l bel tempo rimena,
e i fiori e l'erbe, sua dolce famiglia,
e garrir Progne e pianger Filomena,
e primavera candida e vermiglia.

Ridono i prati e'l ciel si rasserena,
Giove s'allegra di mirar sua figlia,
l'aria e l'acqua e la terra è d'amor piena,
ogni animal d'amar si riconsilia.

Ma per me, lasso! tornano i più gravi
sospiri, che del cor profondo tragge
quella ch'al ciel se ne portà le chiavi;

e cantar augelletti e fiorir piagge
e'n belle donne oneste atti soavi
sono un deserto e fere aspre e selvagge.

English version in text is from *Petrarch, Selected Poems*, trans. Anthony Mortimer (University, Ala.: University of Alabama Press, 1977).

45. In contrast to H. Friedrich, I see in the Mont Ventoux experience the paradigm of the limits and possibilities of Petrarch's lyric experience.

46. Friedrich, *Epochen der italienischen Lyrik*, p. 145.

47. Ritter (1974), p. 183.

48. "Alpine Mentalität und europäischer Horizont im Mittelalter," in *Schriften des Vereins für Geschichte des Bodensees und seiner Umgebung*, no. 92 (Friedrichshafen, 1974), pp. 1–46, esp. p. 37. The first mountain climb, which was prompted by both curiosity and the desire for glory, was Peter III of Acagon's around 1260/70. The description heightens the glorious deed by the phantastic detail of a dragon whom Peter III rouses out of a mountain lake. In Antoine de la Ville's report of the 1492 ascent, the open view characteristically remains unmentioned. What we have instead is praise of the mountain meadow at the peak as a "hortus conclusus" with graceful mountain goats, the sort of description that was customary in bucolic poetry (this might be added to Borst, pp. 37-38).

49. "A composition obeying the rules of the painters," H. F. Clark, *The English Landscape-Garden* (London, 1948), pp. 37ff. See also Ritter (1963), pp. 52ff. who also documents the concept "aesthetic gardens," in Schiller (1795) among others.

50. Hofmann (1974), p. 9.

51. Quoted according to Hofmann (1974), p. 10. In Leonardo's treatise, these comments are entitled "How the painter is lord over people of all kinds and over all things."

52. Hofmann (1974), p. 11.

53. Ibid.

54. In *Schriften zur Kunst*, 2nd ed. (Zurich, 1965), p. 789.

55. Schiller, "Uber das Erhabene," S.W. (Cotta), vol. 4, p. 733.

56. *A Philosophical Enquiry into the Origin of Our Ideas of the Sublime and Beautiful*.

57. Rousseau, *Nouvelle Héloise*, éd. de la Pléiade, vol. II (Paris, 1964), pp. 76-84. Rousseau quotes the second stanza of "Gloriosa columna in cui s'appoggia" (Canz. #9).

58. "Beobachtungen über das Gefühl des Schönen und Erhabenen, 1764," in *Werke*, ed. W. Weischedel (Wiesbaden, 1960), p. 826. Kant's first example of the feeling of the sublime is "the view of a mountain range whose snow-covered peak rises above the clouds."

59. "la beauté de mille étonnants spectacles." Before: "offertes en un vrai théâtre," later: "le spectacle a je ne sais quoi de magique, de surnaturel qui ravit l'esprit et les sens" (the beauty of a thousand astonishing spectacles, presented in a real theater. The spectacle has something magical and supernatural about it that delights the mind and entrances the senses; letter XXIII).

60. "Imaginez la variété, la grandeur, la beauté de mille étonnants spectacles; le plaisir de ne voir autour de soi que des objets tout nouveaux, des oiseaux étranges, des plantes bizarres et inconnues, d'observer en quelque sorte une autre nature, et de se trouver dans un nouveau monde" (allusion to the discovery of America!). (Imagine the variety, the grandeur, and the beauty of a thousand astonishing spectacles. The pleasure of seeing nothing but entirely new things, strange birds, bizarre and unknown plants about one, of observing a different nature, and of finding oneself in a new world; letter XXIII.)

61. "Et je méprisais la philosophie de ne pouvoir pas même autant qu'une suite d'objets inanimés." (And I despised philosophy for being unable to accomplish as much as a sequence of inanimate objects.) This criticism is directed at the "image trop vaine de l'âme du sage, dont l'exemple n'existe jamais" (the excessively vain idea one has of the soul of the sage which does not exist in reality).

62. Ritter (1974), pp. 156ff.

63. Ritter (1974), p. 160.

64. "Über das Verhältnis der bildenden Künste zu der Natur, 1807," in Schelling's *Werke* 3. Erg. Bd. (Munich, 1959), p. 416.

65. This explanation for the "so-called romantic quality of an area" is in Goethe, *Maximen und Reflexionen*, no. 868 (dated between 1818 and 1827).

66. More extensively documented and argued in Jauss (1970), p. 49. The character of the beautiful as something past and the recurrence to the poetry of remembrance receive somewhat short shrift in J. Ritter's thesis on the function of the aesthetic in modern society because he is interested primarily in reviving Hegel's theory of subjectivity as the freedom of being with itself (see 1974, p. 33): "Subjectivity has taken on these tasks, to preserve and keep before us the knowledge of God, of the Beautiful, and the moral which in society, and given the reification of the world, becomes something purely subjective. That is its greatness and its world-historical mission."

67. "Zum Bilde Prousts," in Benjamin (1955), vol. II, pp. 132–47; "On some motifs in Baudelaire," in *Illuminations*, pp. 155ff. I also call attention to my extensive critique (1970, pp. 57–66) of the posthumous piece from the "Passagenwerk" for which R. Toedemann is responsible and which was published as *Charles Baudelaire, ein Lyriker im Zeitalter des Hochkapitalismus* (Frankfurt, 1966).

68. See Jauss (1955) and (1955a), and essay D in this volume.

69. A later thesis of Benjamin's which is quoted from the letter to Max Horkheimer dated April 16, 1938, where the plan for the "Passagenwerk" is explained. See W. Benjamin, *Briefe*, vol. 2 (Frankfurt, 1966), p. 752.

70. Benjamin, *Illuminations*, p. 182.

71. In the plan for the "Passagenwerk," see note 69.

72. On this, see Hess (1953), chaps. 4 and 6.

73. As regards this matter, I refer the reader to my sketch in *Poetik und Hermeneutik VI*, pp. 289ff., and R. Lachmann, "Die 'Verfremdung' und das 'Neue Sehen' bei Viktor Sklovskij," in *Poetica* 3 (1970), pp. 226–49.

74. According to M. Imdahl, "Die Rolle der Farbe in der neueren französischen Malerei —Abstraktion and Konkretion," in *Poetik und Hermeneutik II*, p. 195.

75. On this, see M. Imdahl, "Marrés, Fiedler, Hildebrand, Riegel, Cézanne," in *Literatur und Gesellschaft* (Bonn, 1963), pp. 142-95.

76. According to J. Striedter, *Poetik und Hermeneutik II*, p. 263-88.

77. On this, see W. Iser, "Reduktionsformen der Subjektivität," in *Poetik und Hermeneutik III*, pp. 435-91; M. Smuda, *Becketts Prosa als Metasprache* (Munich, 1970), esp. pp. 27, 67ff.; Iser (1972), pp. 319-413: "Ist das Ende hintergehbar? Fiktion bei Beckett."

78. Wellershoff (1976), pp. 45-61.

79. Ibid., p. 53.

80. Koppe, *Literarische Versachlichung: Zum Dilemma der neueren Literatur zwischen Mythos und Szientismus* (Munich, 1977), esp. pp. 188-89; "the aesthetic reduction of the linguistic articulation of 'world' to what tend to become nothing more than expressions of geometricizing and arithmeticizing perceptions of measure and number feigns that existential concern is dealt with by the 'materialization' of consciousness, by practicing what one may call a western, i.e., a genuinely empirical, Nirvana."

81. Wellershoff (1976), p. 54.

82. Adorno, "Standort des Erzählers im zeitgenössischen Roman," in *Noten zur Literatur I* (Frankfurt, 1958), pp. 61-72; and "Kleine Proust-Kommentare" (1958) in *Noten zur Literatur II* (Frankfurt, 1961), p. 97.

83. Quoted from Victor Shklovsky, "Art as Technique," in *Russian Formalist Criticism: Four Essays*, trans. Lee T. Lemon and Marion J. Reis (Lincoln, Nebr.: University of Nebraska Press, 1965), p. 12.

84. Ibid., p. 13. (Sentence actually reads: "Tolstoy . . . describes an object as if he were seeing it for the first time, an event as if it were happening for the first time."

85. "Soit que la foi qui crée soit tarie en moi, soit que la réalité ne se forme que dans la mémoire, les fleurs qu'on me montre aujourd'hui pour la première fois ne me semblent pas de vraies fleurs." English translation in text is from *Swann's Way*, trans. G. K. Scott Moncrieff (New York: Vintage, 1970), p. 141.

86. M. Walser, "Leserfahrungen mit Marcel Proust," in *Erfahrungen und Leseerfahrungen* (Frankfurt, 1965), p. 139.

87. Ibid., pp. 136ff.

88. "Dingwerdung des Erscheinenden": it is with this formulation (for *realisation*) that K. Badt described the nature of Cézanne's art and thus shed light on the analogous situation of the recovery of the lost aura in the painting of Cézanne's time (*Die Kunst Cézannes* [Munich, 1956], esp. pp. 148ff.).

89. Curtius, *Marcel Proust* (1925), now vol. 28 of the Bibliothek Suhrkamp (Frankfurt, n.d.), pp. 128ff.

90. On this, see Jauss (1955a), p. 272-91.

91. Benjamin (1955), vol. I, pp. 428ff.

92. Adorno, *Noten zur Literatur I*, p. 61.

93. Ibid., p. 69.

94. Benjamin, *Illuminations*, p. 203.

95. "Oui, si le souvenir, grace à l'oublie, n'a pu contracter aucun lien, jeter aucun chaînon entre lui et la minute présente, s'il est resté à sa place, à sa date, s'il a gardé ses distances, son isolement dans le creux d'une vallée ou à la pointe d'un sommet, il nous fait tout à coup respirer un air nouveau, précisément parce que c'est un air qu'on a respiré autrefois, cet air plus pur que les poètes on vainement essayé de faire régner dans le Paradis et qui ne pourrait donner cette sensation profonde de renouvellement que s'il avait été respiré déjà, car les vrais paradis sont les paradis qu'on a perdu." ("Yes: if, owing to the work of oblivion, the returning memory can throw no bridge, form no connecting link between itself and the present minute, if it remains in the context of its own place and date, if it keeps its distance,

its isolation in the hollow of a valley or upon the highest peak of a mountain summit, for this very reason it causes us suddenly to breathe a new air, an air which is new precisely because we have breathed it in the past, that purer air which the poets have vainly tried to situate in paradise and which could induce so profound a sensation of renewal only if it had been breathed before, since the true paradises are the paradises that we have lost.") Translation from Marcel Proust, *The Past Recaptured*, trans. Andreas Mayor (New York: Vintage Books, 1970), p. 132. The connection between remembrance, the experience of time as *atmosphère interposée* (from which the "poetry of remembrance" originally derives), and aesthetic distance whose elimination Proust's "novel of the novel" describes pardigmatically cannot be explained here. See Jauss (1955b), especially chapter V.

96. "Le seul véritable voyage, le seul bain de Jouvence, ce ne serait pas d'aller vers de nouveaux paysages, mais d'avoir d'autres yeux, de voir l'univers avec les yeux d'un autre, de cent autres, de voir les cent univers que chacun d'eux voit, que chacun d'eux est" (vol. XII, p. 69). ("The only true voyage of discovery, the only fountain of Eternal Youth, would be not to visit strange lands but to possess other eyes, to behold the universe through the eyes of another, of a hundred others, to behold the hundred universes that each of them beholds, that each of them is . . ." From *The Captive*, trans. G. K. Scott Moncrieff [New York: Vintage Books, 1971], p. 179.)

97. Gadamer (1975), p. 76.

7. Catharsis: the communicative efficacy of aesthetic experience

1. *Poetik und Hermeneutik VI*, p. 545.

2. Ibid.

3. Kommerell (1970), p. 201: "independently of specific dispositions and inclinations, it is assumed that man has a fundamental readiness for compassion and fear which jeopardizes that desirable composure which is the condition for higher concerns."

4. Starobinski (1970), p. 179; and similarly already in S. H. Butcher, *Aristotle's Theory of Poetry and Fine Art* (1907): "The real emotions, the positive needs of life, always contain some elements of disquiet. By the union of a form with a matter which in the world of experience is alien to it, a magical effect is wrought. The pressure of everyday reality is removed, and the aesthetic emotion is released as an independent reality" (p. 127).

5. Here, we can also refer to the discussion "Gibt es eine 'christliche Asthetik'"? in *Poetik und Hermeneutik III*, pp. 583–610; and Jauss (1977), pp. 29ff.

6. Jauss, (1977), pp. 28–34.

7. M. Fuhrmann, *Poetik und Hermeneutik III*, pp. 585ff.

8. Callois (1946), pp. 112–23.

9. See Jauss (1977), pp. 401ff.

10. Herzog (1975).

11. Ibid., pp. 43, 143ff.

12. Ibid., p. 145.

13. Ibid., p. 147. Herzog here refers to Juvencus I, 88ff.: "Elisabeth, being visited by Maria . . . avoids in her praise of Maria all use of the second person. Maria is already being isolated as a figure of worship. . . . Juvencus sees this figure of worship instrumentally: Maria no longer visits her companion; it is God in her who visits the believer."

14. Quoted according to Fuhrmann (1973), p. 93.

15. As an example, I quote the "Prologus super tertia die passionis" from Greban's *Mystère de la Passion*, ed. Jodogne (Brussels, 1965), ll. 19906ff.:

> Pour continuer la matiere
> qui est prouffitable et entiere
> a cueurs plains de compassion,

laquelle traicte par maniere
la haute passion planiere
qui fit nostre redempcion (etc).

(In order to continue the matter which is whole and of profit to hearts full of compassion, it treats of the manner in which the high passion achieved our redemption.)

16. According to K. Ruh, "Zur Theologie des mittelalterlichen Passionstraktats," in *Theologische Zeitschrift* 6 (1950), p. 20.

17.   Ainsi va ses dueulz moderant,
en ce mirouer considerant,
ou tout cueur, pour son dueil mirer,
se doit parfondement mirer.
Et, affin que vous y mirez
et doulcement la remirez,
ce devost mirouer pour le mieulx
vous ramenons devant les yeulx,
senssiblement, par parsonnaiges.
Mirez vous si serez bien saiges,
chascun sa fourme entrevoit:
qui bien se mire bien se voit.

Quoted in Warning (1974), pp. 186ff., to whose commentary I call attention here. (Thus he moderates his sorrow, looking into this mirror where every heart must look deeply in order to see his sadness. And so in order that you may see yourselves and take a good look there, we bring you back this devout mirror before your eyes, making it sensible through characters. Look at yourselves if you be wise. Every one will see his form. He who looks well sees himself well.)

18. Kommerell (1970), p. 204.

19. On this, see W. Schmeja, "Der 'sensus moralis' im Adamsspiel," in *Zeitschrift für romanische Philologie* 90 (1974), 41-72. "The change of habits is the goal of the moral or tropological explanation, which is the moral meaning pertaining to the mending of ways and to practical instruction" (Raban, PL CXII, 331).

20. Warning (1974).

21. "Cum praecinentium et succinentium, canentium et decinentium, intercinentium et occinentium praemolles modulationes audieris, sirenarum concentus credas esse, non hominum, et de vocum facilitate miraberis, quibus philomena vel sithacus, aut si quid sonorius est, modos suos nequeunt coaequare. Ea siquidem est ascendendi descendendique facilitas, ea sectio vel geminatio notularum, ea replicatio articulorum singulorumque consolidatio, sic acuta vel acutissima gravibus et subgravisu temperantur, ut auribus sui iudicii fere subtrahatur auctoritas, et animus, quem tantae suavitatis demulsit gratia, auditorum merita examinare non sufficit. Cum haec quidem modum excesserint, lumborum pruriginem quam devotionem mentis a curis redimunt, exterminant temporalium sollicitudinem, et quadam participatione letitiae et quietis et amica exultatione in Deum mentes humanas traicium ad societatem angelorum" (quoted from R. R. Bezzola, *Les origines et la formation de la littérature courtoise en occident* [Paris, 1967], p. 28). (If you ever heard the subtle modulations of them singing and harmonizing, echoing and responding, intermingling and contrasting their voices, you would believe it to be the music of the Sirens, not of men; and you would marvel at the smoothness of their voices, which neither the nightingale nor warbler, nor anything else more sonorous, could match. Since there is this smoothness of rising and falling, this dividing and doubling of little notes, this repetition and confirming of each part, in this way sharp or very sharp sounds are balanced by deep or very deep ones, so that the

ear is practically robbed of its judgment, and the listener's mind, which the pleasure of so much sweetness lulls, cannot analyze the merits. If these things rise above a regular measure, they can cause the arousal of the loins more quickly than devotion of the mind. But if they are bounded together by some moderation, they ransom the mind from its cares, deaden the anxiety of temporal cares, and by a certain sharing in the joy and quiet, and by a welcome exultation toward God, they draw the minds of men toward the fellowship of angels.)

22. Jacob de Vitry, *Sermones in epistolas*; Thomas Acquinas, "Exposition in I Tim. 4, 2."

23. W. Durandus, *Rationale divinorum officiorum* I.3.

24. The medieval tradition is based on the Aristotelian treatise "De sensu et sensato." See W.-D. Lange, *El Fraile trobador* (Cologne, 1971), *Analecta Romanica* 28, p. 86.

25. Bruno Carthusianus, PL CLII, 805; The Augustinian topos "fides ex auditu est" probably comes from *De Civitate Dei* XVII, 16.

26. "J'entends dire que la tragédie mène a la pitié par la terreur, soit. Mais quelle est cette pitié? Une emotion passagère et vaine, qui ne dure pas plus que l'illusion qui l'a produite; un reste de sentiment naturel étouffé bientôt par les passions, une pitié sterile, qui se repaît de quelques larmes, et n'a jamais produit le moindre acte d'humanité."

27. Quote from "Discourse on the Origin and Basis of Inequality among Men," in *The Essential Rousseau*, trans. Lowell Blair (New York: New American Library, 1974), p. 164.

28. George H. Mead's later social psychology can be seen as an elaboration of these premises in Rousseau's social theory. For interactionist sociology views compassion as the social attitude par excellence. It demands of man as a social being that he enter into someone else's role. He does this by implicitly reacting to a situation as the person concerned must react explicitly. It is thus through the other that the human being acquires its identity, which means that man experiences himself through the experience of what is other. (See *Mind, Self, and Society*, chap. 38.)

29. Quoted from *Politics and the Arts. Letter to M. D'Alembert on the theatre*. Trans. Allan Bloom (Glencoe, Ill.: Free Press, 1960), p. 20.

30. That Rousseau believed man to be naturally a 'deficient being' and constantly exposed to being led astray by his imagination because his senses are weak becomes clear toward the conclusion of the "Letter to M. D'Alembert" through the example of a half-veiled and therefore obscene nakedness: "Is it not known that statues and paintings only offend the eyes when a mixture of clothing renders the nudity obscene? The immediate power of the senses is weak and limited; it is through the intermediary of the imagination that they make their greatest ravages; it is the business of the imagination to irritate the desires in lending to their objects even more attractions than nature gave them . . ." (p. 134).

31. Brecht, "On a non-Aristotelian dramaturgy," in *Gesammelte Werke* (Frankfurt, 1967), vol. 15, p. 305.

32. Ibid., pp. 245, 260.

33. Ibid., p. 305.

34. Ibid., p. 301; vol. 16, p. 666.

35. Ibid., vol. 15, p. 299.

36. Ibid.

37. Ibid., vol. 15, p. 303.

38. Ibid., vol. 16, p. 663.

39. "Short Organum for the Theatre," in *Brecht on Theatre, the Development of an Aesthetic*, ed. and trans. John Willett (New York: Hill and Wang, 1964), p. 186.

40. Vol. 16, p. 702.

41. John Willett, *Brecht on Theatre*, p. 180.

42. PL XVII, 236.

43. Toward the end of the twelfth century, that is testified to by the protest of religious

poets against the "fictions" of worldly literature, for example, concurrently with which the literary concepts *fable* and *conte* were replaced by *estoire* (*historia*), *dit*, and *essemple* which came from biblical exegesis. See Jauss, *GRLMA* VI, 1, p. 164; and U. Ebel, *Das altromanische Mirakel*, Studia Romanica 8 (Heidelberg, 1965), p. 95.

44. As in the Aristotelian discussion of the example, *Rhet.* 2, 20. While Aristotle expresses his preference for the historical example over the fable here, he ranks the enthymeme above the example. His reasons for according preference to the historical example over the fable do not yet include the greater persuasive power of what is vouched for and exemplary because unique. Instead, it is the relationship of rule and instance which still subordinates the example to a cyclical view of history: "it is more valuable for the political speaker to supply [parallels] by quoting what has actually happened, since in most respects the future will be like what the past has been." (*Basic Works of Aristotle*, trans. Richard P. McKeon [New York: Random House, 1941].)

45. Quoted in H. Friedrich, *Die Rechtsmetaphysik der göttlichen Komödie* (Frankfurt, 1942), p. 31. Regarding the emergence of the concept *experientia* in the historical context of the theory of the exemplary, see ibid., p. 31.

46. "This *exemplis confundi* which rouses men from their indolence and will move them to insight and change by a human case that will touch them, by an actual event, where they cannot be moved by the abstract commandment, began to be included as a demand in the instructions for sermons during the time of Gregory the Great (PL LXXV, 518)." H. Friedrich, ibid., p. 30.

47. On this, see D. Harth, "Romane und ihre Leser," in *Germanisch-romanische Monatsschrift* 20 (1970), pp. 159–79.

48. R. Koselleck, "Historia magistra vitae," in *Natur und Geschichte, Festschrift Karl Löwith* (Stuttgart, 1967), pp. 169–218.

49. "Geschichte als Exemplum – Exemplum als Geschichte," in Stierle (1975), pp. 14–48, quotation on p. 38.

50. Ibid., p. 45.

51. See M. Fuhrmann ("Das Exemplum in der antiken Rhetorik," in *Poetick und Hermeneutik V*, pp. 499ff.) who corrects R. Koselleck and K. Stierle by shedding light on the different function the example had for the reader and for the person who acted, and who advances the thesis: "it is only in school and what came under its influence that the motto 'historia magistra vitae' could so radically prevail – to then be just as radically dethroned in that same sphere."

52. Plutarch, "Alexander." "It must be borne in mind that my design is not to write histories, but lives. And the most glorious exploits do not always furnish us with the clearest discoveries of virtue or vice in men; sometimes, a matter of less moment, an expression or a jest, informs us better of their characters and inclinations than the most famous sieges, the greatest armaments, or the bloodiest battles whatsoever." *The Lives of the Noble Grecians and Romans*, trans. John Dryden (New York: Modern Library, n.d.), p. 801.

53. Stierle (1975), p. 45.

54. Buck (1967), pp. 148–83, esp. p. 180.

55. Ibid., p. 182.

56. See Buck (1967), p. 183.

8. Aesthetic experience among the problems of everyday life: problems of delimitation

1. Dewey (1934), pp. 13–17.

2. Ibid., p. 5.

3. Ibid., p. 40.

4. For this, Dewey's example of a stone rolling down a hill (p. 39) is instructive. This event becomes an experience with aesthetic quality because "the final coming to rest is related to all that went before as the culmination of a continuous movement."

5. Sartre (1940), pp. 234-45.

6. Reaction to the first world fairs of 1851 (London) and 1855 (Paris) is revelatory here. The monumental account by Comte de Laborde, "De l'union des arts et de l'industrie" (1857) attempts to set their traditional unity against the separation of artistic and industrial production that has occurred, and recommends an "embellissement" of industrial products. His critics, Maxime du Camp and Champfleury among them, respect industrial production as a "new art": "Le seul art qui, en France, soit à peu pres à la hauteur de l'époque et des circonstances, c'est l'art nouveau, je veux dire celui des machines" (The only art in France which is more or less on a par with the epoch and its circumstances is the new art, I mean the art of the machines; in Revue de Paris 37 [1857], p. 386).

7. It is with this intent that M. du Camp (ibid., p. 388) praises the "high poetry and superior morality of the locomotive: " . . . gros boyaux tronqués courant sur des roues massives, traînant un tender qui ressemble à un vaste bain de siège, et soufflant la fumée par un immense tuyau de poêle. Rien n'est plus admirable qu'une locomotive lorsqu'on dégage la haute poésie et la morale supérieure qu'elle contient abstractivement(!); mais par ses formes elle est lourde, violente, brutale, et laide" (bulging truncated intestines running on massive wheels, pulling a tender which resembles a huge hip bath, and blowing smoke through an immense stovepipe. Nothing is more admirable than a locomotive when one disengages the high poetry and the superior morality it contains abstractly. But in its forms it is heavy, violent, brutal, and ugly). My argument also implies a critique of Dufrenne (1967) who wants to use the example of the locomotives to give greater substance to the objectivist phrase: "le beau est le vrai sensible à l'oeil" (the beautiful is the truth that the eye can see, p. 20).

8. Poetik und Hermeneutik VI, p. 544.

9. Dewey (1934), p. 270.

10. Ibid., pp. 46ff.

11. Ibid., p. 54: "For to perceive, a beholder must create his own experience. And his creation must include relations comparable to those which the original producer underwent."

12. See the chapter "Pourquoi écrire?" in Sartre (1948), pp. 89ff.

13. Dewey's account of the integrative achievement of aesthetic experience, p. 55: "In every integral experience there is form because there is dynamic organization" already comes quite close to Mukarovsky's definition of the aesthetic function as a contentless principle which organizes extra-esthetic meanings.

14. The following discussion is based principally on Mukarovsky's Aesthetic Function, Norm, and Value as Social Facts, trans. Mark E. Suino (Ann Arbor: University of Michigan Press, 1970), and his Structure, Sign, and Function, trans. John Burbank and Peter Steiner (New Haven, Conn.: Yale University Press, 1978). On the prehistory (particularly in relation to the Russian formalists), development, and elaboration (especially by Vodička) of his theory, see Striedter (1976).

15. Mukarovsky, Structure, p. 32.

16. Mukarovsky, Aesthetic Function, p. 95.

17. Ibid., p. 95.

18. Mukarovsky, Structure, p. 41.

19. Formulations in the Paris lecture "On Structuralism" (1946) as quoted by Kalivoda (1970), pp. 32ff., and: "If the esthetic function does not tend toward any practical aim, this does not mean that it will obstruct the contact of art with the vital interests of man. Precisely because it lacks unequivocal 'content,' the esthetic function becomes transparent and does not act inimically to the other functions but helps them" (Structure, p. 12). And: "The esthetic

function does not obstruct man's creative initiative but helps to develop it" (*Structure*, p. 13).

20. Kalivoda (1970), p. 25 and 36ff.

21. Ibid., p. 37.

22. Mukarovsky, *Aesthetic Function*, p. 59.

23. Ibid., p. 42.

24. As he does on pp. 90–91 where he traces the "merely potential character" of the inherent aesthetic value to "a certain organization of the material artifact."

25. Ibid., p. 60.

26. Ibid., p. 64.

27. Ibid., p. 96.

28. Mukarovsky, *Structure*, pp. 40ff. The distinction proposed on p. 42, according to which "the theoretical function strives for a total and unifying *image* of reality, whereas the aesthetic function establishes a unifying *attitude* toward it," presupposes the cathartic efficacy of aesthetic experience, but because Mukarovsky distinguishes between emotional and aesthetic function, this is not permissible.

29. Mukarovsky, *Aesthetic Function*, p. 22.

30. Mukarovsky, *Structure*, p. 42.

31. Vygotski (1965), p. 82.

32. Ibid., p. 87.

33. Quoted from K. Capek, *Lieder des Prager Volkes* in Mukarovsky's *Aesthetic Function*, p. 57.

34. Ibid., p. 57.

35. With the formulation "the world appears as the horizon of fiction, fiction as the horizon of world," I have already adopted the result of Karlheinz Stierle's (1975a) theory of speech acts.

36. Mukarovsky, *Structure*, p. 40, where he provides this definition: "a function is the mode of a subject's self-realization vis-a-vis the external world." It seems to me that the non-articulated multiplicity of aesthetic worlds is also a shortcoming of Dufrenne's (1967) phenomenological theory. See p. 650: "there are as many worlds as there are aesthetic objects, and certainly as there are authors."

37. Mukarovsky, *Structure*, p. 37.

38. The following quotations will be from this work.

39. Schütz/Luckmann (1975), pp. 42ff.

40. Ibid., p. 43.

41. See below, chap. 8b and E1, and Jauss (1977), I, chap. 9 where I attempt to interpret the small genres of the exemplary as preliterary subuniverses. As "intellectual occupations" (*Geistesbeschäftigungen*) in André Jolles's meaning of that term, they can thematize and deal with various claims of the pragmatic everyday.

42. Mukarovsky, *Aesthetic Function*, p. 22.

43. Iser (1976), p. 88.

44. Schütz/Luckmann (1975), pp. 42ff.

45. Ibid., p. 43.

46. Ibid., p. 47.

47. Stierle, "Was heisst Rezeption bei fiktionalen Texten?" (1975a) and *Text als Handlung* (1975). His critique of textual- and pragma linguistics and Iser's of the theory of speech acts (1976, pp. 89ff.) make it unnecessary to discuss them again here.

48. Stierle (1975a), p. 378.

a) Delimiting the ridiculous and the comic

1. Souriau (1948), p. 148: by the addition of an art factor ("par l'adjonction d'un facteur d'art"); p. 150: A reflective revision of laughter occurs when the moral point of view enters in ("il y a une révision réflexive du rire par survenance du point de vue moral").

2. Ibid., pp. 154–55. In the description of these phases, I see the beginning of an aestheticization in the third step of the "sentiment . . . rendu par lui-même curieux, émouvant pour la conscience."

3. E. Dupréel, "Le problème sociologique du rire," in *Revue philosophique de la France et de l'Etranger* 106 (1928), p. 214.

4. Plessner (1961), p. 123. All English quotations in the text, including this one, are from *Laughing and Crying, A Study of the Limits of Human Behavior*, trans. James Spencer Churchill and Marjorie Grene (Evanston: Northwestern University Press, 1970), p. 92.

5. "Elemente einer Pragmasemiotik der Komödie," in *Poetik und Hermeneutik VII*, pp. 279–333.

6. Ibid., p. 326.

7. Ibid., p. 326, 332.

8. According to M. Fuhrmann, the formulation *vis comica* is clearly not from classical antiquity but possibly due to a misunderstanding in the reception of a passage from Suetonius' *Vita Terentii*: "Lenibus atque utinam scriptis adiuncta forest vis, comica ut aequato virtus poneret honore cum Graecis, neve hac despectus parte iaceres," etc. (*comica* belongs with *virtus*). (Would that the power of your pimps had been harnessed for your writings, so that your comedic excellence might place you in equal honor with the Greeks, and you would not lie despised in this field.)

9. Molière, *Critique de l'Ecole des Femmes.*

10. Pointed out by M. Fuhrmann, see Donatius, ed. Wessner, II, p. 358, chap. 2: "in hac scaena, quae docendi atque instruendi spectatoris causa inducitur, miri extrinsecus lepores facetiaeque cernuntur et sales comici. Id enim est artis poeticae, ut, cum narrationi . . . argumenti detur opera, iam tamen res agi et spectari comoedia vie datur" (in this scene, which is introduced to teach and instruct the audience, the outwardly charms, conceits and comic wit are seen; for this is the poetic art, that when the task of the plot is given over to narration, the action of the comedy still seems to be seen and performed); Hieronymus, Epist. 50, 3 (about a young monk, an adversary): "qui tantae in sermonicando elegantiae est, ut comico sale ac lepore conspersus sit . . ." (who is of such elegance in speaking since he is sprinkled with comic wit and charm . . .).

11. Cicero, "De oratore," 2, 237–39: "Nam nec insignis improbitas et sceler iuncta nec rursus miseria insignis agitata ridetur." (For neither exceptional wickedness, especially joined with crime, nor exceptional wretchedness, when assailed, is laughable.)

12. F. Schalk, "Das Lächerliche in der französischen Literatur des Ancien Regime," in *Studien zur französischen Aufklärung* (Munich, 1964), p. 86.

13. La Bruyère, *Oeuvres complètes*, ed. J. Benda (Paris, 1934), p. 336. See Schalk, "Das Lächerliche," p. 86.

14. *Oeuvres de La Bruyère*, ed. G. Servais (Paris, 1865), pp. 14ff.

15. Hegel, *Aesthetics*, vol. II, p. 1233.

16. In what follows, I adhere to Souriau's distinction and correct as far as necessary Plessner's language in order to avoid confusion. Plessner's terminology here is the precise inverse of Souriau's: he calls the occasion for laughter in everyday life "the comic."

17. Against Dupréel: "Le problème sociologique du rire," p. 25: " . . . il n'y a pas de rire presocial. Le rire est par essence impliqué dans le dialogue de deux individus au moins" (there is no such thing as presocial laughter. By its very essence, laughter involves two or more persons.

18. Plessner, *Laughing and Crying*, p. 87.

19. Marquard, "Exile der Heiterkeit," in *Poetik und Hermeneutik VII*, p. 141.

20. See Boileau, *Sat. IX*, ll. 267ff., for example:

> La satire en leçons, en nouveautez fertile,
> scait seule assaisonner le plaisant et l'utile,

Et d'un vers qu'elle épure aux rayons du bon sens,
Détrompe les Esprits des erreurs de leur temps.

The demand not to give the names of the person being attacked is still discussed in Perrault's *Parallele des anciens et des modernes*, see reprint (Munich, 1964), vol. III, pp. 224ff. "Satire, fertile in lessons and novelty, is alone able to blend the pleasant and the useful, and with a single line cleansed in the rays of common sense it frees minds from the errors of their time."

21. D. Tschizewskij, "Satire oder Groteske," in *Poetik und Hermeneutik VII*, pp. 269-78.

22. J. Starobinski, "Le diner chez Bertin," ibid., pp. 191-204.

23. Ibid., p. 332.

b) Sociological and aesthetic role concept

1. The Plato message from *The Laws* 644d, which is considered to be the source of the topos, was not originally a theatrical metaphor. It deliberately leaves open the antithesis plaything:serious intent, suggests that men as puppets hold the strings in their own hands, and does not thematize the position of the spectator at all: "We may imagine that each of us living creatures is a puppet made by the gods, possibly as a plaything, or possibly with some more serious purpose" (from *Plato, the Collected Dialogues*, ed. Edith Hamilton and Huntington Cairns [New York: Bollingen Foundation, 1961]). In the Christian tradition, the spectator acquires special significance from the Paulus passage 1. Corinthians, 4, 9 in which the apostles are clearly being equated with circus gladiators whom God destines to death, an act which is to serve as a warning to mankind: "for we are made a spectacle unto the world, and to angels, and to men." In Johannes of Salisbury's *Policraticus*, finally, God Himself and the blessed heroes of the faith become the spectators of the earthly play. On this, see Curtius (1958), pp. 146ff. who completely ignored this change in meaning.

2. It is no accident that R. Dahrendorf took the analogies between the theatrical and the sociological concept of role in his *Homo Sociologicus*, 10th ed. (Opladen, 1971), pp. 22ff. from Curtius (see preceding note). For Curtius, the history of the *theatrum mundi* topos climaxes in Hofmannsthal's *Grosses Salzburger Welttheater*.

3. Dahrendorf, *Homo Sociologicus*, p. 23. His introductory example are the fifteen roles of Studienrat Schmidt: "As father, Mr. Schmidt finds himself in a field with mother, son and daughter; as 'Studienrat' (secondary school teacher) he relates to his students, their parents, his colleagues and the school administrators; his post as 3rd chairman of the Y party connects him with colleagues in the hierarchy, etc." (p. 30).

4. Dahrendorf, *Homo Sociologicus*, p. 28.

5. H. P. Dreitzel uses this formulation to describe the sociological dilemma of the role player who is not allowed to simply *play* his role. See *Die gesellschaftlichen Leiden und das Leiden an der Gesellschaft* (Stuttgart, 1972), p. 104.

6. Dahrendorf, *Homo Sociologicus*, p. 95.

7. Plessner (1960), p. 28.

8. Ibid.

9. Ibid.

10. Ibid., p. 33.

11. Dreitzel, see note 5; E. Goffman, *The Presentation of Self in Everyday Life* (New York: Doubleday, Anchor, 1959).

12. Dreitzel, *Homo Sociologicus*, p. 110 and 180-83.

13. Ibid., p. 183.

14. Löwith (1928).

15. Dreitzel, *Homo Sociologicus*, p. 110.

16. Ibid., p. 111.

17. Ibid., p. 110.

18. See second volume, part I.

19. Luckmann, "Persönliche Identität, soziale Rolle und Rollendistanz," in *Poetik und Hermeneutik VIII*.

20. See H. Friedrich, *Romanische Literaturen — Aufsätze I* (Frankfurt, 1972), pp. 61 and 67 (on the formulation which is reminiscent of Cicero's "Laelius de amicitia"): "Nihil umquam, Deus scit, in te quisivi, te pure, non tua concupiscens."

21. *Essays* I, xxviii.

22. See P. Watzlawick, J. H. Beavin, and Don D. Jackson, *Menschliche Kommunikation* (Bern, 1969), pp. 138–70.

23. It reads: "But is it possible at all to play 'man' as one plays railroad conductor or 'critical sociologist'?" His answer to this question will be included in *Poetik und Hermeneutik VIII*.

c) The religious origin and aesthetic emancipation of individuality

1. O. Marquard, in "Identitätsprospekt" (i.e., program) for *Poetik und Hermeneutik VIII*.

2. "Eram enim etiam tunc, vivebam atque sentiebam meamque incolumitatem, vestigium secretissimae unitatis, ex qua eram, curae habebam, custodiebam interiore sensu integritatem sensuum meorum inque ipsis parvis parvarumque rerum cogitationibus veritate delectabar." (For I was even then, I was living and feeling, and I was caring for my safety, the trace of the most hidden unity, out of which I was; I was guarding the wholeness of my senses with an inner sense and in these small things and in the thoughts of these small things, I tasted truth.)

3. In his noteworthy article "Augustine's Confessions and the Grammar of Selfhood," in *Genre* 6 (1973), pp. 1–28, Eugene Vance brought out this aspect.

4. Rousseau, *Mon portrait*, I, 1123 (edition de la Pleiade).

5. Quoted from "Ebauches des Confessions," I, 1155.

6. That is shown by this kind of recurrent figure: "Yet, O my God, in Whose presence I now without hurt may remember this, all this unhappily I learnt . . ." (I, xvi, 26).

7. Rousseau, "Ebauches," I, 1153.

8. According to J. Starobinski, *Jean-Jacques Rousseau — La transparence et l'obstacle*, 2nd ed. (Paris, 1971), p. 230; and "Jean-Jacques Rousseau et le peril de la reflexion," in Starobinski (1961), pp. 91–188. His lecture at Constance University explains the three-phase historical model from the perspective of the Vincennes illumination and provides a new interpretation of Rousseau's account which I adopt and carry further here in order to shed light on the inversion of the Augustinian *confessio*.

9. Rousseau, second letter to Malesherbes, I, 1136.

10. On the figuration of incorporated time which, as "edifice occupant . . . un espace a quatre dimensions," concludes and heightens the work of remembrance, see Jauss (1955), p. 197.

11. See above, chap. 6.

12. Starobinski, *J.-J. Rousseau — La transparence et l'obstacle*, p. 236.

13. Ibid.: "That the self-portrait should show little 'anecdotal' resemblance matters little since the painter's soul reveals itself by its manner, its touch, its style. As he deforms his image, he reveals a more essential reality which is the look that he takes at himself, the impossibility of grasping himself except by self-distortion."

14. See the chapter "Le moi accapare l'Histoire Sainte," in Starobinski (1961), pp. 137ff. which also sheds light on the calvinist background: "The idea of an omniscient and just eye is inseparable from the sky of Geneva" (p. 100).

15. "Iconologically, it is significant that the book has changed places in the trial scene: while it is represented in all of apocalyptic literature as the black book which lists the sins of

mankind and is kept at God's throne and will be opened in the presence of assembled mankind, Rousseau writes this book himself, for his particular case, and brings it to the tribunal with the proud words: 'here is what I have done, what I thought, what I have been,'" in H. Blumenberg, *Säkularisierung und Selbstbehauptung* (Frankfurt, 1974), p. 128.

16. "Let each of them in turn reveal with the same frankness, the secrets of his heart at the foot of the Throne, and say, if he dare, '*I was better than that man!*'" (I, 5).

17. "Children and youths . . . regard the world as raw material which they must shape, as a treasure which they must take possession of. Everything they seem to think belongs to them, everything must be subservient to their will," from *The Autobiography of Johann Wolfgang von Goethe*, trans. John Oxenford (New York: Horizon Press, 1969), p. 314. (*Dichtung und Wahrheit*, chap. xvi)

18. Ibid., p. 425.

19. Ibid. H. R. Picard, *Literarische Selbstdarstellung im zeitgenössischen Frankreich* (Munich, 1977) shows for the later development how modern autobiography (most impressively in Michel Leiris's *La règle du jeu*) disavows in multiple ways the aesthetic illusion of totality because it wishes to thematize the never-ending self-portrait of the writer and to represent what is being remembered in horizons of changing significance.

B. Interaction patterns of identification with the hero

1. See above, introduction to chap. A7 (catharsis).

2. D. Wellershoff, in *Poetik und Hermeneutik VI*, p. 550.

3. See Berger/Luckmann (1971), esp. p. 101.

4. See table, p. 159.

5. Frye (1957), pp. 37ff. His attempt to place the sequence of types into the major periods of the history of European literature and to see it concretized at every step in a parallel of tragic and comic genres is historically false, and this is the major objection to Frye's model. The diachronically described heroic types occur in almost every historical phase synchronically, alongside each other, and compete with each other. The frequently forced parallelization of tragic and comic genres is especially unsatisfactory. It may be acceptable to use the opposite poles dionysiac and apollonian for the mythic phase, and the stylistic forms "elegiac" and "idyllic" for the phase of "romance." But then it appears that there is an insufficient number of such dichotomies so that the remaining phases or steps can only be labeled one-sidedly, as cathartic, pathetic, and ironic.

6. It was only for technical reasons that the model of interaction patterns on p. 159 was not arranged in circular form.

7. Gadamer (1975), p. 98.

8. Warning (1974), pp. 37ff.

9. According to Guiette (1972), p. 7: "Ce 'drama' n'a pas d'autre but que la liturgie elle-même. Il est célébration en même temps que commémoration. Il doit signifier, plus qu'il ne représente. Il est louange et prière: service de Dieu" (this "drama" has no object other than the liturgy itself. It is both celebration and commemoration. It must signify rather than represent. It is praise and prayer, service of God).

10. Warning (1974), pp. 140ff.

11. Ibid., pp. 239ff.

12. Kommerell (1957), pp. 202ff.

13. Ibid., p. 209.

14. Lesser, *Fiction and the Unconscious* (1962); Holland, *The Dynamics of Literary Response* (1968). Because the authors are interested in different problems, a discussion of their work did not seem necessary. The convertibleness of their results must still be looked into.

15. It is missing in Stierle (1975a) as middle level between the pragmatic and the self-referential reception and would constitute there the positive counterpart to the negatively evaluated "quasi-pragmatic reception."

16. Schmidt (1971), pp. 50ff.; and in *Poetik und Hermeneutik VI*, pp. 546ff.

17. See above, introduction to chap. A7 and the preliminary remarks in this chapter.

18. In *Poetik und Hermeneutik VI*, p. 550.

19. Cf. ibid., pp. 547ff. My account of the process of reception as a back-and-forth movement between emotional identification and distancing has its correlate in the psychoanalytic description of aesthetic pleasure in Holland (1968), p. 202: "When literature pleases, it, too, lets us experience a disturbance, then master it, but the disturbance is a fantasy rather than an event or activity. This pattern of disturbance and mastery distinguishes our pleasure in play and literature from simple sensuous pleasures."

20. In *Poetik und Hermeneutik VI*, p. 550.

21. On this, see P. von Matt, *Literaturwissenschaft und Psychoanalyse* (Freiburg, 1972), chap. VII.

22. See above, chap. A1.

23. My book *Literaturgeschichte als Provokation* certainly still shares this one-sidedness with the evolutionary theory of the Russian formalists.

24. Ricoeur (1970), p. 175. He outlines in these terms the task of a psychoanalytic aesthetic that has not yet been undertaken: "But it is possible that this opposition between regression and progression is only true as a first approximation. Perhaps it will be necessary to transcend it, in spite of its apparent force. The work of art sets us on the pathway to new discoveries concerning the symbolic function and sublimation itself. Could it be that the true meaning of sublimation is to promote new meanings by mobilizing old energies initially invested in archaic figures?" P. von Matt also seeks to understand aesthetic experience in a dialectic of "beauty as spontaneous shock, and beauty as work of cognition" (*Literaturwissenschaft und Psychoanalyse*, p. 103).

25. Ricoeur (1970), pp. 521–22.

26. I refer to chapter VII, "Identification," in *Group Psychology and the Analysis of the Ego*, vol. XVIII, p. 106.

27. Ibid., p. 107.

28. According to K. Stierle, *Subjekt, Identität, Text – Zur Theorie der Lyrik*, in *Poetik und Hermeneutik VIII*, manuscript p. 23, the lyric subject is inherently a problematic subject: "it is a subject that searches its identity, that articulates itself lyrically in the movement of this search. For this reason, the classical themes of lyric poetry are those where identity is risked, such as love, death, self-reflection, experience of the socially unmediated other, especially of landscape."

29. It was Archibald MacLeish who established that the showing forth of a "universal analogy," especially in incidental situations, is constitutive for the lyric experience. Thus the poem "To His Coy Mistress" owes its fame less to being "a simple exercise in amorous rhetoric" than to the meaning Marvell creates: "The poem is more because constructed of a series of vivid figures which will not let it lie inert in the inanity of its apparent theme. But how can they prevent it from lying so? Because, like all such figures, they are two-legged creatures, and because they stand, in this poem, with one leg in the little amorous game and with the other in tragic life." *Poetry and Experience* (Boston: Houghton Mifflin, 1961), p. 85.

30. Holland, (1968), pp. 289ff.

31. Here, I follow the fundamental insights into the theory of play. See J. H. Huizinga, *Homo Ludens. A Study in the Play-Element in Culture* (Boston: Beacon Press, 1955), pp. 9–11.

32. Kuhn (1960), p. 73.

33. George Herbert Mead, *Mind, Self, and Society* (Chicago: University of Chicago Press, 1934), p. 151.

34. Additional comment by M. Fuhrmann.

35. Mead (1934), p. 138: "The importance of what we term 'communication' lies in the fact that it provides a form of behavior in which the organism or the individual may become an object to himself."

36. On this, see Huizinga, and S. Neumeister, *Das Spiel mit der höfischen Liebe*, Beihefte au Poetica, 5 (Munich, 1969).

37. On the effect and influence of Astrée, see M. Magendie, *Du nouveau sur l'Astrée* (Paris, 1927), pp. 424ff. The letter to d'Urfée is in H. Welti, *Die Astrée des H. d'Urfé und ihre deutschen Verehrer*, Zeitschrift für neufranzösische Sprache und Literatur 5 (1883), pp. 110ff. From the Middle Ages, the *Roman de Renart* would be an example. During the war against Frederick II which was waged in the Orient, (1228–43) Philippe de Novare assigned its animal characters as roles to friend and foe in order to create situations of conflict which could then be played out. See R. Bossuat, *Le roman de Renard* (Paris, 1957), pp. 155ff.

38. In Welti, ibid., p. 115.

39. For this, I refer the reader to the chapter "Die Überbrückung der Rampe" in Wellershoff (1976), pp. 11–27.

40. Wellershoff (ibid., p. 25) demonstrates this development in a discussion of Andy Warhol's idea of the video camera which made clear "that in the documentary doubling of reality, any and every resistance against it becomes ineffective."

41. Badt (1968), p. 103–40; here, especially pp. 135ff.

42. Freud, "Totem and Taboo," in *Works*, vol. XIII, p. 140.

43. Kant, *Critique of Judgment*, § 29.

44. Quoted by Fuhrmann (1973), p. 171, from Dionysius of Halicarnassus' "On Imitation."

45. Scheler, *Zur Ethik und Erkenntnislehre* (Berlin, 1933), vol. I, p. 170.

46. What is problematic about Scheler's five "models," the saint, the genius, the hero, the leading intellect of civilization, the artist of pleasure (corresponding to the fundamental values of the holy, intellectual values, the noble, the useful, and the pleasant, ibid., p. 157) need not be discussed here.

47. Ibid., p. 156.

48. Descartes, *Des passions de l'âme*, § 53–56.

49. Quoted from the *Pensées de Joubert* by Baldensperger, *La critique et l'histoire littéraires en France* (New York, 1945), p. 22.

50. Chateaubriand, *Atala, René . . . avec une notice de Sainte-Beuve*, bibliothèque française, vol. X (Berlin, n.d.), p. 4.

51. See Scheler, *Ethik und Erkenntnislehre*, p. 166: "In the form of the personal model, the past remains present, living, effective in the purest gold content of the moral values it contains."

52. Similarly in M. Halbwachs, *La mémoire collective*, 2nd ed. (Paris, 1968).

53. On this, see Lewis (1964), p. 181: "The story had, by long prescription, a status in the common imagination indistinguishable—at any rate, not distinguished—from that of fact. Everyone 'knew'—as we all 'know' how the ostrich hides her head in the sand—that the past contained Nine Worthies: three Pagans (Hector, Alexander, and Julius Cesar); three Jews (Joshua, David, and Judas Maccabeus); and three Christians (Arthus, Charlemagne, and Godfrey of Bouillon)."

54. Karl Marx, *Surveys from Exile. Political Writings*, vol. II, ed. and introduced by David Fernbach (New York: Vintage Books, 1974), p. 149.

55. In the classic text of this genre, the *Chanson de Roland*, Roland admonishes the frankish knights with the following words before they go into battle: "Or gart chascuns que

granz colps i empleit / Que malveise cancunc de li chantet ne seit!" (now let everyone see to it that he deal out big blows so that no bad song will be sung about him, ll. 1013ff.). The heroic song is origin and goal of this morality, as P. Zumthor observed with reference to this passage, see (1972), p. 325. According to the testimony of Wace, *Roman de Rou* (1160), ll. 8035ff., a certain Taillefer sang a cantilena Rolandi to the Norman army in the battle of Hastings (1066): "Taillefer, qui mult bien chantout / sor un cheval qui tost alout, / devant le duc alout chantant / De Karlemaigne et de Rolant / et d'Oliver et des vassals / qui moururent en Rencesvals." (Taillerfer, who sang very well, went out straight forward on a steed before the duke and was about to sing of Charlemagne, Roland, Oliver, and of many a vassal who died in Roncesval.)

56. "Le thème général et commun des chansons de geste, par opposition aux chansons de saint, est . . . l'émerveillement suscité dans la communauté humaine par la reonnaissance de son pouvoir d'agir" (The general and common theme of the chansons de geste, as opposed to the hagiographic songs, is the marveling aroused in the human community by the recognition of its capacity to act; Zumthor [1972], p. 324.)

57. On this, see E. Köhler, *Ideal und Wirklichkeit in der höfischen Epik* (Tübingen, 1956) and #4 of the *Studia romanica* on the *Chanson de geste und höfischer Roman* (Heidelberg, 1963).

58. Johannes of Salisbury, *Liber de Confessione* PL CCVII, 1088.

59. On this, see Hartman (1975), p. 250.

60. Lessing, *Hamburgische Dramaturgie*, 75. Stück.

61. On what follows, see U. Ebel, *Das altromanische Mirakel: Ursprung und Geschichte einer literarischen Gattung*, Studia Romanica 8 (Heidelberg, 1965).

62. André Jolles's well-known definition of the vita as virtue incarnate, which I am adopting here, leaves active *imitatio* little scope even if one tries to solve the dilemma of the imitation of something unattainably perfect by partial or gradual imitation, as U. Ebel has done (p. 53).

63. Etienne de Fougere, *Livre des manières*, ll. 1130–32: "Tecle fuit saive et Marguerite / Et meinte autre feme petite / Qui entre nos encore habite." (Tecla was saved, and Margaret and many other little ladies who are still living with us.)

64. Quoted from L. Struss, *Epische Idealität und historische Realität—Der Albigenserkreuzzug und die Krise der Zeitgeschichtsdarstellung in der occitanischen, altfranzösischen und lateinischen Historiographie*, dissertation (Constance, 1975). Struss first recognized the testimonial value of this passage and showed its importance in the literary and social-historical context. Lines 4195–4201 read as follows:

> Mais de ço que tantes genz virent
> E qu'il meismes le soffrirent,
> Cil de l'ost d'Acre, les meschiefs
> Qu'il orent es cuers e es chiefs
> Des granz chalors, des granz freidures,
> Des enfermetez, des enjures,
> Ço vo puis jo por veir conter.

(But of that which so many saw, and of what too they had to suffer, that of the army of Acre, the evils they had in their hearts and souls, of the hottest wrath, of the coldest fury, of infirmities, of injuries, things I could never bear to tell.)

65. Lessing, letter to Friedrich Nicolai, November 1756.

66. Ibid.

67. Lessing, letter to Moses Mendelsohn, December 18, 1756.

68. Lessing, letter to Moses Mendelsohn, November 28, 1756.

69. Discussed and documented in greater detail in Jauss (1961), pp. 388ff.

70. Ibid., p. 391. In the history of the concept, this development shows up soon hereafter in Herder's philosophy of history: "in a certain sense, every human perfection is thus national, secular, and, if looked at very closely, individual" (*Auch eine Philosophie der Geschichte zur Bildung der Menschheit*, 1774, Erster Abschnitt, II).

71. Rousseau, *Emile, Oeuvres complètes*, (éd. de la Pléiade), vol. IV, p. 535.

72. On this, see Neuschäfer (1976). Baudelaire's comment on the popularity of biography ("l'immense appétit que nous avons pour les biographies naît d'un sentiment profond de l'égalite," the immense appetite we have for biographies is born of a profound feeling of equality, 1951, p. 954) also documents what Neuschäfer's interpretations demonstrate, namely that the unprecedented effect on large masses of readers of this early commercialized literature cannot simply be explained by the ideological manipulation of needs.

73. Preisendanz (1963), esp. p. 17; further developed in *Wege des Realismus* (1977).

74. Neuschäfer (1976), chap. 3.

75. Ibid., pp. 85–86.

76. In greater detail in Jauss (1970), pp. 203ff.

77. According to Fuhrmann (1973), p. 65.

78. Schiller, *Über naive und sentimentalische Dichtung*, S.W., Cotta, vol. 4, p. 677.

79. Kommerell (1957), p. 201.

80. Schiller, *Über das Pathetische*, S.W., Cotta, vol. 4, p. 513.

81. See above, p. 99.

82. Guiette (1960), pp. 61ff.

83. See above, p. 156f.

84. See above, p. 4.

85. Guiette (1960), pp. 9–32; also Jauss (1977), pp. 411–27 (in what follows, I use findings from that essay).

86. According to E. Vance, "Le combat érotique chez Chrétien de Troyes," in *Poetique* 12 (1972), p. 548.

87. According to D. Harth, "Romane und ihre Leser," in *Germanisch-romanische Monatsschrift* 20 (1970), pp. 159–79.

88. The famous thesis: "the jurisdiction of the stage begins where the sphere of secular law ends" from Schiller's *Die Schaubünne als eine moralische Anstalt betrachtet* of 1784 (S.W., Cotta, vol. 11, p. 91) has its correlate in the passage from the introduction to *Der Verbrecher aus verlorener Ehre* of 1786, quoted below.

89. "Et voilà, chretiens, ce qui est arrivé, lorsque des esprits profanes, et bien éloignés de vouloir entrer dans les intérêts de Dieu, ont entrepris de censurer l'hypocrisie, non point pour en réformer l'abus, ce qui n'est pas de leur ressort, mais pour en faire une espèce de diversion dont le libertinage put profiter, en concevant et faisant concevoir d'injustes soupçons de la vraie piété par de malignes représentations de la fausse" (quoted in Hervieux [1911], p. 332). (And here is what happened, Christians, when profane spirits who are far from making the interests of God their own undertake to censure hypocrisy, not to reform it for that is not within their purview, but to turn it into a kind of diversion from which free-thinking could profit. This they accomplished by conceiving and causing others to conceive unjust suspicions of true piety by giving a malignant impression and representation of what false piety is like.)

90. See above, p. 40.

91. Paris, 1879, p. 127.

92. With reference to Molière, Ritter (1940) based his well-known thesis on the interpretation of W. Krauss (1949), who saw that the ambivalent effect of the comic characters derived from the fact that superficially they demonstrate what is ridiculous in a conduct that violates social norms but that behind this facade they actually call into question society's claim that it is natural for things to be as they are.

93. Hegel, *Aesthetics*, vol. II, p. 1234.

94. Warning, "Komik und Komödie als Positivierung von Negativität," in *Poetik und Hermeneutik VI*, pp. 341–57.

95. In what follows, I have chosen examples from medieval literature. As regards the later humanistic tradition, I refer the reader to my interpretation of the Vergil travesty in essay C, chap. 2.

96. In greater detail in Jauss (1959), pp. 97ff.

97. See ibid., pp. 226ff.

98. The process of sympathetic identification is programmed into the story, as it were, as can be observed in the passages that mention the growing circle of solidarty. See *Lancelot* ll. 1817, 2212, 2594–606, 2736, 2722, and others.

99. On this, see Jauss (1977), I chap. 7 (animal poetry as threshold to individuation), II, and III (on *Rainaldo e Lesengrino*, an Italian epigone who thematizes the irreconcilability of the old feudal world and the unheroic modern ideal of earning a living. In this last picaresque story, old Renart must work on the field and is cheated out of the reward for his labors by the goat).

100. R. Warning, "Opposition und Kasus – Zur leserrolle in Diderots Jacques le Fataliste et son maitre," in Warning (1975), p. 471.

101.
        C'est l'ENNUI! – l'oeil chargé d'un involontaire
        Il rêve d'échafauds en fumant son houka.
        Tu le connais, lecteur, ce monstre délicat,
        -Hypocrite lecteur, -mon semblable, -mon frère!

102. "For now one no longer witnesses the restoration of a temporarily disturbed order but a surprising change whose extent cannot be gauged." D. Wellershoff on the detective stories of Patricia Highsmith, in "Vorübergehende Entwirklichung-Zur Theorie des Kriminalromans," in Wellershoff (1973), p. 112.

103. The same, ibid., p. 125.

104. Starobinski (1970), p. 57: "Quand l'écart est à la mode, quand il est lui-même devenue tradition, l'auteur du 'Grand Ecart' ne dévie guère: c'est Antonin Artaud, volens nolens, qui fait figure de héros litteraire. . . . Encore le succès d'Artaud, la facon dont il a été accepté comme chaman de notre epoque, les commentaires dont il est entouré tendraient-ils à prouver que le scandale de son apparition correspondait à une attente assez généralement éprouvée." (When deviation is fashionable, when it has itself become tradition, the author of the "Great Deviation" hardly deviates . . . nolens volens, it is Antonin Artaud who is playing the role of literary hero. . . . Yet Artaud's success, the way he has been accepted as the shaman of our period, and the commentaries about him would appear to prove that the scandal of his appearance corresponded to an expectation that was rather generally felt.)

105. Cf. Wellershoff (1973), p. 48: "The white rustling is another borderline case of poetic indefiniteness. That's what happens when as the final stage of the reduction processes of concrete poetry, there remains nothing more than a contextless, unreflected word on the surface. . . . Here, indefiniteness passes over into emptiness, becomes the all and nothing of mystic absorption."

106. I found out about this radio play of the "Süddeutsche Rundfunk" in D. Harth, "Romane und ihre Lesser," pp. 159ff.

C. On why the comic hero amuses

1. "Jokes and Their Relation to the Unconcious," in *The Standard Edition of the Complete Psychological Works*, ed. James Strachey (London: Hogarth Press, 1962), vol. VIII, p. 195. (All quotations from Freud are taken from this edition.)

2. Ibid., p. 194.

3. Ibid., p. 195.

4. Freud, "Psychopathic Characters on the Stage," in *Works*, vol. VII, p. 306.

5. Freud, "Writers and Day-dreaming," in *Works*, vol. IX, p. 153.

6. See above, essay B, chap. 2b.

7. T. Verweyen, *Eine Theorie der Parodie* (Munich, 1973).

8. E. Rotermund, *Die Parodie in der modernen deutschen Lyrik* (Munich, 1963), p. 8. In his understanding of parody which E. R. develops on the basis of Goethe's well-known remark about Wieland, I see an alternative definition of the parodistic style which retains its specific justification alongside that of Verweyen, who sees parody as critical imitation.

9. Verweyen, *Theorie der Parodie*, pp. 67, 84: "to understand (parody) not as the critical reference to their reception as paradigms of communicative interaction."

10. The degree to which such comic can be enjoyed does not necessarily depend on a person's knowledge of literary history if the later reader can himself infer the negated ideals and norms of action from the text. One need only call to mind *Don Quixote* which makes available to us in its near-totality the "code" of forgotten chivalric romances.

11. Freud, *Works*, vol. VIII, p. 202.

12. Ibid., p. 200.

13. Baudelaire, "De l'essence du rire" (1852), éd. de la Pléiade, p. 711. English version in text is from *Charles Baudelaire, The Painter of Modern Life and Other Essays*, trans. Jonathan Mayne (London: Phaidon Press, 1946), p. 156.

14. "Le rire est l'expression de l'idee de superiorité, non plus de l'homme sur l'homme, mais de l'homme sur la nature," éd. de la Pléiade, p. 712.

15. Quotes from Mikhail Bakhtin, *Rabelais and His World*, trans. Helene Iswolsky (Cambridge: M.I.T. Press, 1968).

16. Ibid., p. 88.

17. Hegel, *Aesthetics*, vol. II, p. 1220.

18. Ibid., vol. II, p. 1234.

19. Ibid., vol. II, p. 1200.

20. "Humor," in *Works*, vol. XXI, p. 162.

21. Ibid., p. 166.

22. Stackelberg, *Literarische Rezeptionsformen* (1972), p. 168.

23. Gillot, "L'Iliade travestie—Un étrange divertissement," in *La Regence*, Colloque d'Aix-en-Provence, 1970, p. 190.

24. Paul Scarron, *Oeuvres*, réimpression de l'édition de Paris 1786 (Geneve, 1970), vol. 4 (I-VIII), vol. 5 (VIII-XII by Moreau de Brasei); the following quotations are identified by roman numeral and page number.

25. Quoted from the edition by F. Bobertag (Berlin & Stuttgart, 1890) *Dt. Nat.-Lit*, vol. 141. The continuation by C. W. F. Schaber from A. Blumauer, *Gesammelte Werke* (Wien, 1882), vol. 3. In what follows, I have used a seminar paper by B. Steinwachs. I am grateful to the participants for their stimulating suggestions that were made in the course of this seminar on the epic hero which I gave jointly with Manfred Fuhrmann during the summer of 1973 at Constance University.

26. Cf. p. 212:

> Was weiter jetzo folgt, geschah
> Durch lauter lose Kniffe,
> Durch närrische Mirakula,
> Der Götter eig'ne Pfiffe,
> Denn wenn ein Gott nicht haben will,
> Dass ihm ein Laie seh' ins Spiel,
> Macht er ein'n blauen Nebel.

(The rest that follows now occurred through sheer trickery, through puckish miracles, the Gods' own ruses, for when a God does not want a layman looking into his cards, he creates a blue fog.)

27. v. Stackelberg (1972), p. 184.

28. Quoted and commented in J. v. Stackelberg, *Von Rabelais bis Voltaire – Zur Geschichte des französischen Romans* (Munich, 1970), p. 273.

29. According to Bakhtin, *Rabelais and His World*, pp. 9-11.

30. See the review by S. Jüttner, *Romanistisches Jahrbuch* 23 (1972), pp. 243-49.

31. *Pantagruel*, chap. xxx. All English quotations in text are from the translation by Jacques Le Clercq (New York: Modern Library, n.d.).

32. See J. v. Stackelberg, *Von Rabelais bis Voltaire*, pp. 46ff. whose Rabelais chapter paradigmatically represents present research results.

33. The relevant interpretation in the chapter "La faim et la soif" by Michel Butor and Denis Hollier, *Rabelais ou c'était pour rire* (Paris, 1972), pp. 112ff. here also correctly emphasizes the overlapping in the relationship between father and son: "Pantraguel qui règne sur les altérés, dont l'emblème est le sel, est fils de Gargantua qui règne sur ceux qui se restaurent . . . " (Pantagruel who reigns over the Thirsties, whose emblem is salt, is the son of Gargantua who reigns over those who are refreshed, p. 117).

34. Bakhtin, *Rabelais and His World*, p. 88.

35. v. Stackelberg, *Von Rabelais bis Voltaire*, p. 48.

36. *Rabelais – Jeu dramatique en deux parties tiré des cinq livres de Francois Rabelais* (Paris, 1968), pp. 36-37 with the stage direction: "Tableau burlesque de la crucification . . . Le Calvaire: espèce de tableau grouillant, passablement choquant mais sauvé par la Joie et la jeunesse véritables" (A burlesque picture of the Crucifixion . . . the Calvary: a sort of swarming picture, somewhat shocking but saved by true Joy and youth).

37. Bakhtin, *Rabelais and His World*, p. 26.

38. *Das Zitat in der Erzählkunst* (Stuttgart, 1961), p. 47.

39. According to Bakhtin, *Rabelais and His World*, p. 23.

40. Auerbach (1953), pp. 262ff.

41. Bakhtin, *Rabelais and His World*, p. 92.

42. Ibid., p. 89.

43. Ibid., p. 39.

44. Cf. Butor-Hollier, *Rabelais*, p. 10: "Le rire de Rabelais est en grande partie un superbe déguisement pour essayer de détourner les ennemies, brouiller les pistes, éviter les censures si terribles alors." (In large part, Rabelais's laughter is a superb disguise which attempts to side-track his enemies, to cover his tracks, and to avoid the censorship which was so severe in those days.)

45. Some of the *caractères* of La Bruyère, as for example "Le fleuriste" and other "genres de curieux" (De la mode) belong here. But the satiric or social-critical intent in most cases overshadows the portrayal of the characters, and this is equally true in Molière's comic figures who lack the innocence of naive *humors*.

46. Quoted from *The New Oxford Illustrated Dickens* (London, 1964).

47. The extremely shrewd Mr. Jingle, a literary ancestor of Felix Krull, confidence man, goes the three Pickwickians and their arrogated roles one better at their very first encounter: "'My friend Mr. Snodgrass has a strong poetic turn,' said Mr. Pickwick. 'So have I,' said the stranger, 'Epic poem – ten thousand lines – revolution of July – composed it on the spot – Mars by day, Apollo by night – bang the fieldpiece, twang the lyre'" (p. 11).

48. On the comic of the pair, see J. Huizinga's essay on Rosencrantz and Guildenstern in *Jahrbuch der deutschen Shakespeare-Gesellschaft* 46 (Berlin, 1910), pp. 60-86; revised version in *Wege der Kulturgeschichte* (1930).

49. *Works*, vol. XXI, p. 162.

50. A part of this is the humoristic hero's ability to laugh at himself. As when he proposes to bring action against Captain Baldwig for false imprisonment and is kept from this by Mr. Wardle "because they might turn around on some of us, and say we had taken too much cold punch. Do what he would, a smile would come into Mr. Pickwick's face; the smile extended into a laugh; the laugh into a roar; the roar became general" (p. 261).

51. But meeting the confidence man Mr. Jingle again in Fleet prison does not come up to the level of poetic justice: his misery furnishes Mr. Pickwick an occasion for an act of generosity. At the end, the two lawyers Dodson and Fogg remain on the side of unpunished evil.

52. "Character and Consciousness," in *New Literary History* V (1974), pp. 225-35.

53. *Aesthetics*, vol. I, p. 591.

54. Krauss (1949), p. 18.

55. In a new interpretation of *Jacques le Fataliste*, R. Warning has shown the relevance of Diderot's relation to a tradition that goes back to Plato's *Republic* and which was still known to and through Hobbes and Leibniz. It defines the relationship between master and servant by allocating reason on the basis of class. See "Opposition und Kasus — Zur Leserrolle in Diderots *Jacques le Fataliste et son maître*," in Warning (1975), p. 475.

56. Cf. chap. 39: "I never see such a fine creetur in my days. Blessed if I don't think his heart must ha' been born five-and-twenty year arter his body, at least" (p. 556).

D. On the question of the "structural unity" of older and modern lyric poetry

1. Malraux (1951), p. 275.

2. Friedrich, (1956).

3. Burger, "Von der Struktureinheit klassischer und moderner deutscher Lyrik," in *Festschrift für Franz Rolf Schröder* (Heidelberg, 1959), pp. 229-40.

4. Ibid., p. 229.

5. Ibid., p. 230.

6. Cf. ibid., p. 230: "But to create a new world in and through language also means that an existing one is destroyed or 'sublated' in Hegel's sense. It is certainly burst open."

7. Ibid.

8. Ibid., p. 231.

9. Hocke, *Manierismus in der Literatur*, Rowohlts Deutsche Enzykopädie vol. 82/83 (Hamburg, 1959).

10. We will return to this matter at the end of the essay.

11. According to Paul Robert, *Dictionnaire alphabétique et analogique de la langue française* (Paris, 1951), *étrangeté*.

12. Hocke, *Manierismus*, p. 272.

13. "De même qu'il avait demontré que le refrain est susceptible d'applications infiniment variées, il a aussi cherché à rajeunir, à redoubler le plaisir de la rime en y ajoutant cet élément inattendu, l'*étrangeté*, qui est comme le condiment indispensable de toute beauté." The emphasis is Baudelaire's, which suggests that he thought the word had a new meaning when applied to poetics. Although it is true that that meaning cannot as yet be understood as the precise French correlate of *estrangement* or *alienation*, the combination of *ajouter* . . . *l'étrangeté* goes beyond the narrower meaning of *strangeness* which refers to a state.

14. Baudelaire, *Oeuvres Complètes*, ed. de la NRF, t.X (Paris, 1928), p. 29. English version in text is from the Lois Boe Hyslop and Francis E. Hyslop translation, *Baudelaire as a Literary Critic*, (University Park, Pa.: Pennsylvania State University Press, 1964), p. 134.

15. Cf. Hocke, *Manierismus*, p. 70.

16. After Théophile's death in 1626, between 1631 and 1650, his work went through at least twenty-five editions, and through eleven between 1651 and 1660. On this, see D. Mornet, *Histoire de la littérature française classique* (de 1660 à 1700) (Paris, 1940).

17. Gide, *Anthologie de la poésie française*, éd. de la Pléiade (Paris, 1949), preface, p. 8.

18. Ibid., p. 9.

19. Ibid., p. 11.

20. Ibid., p. 10.

21. *Anthologie* . . . pp. 300ff. In what follows, the text chosen by Gide is in italics. Quotations are from Théophile de Viau, *Oeuvres poétiques*, Seconde et Troisième Parties, ed. Jeanne Streicher (Geneva/Paris, 1958). Ode III is printed there on pp. 147–51. The other nine odes of the *Maison de Silvie* will be identified by roman numeral (for number of ode) and arabic (for line of verse). R. A. Sayce's objections to this edition raised in his review (*French Studies* 13 [1959], p. 267ff.), do not have a direct bearing on our concern. On the dating of the odes, some of which were written in Chantilly (ode III), some in prison, and which were published in September 1624, see A. Adam, *Théophile de Viau et la libre pensée française en 1620* (Paris, 1935), p. 391.

22. This dissolution of objects and beings becomes visible in stanzas v to viii in part because after immersing their "jeunes corps qui bouillent" in the "humidité des eaux" (ll. 49 to 50), the bathing amourettes no longer present themselves in their entire contours but only through their movement or in a *pars pro toto* impression. The following sequence of images results: the gesture of drinking (l. 52), the reflection of their "whiteness" in the water (ll. 53–54), the movement of the swimmers "dans les ondes qu'il vont fendants" (l. 57), the contrast of their skin color and the disappearance of their shadows in the water (ll. 61ff.), the water breaking against their shoulders (ll. 71–72), their glances (l. 76), and their hair, floating on the waves (l. 77).

23. See H. Lützeler, "Bedeutung und Grenze abstrakter Malerei," in *Jahrbuch für Ästhetik und allg. Kunstwissenschaft*, vol. III (1955–57), pp. 1–35, esp. pp. 4ff., on the beginnings of modern painting in Monet, Seurat, and Cézanne: "It is common to all three schools of modern art that they accord less importance to the object than the form: they all want to stop being descriptive, representational." On the concurrent detachment of the novel from the epic fable in Flaubert's "roman sans sujet," see Jauss, *Heidelberger Jahrbücher* 2 (1958), pp. 101ff.

24. "This close union of word and sound in Marino's sense was the stimulus for the lyrical 'musicisme' which gave rise to 'abstract,' 'evocative' poetry from Baudelaire via Rimbaud and Mallarmé to Joyce. It was that poetry which wished to create in the reader certain states of consciousness by the mere sound of the language, and without a concern for information or content." Hocke, *Manierismus*, p. 182.

25. See W. Benjamin, "The Work of Art in the Age of Mechanical Reproduction," in *Illuminations*, esp. pp. 233–34, and the examples in Malraux (1951), pp. 23ff.

26. Hocke, *Manierismus*, p. 89.

27. In his comments on the ode "Le Matin," G. Hess already showed (1953, p. 12) that the so-called realism of Théophile's landscape painting lacks a unified perspective, "a characteristic feature of modern literature."

28. The incoherence is increased even further by the change in terms used for the grammatical subject. Thus, one cannot immediately tell, for example, that "les oyseaux" (l. 31) mean "les Cygnes" (l. 23) since the preceding sentence (ll. 25–30) no longer referred to the swans. "Leur," in l. 71, similarly does not connect with "ses estoilles nues" (l. 70) as might have been expected but—again skipping the preceding sentence—with 'ils" (l. 62), which means ultimately with "mill' amours" (l. 47).

29. The unity of images within the stanzas is further strengthened by the "classical" symmetry of their outer form. As a result of the rhyme scheme (abab cc deed), we get a

rising movement to the two middle verses (cc) which emerge as an articulative climax but which also function as a "pivot" because they regularly form a syntactic unit with the following lines whose falling movement is given a tension of its own by the delayed end rhyme.

30. "Là," ll. 21, 31; "en," l. 61; "et," l. 81.

31. His favorite haunts were still the pools and spreading lakes; and, hating fire, he chose the water for his home, as the opposite of flame. The Sandys' translation is cited in the text.

32. On this, see J. Rousset, *La Littérature de l'age baroque en France* (Paris, 1953), esp. p. 76: "One can see that in the France of that period, people not only had a taste for the composite and transformations but that there were elements of an aesthetic of composites and transformation which existed parallel to, and often mixed in with, more 'classical' currents." On the conception of the ode before 1660, see D. Mornet, *Histoire de la littérature française classique*, pp. 84ff., and p. 13: "for a long time, the ode was no more than a poem written in stanzas, using a meter which was not regularly Alexandrines and whose subjects could be lyrical, narrative, realistic, even simple 'galimatias,' it didn't matter."

33. It would be engaging to pursue this principle in its stylistic change through time. On La Fontaine, who raised the play of *diversité* to a motto, see, in this connection, E. Loos, "Die Gattung des 'Conte' und das Publikum im 18. Jahrhundert," in *Romanische Forschungten* (1959), p. 120.

34. In the tenth ode, Théophile wrote a variation on this notion by introducing the book-topos:

> Ces lieux si beaux et si divers
> Meritent chacun tous les vers
> Que je dois à tout le volume
>
> (ll. 5-7)
>
> Chaque fueille, et chaque couleur
> Dont Nature a marqué ces marbres
> Merite tout un livre à part,
> Aussi bien que chaque regard
> Dont Silvie a touché ces arbres
>
> (ll. 16-20)

(These places so comely and diverse, merit each, all the verse I owe to the whole volume. Every leaf, and every color with Nature marked these marbles is worth yet another book, and so is every look with which Silvie touched these trees.)

35. With *beau désordre* we refer to the well-known verse which Boileau later used to define the genre of the ode: "chez elle, un beau désordre est un effet de l'art" (in it, a comely disorder is an effect of art, *Art poétique*, II, 72).

36. According to R. Lebègue in his judgment of Théophile's odes, in *La poésie française de 1560 à 1630* (Paris, 1951), vol. II, p. 112.

37. G. R. Hocke, *Manierismus*, p. 30; on deliberate obscurity, see pp. 18ff., 26, 32.

38. According to J. Tortel, "Quelques constantes du lyrisme préclassique," in *Le préclassicisme français* (Paris, 1952), p. 126.

39. On this procedure, see D. Mornet, *Histoire de la littérature française classique*, p. 13: "In his *Descriptions poétique* (1649), P. de Bussieres still feels that 'description,' even in the form of an ode, is not subject to the rules of bienséance and 'has no law other than the vigor of its flashes of wit.'" But this contemporary view does not preclude the possibility that even the apparent arbitrariness of the 'ode descriptive' may have its implicit poetics which in turn need not be identical with the rhetorical tradition of 'descriptio.'" (On this, see H. Lausberg, *Elemente der literarischen Rhetorik* [Munich, 1949], pp. 73-76.) For the oratorical order "proposition, demonstratio, conclusio" which Théophile employs in his "Ode à Cloris" is absent from Ode III (see D. Mornet, *Histoire de la clarté française* [Paris, 1929], p. 173).

40. J. Tortel, "Quelques constantes du lyrisme préclassique," p. 148.

41. The concept "Bildfeld" (translated as "image-field" in the text), which presupposes a "supraindividual world of images as the objective, material store of metaphors of a community," was introduced by H. Weinrich in the study "Münze und Wort" and given a methodological underpinning. (In *Romanica, Festschrift für G. Rohlfs* [Halle, 1958], pp. 508-21.) The passages discussed below are revelatory also because some of them embody a precious exaggeration of the tradition Weinrich pointed to ("impress" is paradoxically used with reference to something liquid).

42. "Basically, concetti or conceits are metaphors of concepts or ideas. What does that mean? The metaphor is seen as a surprising 'concordia discors' of images. The 'concetto' brings a surprising concordia discors of ideas. In both cases, extremes are united" (Hocke, *Manierismus*, p. 152). The quoted stanza confirms a distinction J. Rousset made between the baroque and the precious style: "The water of a baroque poet is the image of metamorphoses, of ebb and flow, of a world of movement. The water of the precious poet is of crystal or drinkable silver. . . . When the Baroque immobilizes and geometricizes itself, it tends toward the precious" (*La Littérature*, p. 242). That the quoted passage is typical of Théophile could be amply documented by the image of the water's surface which informs the *Maison de Silvie* like a leitmotif.

43. On the following also I, 65-70, IX, 68ff.

44. VII, 11-20; compare ll. 21-30, esp. 25-27:

> Elle donne le mouvement
> Et le siege à chaque element,
> Et selon que Dieu l'authorise.

(She gives the movement and the setting for every element according to how God ordains them.)

45. This corresponds with the rejection of Apollo and the muses which is characteristic of Théophile's motto "Il faut écrire à la moderne" (in ode I). The poet wishes to be inspired by the higher power of the Christian god.

46. Tortel, "Quelques constantes du lyrisme préclassique," p. 138.

47. Macon, *Chantilly et le Musée Condé* (Paris, 1910). See the summary of the editor in her "notice" on the *Maison de Silvie* (p. 134 of the edition used here).

48. From the memoirs of Lord Herbert of Cherbury, quoted by G. Macon, *Chantilly*, p. 58.

49. Ibid., p. 36.

50. Ibid., p. 59.

51. Ibid., p. 60.

52. Ibid., p. 71.

53. This is the necessary other side of J. Tortel's one-sided judgment: "the preclassical lyric never transforms the dream into life. True life is not dreamt life, for the dream itself is a reality. Things exist. The world is inhabited by human beings. The fields are there to be harvested, the woman, to be possessed in love . . . " ("Quelques constantes du lyrisme préclassique," p. 139).

54. Simply mentioned by J. Streicher in her "Notice" (Théophile de Viau's *Oeuvres poétique*, p. 135). On the tapestries at Chantilly, also see G. Macon, *Chantilly*, pp. 38, 58. The author quotes on p. 35 that "trois de votre tapisserie du Microcosme" (three of your tapestry of the Microcosm) were finished. It would still have to be determined whether Théophile's *Maison de Silvie* perhaps also referred to this Orbis pictus tapissery. The following passages in the *Maison de Silvie* could refer to pictorial representations of Ovid's *Metamophoses*: Orpheus (I, 78-80), Diana and Acteon (II, 51-57), Melicertes (III, 21-24, 92-94; IV, 131-34), Scylla (III, 35-40), Phaeton and Cygnus (III, 85ff.), Morpheus (V, 71), Aurora (VI, 36-40; VII, 47-54), Narcissus (VI, 45-64), Philomela (VIII).

55. Quoted bỹ A. Adam, *Théophile de Viau*, p. 234; on Théophile's poetological theory, see up to p. 235.

56. For example, in the "Lettre de Théophile à son frere," pp. 185-97 in our edition.

57. Cf. VIII, 96-100 (and the evocation following these verses):

Je ne scay quelle molle erreur
Parmy tous ces objects funebres
Me tire tousjours au plaisir,
Et mon oeil qui suit mon desir
Void Chantilly dans ces tenebres.

(I don't know by what wrongful weakness I am ever drawn, even among all these funereal objects, to pleasure; and my eye, in the wake of my desire, sees Chantilly in these shadows.)

58. The substitutability of these identifications is especially marked in the next to last stanza of ode IV (ll. 91-100) against which A. Adam unjustifiably objected because he failed to see this principle at work ("Si quelqu'un comprend quelque chose à ce galimatis, qu'il le dise," If anyone understands something in this gibberish, let him speak up, *Théophile de Viau*, p. 358, note 6). Just as at the beginning of this ode, Phaeton suddenly comes in through "Pour avoir aymé ce garçon" (For having loved this boy, l. 21) (here, the poet speaks of himself in the third person), after which the poet suddenly switches to the first person in the same stanza ("Mon coeur n'a point passé ma rime," My rhyme did not pass through my heart, l. 30), which he retains in what follows (cf. ll. 63, 80, 84, 88); the inverse switch from poet (ll. 91, 97) to Damon (l. 100) occurs at the end of the ode. This means that we have a change from the biographical "I" that justifies his friendship with Des Barreaux, to his mythological personification, which corresponds to his role in the dream Thyrsis (Des Barreaux) tells in ode V. Such mythological transpositions are so natural to Théophile that he never goes to the trouble of giving reasons for them.

59. According to Du Bellay, quoted by R. J. Clements, *Critical Theory and Practice of the Pleiade*, Harvard Studies in Romance Languages, XVIII (Cambridge, Mass.: Harvard University Press, 1942) p. xvi; cf. p. 158.

60. See following page of text.

61. Although it is true that Thyrsis (Des Barreaux) also has the gift of prophecy (cf. IV, 91-94), it is no longer expressly brought into connection with the Cygnus theme. The verses: "Et de qui les soins amoureux / Ont fait ainsi blanchir la plume" (And of whom the loving needs thus made my plumes whiten; III, 83ff.) are distantly reminiscent of Du Bellay's poem *Aux Dames Angevines* in which the poet, a worshiper of women, compares himself with a swan whose plumage is beginning to turn white, like that of Apollo's birds (quoted by Clements, *Critical Theory and Practice*, p. 162).

62. Here we have a further reason for assuming that the representation of the *Metamorphoses* on the tapestries in Chantilly was one of the principal sources of his inspiration.

63. On Théophile's trial, see in this connection A. Adam, *Théophile de Viau*, pp. 356ff.

64. On this break with the tradition of the lyric poetry of the Renaissance, see J. Tortel, "Quelques constantes du lyrisme préclassique," p. 150.

65. Quoted by Clements, *Critical Theory and Practice*, p. 159.

66. "The Poetic Treatment of a Platonic-Christian Theme," now in Spitzer (1959), p. 130.

67. On Icarus as the mythological counterimage to the Platonic parable about the wings of the soul (Phaedon), see Spitzer (1959), p. 144, note 1.

68. According to Spitzer (1959), pp. 134ff.

69. Cf. Spitzer (1959), p. 141.

70. Phaedon 84e/85. Translation in text is from *The Complete Dialogues of Plato*, ed. Edith Hamilton and Huntington Cairns (New York: Pantheon Books, 1961), p. 67.

71. Quoted from Clements, *Critical Theory and Practice*, p. 152.

72. That the white plumage should turn into a black that penetrates everywhere (last stanza, ode III) is probably to be traced to the black bile (*bilis innaturalis* or *atra*), the element of the melancholy temper.

73. According to J. Tortle, "Quelques constantes du lyrisme préclassique," p. 157: "But here, Théophile is at one with his contemporaries: the dislocation of the universe, the only end to the will to live, is something they all think about, they all foresee, they all prepare for, as they expect, and prepare to, die." See also the texts, pp. 360-69, dealing with "l'attente du verdict."

74. Diderot, *Oeuvres esthetiques*, ed. P. Vernier, (Paris, 1959), p. 402.

75. Baudelaire (1951), p. 1188.

76. The passage quoted is in the essay on Théophile Gautier and attacks Victor Cousin's well-known treatise: "Du vrai, du beau et du bien" (1818). (There was a new edition with this title in 1836.) (See Baudelaire [1951], p. 1021.) Concerning the further disagreements with Platonism, see especially the "Notes nouvelles sur Edgar Poe," the "Salon de 1859," and "Le peintre de la vie moderne." We quote another passage here which makes clear the break with Diderot: "Most of the errors about beauty spring from the eighteenth century's false conception of morality. At that time, nature was considered as the basic source and type of every possible form of the good and the beautiful" (Hyslop translation, p. 297).

77. Hess (1953), chap II: "Dichten und Malen."

78. Hess (1953), p. 39; Baudelaire's poem "le Cygne" is quoted from the critical edition of the *Fleurs du Mal*, 2nd ed., ed. Crepet-Blin (Paris, 1950), pp. 95-97 (with extensive commentary, pp. 448-52). English version in text is from *Charles Baudelaire, The Flowers of Evil*, a selection edited by Marthiel and Jackson Mathews (New York: New Directions, 1955), pp. 79-82, translation by F. P. Sturm.

79. On the relation between rhythm and image, also see the comments by A. Nisin in his noteworthy attempt at writing a modern poetics from the reader's perspective (1959), esp. pp. 114ff.

80. The famous passage from the first "Projet de Préface pour les Fleurs du Mal," from which we quote here, characteristically puts the anti-Platonic severance of the beautiful from the good at the very beginning of the definition of poetry: "What is poetry, what its purpose? It is about the difference between the good and the beautiful; of beauty in evil, that rhythm and rhyme respond in man to the immortal needs of monotony, symmetry and surprise . . ." (1951), p. 1363.

81. Baudelaire, *Notes nouvelles sur Edgar Poe* (1951), p. 29.

82. According to Friedrich (1956), p. 41.

83. "Imagination decomposes all creation, and with the raw materials accumulated and disposed in accordance with rules whose origin one cannot find save in the furthest depths of the soul, it creates a new world, it produces the sensation of newness," from *Art in Paris, 1845-1862, reviewed by Charles Baudelaire*, trans. and ed. Jonathan Mayne (New York: Phaidon, 1965), p. 156. ("L'imagination décompose toute la création, et, avec les materiaux amassés et desposés suivant des règles dont on ne peut trouver l'origine que dans le plus profond de l'âme, elle crée un monde nouveau, elle produit la sensation du neuf," from "Le Salon de 1859" [1951]. p. 765.)

84. Here, our interpretation agrees with that in J.-D. Hubert, *L'esthétique des 'Fleurs du Mal'—Essai sur l'ambiguité poétique* (Geneva, 1953), pp. 98-101. Since two other rather extensive interpretations of the poem that have come to my knowledge pursue other goals, I believe I need not discuss them. See R.-B. Chérix, *Essai d'une critique integrale—Commentaire des 'Fleurs du Mal'* (Geneva, 1949), pp. 323-27; and J. Prévost, *Baudelaire—Essai sur l'inspiration et la création poétique* (Paris, 1953), pp. 114-17.

85. "It has been noted that in the variant readings, in 'La Causerie,' the piece was accompanied by the epigraph: 'Falsi Simoentis ad undam' [and Simois seemed the well-dissembled flood (Dryden)] and if the reader will turn to the 'Projets de Préface,' he will notice that the poet intended to indicate himself the source from which he had taken it: 'Virgil, the entire piece about Andromache' (Aen. III, l. 397)," Crepet-Blin's edition of the *Fleurs du Mal*, p. 449.

86. Hubert, *L'esthétique des 'Fleurs du Mal'*, p. 99.

87. Ovid, *Metamorphoses* I, 84-85, cf. Crepet-Blin, *Fleurs du Mal*, p. 451.

88. We are referring here to Baudelaire's definition of the "art pure suivant la conception moderne" in the essay "L'Art philosophique" (1951), p. 918.

89. G. Hess (1953), in his interpretation of the second Spleen poem (where one also finds the verse "L'ennui, fruit de la morne incuriosité"), called attention to this new function of allegory. See especially p. 82: "because Baudelaire equates allegory with the self and thus makes the images of outer reality into realities of his inner psychological landscape, he attains to that intensity of 'abstract sensuality' which strikes Lalou as a characteristic of his poetry." A number of aphorisms in W. Benjamin's "Zentralpark" (1955), I, pp. 473ff. touch on the inner relationship between allegorical intent, remembrance, and relic.

90. (1956), pp. 35-36.

91. Baudelaire (1951), p. 883.

92. "Like almost all of Mallarmé's poetry, 'Eventail' is a poem about the writing of poetry. The ontological scheme reveals itself: to the extent they have a real presence, objects are impure. Only in their destruction do they make possible the birth of their pure essences in language" in Friedrich (1956), p. 78.

93. The revision of the conclusion covers what were originally pages 262-66.

94. Burger, "Von der Struktureinheit klassischer," p. 229.

95. The quoted line is from Mallarmé's "Les Fenêtres."

96. Burger, "Von der Struktureinheit klassischer," p. 234.

97. Ibid., p. 238.

98. Ibid., p. 233; the concluding stanza in its final version reads as follows:

> Staunend seh' ich dich an, Stimmen und süssen Gesang,
> Wie aus voriger Zeit, hör ich und Saitenspiel,
> Und die Lilie duftet
> Golden über dem Bach uns auf.

(Astonished, I look at you, voice and sweet song as from an earlier time I hear, and strings. And golden rises the lily's fragrance above the brook.)

99. Ibid., p. 235.

100. Ibid., p. 238; the stanza in question reads:

> Sie schlossen ihre Mäntel, starrten gedankenlos
> Die Wolke an, die über ihre Köpfe
> Dahinfuhr schwarz und herrlich
> Die schöne Wolke, dachte der Photograph
> Und machte die Aufnahme privat.
> Ein fünfzigstel Sekunde, Blende zehn.
> Doch auf der Platter war dann nichts zu sehen.

(They closed their coats, stared unthinkingly at the cloud that sailed above their heads, black and splendid. What a beautiful cloud, the photographer thought, and took the picture because it amused him. One/fiftieth of a second, f-10. But the plate didn't show a thing.)

101. As, for example, in the parallel volume, *Die Welt as Labyrinth*, Rowohlts Deutsche Enzykopädie vol. 50/51, pp. 206-7, 220, and 226: "The classic author represents God in his

essence, the mannerist represents Him in His existence. If there are two forms of the manifestation of the absolute, they both depend on the absolute; in both, the absolute is present and active."

102. Malraux, *Voices of Silence*, trans. Stuart Gilbert (New York: Doubleday, 1953), p. 53.

103. In Adorno (1971), pp. 77ff.

104. Ibid., p. 78.

105. On this matter, one might recall Adorno's interpretation of "Wanderers Nachtlied," ibid., p. 81: "Even the 'Warte nur, balde/ruhest du auch' has the gesture of consolation: its profound beauty cannot be separated from what it passes over in silence, the idea of a world which refuses peace."

106. This determination of the lyric experience which I introduced in passing in chap. B1 (see above) will be developed through the use of historical examples.

107. De Man (1971), chap. IX: "Lyric and Modernity," esp. pp. 175ff., where he refers to *Poetik und Hermeneutik II*. Ibid., K. Stierle, "Möglichkeiten des dunklen Stils in den Anfängen moderner Lyrik in Frankreich" (pp. 175-94).

108. De Man (1971), p. 161.

109. "Literarische Tradition und gegenwärtiges Bewusstsein der Modernität," in Jauss (1970), pp. 11-66.

110. De Man (1971), p. 185.

111. See above, p. 122, also, "Position und Negation in Mallarmés 'Prose pour des Esseintes,'" English version in *Yale French Studies* 54 (1977), pp. 96-117.

112. See above, p. 84f.

113. See above, note 89.

114. Mallarmé, *Oeuvres complètes*, éd. de la Pléiade (Paris, 1945), p. 368. English version in text is from *Mallarmé: Selected Prose Poems, Essays, and Letters*, trans. Bradford Cook (Baltimore: Johns Hopkins Press, 1956).

E. *La douceur du foyer*: lyric poetry of the year 1857 as a model for the communication of social norms

1. The following essay is based on an extensive sociological-literary cross-sectional analysis of lyric poetry in 1857 which was undertaken in my seminar *Lyrik als Kommunikationssvtem* during the summer term, 1972, at the Fachbereich Literaturwissenschaft, Constance University. Thomas Luckmann assisted in an advisory capacity. This is the appropriate place to thank him and Charles Grivel, guest professor at the Fachbereich at the time, my colleagues H. U. Gumbrecht and Reinhold R. Grimm, and the participating students for their contributions and criticism. The wording of the version originally published in Warning (1975) was improved in only a few places (especially the definition of the poetic message as reduced to a question-and-answer relation, p. 403 in the earlier version, and the notes whose numbers there are #24 and #29).

2. Riffaterre (1971). Also "Le poème comme représentation," in *Poétique* 4 (1970), 401-18. See also "Sémantique du poème," in *Cahiers de l'Assoc. intern. des études françaises* 23 (1971), "The Stylistic Approach to Literary History," in *New Literary History* 2 (1970), "Modèles de la phrase littéraire," in *Problèmes de l'analyse textuelle*, ed. P. Leon a.o. (Montreal and Paris, 1971).

3. "Le poème comme représentation," p. 403.

4. Ibid., p. 403 and 418: "the literary description of reality thus only appears to refer to things, to signifieds. Actually, poetic representation is based on a reference to signifiers." This means that M. Riffaterre's analysis extends to the "forme du contenu," as Hjelmslev called it. See the discussion on "Modèles de la phrase littéraire" (p. 197).

5. Riffaterre (1971), p. 33.

6. H. Weinrich, "Münze und Wort. Untersuchung an einem Bildfeld," in *Romanica-Festschrift für G. Rohlfs* (Halle, 1958), pp. 508-21.

7. "Le poème comme représentation," p. 404.

8. According to W. D. Stempel, "Pour une description des genres littéraires," in *Actes du XIIe congrès intern. de linguistique romane* (Bucharest, 1968).

9. Riffaterre (1971), p. 58.

10. Ibid., p. 57.

11. "Le poème comme représentation," p. 407.

12. Ibid., p. 408.

13. This is best explained by an example showing the overlapping of descriptive systems which Riffaterre himself gives: "the system 'mother' whose hyperbole is 'young mother' is set against the system 'old mother.' In the later, for example, the 'mother:child' relationship is inverted since it is the child that protects and nourishes, or doesn't. The situation is complicated when it is negative: if there is ingratitude, the 'prodigal son' is connected with 'father' rather than 'mother,' and if there is death, the relation belongs to the 'mater dolorosa' system" (Modèles de la phrase littéraire, p. 144, #34). These descriptive systems clearly reflect original interaction patterns or social norms that have been handed down and are therefore not simply "bâtis sur les signifiants et non sur les référents."

14. According to P. L. Berger and T. Luckmann (1967).

15. Berger/Luckmann, p. 25, where art is mentioned as "finite province of meaning" but not seen in its actual social function as something that conveys, shapes, and legitimates norms.

16. It is part of my cross-sectional analysis of literary production during the year in which the *Fleurs du Mal* and *Madame Bovary* were published. On the possibilities of collaboration between the field of literary studies and the sociology of knowledge, see H. U. Gumbrecht, "Soziologie und Rezeptionsästhetik," in *Neue Ansichten einer künftigen Germanistik*, ed. H. Kolbe (Munich, 1973), pp. 48-74.

17. Berger/Luckmann (1967), p. 93.

18. See note 2, above.

19. According to the interpretation by L. Spitzer in *Interpretation zur Geschichte der französischen Lyrik* (Heidelberg, 1961), p. 134.

20. Berger/Luckmann (1967), pp. 24-25.

21. Lotman (1977), pp. 217ff.

22. According to the definition of W. Benjamin, *Illuminations*, p. 222.

23. The following passage from "Quatrevingt-treize" (III, vii, 6) allows no doubt about this: "Nature is pitiless. It refuses to withdraw its flowers, music, its fragrances and its rays. It overwhelms man by the contrast between God's beauty and society's ugliness" (quoted in the commentary of the Garnier edition, p. 594).

24. On this and on what follows, see R. Prigent, ed., *Renouveau des idées sur la famille*, Inst. nat. d'études démographiques, Travaux et documents, Cahier #18 (Paris, 1954), especially pp. 50ff.

25. G. Desmottes, ibid., p. 57. P. Ariès, "L'évolution des roles parentaux," in *Familles d'aujourd'hui, Colloque consacré à la sociologie de la famille*, éd. de l'Inst. de Sociologie (Brussels, 1968), pp. 35-55 has shown meanwhile that Desmottes probably overestimated the *patria potestas* in the social reality of the early nineteenth century, as is also shown by the right of inheritance where even during the Restoration, heads of families could no longer dispose over their estate as they saw fit. I am indebted to my colleague at Constance, Horst Rabe, for this information and the correction of note 29.

26. J. Stoetzel, *Les changements dans les fonctions familiales*, cf. note 23, pp. 343-69.

27. *Manteia*, Revue trimestrielle, XII/XIII (Marseille, 1971), pp. 13-138.

28. Ibid., p. 19.

29. "Thus the father (his body: what he touches, consumes, surveyes) appears behind the show that is made of his 'soul' (his dignity, honor, sense of being) as indissolubly linked to the economic structure whose existence he does not mention," ibid., p. 18.

30. P. Ariès, *Le XIXe siecle et la révolution des moeurs familiales*, see note 23, pp. 112–18. One of the finest illustrations can be found in Balzac's *Memoires de deux jeunes mariees*: "On peut avoir en mariage une douzaine d'enfants, en se mariant à l'âge où nous sommes, écrit Mme de l'E. à son amie Louise de Ch.; et si nous les avions, nous commettrions douze crimes, nous ferions douze malheurs. Ne livrerions-nous pas à la misère et au désespoir de charmants êtres? Tandis que deux enfants sont deux bonheurs, deux bienfaits, deux créations en harmonie avec les moeurs et les lois actuelles." (Getting married at our age, it is possible to have twelve children, Mme. de l'E. writes to her friend Louise. And if we were to have them, would we not be committing a dozen crimes, creating unhappiness a dozen times over? Wouldn't it mean abandoning charming beings to misery and despair? Two children, on the other hand, mean two instances of happiness, two acts of kindness, two creations that are in harmony with current morals and laws.) (Letter XVIII, quoted according to note 23, p. 69.) But more recent research in the field of historical demography has confirmed the belief that there was family planning also in the society of the Ancien Regime. See most recently A. Chamoux and D. Cauphin, "La contraception avant la Révolution française," in *Annales* 24 (1969), pp. 662–84.

31. "The paternalist governance of the family was thus a compromise between the reproductive functions of the couple on the one hand, and the necessity of conserving the patrimony and improving the condition of that child whom custom or the testament made the heir on the other. It did not occur to people that insurmountable social and financial difficulties could be overcome if the number of children were reduced," ibid., p. 115.

32. "The family thus became less and less sacred, social, and institutional, and more personal, created, intended. In this new climate, it was therefore not surprising that one attempted to dissolve it, considering that one had admitted that it could be created. It was at this moment that divorce appeared as the reverse of adoption" (p. 116).

33. A. Schütz, *Das Problem der Relevanz* (Frankfurt, 1971), esp. p. 208; and P. L. Berger/T. Luckmann (1967), pp. 22ff.

34. Cf. Berger/Luckmann (1967), pp. 92–93.

35. Pierre Dupont's attempt to sing the praises of the railroad, the epochal symbol of technical progress, is interesting. To do so, he has recourse to that genre of poetry which describes occupational roles and still belongs to the preindustrial world. In "Le chauffeur de locomotive" (*Chants et Chansons*, II, 25), he describes the locomotive with the image-field of the horse since he clearly had no metaphors other than those relating to nature at his command:

> Donne l'avoine à ton cheval!
> Sellé, bridé, siffle! et qu'on marche!
> Au galop, sur le pont, sous l'arche
> Tranche montagne, plaine et val;
> Aucun cheval n'est ton rival.

(Give oats to your horse! Saddled, bridled, whipped! Forward! At a gallop, on the bridge, under the arch he cuts through mountain, plain and valley; no horse will ever be your rival.)

36. " . . . neither the epic nor the drama can speak of God any longer. Henceforth, it will be lyric poetry which will raise its sublime inspirations toward heaven, it is lyric poetry that will exalt the life of the heart above that of the inteligence and thus prepare that reign of love which the Middle Ages sketched" quoted from an article in the *Revue francaise* from the year 1857 (vol. XI, p. 299).

37. Victor Hugo, *Les Contemplations*, Preface.

38. Pierre Dupont, "La mère Jeanne" (II, 1):

> Dans la vie on ne reste guères
> A l'âge riant des amours.
>
> . . .
>
> Du jour qu'on est mère et fermière,
> On a d'autres chiens à fouetter.

(In life we scarcely ever remain in the laughing age of love. . . . From the day one is a mother and a farmer, we have other things to tackle.)

39. For this, see J. H. van den Berg, *Metabletica ou la psychologie historique* (Paris, 1962), p. 31 and chap. 4.

40. Victor Hugo thematized this threshold in the wedding poem for February 15, 1843 (in *Contemplation* IV, ii) as the passage from one family to the other:

> Aime celui qui t'aime, et sois heureuse en lui,
> —Adieu! —sois son trésor, ô toi qui fus le notre!
> Va, mon enfant bénie, d'une famille à l'autre.
> Emporte le bonheur et laisse-nous l'ennui!

(Love him who loves you, and be happy with him, —Goodbye! —be his treasure, oh you who were ours, go, my blessed child, from one family to another. Take with you happiness and leave us sorrow!)

41. Baudelaire, "Moesta et errabunda" and "L'ennemi," Henri Cantal, "Après trente ans."

42. Hugo, "L'enfance" (I, xxiii); it should be mentioned that for biographical reasons, the father-daughter relationships is the most important in the *Contemplations*.

43. In his excellent sociological analysis (*Les changements dans les fonctions familiales*), J. Stoetzel also calls attention to this distinctive ideality. Cf. note 23, p. 344: "The fundamental value of the family expresses itself in the notion of the 'foyer.' . . . It implies first of all an idea of warmth and security. It also refers to the economic role of the family: the family is an organization that consumes. The 'foyer' is also a center and this calls attention to the fact that the family expresses the idea of a gathering, an hierarchical integration. Since the fire must be maintained, the uninterrupted cooperation of all and the loyalty of all its members is implied when the family is considered as a 'foyer.' And finally, there is the traditional tie in our culture between the notion of fire and a religious idea: a 'foyer' is also a domestic altar. It can thus be seen that the 'foyer' takes on meaning at every level of the hierarchy of values: values of the pleasant and the unpleasant, of life and health, social and spiritual values, and finally religious ones all come together in the notion of the 'foyer.'"

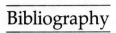

Bibliography

Bibliography

Adler, Alfred, *Epische Spekulanten—Versuch einer synchronen Geschichte des altfranzösischen Epos* (Munich, 1975).

Adorno, Theodor W., *Ohne Leitbild—Parva Aesthetica* (Frankfurt, 1967).

——, *Ästhetische Theorie, Gesammelte Schriften* vol. 7 (Frankfurt, 1970).

Apel, Karl-Otto, ed., *Hermeneutik und Ideologiekritik* (Frankfurt, 1971) (Theorie-Diskussion).

Auerbach, Erich, *Mimesis—The Representation of Reality in Western Literature*, trans. Willard Trask (Princeton, N.J.: Princeton University Press, 1953).

Badt, Kurt, *Kunsttheoretische Versuche* (Cologne, 1968).

Bakhtin, Mikhail, *Rabelais and His World*, trans. Helene Iswolsky (Cambridge, Mass.: M.I.T. Press, 1968).

Barthes, Roland, *Mythologies*, trans. Anette Lavers (New York: Hill and Wang, 1972).

——, *The Pleasure of the Text*, trans. Richard Miller (New York: Hill and Wang, 1973).

Baudelaire, Charles, *Charles Baudelaire, The Painter of Modern Life and Other Essays*, trans. Jonathan Mayne (London, 1946).

——, *Oeuvres complètes*, Edition de la Pléiade (Paris, 1951).

——, *Baudelaire as a Literary Critic*, selected essays introduced and translated by L. B. Hyslop and F. E. Hyslop (University Park, Pa.: Pennsylvania State University Press, 1964).

——, *Art in Paris 1845-1862, reviewed by Charles Baudelaire*, trans. and ed. Jonathan Mayne (New York: Phaidon Press, 1965).

Benjamin, Walter, *Schriften*, 2 vols. (Frankfurt, 1955).

——, *Illuminations*, trans. Harry Zohn (New York: Schocken Books, 1969).

Berger, Peter L., and Luckmann, Thomas, *Die Gesellschaftliche Konstruktion der Wirklichkeit* (Frankfurt, 1970; 2nd ed. 1971).

——, *The Social Construction of Reality* (New York: Doubleday, Anchor Books, 1967).

Binder, Wolfgang, "'Genuss' in Dichtung und Philosophie des 17. und 18. Jahrhunderts," in *Archiv für Begriffsgeschichte* 17 (1973), pp. 66-92.

Bloch, Ernst, *Das Prinzip Hoffnung* (Frankfurt, 1959).

Blumenberg, Hans, "'Nachahmung der Natur'—Zur Vorgeschichte des schöpferischen Menschen," in *Studium Generale* 10 (1957), pp. 266-83.

——, "Sokrates und das 'objet ambugu'—Paul Valérys Auseinandersetzung mit der Tradition der Ontologie des ästhetischen Gegenstandes," in *Epimeleia, Helmut Kuhn zum 65. Geburtstag*, ed. F. Wiedmann, suhrkamp taschenbuch wissenschaft 24 (Munich, 1964), pp. 285-323.

——, *Der Prozess der theoretischen Neugierde* (Frankfurt, 1973).

Borinski, Karl, *Die Antike in Poetik und Kunsttheorie*, vol. I (Leipzig, 1914); vol. II (Leipzig, 1924).

Buck, Günther, "Kants Lehre vom Beispiel," in *Archiv für Begriffsgeschichte* 11 (1967), pp. 148-83.

Callois, Rober, *Vocabulaire esthétique* (Paris, 1946).

Conze, Werner, "Arbeit," in *Geschichtliche Grundbegriffe—Historisches Lexibon zur politisch-sozialen Sprache in Deutschland*, ed. O. Brunner, W. Conze, R. Koselleck (Stuttgart, 1972), vol. I, pp. 154-215.

Curtius, Ernst Robert, *European Literature and the Latin Middle Ages*, trans. W. R. Trask (New York: Pantheon Books, 1953).

Dehn, Wilhelm, ed. *Ästhetische Erfahrung und literarisches Lernen* (Frankfurt, 1974).

Dewey, John, *Art as Experience* (1934), 16th ed. (New York: Capricorn Books, 1958).

Dockhorn, Klaus, Rezension von H. G. Gadamer, "Wahrheit und Methode," in *Göttingische Gelehrte Anzeigen*, 218 (1966), pp. 169-206.

Dufrenne, Mikel, *Phénoménologie de l'expérience esthétique* (Paris, 1967).

Fellmann, Ferdinand, *Das Vico-Axiom. Der Mensch macht die Geschichte* (Freiburg/Munich, 1976).

Freud, Sigmund, *The Standard Edition of the Complete Psychological Works* (London: Hogarth Press, 1962).

Friedrich, Hugo, *Die Struktur der modernen Lyrik*, rowohlts deutsche enzykopädie 25 (Hamburg, 1956). Quotations from the first edition of the expanded 1966 edition.

——, *Romanische Literaturen—Aufsätze I and II* (Frankfurt, 1972). Translated as *The Structure of Modern Poetry*, trans. Joachim Neugroschel (Evanston, Ill.: Northwestern University Press, 1974).

Frye, Northrop, *Anatomy of Criticism* (Princeton, N.J.: Princeton University Press, 1957).

Fuhrmann, Manfred, *Einführung in die antike Dichtungslehre* (Darmstadt, 1973).

Gadamer, Hans Georg, *Truth and Method*, ed. Garrett Barden and John Cumming (New York: Seabury Press, 1975).

Geiger, Moritz, "Beiträge zur Phänomenologie des ästhetischen Genusses," in *Jahrbuch für Philosophie und phänomenologische Forschung* 1, no. 2 (1913), pp. 567-684.

Giesz, Ludwig, *Phänomenologie des Kitsches*, 2nd ed. (Munich, 1971).

Grimm, Reinhold R., *Paradisus coelestis—paradisus terrestris. Zur Auslegungsgeschichte des Paradieses im Abendland bis um 1200* (Munich, 1977).

Guiette, Robert, *Questions de Littérature*, vol. I (Gent, 1960); vol. II (Gent, 1972).

Habermas, Jürgen, *Technik und Wissenschaft als 'Ideologie'*, edition suhrkamp 287 (Frankfurt, 1968).

——, *Kultur und Kritik. Verstreute Aufsätze*, suhrkamp taschenbuch 125 (Frankfurt, 1973).

Harth, Dietrich, *Philologie und praktische Philosophie*, Humanistische Bibliothek, I, 11 (Munich, 1970).

Hartman, Geoffrey H., *The Fate of Reading and Other Essays* (Chicago: University of Chicago Press, 1975).

Hegel, G. W. F., *Asthetics*, trans. T. M. Knox (Oxford: Clarendon Press, 1975).

Henrich, Dieter, "Kunst und Kunstphilosophie der Gegenwart (Überlegungen mit Rücksicht auf Hegel)," in *Poetik und Hermeneutik II* (1966), pp. 11-32. Translated as "Art and Philosophy of Art Today: Reflections with Reference to Hegel," in Richard E. Amacher and Victor Lange, eds., *New Perspectives in German Literary Criticism: A Collection of Essays* (Princeton, N.J.: Princeton University Press, 1979), pp. 107-33.

Hervieux, Marcel, *Les ecrivains français jugés par leurs contemporains*, vol. I: *Le XVIe et le XVIIe siecle* (Paris, 1911).

Herzog, Reinhart, *Die Bibelepik der lateinischen Spätantike — Formgeschichte einer erbaulichen Gattung*, vol. I (Munich, 1975).

Hess, Gerhard, *Die Landschaft in Baudelaires 'Fleurs du Mal'* (Heidelberg, 1953).

Hofmann, Werner, "Zur Geschichte und Theorie der Landschaftsmalerei," in *Caspar David Friedrich, 1774-1840* (Munich, 1974) (catalog published by Prestel-Verlag).

Hohendahl, Peter Uwe, ed., *Sozialgeschichte und Wirkungsästhetik* (Frankfurt, 1974).

Holland, Norman N., *The Dynamics of Literary Response* (New York: Oxford University Press, 1968).

Imdahl, Max, "'Is It a Flag, or Is It a Painting?' — Über mögliche Konsequenzen der konkreten Kunst," in *Wallraf-Richartz-Jahrbuch* 31 (1969), pp. 205-32.

Iser, Wolfgang, *Der implizite Leser — Kommunikationsformen des Romans von Bunyan bis Beckett*, Uni-Taschenbücher 163 (Munich, 1972). Translated as *The Implied Reader: Patterns of Communication in Prose Fiction from Bunyan to Beckett* (Baltimore, Md.: Johns Hopkins University Press, 1974).

———, *Der Akt des Lesens — Theorie ästhetischer Wirkung*, Uni-Taschenbücher 636 (Munich, 1976). Translated as *The Act of Reading: A Theory of Aesthetic Response* (Baltimore, Md.: Johns Hopkins University Press, 1979).

Jauss, Hans Robert, *Zeit und Erinnerung in Marcel Prousts 'A la recherche du temps perdu'* (Heidelberg, 1955 [1st ed.], 1970 [2nd ed.]).

———, "Proust auf der Suche nach seiner Konzeption des Romans," in *Romanische Forschungen* 66 (1955), pp. 225-304 (=1955a).

———, *Untersuchungen zur mittelalterlichen Tierdichtung*, Beihefte zur *Zeitschrift für romanische Philologie*, 100. heft (Tübingen, 1959).

———, "Diderots Paradox über das Schauspiel," in *Germanisch-romanische Monatsschrift* 11 (1961), pp. 380-413.

———, *Ästhetische Normen und geschichtliche Reflexion in der 'Querelle des Anciens et des Modernes'* (Munich, 1964).

———, *Literaturgeschichte als Provokation*, edition suhrkamp 418 (Frankfurt, 1970). English translation forthcoming in Hans Robert Jauss, *Towards an Aesthetic of Reception*, trans. Timothy Bahti with an introduction by Paul de Man (Minneapolis: University of Minnesota Press, 1982).

———, *Kleine Apologie der ästhetischen Erfahrung*, Konstanzer Universitätserden 59 (Constance, 1972).

———, *Alterität und Modernität der mittelalterliche Literatur — Gesammelte Aufsätze 1956-1976* (Munich, 1977).

Jolles, A., "Die literarischen Travestien Ritter/Hirt/Schelm," in *Blätter für deutsche Philosophie* 6 (1923/33).

Kalivoda, Robert, *Der marxismus und die moderne geistige Wirklichkeit*, edition suhrkamp 373 (Frankfurt, 1970).

Kommerell, Max, *Lessing und Aristoteles — Untersuchung über die Theorie der Tragödie* (Frankfurt, 1957).

Kracauer, Siegfried, *Theory of Film — The Redemption of Physical Reality* (New York, 1960).

Krauss, Wetner, *Gesammelte Aufsätze zur Literatur und Sprachwissenschaft* (Frankfurt, 1949).

Kuhn, Helmut, *Vom Wesen und Wirken des Kunstwerks* (Munich, 1960).

Labroisse, Gerd, ed., *Rezeption — Interpretation. Beiträge zur Methodendiskussion*, Amsterdamer Beiträge zur Neueren Germanistik 3 (Amsterdam, 1974).

Lemon, Lee T., and Marion J. Reis, translators, *Russian Formalist Criticism: Four Essays* (Lincoln, Neb.: University of Nebraska Press, 1965). (Contains Sklovskij's "Art as Technique.")

Lesser, Simon O., *Fiction and the Unconscious* (New York: Vintage Books, 1962).

Lewis, C. S., *The Discarded Image* (Cambridge, England, 1964).

Lotman, Jurij, *The Structure of the Artistic Text*, trans. Ronald Vroon (Ann Arbor: University of Michigan, 1977).

Löwith, Karl, *Das Individum in der Rolle des Mitmenschen* (1928) (Darmstadt, 1962 [2nd ed.]).

——, *Paul Valéry — Grundzüge seines philosophischen Denkens* (Göttingen, 1971).

Malraux, André, *Les voix du silence* (Paris, 1951). Translated as *The Voices of Silence*, trans. Stuart Gilbert (New York: Doubleday, 1953).

Man, de, Paul, *Blindness and Insight — Essays in the Rhetoric of Contemporary Criticism* (New York: Oxford University Press, 1971).

Mandelkow, Karl Robert, "Rezeptionsästhetik und marxistische Literatutheorie," in *Historizität in Sprach-und Literaturwissenschaft*, ed. W. Müller-Seidel (Munich, 1974), pp. 379–88.

Marcuse, Herbert, "On the Affirmative Character of Culture," in *Negations. Essays in Critical Theory*, trans. Jeremy J. Shapiro (Boston: Beacon Press, 1968).

——, *Counterrevolution and Revolt* (Boston: Beacon Press, 1972).

Marquard, Odo, *Schwierigkeiten mit der Geschichtsphilosophie* (Frankfurt, 1973).

Mead, George H., *Mind, Self, and Society* (Chicago: University of Chicago Press, 1934).

Mittelstrass, Jürgen, *Neuzeit und Aufklärung — Studien zur Entstehung der neuzeitlichen Wissenschaft und Philosophie* (Berlin/New York, 1970).

Mukarovsky, Jan, *Aesthetic Function, Norm, and Value as Social Facts*, trans. Mark E. Suino (Ann Arbor: University of Michigan Press, 1970).

——, *Structure, Sign, and Function*, trans. and ed. John Burbank and Peter Steiner (New Haven, Conn.: Yale University Press, 1978).

Naumann, Manfred, ed., *Gesellschaft — Literatur — Lesen. Literaturrezeption in theoretischer Sicht* (Berlin/Weimar, 1973).

Neuschäfer, Hans-Jorg, *Populärromane im 19. Jahrhundert*, Uni-Taschenbücher 524 (Munich, 1976).

Nisin, Arthur, *La littérature et le lecteur* (Paris, 1959).

——, *Les oeuvres et les siecles* (Paris, 1960).

Panofsky, Erwin, *Idea — Ein Beitrag zur Begriffsgeschichte der älteren Kunsttheorie*, 2nd ed. (Berlin, 1960). Translated as *Idea: A Concept in Art Theory* (Columbia: University of South Carolina Press, 1968).

Plessner, Helmuth, "Soziale Rolle und Menschliche Natur" (1960), in *Diesseits der Utopie* (Cologne, 1966).

——, *Laughing and Crying, A Study of the Limits of Human Behavior*, trans. James Spencer Churchill and Marjorie Grene (Evanston, Ill.: Northwestern University Press, 1970).

Poetik und hermeneutik — Arbeigsergebnisse einer Forschungsgruppe

    I. *Nachahmung und Illusion* (1964), ed. H. R. Jauss;

    II. *Immanente Ästhetik — Ästhetische Reflexion* (1966), ed. W. Iser;

    III. *Die nicht mehr schönen Künste* (1968), ed. H. R. Jauss;

    IV. *Terror und Spiel* (1971), ed. M. Fuhrmann;

    V. *Geschichte* — Ereignis und Erzählung (1973), ed. R. Koselleck und W. D. Stempel;

    VI. *Positionen der Negativität* (1975), ed. H. Weinrich;

    VII. *Das Komische* (1976), ed. W. Preisendanz and R. Warning.

Poirion, Daniel, "Chanson de geste ou épopée?" in *Travaux de linguistique et de litterature* X, no. 2 (Strasbourg, 1972), pp. 7-20.

Preisendanz, Wolfgang, *Humor als dichterische Einbildungskraft* (Munich, 1963).

——, *Wege des Realismus — Zur poetik und Erzählkunst im 19. Jahrhundert* (Munich, 1977).

Ricoeur, Paul, *Le conflit des interprétations — Essais d'herméneutique* (Paris, 1969). Translated as *The Conflict of Interpretations: Essays on Hermeneutics* (Evanston, Ill.: Northwestern University Press, 1974).

——, *Freud and Philosophy. An Essay on Interpretation*, trans. Denis Savage (New Haven, Conn.:/London: Yale University Press, 1970).

Riffaterre, Michael, *Essais de stylistique structurale* (Paris, 1971).

Ritter, Joachim, "Ästhetik," in *Historischen Wörterbuch der Philosophie* (Basel/Stuttgart, 1971), vol. 1, Sp. 555-80.

——, *Subjektivität* (Frankfurt, 1974). This volume contains "Über das Lachen" (1940) and "Landschaft — Zur Funktion des Ästhetischen in der modernen Gesellschaft" (1963).

Rüfner, Vinzenz, "Homo secundus Deus — Eine geistegeschichtliche Studie sum menschlichen Schöpfertum," in *Philosophisches Jahrbuch* 63 (1955), pp. 248-91.

Sartre, Jean-Paul, *L'imaginaire. Psychologie phénoménologique de l'imagination* (Paris, 1940). Translated as *The Psychology of Imagination*, trans. Bernard Frechtman (London: Methuen, 1972).

——, "Qu'est-ce que la littérature?" in *Situations II* (Paris, 1948). Translated as "What is Literature?" trans. Bernard Frechtman (London: Methuen, 1950).

Schapiro, Meyer, "On the Aesthetic Attitude in Romanesque Art," in *Art and Thought* (Feb. 1948).

Schiller, Karl Friedrich v., *On the Aesthetic Education of Man*, trans. Reginald Snell (New York: Fredrick Ungar, 1965).

Schlaffer, Heinz, ed., *Erweiterung der materialistischen Literaturtheorie durch Bestimmung ihrer Grenzen*, Literaturwissenschaft und Sozialwissenschaften 4 (Stuttgart, 1974).

Schmidt, Siegfried J., *Ästhetizität — Philosophische Beiträge zu einer Theorie des Ästhetischen* (Munich, 1971).

Schütz, Alfred, and Luckmann, Thomas, *Strukturen der Lebenswelt*, Soziologische Texte 82 (Neuwied/Darmstadt, 1975). Translated as *Phenomenology of the Social World*, trans. George Walsh and Frederick Lehnert (Evanston, Ill.: Northwestern University Press, 1967).

Souriau, Emile, "Le risible et le comique," in *Journal de psychologie normale at pathologique* 41 (1948).

Spitzer, Leo, *Romanische Literaturstudien* (Tübingen, 1959).

Stackelberg, Jürgen von, *Literarische Rezeptionsformen* (Frankfurt, 1972).

Starobinski, Jean, *L'oeil vivant*, vol. I (Paris, 1961); *La relation critique*, vol. II (Paris, 1970).

Stempel, Wolf-Dieter, ed., *Texte der russischen Formalisten*. Vol. II: *Texte zur Theorie des Verses und der poetischen Sprache* (Munich, 1972).

Stierle, Karlheinz, *Text als Handlung — Perspektiven einer systematischen Literaturwissenschaft*, Uni-Taschenbücher 423 (Munich, 1975).

——, "Was heisst Rezeption bei fiktionalen Texten?" in *Poetica* 7 (1975), pp. 345-387 (=1975a).

Striedter, Jurij, ed., *Texte der russischen Formalisten*. Vol. I: *Texte zur allgemeinen Literaturtheorie und zur Theorie der Prosa* (Munich, 1969).

——, Introduction to Felix Vodička, *Die Struktur der literarischen Entwicklung* (Munich, 1976).

Valéry, Paul, *Oeuvres*, 2 vols. Edition de la Pléiade (Paris, 1960). Translated as *Collected Works*, 15 vols., ed. Jackson Mathews (Princeton, N.J.: Princeton University Press, 1971-1975).

Warning, Rainer, *Funkton und Struktur — Die Ambivalenzen des geistlichen Spiels* (Munich, 1974).

——, ed., *Rezeptionsästhetik — Theorie und Praxis*, Uni-Taschenbücher 303 (Munich, 1974).

Wellershoff, Dieter, *Literatur und Lustprinzip* (Cologne, 1973).

——, *Die Auflösung des Kunstbegriffs*, edition suhrkamp 848 (Frankfurt, 1976).

Werckmeister, Otto K., *Ende der Ästhetik* (Frankfurt, 1971).

Vygotsky, Lev S., "Kunst als Katharsis" (1965), in *Ästhetische Erfahrung und literarisches Lernen*, ed. W. Dehn (Frankfurt, 1974), pp. 81–89.

Zimmermann, Hans Dieter, *Vom Nutzen der Literatur — Vorbereitende Bemerkungen zu einer Theorie der literarischen Kommunikation*, edition suhrkamp 885 (Frankfurt, 1977).

Zumthor, Paul, *Essai de poétique médiévale* (Paris, 1972).

Index

Index

Hans Robert Jauss is a professor of literary criticism and romance philology at the University of Konstanz, West Germany, and is founder and co-editor of *Poetik and Hermeneutic.* He has taught at Columbia, Yale, and the Sorbonne. His writings include studies of medieval and modern French literature as well as theoretical works.

Michael Shaw has a doctorate in comparative literature from Yale University. He has translated many German works, among them Max Horkheimer's *Dawn and Decline.*

Wlad Godzich teaches comparative literature at the University of Minnesota and is co-editor, with Jochen Schulte-Sasse, of the series Theory and History of Literature.